LAST FLAG DOWN

★ ★ ★ ★ ★ ★ ★ ★ ★ ★ ★ ★ ★ ★ ★ ★ ★ ★ ★ ★

LAST FLAG DOWN

THE EPIC JOURNEY OF THE LAST CONFEDERATE WARSHIP

John Baldwin and Ron Powers

THREE RIVERS PRESS / NEW YORK

Published in the United States by Three Rivers Press, an imprint of the
Crown Publishing Group, a division of Random House, Inc., New York.
www.crownpublishing.com

Three Rivers Press and the Tugboat design are registered trademarks of
Random House, Inc.

Originally published in hardcover in the United States by Crown Publishers,
an imprint of the Crown Publishing Group, a division of
Random House, Inc., New York, in 2007.

Library of Congress Cataloging-in-Publication Data

Baldwin, John.
Last flag down : the epic journey of the last Confederate warship /
John Baldwin and Ron Powers.—1st ed.
Includes bibliographical references and index.
1. Shenandoah (Cruiser)   2. United States—History—Civil War, 1861–1865—
Naval operations, Confederate.   3. Voyages around the world—History—19th
century.   4. Ocean travel—History—19th century.   I. Powers, Ron.   II. Title.
E599.S5B35 2007
973.7'57—dc22
2006025706

ISBN 978-0-307-23656-2

Printed in the United States of America

Map and illustrations by Jackie Aher
Design by Leonard Henderson

10 9 8 7 6 5 4 3 2 1

First Paperback Edition

In loving memory of my son, Kevin Powers (1984–2005)
—RP

To my true love, "Babes"
—JB

CONTENTS

CHAPTER 1 1

CHAPTER 2 23

CHAPTER 3 49

CHAPTER 4 65

CHAPTER 5 83

CHAPTER 6 104

CHAPTER 7 120

CHAPTER 8 136

CHAPTER 9 154

CHAPTER 10 172

CHAPTER 11 189

CHAPTER 12 206

CHAPTER 13 222

CHAPTER 14 238

CHAPTER 15 255

CHAPTER 16 267

CHAPTER 17 280

CHAPTER 18 291

CHAPTER 19 303

CHAPTER 20 315

NOTES 333

GLOSSARY 335

BIBLIOGRAPHY 343

ACKNOWLEDGMENTS 344

INDEX 346

The Journey of Lt. William Conway Whittle and the CSS *SHENANDOAH*

Crossed the
Arctic Circle
June 19, 1865

ARCTIC CIRCLE

RUSSIA

Sea of Okhotsk
May 27, 1865

Bering Sea
June 18, 1865

ASIA

JAPAN

CHINA

INDIA

Pacific Ocean

KINGDOM OF
HAWAII

Ponape/
Ascension
Island

April 1, 1865

Indian
Ocean

AUSTRALIA

St. Paul Island
Jan. 2, 1865

NEW
ZEALAND

Melbourne
Jan. 25, 1865

"The Roaring

ANTARCTICA

ANTARCTIC CIRCLE

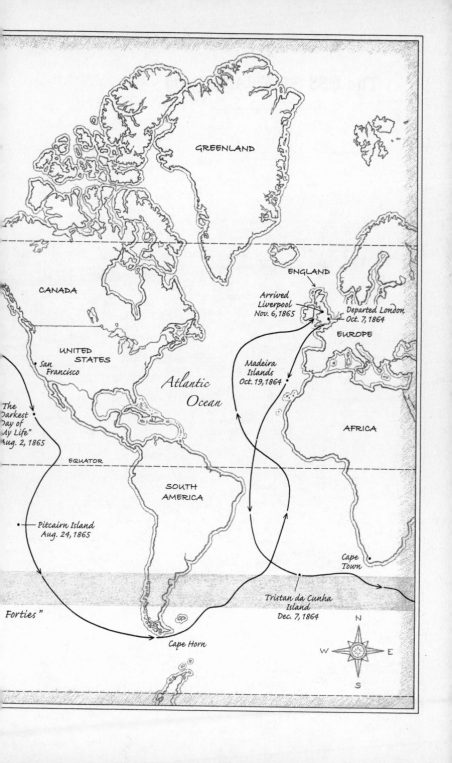

GREENLAND

ENGLAND

Arrived
Liverpool
Nov. 6, 1865

Departed London
Oct. 7, 1864

CANADA

EUROPE

UNITED
STATES

San
Francisco

*Atlantic
Ocean*

Madeira
Islands
Oct. 19, 1864

AFRICA

The
Darkest
Day of
My Life"
Aug. 2, 1865

EQUATOR

SOUTH
AMERICA

Pitcairn Island
Aug. 24, 1865

Cape
Town

Tristan da Cunha
Island
Dec. 7, 1864

Forties"

Cape Horn

N

W   E

S

The CSS *SHENANDOAH*

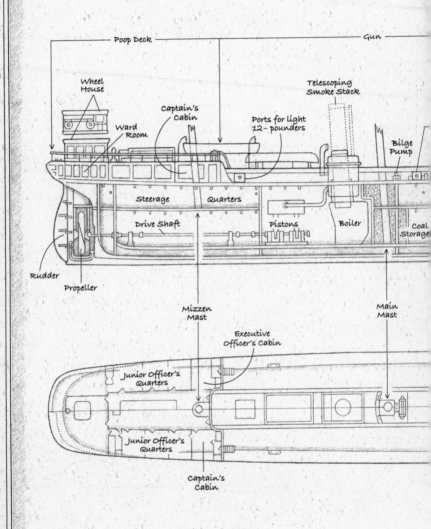

Poop Deck

Gun

Wheel House

Captain's Cabin

Ward Room

Ports for light 12 – pounders

Telescoping Smoke Stack

Bilge Pump

Steerage

Quarters

Drive Shaft

Pistons

Boiler

Coal Storage

Rudder

Propeller

Mizzen Mast

Main Mast

Executive Officer's Cabin

Junior Officer's Quarters

Junior Officer's Quarters

Captain's Cabin

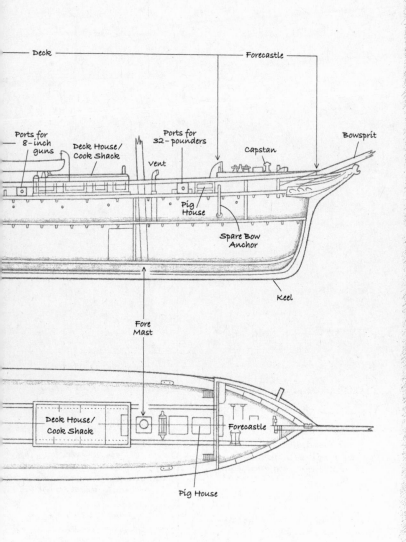

Deck

Forecastle

Ports for
8-inch
guns

Deck House/
Cook Shack

Ports for
32-pounders

Vent

Capstan

Bowsprit

Pig
House

Spare Bow
Anchor

Keel

Fore
Mast

Deck House/
Cook Shack

Forecastle

Pig House

SAIL PLAN for the CSS *SHENANDOAH*

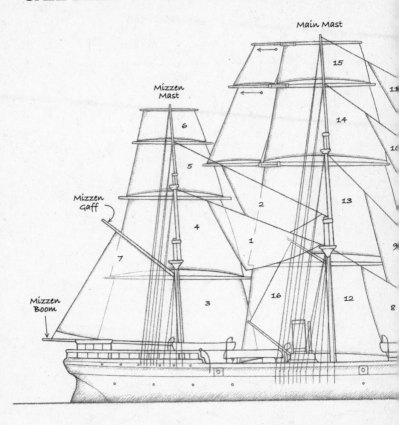

MIZZEN MAST

Fore-and-Aft Sails:
1. Mizzen Staysail
2. Mizzen – Topmast/ Staysail

Square Sails:
3. Mizzen Sail
4. Mizzen – Topsail
5. Mizzen – Topgallant Sail
6. Mizzen Royal

Fore-and-Aft Sail:
7. Spanker or Mizzen Gaff

MAIN MAST

Fore-and-Aft Sails:
8. Main Staysail
9. Main – Topmast Staysail
10. Main – Topgallant Staysail
11. Main – Royal Staysail

Square Sails:
12. Main Sail
13. Main – Topsail
14. Main – Topgallant Sail
15. Main Royal

Fore-and-Aft Sail:
16. Spencer or Main Gaff

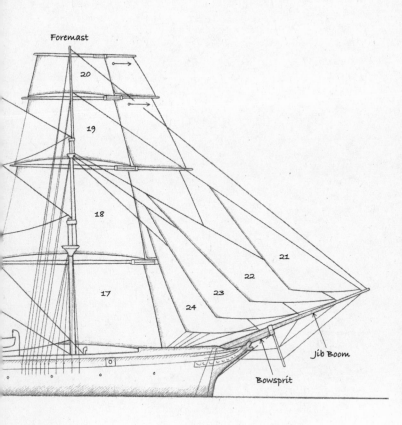

Foremast

Jib Boom

Bowsprit

FOREMAST

Square Sails:
17. Foresail
18. Fore – Topsail
19. Fore – Topgallant Sail
20. Fore Royal

BOWSPRIT AND JIB BOOM

Fore-and-Aft Sails:
21. Flying Jib
22. Standing Jib
23. Fore – Topmast Staysail
24. Foremast Staysail

← o Studding Booms (extendable yards used to fly more canvas)

1

Coal.

The Noble Cause bleeding to death, starving to death. The Northern aggressors with their dirty heels in the sacred ground of Louisiana, Georgia, Virginia; his generation largely in its graves, or soon to be. And here he was watching the empty horizon from a coal-laden merchant steamer off the coast of West Africa. Three decks below him, his crew bent to dismal duty, the drudgework of the high seas. They were securing the ship's bunker coal—her fuel supply—and preparing her cargo, of yet more coal, for heavy weather. The description given to those sweating wretches who had to carry it out said it all: "coal heavers."

Coal.

A mundane cargo for this fine fast ship running now in front of the wind, racing for her life, almost due south, and almost diametrically away from the Confederate States of America. Within her, a cargo weighing almost as much as the ship itself and a valuable cargo indeed: 800 long tons of almost smokeless Welsh coal. A cargo so expensive its owners had sent a man on the voyage to look after it, to see it wasn't pilfered for fuel, to see it was delivered as planned. A cargo almost as mundane as the young "coal agent's" undercover alias: "George Brown."

To be hauling coal, not Enfields, at this moment of the Confederacy's most parlous plight: Atlanta, proud citadel of the Confederacy, lost to Sherman; Lee in the trenches at Richmond since June; Sheridan's cavalry chasing Jubal Early's ragged men up the Shenandoah Valley, burning the fields and barns and mills behind them.

Norfolk, Virginia, or those remnants that had not been burned, was now under martial law; indeed, the homes of "Brown's" family, the Whittles, the Sinclairs, the Pages, those still standing, were occupied by Federal troops. The South that the young man had known as a glittering nation unto itself, a kingdom of honor and deep traditions, where family names reached back in time until they seemed to merge with the land itself—this Old South was now a scorched, bleeding thing, its armies ground up by the cold advancing Union machine. The war was in its brutal, inexorable end-game.

Sea King, since leaving London days ago, seemingly irrelevant to it all, had plodded toward the southern seas with a consignment of coal. Simply a modern merchantman going peacefully about its business.

Or so the slim boyish "George Brown—coal agent" had hoped any dangerous adversary in the vicinity of the London docks would believe—falsely. When he left the Thames on *Sea King,* he had staked his life, the life of a Confederate spy, on that risk. Any hostile interception, any "search and seizure" of that vessel and her stores, would have guaranteed his imprisonment, even death. But *Sea King* was gone now, reported lost, in reality sold to the Confederacy, renamed and reflagged.

"George Brown" had, for the first eleven days, risked only his own life, but now there were others, a new crew, and soon he would be risking these men's lives as well. Any hostile interception of this once-peaceful vessel now would be an act of war.

And war was his profession.

He was in fact an experienced and dangerous warrior of the sea: Lt. William Conway Whittle, CSN. And this risk was only the first in a Homeric voyage that promised more, and ever more terrible, risks.

What a busy day these twenty-four hours have been. Thank God we have a fine set of men and officers, and, although we have an immense deal to contend with, we are industrious and alive to the emergency.

Just the sort of mild pleasantries (aside from that "emergency") one might expect from the mind of a slightly built twenty-four-year-old with narrow, sloping shoulders; a high, almost scholarly forehead crowned by a severely combed pompadour; narrow-set, vaguely disapproving eyes; and a small mouth that gave no hint of the eloquent mind inside. He could have been a schoolmaster or an assistant bank clerk. But on this day—October 26, 1864—young Lieutenant Whittle commenced the log of an odyssey that would take its place among the most evocative testimonials produced by the Civil War.

※◎※

Sea King's cargo of coal had been a ruse. The emergency was real. The coal had been the final camouflage in a desperate, nonesuch skein of conspiracy conceived and carried out over many months by Whittle and senior agents of the Confederacy working discreetly in London and Paris late in the Civil War: a scheme to obtain this speedster of a ship—this *Sea King*—from the English merchant navy with the quiet consent of Queen Victoria herself; load up a cargo of the black, fumy stuff; and, keeping her disguised as a harmless freighter, ease her out of the harbor at London, down the Thames into the English Channel, and from there toward her destiny as a killer of Yankee vessels. She would be met by her Rebel crew and her supply of armaments somewhere on the open ocean, far from the prying eyes of Yankee spies. *Sea King*'s cover story was virtually airtight. There was just one tie to the Confederacy when she finally left England, in fact there was only one Rebel on board at all, and he was undercover: Lt. William Conway Whittle, CSN, also known as "Mr. Brown."

Conway Whittle was an ideal figure for this mission. He'd been personally selected by top Confederate operatives in Europe to be the ship's executive officer, second in rank only to the captain. On the heels of his dashing exploits as a blockade runner, Whittle had been secretly summoned to Paris in September 1864. There he met with Commodore Samuel Barron, a lifelong friend of Whittle's father, Commodore W. C. Whittle, and one of young Lieutenant Whittle's primary mentors. Commodore Barron was also one of the key figures in the Confederacy's hopes to patch together a navy from a European base. Barron handed young Whittle a letter that contained his instructions. He was to make his way via Liverpool to London and check into the fashionable Wood's Hotel under the "Brown" alias. On the Friday morning of October 7, carrying a newspaper and dressed in unobtrusive business attire, the young man was to take a seat in the hotel dining room, pull the corner of his napkin through a buttonhole in his jacket, and await a stranger who would ask him, "Is this Mr. Brown?"

This figure would be Richard Wright, an elderly Liverpool businessman who'd become wealthy through his investments in Southern cotton. It was Wright who had discreetly purchased the ship then known as *Sea King* and was in London to arrange its transfer to the Confederate Navy. After the Wood's Hotel rendezvous, Wright took "Brown" toward the East India Dock, so that the younger man could get a covert glimpse of the exquisitely built black, three-masted extreme clipper he would board before dawn the next day. Then, in his final act as the ship's owner, Wright took Whittle to a safe house where he introduced him to Capt. Peter S. Corbett, *Sea King*'s interim captain, and formally gave Corbett power of attorney to sell the ship at any time, to any suitable offer. As all three knew, it was an offer already accepted.

At 3:00 a.m. on Sunday, October 8, "Brown" performed the final act in the elaborate ruse concocted for him. He checked out of the hotel and headed for the waterfront, stumbling and reeling like a drunken man. At the dock, he gazed upward at *Sea King*'s bowsprit, then pretended to steady himself for what would appear to be any old besotted sailor's last-minute return on board after a night of AWOL pub-crawling. No one moved to stop him. Still, rather than risk the conspicuous gangway, he crawled over *Sea King*'s low-slung hull near the forerigging. Within moments the ship cast off and began to idle her way down the Thames—the first small leg of a voyage that would take her around the world.

Sea King's slow passage toward the Atlantic was excruciatingly hazardous, a gauntlet that could doom her at any moment. Both Yankee and Rebel spies (and counterspies) prowled the docks at London and Liverpool, the eyes and ears of both the embattled governments across the sea. From the first days of secession, the officially neutral Great Britain had been frantically courted by American diplomats from both the North and the South. Even at this late stage, her two great shipyards held the potential to turn the war one way or the other. Thus, hardly any ship moved in and out of either port city without scrutiny and rapidly relayed comment.

The Confederacy needed Britain far more than the Union did. Southern strategists dreamed of giant ironclads and took steps to have them built at Liverpool; ironclads that could steam west across the Atlantic, smash the Union blockade, reestablish the cotton trade with Britain, and even perhaps move up the Atlantic coast and the inland waterways, shelling Northern cities as cannonballs bounced helplessly off their plated sides. British merchants, long since grown fat on the slave-harvested Dixie cotton spun into textiles in their mills, heavily favored an economic/military alliance with the South.

The industrial Union, by contrast, competed with England for the South's raw materials, had little to offer England in the way of lucrative trade, and in fact suffered British ill will that still lingered from the unpleasantness involving General Cornwallis, Yorktown, and the Declaration of Independence. And then of course the War of 1812. Lord Palmerston, the head of the British government, could hardly hear the words "American democracy" without harrumphing.

Thus a British-Confederate alliance, in the war's early weeks and months, seemed to need just the formalizing strokes of a few pens. The inevitability was delayed only by American diplomacy and American intelligence.

But *what* diplomacy! And *what* intelligence! Holding the fabric of British neutrality together virtually with their bare hands were a determined duo of American diplomats as brilliant, tough, resourceful, and utterly inexhaustible as they were different from each other. They arrived separately in Great Britain in 1861, each appointed by Abraham Lincoln. One of them, a bearded, jug-eared Quaker from New Jersey, set up a vast and intricate network of information agents from his Liverpool office as American consul. He fed the results—munitions transactions, secret and illicit shipbuilding agreements, blockade-running plans—to his "odd-couple" colleague at the Court of St. James in London: a cold, aloof patrician from America's most distinguished family who held the lofty ambassadorial title Envoy Extraordinary and Minister Plenipotentiary. The ambassador in turn used this information to forestall the dreaded alliance: he mounted eloquent arguments to Parliament that Britain was violating its own legal standards of neutrality, and demanded that Her Majesty's government uphold its sacred ideals.

Their names were Thomas H. Dudley and Charles Francis Adams. It was their combined power—the power of the United States itself, in the end—that young Lt. William Conway Whittle would soon find himself matched against in a desperate cat-and-mouse game that would span the globe.

In fact, Thomas Dudley had already got wind of *Sea King*. Before she was moved to London, the United States consul in Liverpool had received a tip from a detective regarding a suspiciously sleek-looking craft docked on the Mersey. Dudley took a look for himself, and notified Charles Adams in London that he was keeping an eye on a likely privateer. But Dudley was lulled by subterfuge, and waited too long to act. The ship's operatives, wary of just such attention, allowed *Sea King* to saunter in and out of various ports on the English coast, like a merchantman searching for a cargo, until the consul's suspicion waned. None of the crew had an inkling of the ship's true purpose; they were professional British sailors who had signed on to what they'd been told was a straightforward commercial voyage: London to Bombay and back, a fine payday on a fine new ship. And so even though *Sea King* had left London without interference, she had not sailed with indifference.

Enemy spyglasses had followed her as she made her way along the Thames in the early-morning sunlight, sweeping her sides and decks for any sign of armaments. They saw none. But Adams, still not convinced *Sea King* was neutral, and despite the fact that she had left her dock, wanted a closer look. He called in the U.S. Navy. Adams alerted two warships, USS *Niagara*, one of the navy's fastest and most heavily armed steam frigates, and USS *Sacramento*, another steam-powered warship, both on patrol in the English Channel.

Niagara and *Sacramento* were lethal predators. Only a few days after *Sea King*'s nerve-racking creep down the Thames, these two sprang at a peaceful Spanish steamer, overwhelming the merchant ship, holding her in custody and searching her for two days, all in British waters. It was Adams himself who ordered her released.

Official Britain's deference to the U.S. Navy's interests infuriated the Confederacy, especially given the country's long history as an enthusiastic buyer of Southern cotton. "The British Government will scarcely give our public ships common shelter," complained one Southern naval man to another,

> and we can not send an unarmed vessel in the direction of North America without embarrassing and annoying enquiries from the customs and board of trade officials. Yet United States ships of war are permitted to lie in English ports and watch British ships, as in the case of the Georgia, previously reported, and are allowed to cruise and make captures of neutral ships off the largest port of the kingdom and in waters which were once considered exclusively British.[1]

It was sheer luck—augmented by careful planning—that enabled Sea King to slip past these watchdogs and not find her adventure over before it began. By nightfall the nascent Rebel cruiser had raced out of the Channel and entered the Atlantic. Yet the hunt for her was not over. It had scarcely begun. But by now, some eighteen days later, she sailed alone far out in the open Atlantic, with the docks of London nearly three thousand miles astern. The coal had been mostly shifted, making way for the new, more pertinent cargo. An awe-inspiring vessel was emerging: a tiny, diehard crew, working a dramatic transformation under Whittle's eye and guidance, was creating a warship, even as she raced south ahead of the wind.

Sea King had transmuted into Shenandoah. She had joined that small, scattered cadre of fast, light cruisers bent on a quest that seemed wildly impossible, if not deluded, on its face: to reverse the course of the Civil War.

Never in the history of armed national conflict, not even at Agincourt, had the investment of hope in a handful of gallant and daring individuals seemed so utterly pointless, so drastically out of scale. Their goals were manifold, and breathtaking: to rip a hole in the skin of the

Federal blockade and thus open up channels of desperately needed arms and goods flowing from England to Dixie; to cripple Yankee shipping, along with the economically vital Yankee whaling fleet; to end Britain's official neutrality and ignite the rapid construction of a Confederate navy in British shipyards; and, in sum, to shock and disable Abraham Lincoln's war machine as traumatically as Stonewall Jackson's infantry had shocked it at Bull Run and Chancellorsville.

✥

As for the "emergency" Whittle had noted—well, on *Shenandoah*'s first day there were plenty of emergencies. A dangerously undermanned crew, for one. Barely enough men to hoist the anchor, and far too few to "fight the ship," the inclusive term for naval combat and its manpower requirements: men to load and fire the heavy guns, men to return small-arms fire, men to repel boarders, men to operate the ship's sails while all the others were under fire. Whittle's fondness for that term underscored his fundamental perception of *Shenandoah* herself. It was as if the ship, beautiful, fast, and complex as she was, was basically an elaborate weapon. A weapon he could not hope to operate, shorthanded as he was.

His cannon were still in boxes, his rifles had no marines.

And despite the fact that *Shenandoah*'s speed and agility might well be enough to keep her out of combat with a Yankee warship, shorthanded as she was, she probably wouldn't have manpower enough to survive a severe storm.

Twenty-two very young seamen of dubious allegiance and twenty-four officers, doing the work of a hundred fifty. (Among these, to be sure, was Southern royalty: Lt. Smith Lee, nephew of a certain commander of the Army of Northern Virginia.)

There was the "emergency" of imminent capture—or worse. Yankee warships crisscrossed the Atlantic like wasps, ever vigilant for targets such as this one. And while *Shenandoah,* one of the fastest ships afloat, could outrun any of these, if she were somehow to be surprised, she could not fire a shot in her own defense; her guns remained belowdecks in crates, camouflaged as farm equipment.

Which led to the emergency of Mr. O'Shea's foot:

Mr. O'Shea our carpenter hurt his foot very much today but I trust he will not lay up for it as the heaviest of our work now comes in his department.

The heaviest, and, aside from navigation, the most vital. Mr. O'Shea's department was charged, for example, with sawing hinged ports in the ship's eleven-inch teak sides, ports through which those vital cannon barrels would soon glower: two thirty-two-pounders and six sixty-eight-pounders. For want of Mr. O'Shea's foot, in short, a Cause could be lost. But the master carpenter had refused to buckle. Nor had anyone buckled, for that matter, not even the new recruits.

We are getting along wonderfully. Never did I see a set of officers and men work harder or more cheerfully than our noble hands. . . . The holy devotion to the cause has been handed by the officers to the men, and the work is not only done but cheerfully done.

❧

The hard work had commenced a few days earlier, at Funchal, principal port of the Madeira Islands, a Portuguese possession nearly five hundred miles off the African coast. There, still in its merchant trappings, the camouflaged raider waited for a carefully timed rendezvous with another undercover Confederate naval asset. *Laurel,* a fast supply steam packet, had eased out of Liverpool and down the Mersey less than two hours after *Sea King*'s departure from London. Seeking further refuge from inquisitive Portuguese eyes, the two ships left Funchal after sharing a secret signal, again several hours apart—then closed their distance on the open sea and slipped into the shallow waters off the appropriately named island Deserta. There, both crews sweated and strained around the clock to transfer the goods from *Laurel* to *Sea King.* The two ships were lashed together; any passing U.S. Navy warship could have used them for target practice. None did.

On October 19, in a brisk but formal ceremony, *Shenandoah* received her commission and her new name. Two days after that, she put to sea again, and the real transformation began.

In her final form, *Shenandoah* was a black-hulled stiletto: a year old, 230 feet long and 32.5 feet wide. She weighed 1,018 tons. In her bowels churned a 250-horsepower steam engine that turned a fourteen-foot bronze propeller. When others were becalmed, *Shenandoah* was capable of eight knots. Under favorable winds, with her extreme clipper hull and immense spread of canvas, she could double that. On her maiden voyage, under her first owners, *Sea King* had demonstrated her composite design's breakthrough attribute: speed. She was built specifically to race the first tea shipments from the latest Chinese harvest back to the ravenous markets of London. The first cargo to arrive was allowed to "make the market" by setting the price. Until the next ship began offloading, the winner was guaranteed the handsome benefits of cornering the market.

In London in the 1860s, fortunes rode on the price of tea, and in 1863 a bet on *Sea King* had been a winner. The necessity for speed above all else drove the invention of ever more sophisticated ships. It all came down to modern design, new approaches to age-old technology. Something as simple as wire rope spun from drawn wire, something as basic as cast-iron ribs and cross-bracing gave these ships an almost uncanny ability to survive a storm. And to exploit one. The ships known at the time as extreme clippers now offered the captain two options in a gale: The first was hang on, buttoned up and riding safely pointed into the waves, waiting for the wind to die down, the old way. The second way was storm riding. Suicidal in an earlier age, it now meant sailing with the wind, riding the storm. In fact, it meant keeping far too many sails aloft even to turn back into the storm for safety. Speed was everything, but it carried a cost. This choice meant keeping the sails up, not down. It meant letting the storm drive the ship from behind. It meant giving over control of the ship to the wind itself. You rode with the violence of the storm, a hair-raising experience for most old-school sailors who would always heave to and wait out a storm. But not with the new clippers. Stories are told of a captain on one of these extreme clippers who took to padlocking the halyards, the ropes controlling the sails, so the terrified crew would not be able to take in canvas and slow down while their speed-maddened captain got some rest. The crew would have to ride it out. Some of the storm-driven extreme clippers are known to have covered over 400 miles in a single day.

On the first round-trip, *Sea King,* with her solid teak, copper-bottomed hull and her elaborate high-tech sails, some furled and unfurled almost automatically by men working from the decks, was going to prove unbeatable. She boasted three huge iron-made lower masts that were strong enough to hold the topmast thirteen stories above the deck. She was the final product of the explosive growth in ship design created by combining steam and sail.

Sea King also had two remarkable innovations, both of which ultimately became technological dead ends. First, she had a hoisting propeller: the huge bronze blade rode in an elaborate cradle and could be hoisted free of the drive shaft and stored above the waterline to reduce drag when she was under sail. Second, *Sea King* had been equipped with a lowering smokestack that gave her more room for canvas when the boiler was off; lowering the stack also made her look more like a traditional merchantman and not at all like a modern steam-driven warship. *Sea King* could set an immense, and immensely strong, spread of canvas, and her critical backup steam power meant that for days with no wind, *Sea King* would be unbeatable. Indeed, she set the London-Bombay-London round-trip speed record. She had earned her (somewhat androgynous) name.

But now her speed, strength, and long-range capabilities would be put to another purpose: not the creation of wealth, but its destruction.

Her mission was as simply stated as it was brutal: to prowl the seas of the world in search of Yankee merchant ships and whalers; and, upon contact, to capture, pillage, and sink them.

※◎❦※

Things were going "all very well," Conway Whittle recorded in his log book on that first day, "with one exception . . ."

The exception to all the good cheer would be Captain Waddell.

James Iredell Waddell. The powerfully built, brooding, infinitely complicated "Lieutenant Commanding"—the captain—of this warship was the second of the three men who knew *Shenandoah's* secret mission. A seasoned naval veteran of forty, his dark, sideburned face seared under too many unforgiving suns, Waddell was the oldest, by far, among the officers spirited aboard the *Laurel* at night from a tug-boat on the Mersey, as part of the Rebels' complex subterfuge.

He'd been born in landlocked Chatham County, North Carolina, in 1824, adopted by his paternal grandmother, and "taught the rudi-ments of education in a school conducted by a very estimable lady, who did not believe in moral suasion,"[2] as he recalled in a brief and somewhat opaque memoir. The implication is that he was orphaned, then beaten by his teacher—which perhaps explains the reputation of an "incorrigible youngster"[3] given to "deviltry" that hung about him. Awarded an acting midshipman's appointment while still in his teens, he reported for active duty to the first ship he had ever boarded, and was overwhelmed by it: the three-decked man-of-war *Pennsylvania*, moored in the Elizabeth River at Norfolk. ("Can you wonder at my surprise? It seemed an endless undertaking [climbing] from the water up the companion ladder to the spar deck."[4]) He entered Annapolis in 1841; a year later, his incorrigibility having darkened into moodiness and a taste for violence, he fought a duel with another midshipman and took a round in his hip. The lead ball stayed inside him and caused him to limp painfully for the rest of his life.

He served a brief stint as professor of navigation at Annapolis, but grew to detest the classroom; he wanted action. "The all important, useful and necessary branches of my profession," he declared later in life, "I learned at sea, on ship board, while a boy."[5] Action he soon got: the Gulf of Mexico, including engagement at Vera Cruz in the Mexi-can War; promotion to second lieutenant aboard the USS *German-town* off the coast of Brazil; duty with the East India Squadron, where he learned of the imminent North-South conflict. He returned to the States in 1861, hoping for peace and opposed to secession, but re-solved to fight for his South if war broke out. He married his fiancée, Ann Sellman Inglehart, in December 1861.

⚓

The war's eruption found James Waddell holding on to a time-honored code of military honor—protect your homeland—that abruptly no longer applied. After the Rebel victory at the Battle of

Bull Run, he wrote a polite letter of resignation to the secretary of the navy, explaining his sense of obligation to family and region. Still, his sense of duty impelled him to remain loyally at his post aboard the gunship USS *Adams* until it returned to port. He wrote a second, even more elaborate letter, filled with courtesies, to President Lincoln himself.

Waddell's courtliness was rewarded with a curt dismissive slap in a letter from Navy Secretary Gideon Welles: Waddell's resignation had been received, and his name stricken from the rolls. When Waddell inquired about the military pay due him, Welles informed him that the money would be forthcoming—provided Waddell signed a document promising he would not take part in the war.

Waddell was furious; he'd earned his salary, and honor required that it be paid him. As for Welles's requirement that he sign a non-combatant promise, that was nothing less than bribery! James Waddell decided to flee, and lost no time forging a difficult, rain-lashed, and peril-laden trek by schooner and wagon from New York Harbor through occupied Maryland to Richmond, where, on March 27, 1862, he was commissioned a lieutenant in the Confederate Navy. He carried his rage against Welles for the rest of his life. It had fermented deeply, along with his already volatile nature, when he reported to duty under the Confederacy's supreme offshore operative, James D. Bulloch, and was sent aboard the black raider.

Bulloch—author of that complaining letter to Secretary Mallory about Britain's partiality to the Union Navy—was the third Confederate operative who knew *Sea King*'s true identity. An archangel of the Cause, he had been assigned the impossible task of forging a Confederate navy virtually out of thin air. In the spring of 1861, at age thirty-eight, he'd found himself appointed the Rebels' chief procurement agent. A tough, shrewd, fearless Georgian, a veteran of two decades as a U.S. naval officer and merchant mariner, the balding and brilliantly bearded Bulloch was a godsend in many ways. As important as his thorough knowledge of ships and the sea was his partisan ferocity. Bulloch radiated a political worldview that made Jefferson Davis look conciliatory by comparison, and he thought nothing of risking his life or his fortune, or his family, to help attain it. He'd walked away from

wealth and prestige as a leading New York merchant to defend the
Cause. (In departing New York, he left behind his wife, Harriet, and
his sister Martha, who was married to the eminent Theodore Roosevelt Sr. and was the mother of an adventurous little boy.)

Bulloch, with two seasoned naval officers both eager for sea duty,
had more or less assigned Whittle and Waddell joint control of the
ship, but had given Waddell just a shade more rank than Whittle.
Ideal preconditions for rivalry. Could Whittle, at only twenty-four,
withstand the larger, older man's domineering instincts?

Waddell had already tested Whittle, in Deserta, while still at anchor. And lost. The confrontation stemmed from the prospect of taking a dangerously undermanned ship on the ocean to make war. Every
instinct in Waddell's military mind told him that this was folly—
madness. To his superiors, there had seemed little alternative. Attempts to recruit a full complement of sailors for the raider after the
transfer at Deserta had gone badly. Of the fifty-five men who'd sailed
the *Sea King* out of London (realizing ten days out that they were no
longer headed for Bombay and none too happy about it), only four
had signed up—two of them cabin boys. Not even Waddell's volup-
tuous sifting of gold coins in a chest as he stood before the assembled
Englishmen could generate a groundswell of volunteering.

Thus *Shenandoah's* manpower, even before she set sail, remained
critically below any rational minimum. At Deserta the officers had
been obliged to help the crewmen set the sails and raise the anchor—
an unheard-of breach of military tradition, but necessary. Nearly obsessed with manpower—this was, after all, his first command, and he
felt the weight of it—Waddell had argued for making a bold entry into
some island port and brazenly rounding up seamen and supplies before
launching any serious open-water search for Yankee prey. Whittle saw
this as tantamount to annihilation. Even the Portuguese roustabouts at
Funchal had recognized the black ship as a raider in mufti. Did Waddell imagine that another such incursion—now a violation of the rules
of neutrality—would go unresisted, and unreported?

*We could not have gotten men, we could not fit our ship and would
have had a Yankee fleet waiting at the entrance to the harbor and*

our position would have been most humiliating. No indeed, I shall never regret the advice I gave and which advice I flatter myself kept us at sea.

Conway Whittle had won this first engagement of wills with his intimidating co-commander. It was a victory that privately outraged Waddell's notions of military standards; it worked into his psyche. "Responsibility weighed upon my mind," he wrote in his own journal, "and reflection often created an absence of everything in active movement around me . . . national property and an important cruise were trusted to me . . . upon the accuracy of all the calculations of my judgment . . . depended success or failure." Strange broodings, those: the thoughts of a man haunted by fears of catastrophe, and strikingly at odds with the intimidating face he presented to the world. That phrase, "and reflection often created an absence of everything in active movement around me"—it conveyed hints of a dark poet. As if to confirm this, Waddell inserted a further note of vulnerability even more deeply at odds with his image as a cold, domineering officer: "I have no doubt I very often appeared to those with me an unsocial and peculiar man."[6]

Whittle's victory over the captain had immediately birthed another crisis. Now he must demonstrate that his instinct to remain at sea was not equally foolhardy. How long could *Shenandoah* remain operational on a skeleton crew? How long would the sailors' morale hold out under these conditions? How deep was their loyalty to *Shenandoah*'s mission, given that capture, following any act of war on their part, could well mean imprisonment, even death by hanging? How many days—hours—could Whittle count on before the hard work and good cheer turned sour? Turned, in its most terrifying form, into mutiny?

The answers to all these questions hinged on the speed with which Whittle could bring the crew up to full strength. And there remained only one possible means to accomplish that task: enlisting sailors from the Yankee merchantmen that *Shenandoah* spotted, outraced, brought to heel, and sank.

Whittle was taking a chance here by violating neutrality standards on the high seas, and he doubtless knew it. His plan struck some ears as a version of impressment, the despised naval practice of snatching men from other countries' sailing ships and even coastal towns, and forcing them to serve against their will. Impressments were a tactic of the British navy that predated the eighteenth century and had been used ruthlessly, especially against American merchantmen. The British claimed a fig leaf of legitimacy in these seizures: they were looking to reclaim deserters from the Crown who had signed on with American ships for better pay, but hundreds of their victims had been natural-born U.S. citizens. Impressment was simply another form of piracy. In 1812, President James Madison declared war on Britain largely to force a halt to the practice.

But what if seamen from a captured ship *wished* to sign on with the conqueror? What if their shift of loyalties were prompted not by pistols, but by incentives—the promise of steady pay on a magnificent ship, and of high adventure undreamed of in the merchant trade, and, most tantalizingly, a share of all the riches harvested from their plump, prosperous prey?

This would be Conway Whittle's adaptation of impressment. He would respect the neutrality of any nonbelligerent vessel, limiting his approaches to men from Yankee merchantmen. No coercion, only persuasion. And if the United States of America complained—well, there was already a war on.

Shenandoah, then, would gather its crew even as it plied the seas. That was the optimistic plan, at any rate—James Waddell's affronted judgment notwithstanding. But as afternoon gave way to twilight on October 26, 1864, Conway Whittle understood that the mission's survival depended on his optimism being justified in very short order: he needed a conquest, and he needed it urgently. He needed it, if possible, even before the ship's guns were fixed and ready to fire.

⚜

James Waddell's impulse to test Whittle probably sprang from a deep well of frustration the veteran seaman had by now accumulated regarding the Confederate navy, its prospects, its lost opportunities. He had watched helplessly in the early months of the war as the C.S.A.

poured much of its scarce finances into wooden warships in England built by agents friendly to the South. "I have mentioned a belief," he wrote darkly after it was all over, "from the fact that as the South had no seamen, it was unwise to buy or build fighting ships." He'd looked on in 1863 as a far more hopeful project, two magnificent ironclads, discreetly funded by wealthy Dixie businessmen and constructed at Laird Brothers Shipyards, across the Mersey from Liverpool, were embargoed by the British government. Waddell himself was skeptical of the general belief that those ironclads might have changed the course of the war: impervious as they were to bombardment, they could not only have run the Federal blockade, but attacked and reduced Northern coastal cities.

The type of Southern naval warfare that did make sense to Waddell—fast, lightly armed ships such as *Shenandoah* and others, racing over the oceans to make surgical strikes against Yankee freighters—was mobilized too late, in his opinion: "I will say with pardonable modesty that had any number of vessels capable of carrying one gun been purchased abroad by the Confederacy early in the war, they would have driven from the seas or captured the merchant marine of the enemy . . . If the South could have contested the supremacy of the ocean with the enemy, it would have been [a different] war."[7]

As *Shenandoah* sailed southwestward toward her destiny, she headed into the gunsights of some of the most powerful figures of the mid-nineteenth century. Intelligent, experienced men on both sides of the American conflict, and also in Great Britain, were far from inclined to dismiss the power of Confederate raiding ships out of hand. They knew from experience the maritime devastation these scourges could deliver.

Some half-dozen other Confederate raiders had preceded *Shenandoah* into the hunt for Yankee prey. Yet their combined raids devastatingly justified Waddell's wish that more of them had come sooner; they destroyed, captured, or drove abroad to flags of convenience more than a million tons of Union cargo ships, in a sort of dress rehearsal for naval strategies in a war yet seventy-five years in the future.

Among the seven were *Shenandoah*'s two sister ships from the Liverpool yards, the *Florida* and the legendary *Alabama*. *Florida* (formerly the *Manassas*) enjoyed sporadic success. Shortly after being launched at Liverpool in the summer of 1862, she crossed the Atlantic undetected and staggered through the Union blockade into quarantine at Mobile Bay, her small crew stricken with yellow fever. She surged back into action on a stormy sea on the night of January 17, 1863, outraced a Yankee warship, and captured twenty-four merchantmen through the following August. After a six-month hiatus at Brest for repairs, *Florida* rounded up thirteen more enemy ships and then, hemmed in by the Federal cruiser *Wachusett* off the coast of Brazil, was rammed in the harbor, and eventually sunk. That the neutrality of a sovereign nation had been violated by the U.S. Navy meant little to the world at large, but on a personal and professional level, the stories of the harsh—some said barbarous—treatment handed out to the captive crew of *Florida* lodged deeply in the consciousness of officers and gentlemen such as Waddell and Whittle.

Alabama fared a bit better. The craft soon to gain fame as "the Greyhound of the Seas" had slid into the waters along with *Florida* in the summer of 1862, under the ferocious command of Captain Raphael Semmes. Powered along by twin 300-horsepower engines under her massive sails, a deadly fighter with her pivoting, hundred-pound Blakely rifle and six thirty-two-pounders, her crew of 120 men and 24 officers resplendent in their crisp duck frocks, straw hats, and polished shoes, *Alabama* proved a nightmare ship to the Yankee merchant fleet. She captured and burned her way through the North Atlantic and the West Indies and rounded the South African coast, laying waste to more than sixty ships in two years—the highest number of conquests in recorded naval history. In June 1864, four months before *Shenandoah*'s launching, CSS *Alabama* was drawn into battle and sunk off Cherbourg, France, by the pursuing Union warship *Kearsarge*. Several *Alabama* survivors were now among the young officers aboard *Shenandoah;* men apart, already, despite their tender ages; figures of legend.

The South did not have the luxury of regarding the raiders' outsized conquests as windfall victories. For the Confederate States of America to have the faintest prayer of converting its present debacle into victory—or, more likely, an endless deadlock—its scattered pastiche of a navy would need to achieve the impossible again, and again, and again. And then again. Overwhelmed by a well-equipped, deeply structured, and highly rationalized United States Navy—the shipyards from Maine to Maryland mobilizing to expand the fleet—the South faced slow strangulation from the sea: its great sweeping arc of coastline, 3,600 miles from Chesapeake Bay to the Gulf Coast of Texas, was rapidly ringed by a Union blockade.

At first the blockade, improbably, had been thought a godsend for the Rebels. Europe's booming textile mills, chiefly those in Britain and France, depended on imports of Southern cotton, and the architects of secession assumed that these countries would unleash their naval might against the North as a matter of self-interest. This had not happened, though Britain had come tantalizingly close to recognizing the Confederacy as a legitimate nation in the early stages of the war. Only the unstinting persuasion and argument of dedicated Washington diplomats had preserved neutrality, and for three years the Yankee stranglehold, though famously porous, had worked: the Southern treasury was depleted. Moreover, the expected large-scale importation of manufactured goods—guns and ammunition in particular—had never materialized. And the Confederacy labored on to cobble together a naval force, and naval strategy, by whatever means lay at hand.

"Whatever means" fell to a shrewd fat man of fussy tastes named Stephen R. Mallory, a former helper at his mother's Key West, Florida, boardinghouse. Mallory had grown up to study admiralty law, serve two terms in the United States Senate, and, in 1853, win an appointment as chairman of the Naval Affairs Committee. He spearheaded the midcentury modernization of the United States Navy, infusing it with elegant new steam-powered frigates and sloops of war, which Mallory himself would soon be dreaming up ways to sink, and streamlining the naval chain of command, which he would soon be trying to outwit. Following his native state into secession in 1861 and nominated by Jefferson Davis to be the Confederacy's secretary of the navy, Stephen Mallory now faced the undignified and certainly daunting prospect of fighting against his own nautical war machine.

That machine was now in most capable hands. Gideon Welles, with his seaweed-styled beard, was the very picture of the nautical commander. He looked like Neptune. To Abraham Lincoln, who appointed him secretary of the navy, he *was* Neptune—"Old Father Neptune," as Honest Abe liked to call him. Welles was in fact a classic upper-crust New Englander (Connecticut, the Cheshire Academy) who, though sharp-witted, had no training whatsoever in anything to do with the sea. (He'd expected to be named postmaster general.) He did understand administration, and had an eye for the big picture. With the wealth of the industrial North backing him, Welles quickly expanded the work that Mallory, now his adversary, had begun: he expanded the Union navy's size, scope, and firepower capacity; he quickly implemented a blockade plan; and he set about tightening the vise on the Confederacy's underdefended ports and drastically overmatched sea power.

Welles was aided by a number of savvy naval professionals in his department; but his Rebel counterpart, in this aspect at least, held the advantage. In James Dunwoody Bulloch, Mallory had his own Mallory.

Bulloch would need to exhaust all his gifts of relentless brilliance, because the shopping list that Mallory handed him was staggering; it added up to a new navy. Complete with sailors. Bulloch would have to conduct his shopping abroad, given that "Southern shipbuilding" was virtually a contradiction in terms. Shopping abroad, in turn, meant that the patrician Bulloch would have to function as a secret agent: the neutrality provisions maintained by the European powers prohibited any purchase of war goods by a belligerent in the American war. Furthermore, Britain's forty-two-year-old Foreign Enlistment Act criminalized the recruitment of seamen (or any other armed combatant) within the borders of Victoria's globe-girdling Empire.

It would require a mastermind—and a steel-nerved one, at that—

to find a way around, or through, these seemingly airtight provisions. By early June 1861, Bulloch was in Liverpool under an assumed name. By the summer of 1862, remarkably just over twelve months, he had arranged for the construction, acquisition, and deployment of the CSS *Alabama,* one of the most successful commerce raiders in the history of naval warfare. The costs to the North began to mount up. Maritime insurance rates skyrocketed, and Yankee ships rotted at the dock rather than risk destruction. Bulloch had done his job well, and despite the loss of *Alabama* and the ever-tightening blockade, by the fall of 1864 he was about to send the fastest ship on the ocean after the U.S. Merchant Marine.

❧

From Lieutenant Whittle's log of October 26, 1864: "This afternoon made our first chase. She was a fully rigged ship to leeward but we had not the daylight to catch her."

Nor were the guns in any shape to engage her if necessary, for that matter. The "tackles" required to hold the cannon fast after firing were lost—left behind in the confusion and haste at Deserta, apparently, or perhaps intercepted by Yankee agents on the pier in Liverpool. This would not pose a fatal problem vis-à-vis the generally unarmed merchant ships. But if a Yankee man-of-war should happen to close on her in darkness, *Shenandoah* would be a floating target for a cannonade. Whittle had ordered the crew to shove her unsecured cannon barrels through those newly sawed ports anyway, if only as a bluff.

> *I trust we may soon get a prize from which we may get some men. Imagine my anxiety to have more when I say that one more man* [in each watch] *would do an immense amount of good. Think of a ship of this size having only four men in a watch . . .*

It was a time for trusting in God's aid; and God had not thus far displayed much more inclination than Britain to intervene in the Southern cause. Night came on; *Shenandoah* raced blindly through the gathering darkness toward its quarry until pursuit grew impossible.

The raider had covered her first 1,500 miles since hoisting the Confederate navy battle flag in the Madeiras, their last known location. Even now the U.S. Navy would need to search over a million square miles of the Atlantic to find them. The loneliness had only begun. And the time for decisive action was already running out.

2

I f the South's greatest weapon in the Civil War was the knightly spirit of its fighting men, Conway Whittle was the Southern arsenal incarnate.

Like many young officers of his time and region, Whittle was an innate patriot, and not an ideologue. That the "peculiar institution" of slavery predominated over all other issues as an ignition point for the Civil War is scarcely a matter of serious debate. Nor is the wrongness of the South's insistence that slavery was divinely ordained and thus a legitimate social institution. But as in all wars, it was the political leadership on each belligerent side that staked out the predicates for armed conflict; it was the press and the pulpit that inflamed public opinion; and it was the young men who did the fighting and bleeding and starving and dying, and who worked out their private rationales for fighting and bleeding and starving and dying.

Vast numbers of Southern boys supported slavery, and the racial assumptions that enabled it, without question—as did vast numbers of Northern boys. For many others—and this was especially true of the officer class, who generally had more discretion in choosing which side to fight for—the motivating impulse was not perpetuation of human bondage, but a defense of nationhood, and of place.

Waddell was a good example of this ethic—Waddell, who had been so rudely treated by Gideon Welles when he tried to explain it in his letter of resignation from the U.S. Navy. Years after the war, in his memoirs, Waddell meditated on the typical officer's mindset—detachment from ideology, yet passion for homeland:

Naval officers are very conservative men. They had nothing to do with the contest between the political elements of the North and the South. . . . Those discussions which excited sectional discord and animosities among the people, exercised small influence upon the minds of naval officers. Their opinions on political questions were generally in condemnation of the doctrines set for them by noisy demagogues and wild theorists.

For Waddell, and for thousands of Southern men caught up in the terrible war, the Southern "cause" had little to do with an appetite for subjugating other human beings, or even for rejection of the American nation. As he wrote in his memoirs,

It is well known with what regret they threw aside those emblems and decorations [of their service to the Union] . . . *the Federal flag was dear to them, but they were forced to abandon it or sail beneath its folds to the destruction of their homes and their kindred.*[8]

Such a choice had confronted Conway Whittle.

He was the offspring, one of eleven, of the legendary Commodore William Conway Whittle, a hero of both the United States and (later) the Confederate navies. (A portrait of the elder Whittle shows a gaunt mariner in the epaulets and double brass buttons of his CSA uniform, chin tucked deep into his starched white collar, his mouth as straight and tight as a bayonet, his eyes blazing forth from beneath a dark avenger's brow.) Born at Norfolk in 1805, Commodore Whittle had entered the navy at age fifteen. Twenty-seven years later, at Vera Cruz, the pivotal battle of the Mexican War, he was in the thick of the first major amphibious landing of troops in the history of the U.S. Army. He survived heavy fire heading for the beach outside the walled city in an open boat, and was wounded while charging a parapet at the head of the soldiers from his ship.

The following year, on patrol against the slave trade, he was commanding a sloop-of-war off the coast of Africa when a plague of yellow fever swept through Norfolk and claimed the lives of his wife, Elizabeth Beverly Sinclair, and his eldest son, Arthur Sinclair Whittle.

Conway junior, then fourteen, survived. Whatever sort of boy he'd been, mass death and maternal bereavement interrupted that boyhood forever. Now commenced his maturation. His stoic father, returning home, enrolled him in the Naval Academy at Annapolis. The boy graduated at eighteen. But his achievements at Annapolis were only a prologue to the almost superhuman skein of wartime adventures that soon ensued—adventures that displayed not only Conway Whittle's fearlessness, but the rare combination of aggressiveness, gentleness, cunning, and chivalry that marked him as a latter-day knight errant.

Conway Whittle unleashed his first demonstration of valor under fire, and his remarkable knack for leadership, before his twentieth birthday.

In March 1860, as sectional tensions in the United States escalated toward civil war, Whittle was a midshipman aboard the USS *Preble* in the harbor of Vera Cruz—one of three American warships patrolling the tropical waters off the troubled shores of Mexico. In the wake of its 1848 military defeat by the United States, Mexico had been ravaged by uprisings within its borders. From without came armed men, fighters for both sides. The enlightened jurist and soon-to-be president Benito Juarez was struggling to preserve his reformist government's survival against both soldiers of fortune and regulars from Cuba and Spain—in fact, the armed proxies of the economically powerful Catholic church. The Illinois congressman Abraham Lincoln—to whom Juarez would one day be compared— was among the many Americans who recognized Juarez's democratic vision; and a concerned United States was about to give diplomatic recognition to his embattled government, which could well mean armed support.

Among the most dangerous revolutionaries stalking Juarez was Gen. Miguel Miramon, leader of the Church Party. General Miramon's troops had Juarez's weaker army pinned down inside the seaside capital city of Vera Cruz, holding threatening positions above and below the fortified harbor castle of San Juan Ulua. At the same time, a rebel naval expedition, fitted out in Cuba, was en route to attack Vera Cruz from the sea.

Providing unofficial support to Juarez's regime alongside *Preble* were the frigate *Savannah* and the sloop-of-war *Saratoga*. A desperate Juarez had appealed to the ships' senior commanding officer, Captain Joe Jarvis, to intercept the invading force.

While Jarvis hesitated—unsure of his authority to take action—a pair of mysterious two-masted steamships, showing no flags, hove into view off the harbor, heading toward the port. The loyalist troops inside the castle, in what Whittle would recall as "a spirit of bravado," fired a cannon in the ships' direction. The round fell far short, but the two ships quickly bore away to the southwest, toward the Rebel forces positioned some dozen miles below the harbor, near a reef called Anton Lizardo. Their colors remained concealed, but their purpose was clear, and being "combines"—steam-and-sail composites—their tactical advantage over Jarvis's far stronger but wind-driven squadron was significant. At least for a time.

Jarvis finally decided to investigate. At around seven o'clock in the March evening, he sent *Saratoga* out to overtake and inspect the strangers. In light air *Saratoga*, well armed but sail-powered, was ignominiously towed into harm's way by two small chartered steamers that Jarvis had hired as they lay at anchor inside the port: *Indianola*, a propeller-driven craft, and *Wave*, a side-wheeler. Crew for both came from the men of the squadron. Conway Whittle volunteered for *Wave*, which would be under the command of Lt. Joel Kennard. The small boat was hastily armed with a single howitzer of which Whittle would be in charge, and a force of twenty sailors with rifles. *Indianola* was similarly armed.

Whittle's journal records the action that soon erupted.

A beautiful moonlight soon overtook us . . . on approaching Anton Lizardo we saw the two vessels in a bend of the reef. One had anchored and the other, apparently, about to do so. As soon as they saw us, the one not anchored started off from us to the southward. Capt. Turner [aboard *Saratoga*] *fired a shot across her bow to bring her to, but she kept on. He then ordered the towing steamer to anchor the* Saratoga *near the steamer at anchor. This was done and both towboats were ordered to pursue the flying steamer and we, under full steam, gave chase.*

Indiana caught up first, at sometime after 11:00 p.m. Her officer in charge, Lt. Andrew Bryson, hailed the stranger in English, asking her name and nationality. He received no reply, and hailed her again in Spanish. The reply to this was "a full broadside from her guns. On hearing this, *Saratoga*, anchored near the other [stranger], fired at her and she promptly surrendered."

The broadside fired at *Indianola* by the second ship damaged her hull above the water. Both towing steamers now opened up on the remaining enemy, while *Saratoga*, some distance away, and anchored, guarded her captive. Aiming and firing the howitzer aboard the *Wave* throughout the engagement was young Conway Whittle.

With howitzers and musketry, we peppered her so vigorously that she [the second "mystery ship"] *turned around and ran to the northward. We followed, and keeping up and receiving vigorous fire. On the new course, the* Indianola *was thrown out of the fight by running aground on a spur of the reef, and despite her every effort, so remained until after the surrender.*

Soon the second mystery ship herself ran hard aground.

With the *Saratoga*, the squadron's flagship, still at anchor, her sails useless on a windless night, and the steamer *Indianola* badly shot up and aground, *Wave* took action alone. Overmatched in firepower if not determination, and in hot pursuit, she closed with her quarry. Instead of standing off from her prey, *Wave* chose close-quarters combat, setting herself up well inside small-arms range. Her marines fired at will. With *Wave* under her port quarter, the target unleashed her pivot-gun and musketry upon the Americans. Whittle, returning fire from *Wave*, found his howitzer jammed. Its lockstring had become entangled with the hammer. Improvising coolly under fire, the teenager grabbed a nearby carpenter's hammer and used it to explode the primer for the fight's duration. It lasted "until about 2:30 a.m. when [the enemy's] fire slackened and finally ceased and she showed an improvised white flag and surrendered."

On hearing the victorious crew's three cheers, *Saratoga* sent over a small boat in order to transport an officer of the *Wave* over to the defeated craft to receive her surrender. *Wave*'s crew nominated Midshipman Conway Whittle, who soon found himself the only American on board the vanquished ship. Her name was totemic indeed.

> *I found the prize to be the steamer* General Miramon *from Havana. The steamer which had surrendered to the* Saratoga, *was the* Marquis de Habana *from Havana. Both were under the command of Admiral Marin and each had about 100 men and several broadside and one pivot gun of good caliber, and laden with munitions of war for the revolutionists.*

Many of the enemy combatants had been wounded, including Admiral Marin, who was belowdecks. Whittle found the officer of the deck and demanded his sword. The officer had none, but handed Whittle his speaking trumpet in surrender. Alertly, the young midshipman summoned an engineer from *Wave* to check *Miramon*'s boiler pressure. The pressure proved to be near the point of explosion. Conway Whittle's thorough seamanship had saved the Spanish crew, and himself, from a terrible explosion.

The youth enjoyed a Tom Sawyerish moment of glory when *Indianola*, having finally ungrounded herself, steamed near the combatants and harrumphed out a demand for the Spaniards' surrender: "Much to their surprise, I replied that I was on board and had received the surrender."

The Mexican federal forces eventually overcame their powerful revolutionary enemies, and in 1861, Benito Juarez was elected president of Mexico. As for Conway Whittle, he reaped one final accolade for his exploits—one that doubtless gratified him far more than the cheers of his comrades. It was contained in a letter sent on March 23, 1860, by Lt. R. D. Miner, the official "Prizemaster" of *Miramon,* to one Captain William C. Whittle, U.S. Navy, describing his son's exploits in his first firefight:

> *Dear Sir:*
>   *It will no doubt be gratifying for you to know that your son, midshipman Whittle, is very highly spoken of for his conduct in the*

*action off Anton Lizardo. He had charge of a howitzer and fought it
well, and it was he who demanded the surrender of the steamer.*

Heroism enough for a young man not yet twenty. But Conway
Whittle had not even begun to fight.

❧

He had completed two years of active duty when the Civil War broke
out in 1861. Both father and son resigned their commissions in the
U.S. Navy and offered themselves to the Southern cause. The senior
Whittle accepted a commission as commodore from the Confederate
government. He commanded the early river defenses below Richmond, and later the Confederate naval debacle at New Orleans.

The son's first assignment hurled him to the epicenter of the belligerents' struggle for control of the seas. In October 1861, Conway
Whittle reported for duty aboard the CSS *Nashville,* a ship whose
name would soon be linked with his own in Southern folklore.

Nashville was an elegant 1,220-ton, two-masted side-wheel
steamer, built at Greenpoint, New York, in 1853 for peaceful pur-
poses: to carry fashionable passengers between Charleston, South
Carolina, and New York City. Her job description changed abruptly as
she lay in port at Charleston, South Carolina, in January 1861, when
the state seceded from the Union and *Nashville* became the first combat ship commissioned by the Confederacy. After witnessing the fall
of Fort Sumter in April, *Nashville* was hastily armed and swept up immediately into the cloak-and-dagger intrigue that swirled about the
South's frantic international efforts to build, beg, borrow, or steal a
navy.

She was dispatched eastward toward Great Britain the following
October, under the command of Lt. Robert Baker Pegram of Virginia.
Conway Whittle was on board as third lieutenant. Soon the young
man would be promoted to second lieutenant; not long after that, he
would assume command.

Among his comrades was a nearsighted young midshipman named
Irvine S. Bulloch. The Georgian was James Bulloch's half brother and
fully his equal as a Southern zealot. Obscure at this early stage of the

war, young Irvine Bulloch was destined to attain glory of his own, first aboard the legendary *Alabama*, and then aboard *Shenandoah*.

Lieutenant Pegram's original mission was to transport a pair of Confederate diplomats to London and Paris: Rebel ambassadors sent across the sea on behalf of their new country to see the leaders of old Europe, where they were expected to negotiate formal recognition of the Confederate States of America as a nation—and ally. These plans changed just before *Nashville* disembarked. Giving in to doubts that the ship could either outrun or outgun a Yankee warship (she was rather bulky, and carried only a couple of twelve-pound howitzers), Confederate authorities rebooked the diplomats to England via Havana, and dumped on *Nashville* an inglorious cargo of mail instead.

The chagrined Pegram proved that his ship could damn well run by slashing through the Union blockade of Charleston harbor on October 21 and bursting into the open sea toward his transatlantic mail drop. Off the coast of Britain, he decided to show the world that his ship and his nation could by-God fight, as well. Whittle was about to find himself not only on the first Confederate warship, but at the South's first offshore naval victory of the Civil War.

On November 19, *Nashville* caught a Yankee merchant ship, *Harvey Birch*, in the English Channel. She evacuated the crew, burned the vessel, and left her flaming wreckage before the shocked eyes of both England and France. Pegram and *Nashville* then docked at Southampton, where they were treated like conquering heroes. The incident made headlines in America and western Europe. And it caused discreet smiles under certain powdered wigs at Whitehall in London. The vast British industrial mills had been spinning Southern cotton into economic gold for decades, and Her Majesty's lords and ministers were tilting ever more precariously toward Dixie. In fact they had already launched the stately, cautious process toward alliance: on May 9, Britain had recognized both the North and the South as "belligerents." This action conferred a certain sovereign legitimacy on the Confederacy that led many in the South to believe that full recognition would soon follow, and with it a bounty of British industrial might that would neutralize the North's factory advantage and tip the balance of the war.

◈

Dashing as it was, Lieutenant Pegram's exploit served merely as an aftershock to an incident that spurred European sympathy for the South. This one was perpetrated by the North.

It involved those same Confederate diplomats who'd been displaced from Pegram's ship. Their names were John Slidell and James M. Mason. These two might well have enjoyed a faster ship than *Nashville* on the first leg of their crossing, but out of Havana they'd ended up on a plodding British-owned packet, the *Trent*. On November 8, as it chugged through the Caribbean toward the island of St. Thomas, *Trent* was intercepted by a Yankee sloop-of-war commanded by the swashbuckling if shortsighted Captain Charles Wilkes. Wilkes stormed aboard the packet, arrested the dignitaries, and hauled them off to a Union prison fortress.

His aim had been the same as Pegram's: to make a bold stroke that would rally the spirit and confidence of his embattled nation. He achieved recognition indeed, but with the wrong nation. Wilkes had embarrassed his country by stupidly violating its own restrictions against search of a neutral ship at sea and impressment of its crew. He had in a sense done Slidell and Mason's work for them.

The "*Trent* affair" spurred the momentum of British public opinion away from its tepid support of the United States. Only a latter-day revulsion against the practice of capturing and importing African slaves for hard labor—a practice Britain had helped pioneer—held the nation's sentiments in check. Just a year earlier, as the American crisis barreled toward flash point, the London *Times* had anguished: "Can any sane man believe that England and France will consent, as is now suggested, to stultify the [neutrality] policy of half a century for the sake of an extended cotton trade, and to purchase the favors of Charleston and Milledgeville by recognizing what . . . impels African labor toward the tropics on the other side of the Atlantic?"

Now the answer was edging toward "yes." The South seemed on the verge of nailing down a partnership with England that could make it the military and economic equal of the Union. Perhaps the rest of Europe would follow.

It was in this hopeful climate that CSS *Nashville,* having burned and sunk a fine U.S. merchant vessel, then docked at Southampton on November 21, the first ship to display the Confederate flag in British waters. For weeks, young Third Lieutenant Whittle witnessed a stream of welcoming visits laid on by British dignitaries. Towering over all of them, his white muttonchops fierce and his gaze steely, would be one of the titans of nineteenth-century geopolitics: the seventy-seven-year-old Henry Temple, the third Viscount Palmerston.

The once and future British prime minister deeply favored the Confederacy. It was Palmerston who had engineered the May recognition of the South as a belligerent. It was Palmerston who had thrown a torch on the *Trent* tinderbox by thundering to Parliament, "You may stand for this, but damned if I will!" and firing off an ultimatum to Washington demanding the diplomats' release—to which Lincoln wisely, if bitterly, acceded. Yet Palmerston's sympathy with the South was anything but sentimental. Since 1850 he had been the leading voice of Imperial Britain, obsessed with making his country the hub of what he grandly called "the new Rome"—the ruler of the world. He quietly hungered not so much to align Britain with the South as to claim those cotton and tobacco fields for the Crown, along with Europe, Russia, and the old Ottoman empire. Moreover, a severed America would be a crippled military threat. And slavery? Lord Palmerston did not understand the bother. His own servants seemed perfectly content.

Lord Palmerston's visit aboard *Nashville* occurred on Saturday, December 14, and coincided with some very bad news: bad for his empire-building schemes, and therefore bad news for the Confederacy.

Prince Albert, the Queen's beloved husband, had died at forty-one, succumbing to typhoid fever. Albert was no player in the diplomatic world, but he was the emotional fulcrum for Queen Victoria's life and the father of their nine children. His adoring widow immediately secluded herself, and would mourn his death for forty years. Victoria's sympathies favored the South, but Palmerston understood the calamity almost at once: her grief would virtually disable her, and prevent the viscount from urging her royal imprimatur on an alliance. Even in happy times, Victoria disliked her calculating prime minister. Palmerston's zeal for world dominion far exceeded her own—and besides, he'd been caught once trying to seduce one of her ladies-in-waiting. Hardly what one would call proper Victorian form.

The Confederates aboard *Nashville* could scarcely divine these currents, yet Lieutenant Pegram gallantly—and immediately—lowered the Confederate flag at the news. It did not go unnoticed. "Ours was one of the first flags half-masted at Southampton in recognition of the sad event which stirred the running hearts of a nation who revered their queen's husband," Whittle later wrote.

The implications of *Nashville*'s presence in the harbor changed abruptly from polite and political to precarious when a formidable predator materialized: the USS *Tuscarora*, commanded by Captain. T. A. M. Craven, bent on avenging the loss of *Harvey Birch*. Fast and heavily armed, *Tuscarora* docked imposingly close to the Confederate ship. Clearly, capture or destruction was on its agenda: a large, deadly cat beginning to toy with the rat in its trap. "She resorted to every expedient to watch us," wrote Whittle, "and took a position to prevent our escape."

Luckily for the Rebels, either the Admiralty acted without her, or the moment was so incendiary that the queen set aside her grief long enough to remind Captain Craven, through her ministers, of Britain's neutrality. Any confrontation within British waters would be treated as a violation of this neutrality, and dealt with harshly by Her Majesty's navy. The two ships were enjoined to leave the harbor twenty-four hours apart. *Tuscarora*, its tail twitching, slunk out of Southampton. Craven sailed her only as far as the Isle of Wight, where he began to prepare for combat as he watched the harbor entrance. Still within British jurisdiction, he waited at anchor for his prey, knowing *Nashville* would have to emerge or be seized.

But Captain Craven, like so many of the Federals, had reckoned without the vast web of Southern espionage that had quickly formed and spread throughout the Isles. "Our watchful friends reported this movement," Whittle recalled. These "friends" most likely included members of the British admiralty acting as spies for the Confederacy.

Armed with the information, Lieutenant Pegram passed it along to the pertinent naval authorities, along with notification that *Nashville* would be embarking the next day. The British wanted safe passage for *Nashville*, and they made certain that it happened. As Whittle wrote with obvious glee,

> At the time fixed, the Nashville, *with her flag flying in broad daylight, passed out in close view of the* Tuscarora, *near which was anchored the British frigate* Shannon, *sent down to see that the law was not violated . . . Captain Craven doubtless gnashed his teeth in impotent rage, for we left him to meditate upon the situation.*

CSN *Nashville*, with Her Majesty's navy providing backup, was now safe to strut about the ocean—for the time being.

At Bermuda for coaling in late February, having seen neither prey nor foe on the crossing, they encountered the crew of a North Carolina schooner, the *Pearl*, recently wrecked on the rocks. Pegram welcomed these sailors aboard, including the able pilot, Captain J. Beverage, and sailed out on the twenty-fourth, away from the Union sympathizers swarming the island. Their destination was Beaufort, North Carolina—on the fighting side of the Union blockade.

> *On February 26th, we captured and burned the American schooner,* Robert Gilfillan, *and took her crew onboard.*

Nashville was out to make as much trouble for the U.S. merchant navy as possible, but two days later, near the harbor entrance at Beaufort, they would sight as much trouble as the Confederates could ever wish: a hulking Yankee warship with inhospitable intentions. Some creative seamanship was called for.

> *Arriving south of and off Beaufort, February 28th a.m., we found the U.S. steamer* State of Georgia *blockading. As the entrance was narrow, we resorted to a* rouse de guerre.

Luckily, a "sister ship" to *Nashville*—a craft that closely resembled her, but that belonged to the Union—was known to be working the blockaded coast, carrying mail, relaying military orders, and "recruiting invalids of the blockading fleet," as Whittle later termed it in a phrase that dripped sarcasm.

With breathtaking audacity, the *Nashville* officers decided to "personate that vessel." Striking their own colors and raising a U.S. flag—retained on board for just such a moment—they "became" the docile mail shuttle. With the Stars and Stripes flying over a band of armed Rebels, the ship sailed directly toward the loaded cannons of her enemy.

We ran boldly for the blockader at slack speed in shore and abreast of her.

Pegram now had maneuvered the ships broadside to each other, but they still had yards of sea separating them. The *State of Georgia*'s long-range guns were now trained nearly point-blank on the virtually unarmed *Nashville* from whose masthead fluttered the Stars and Stripes. Then the unsuspecting *Georgia* fell for *Nashville*'s trick: she lowered a longboat and sent a detail of sailors to pick up "the mail." As the sailors heaved on the oars, *Nashville* continued to "drift" toward shore, until the crewmen of the launch rowed themselves directly in front of the muzzles of their own guns. The men in the longboat quickly became unsuspecting human shields—as the *Nashville* crew had intended.

When the boat was in the line of fire, we changed our course, hoisted our flag, headed full speed, ran into the harbor which was defended by Fort Macon on the east end of Bogue Island.

The *Georgia*'s sailors looked on in what Whittle imagined to be "an impotent state of rage." Finally—when the longboat had drifted out of harm, and *Nashville* had sailed out of effective range—*Georgia* let loose a volley. In the spirit of the moment, Pegram personally returned fire with one of *Nashville*'s signal guns, a peashooter. It managed about a third of the distance.

The playfulness of that escapade—coexisting as it did with deadly intent—is hard not to notice. It was characteristic of the Confederate navy, this chivalric *savoir faire:* a means of saluting one's adversaries, and laughing at death, that survived as a grace note of combat in the Western world up through the champagne-sipping, silk-scarf-wearing aviators of the early World War I years.

⁂

But the fun—if that's the term—was only beginning.

CSS *Nashville* had run the blockade, and in broad daylight, true enough, but even behind the guns of Fort Macon, she was now basically bottled up in port. Most certainly the game was still afoot.

Nashville made fast at the wharf at Morehead City, a tidy little right-angled town that formed the eastern terminus of the three-year-old Atlantic & North Carolina Railroad. Here, amid the sand dunes and sparkling waters of the Carolina shore, a grim struggle was soon to commence. A mighty force commanded by the Union major general Ambrose Burnside was gathering itself for an amphibious invasion of the Old North State*: 13,000 troops, transported on eighty ships, would soon converge here, and lay siege to the vulnerable Fort Macon. Scattered Union forces already prowled the land and shore. The Rebels were preparing to destroy the railroad in hopes of blunting the enemy's advance. *Nashville* was on hand to do what she could. Exposed, with at least one vengeful enemy ship in the vicinity, her existence dangled—once again—by a slender thread.

Captain Pegram immediately left the ship and boarded a train on the doomed line for the 250-mile trek northward to the Confederate capital at Richmond, Virginia, to receive new orders. He returned several days later with startling news: the government had sold *Nashville* to a group of Southern entrepreneurs, steamship men and investors, a firm called Fraser, Trenholm & Co. based in Liverpool and Charleston—the sort of money-men who always knew how to make warfare pay. Blockade runners *par excellence.* The ship would become their privateer, pending delivery in seaworthy condition. Pegram's or-

---

*The more familiar nickname "Tar Heel State" derives from a remark made, in tradition, by Robert E. Lee later in the war, in reference to the state's stubborn infantrymen who held their ground as though they had tar on their heels.

ders were to disarm the ship, strip it of every piece of government issue: chronometers, charts, provisions, weaponry. The ship's officers and crew would assist in transporting these items to Richmond, and then await their reassignments, while Fraser, Trenholm & Co. resupplied the ship. Until they did, the ship's stores and manpower would remain almost fatally depleted; in military terms, she was a nonentity. Pegram, no doubt without giving it much thought, decided to leave her in the charge of the young third lieutenant on board—this William Conway Whittle.

Whittle accepted, and then presented Pegram with what seems a reasonable request, under the circumstances:

Hearing that Burnside would capture New Bern, that the agent and crew of the purchasers would thereby be prevented from getting to us and also that an expedition would be sent for our capture, we having no men or means for defense, I asked Captain Pegram as he was about to get out, to leave me with means of navigating so that in a dernier-resort [last resort], *I might run to the sea. He declined to do this on the ground that escape was impractical.*

If Conway Whittle wondered, "Impractical, compared to what?" he kept the thought to himself. (If the ship were to be destroyed, which now seemed likely, Fraser, Trenholm & Co. was not obliged to honor its purchase agreement.) The lieutenant was thus left without charts, dividers, chronometers, or sextants, and with a "crew" consisting of two midshipmen, a chief engineer, a bosun, a sawyer, a cook, a ship's boy, four firemen, and three sailors. Thirteen shipboard souls, essentially empty-handed, on a 215-foot oceangoing steamship, awaiting whatever the United States of America might choose to throw at them.

Pegram, meanwhile, had hopped aboard the last train out.

Soon, word reached the ship that the hostile vessels outside the harbor now numbered three. Further bad news arrived shortly afterwards: advance units of Burnside's army were probing toward New Bern, the railhead thirty-six miles to the northwest, on the Neuse river. This meant that the ship's new owners would no longer be able to send reinforcements to the ship. *Nashville* was undermanned, underarmed, cut off from any help. A sitting duck.

William Conway Whittle decided on the only option left to him, given that "surrender" was not in his ancestral gene pool. He decided to take the action to the enemy.

Then New Bern fell.

I learned [from the Commander of Fort Macon] *an expedition was coming for my capture. I left the wharf and anchored as near Fort Macon as I could get and quietly prepared for an escape.*

Even with the U.S. Navy momentarily held at bay by the cannons of Fort Macon, Whittle was surrounded. Federal ground troops were coming up behind him, and the Yankee navy blocked his only escape route. Time was running short, and the young officer scavenged wildly now for a way to make the 1,200-ton ship do his bidding. Among the conveniences he lacked to accomplish this was a local harbor pilot—someone who knew the shifting bars and currents of the river's mouth, someone experienced, someone who could be persuaded to guide them out to the ocean, and out to the enemy. He needed to conjure one virtually out of thin air, and proceeded to do so:

There were several sail vessels [in the vicinity] *belonging to Fraser, Trenholm & Co., of Liverpool and Charleston locked up in Beaufort. One of these was in command of a Captain Gooding, good coast pilot and true. I took him into my confidence.*

After the gallant engineer Hood had told me he could run the engine with his gang, reinforced from the deck, I engaged Gooding to go with me as pilot, with the promise that if we succeeded in delivering her to her purchasers, I would do all I could to have him put in command of the vessel.

Gooding was an unknown quantity. Whittle had no way of knowing how reliable he would be in the long run. That didn't matter. There was probably not to be a long run. Whittle, while he was hoping to escape, expected full well to be captured, and he planned to set *Nashville* on fire before he let that happen.

> *I had preparations made in the holds and in different parts of the ves-*
> *sel with dry wood, etc., so that at a moment's notice the vessel could be*
> *fired all over beyond extinguishment.*
> *Everything was quietly and quickly done and such orders given as*
> *necessary to ensure her destruction in case of any accident to me.*

Conway Whittle did not expect to live through this last voyage of *Nashville*. After all, his intention was to sail her directly into the enemy's line of fire, with himself stationed in the pilot house beside Gooding. He calmly gave instructions to the rest of the crew as to their duties in the event of his death. He was twenty-two years old.

He could count on at least a sliver of protection: the Confederate guns of the seaside Fort Macon, which had so far been his only shield against the three marauders sitting outside the harbor. On the eve of *Nashville*'s desperate seaward run, Whittle was visited by the fort's commanding officer, Col. Moses J. White, who invited him and his crew to join the undermanned defenders inside the walls. Whittle declined, with thanks. "I told him of my plan, that I would carry it out that evening and asking him to see to it that the Fort did not fire on me. He was delighted and wished me Godspeed. The two Confederate officers—each facing a likely imminent death—saluted, and parted. Colonel White would surrender Fort Macon the following April 26, after a brutal cannonading by Burnside's forces—the highlight of Burnside's rather spotty record as a commander, but the onset of the Federal deluge in North Carolina.

There was nothing left for Whittle to do but wait for the optimal moment to make his move. That, and contemplate mortality, as the winter night began to settle over the harbor: "Between sunset and moonrise, the moon being nearly full, was my only chance for darkness. I tripped my anchor and with all lights extinguished we started."

Nashville was now a phantom of the night.

Certain phantom-watchers reacted immediately.

As soon as we moved, a rocket was sent up from the lower end of Bogue Island below Fort Macon, evidently from an enemy's boat, sent from the blockaders to watch us, giving me assurance that our movements were known.

The enemy moved as well.

Steaming for the entrance over the bar, I saw the blockaders under way, close together and covering the narrow channel. Just before getting to the bar on which, from our draught, I expected to strike bottom, I slipped my anchor (it having caught under the forefoot . . .) to prevent its punching a hole in the bottom.

Whittle had neither enough men to raise the hook properly, nor much likelihood of needing any anchors at all anytime soon. The little annoyances of the sailing life. Whittle ordered the damned anchor cut loose, went to flank speed, and made for the shallows.

The boards of *Nashville*'s paddlewheels were soon slicing through the tips of the submerged duck grass, her keel barely above the sandbar, drawing ten feet. For the moment. The charts were outdated, no help. At any turn of her giant blades, the ship could be grounded and immobilized.

She scraped, but she passed.

Getting across the sandbar hardly promised relief. Waiting for *Nashville* were the teeth of the Union navy. Whittle made directly for them.

We were going at full speed, fourteen miles per hour. I was in the pilot house with Gooding by my side and two men steering at the wheel. The blockaders were under way and broadside to me across the only narrow passage out. As soon as I got in range, they opened on us.

Three broadsides tore across the water for *Nashville*. The Yankee sailors scrambled to reload.

I ran straight for the one furthest to the northward and eastward with the determination to go through or sink both ships in the attempt. My speed and steering for the left hand vessel caused the enemy to get out of my track.

The Yankees, it seemed, were going to allow Whittle the right-of-way; it was either that or be rammed, and no captain between Baltimore and Texas wanted that sort of thing on his record. But they were going to treat him to a close-quarters cannonade. The night air filled with smoke and deafening percussion.

As I passed through and out, they poured their shots at us. They kept it up until we were out of range, firing as near as I could tell over 20 shots.

One of the shots struck the pilot house. Whittle and his three helmsmen were unharmed. Another ball shattered the smokestack. And then it was over.

The moon rose clear and full a short time after we got through and found us well out skirting the southern side of Cape Lookout. No attempt was made to follow us that I know of.

Whittle shot *Nashville* eastward from the Carolinas, to the inner edge of the Gulf Stream, where she tiptoed along until the following day, away from the busy corridor of vessels bound either way. On the afternoon of March 18, the crewmen shaped their course for Charleston, South Carolina. And as darkness fell they were riding blind once again.

Toward dawn on the nineteenth, as visibility began slowly to return, they suddenly realized they had steamed inadvertently into the midst of the blockading Yankee fleet. A cascade of rockets shattering the daybreak told the astonished *Nashville* that Yankee blockaders had in turn discovered their presence. They were surrounded. Whittle's skeleton crew threw coal as if their lives depended on it, as he brought *Nashville* about and fled northward before the sleeping U.S. Navy, its yards draped in limp, useless canvas, could pursue. Even had they managed to run this deadly gauntlet, and made Charleston, an underwater scrap heap would have ripped the ship's bottom to shreds. The

Union navy had requisitioned a flotilla of ancient whaling ships from the junk dealers at New Bedford and towed them down to the channels of Charleston Harbor. There the navy loaded the old tubs down with crushed stone until they sank, masts up, closing off one channel and leaving only a narrow, tortuous alternate open. Whittle could see that running this channel would subject *Nashville* to close-range naval artillery fire that would almost certainly destroy the ship. His tiny crew was sleep-deprived to exhaustion. The ship was nearly out of coal.

> *I put back and ran out clear of the blockaders and shaped our course for the land north of Charleston.*

Daybreak, March 19, found *Nashville* steaming close to the shore toward Cape Roman. The destination now was the seaport village of Georgetown, South Carolina; but once again the prospect of overwhelming danger—more Yankee gunships—prompted Conway Whittle to begin improvising another desperate survival ploy:

> *Seeing smoke of those steamers ahead, I stopped and made preparation to take to the boats, destroy the ship and go ashore in the event that these vessels approached us and saw us for I knew that the crew was too worn for a successful run.*

Whittle's rational, dispassionate prose, written many years after these events, hardly conveys the nerve-sapping tensions that he and his men had endured through the last two days. Naval warfare, like ground combat, was an excruciatingly intimate experience, given the crude technologies of the mid-nineteenth century. Intimate, and maddeningly slow to commence. An officer looking through his binoculars could clearly see the preparations his enemy was making across the water. Often, ships maneuvered for hours in relatively close range; the men whom you were soon to kill, or who were soon to kill you, could be observed going about their duties, like so many workers in a mill or on a construction site. The prolonged anticipation could drive an impressionable man to the brink of madness.

On this day the tension was deepened by uncertainty. The thick black smoke from the distant ships obscured their precise movements, even their identity. The men of *Nashville* had no choice but to wait helplessly, and prepare to row for their lives.

Finally the tension broke. A strong wind whipped up and scattered the smokescreen. Reading the wind, Whittle could see that the enemy was moving northward, away from *Nashville*. He ordered the crew to steer the ship into the river and toward the Georgetown harbor.

Halfway in, the absence of charts caught up with them. The ship ran aground on a sandbar. *Nashville* was trapped. And now, armed men were closing on the immobilized ship: a longboat, rowing toward them; a body of cavalry, galloping toward the beach. A shoreline fort, occupied by God knew who, almost surely had them in its gunsights.

Who were they? And what would Whittle's men do for weaponry?

I . . . made preparations for defense against boarders. Not having guns, we got up grate bars and rigged up a hot water hose.

Using whatever coal remained for the steam engine, *Nashville*'s crew would scald anyone who tried to board the ship—much as castle defenders of medieval times would pour hot oil down upon enemies scaling the parapets.

A shout from the longboat, demanding that the vessel identify itself. The moment of truth was at hand.

I replied:
    "Are you Federals or Confederates?"
    The reply came:
    "We are South Carolinians." This was intense relief and I answered:
    "This is the Confederate States steamer Nashville. *Come alongside."*

South Carolina militiamen! *Nashville*'s charmed existence had been given another extension. The militiamen, still skeptical, boarded the ship; one of their officers told Whittle that the colonel in charge of the fort expected to see the ship hoist a backup to their Confederate flag in short order, as a signal that she was truly a Rebel, or they would commence firing.

And now the irony of the ruse they had created earlier—posing as a Yankee to run past the U.S. gunboat *State of Georgia*—struck home. All Whittle had on board for a backup flag was the Stars and Stripes.

I told him I had no other flag except the United States flag and that might mislead him.

Whittle added that what he really needed was a local pilot, one who knew these waters and could steer the ship safely upriver to Georgetown. He prevailed on the longboat officer to convey this information, and this request, to the fort—and quickly; Yankee marauders offshore could well have spotted *Nashville*'s smoke, and one or more might be bearing down on them at any minute. Soon help was on the way.

In the meantime, I had gotten the ship afloat and she promptly steamed in and up for Georgetown in charge of the pilot. I went ashore and was cordially met by Colonel Manigault. His troops, as I stepped ashore, said:

"Three cheers for the captain of the Nashville.*"*

These were heartily given and as I was young and it was my first command, I felt profoundly thankful.

William Conway Whittle had just completed a remarkable feat of seamanship. In less than three weeks' time, he had seized control of a situation in which he, his ship, and his garrison crew had essentially been left for dead in the harbor at Morehead City; brilliantly maneuvered *Nashville* through a cat's cradle of enemies; crept along the Carolina coast in constant danger of annihilation; barely escaped catastrophe by steaming through the Yankee fleet blockading Charleston; and brazened his way, in broad daylight, into Georgetown's harbor, despite the U.S. patrols.

"Three cheers for the captain of the Nashville." Indeed.

The story of Conway Whittle's escapade spread quickly up and down the coast. He was a hero.

Not that there was any time for dwelling on such things. In a debriefing at Georgetown, Colonel Manigault urged the young officer to get the ship out to sea again as quickly as he could—the blockaders were seldom far from striking distance. Whittle found a telegraph office, and very soon Stephen Mallory, secretary of the Confederate States Navy at Richmond, found himself digesting some astonishing news: the ship he'd assumed burned and sunk at Morehead City was safe in another Southern port. The lucrative deal with Fraser, Trenholm & Co. had not fallen through after all.

Whittle entrained for Richmond, heading directly toward the oncoming Yankee armies, to receive more detailed instructions from the secretary. Somehow he arrived at Richmond, in the middle of the night, conferred with Mallory, and hours later was on his way to Charleston, South Carolina, where he personally negotiated final purchase terms with Fraser, Trenholm & Co. and made arrangements for getting the ship to sea again as soon as possible. For both her new owners, the blockade runners, and her former owners, the Confederate States Navy, the arrangement had enormous potential. Every time the privateers, untroubled by the nuances of international law, brought a valuable consignment of cotton through to Britain, the CSN—through Bulloch—would arrange a covert return cargo of weapons for the Southern armies. By 1863 sleek steam-powered blockade runners built by Fraser, Trenholm & Co. specifically for stealth and speed would be successful on roughly five out of six runs, even from Charleston; from '63 through early '64 there were almost 600 attempts, and some 500 of them made it. And, conveniently, a voyage all the way to England wasn't always required. A quick run, just as far as the big British cargo ships waiting in the Bahamas, would do. There reliable dock workers would gladly unload the cotton, and reload the blockade runners with crates of uniforms, bandages, and rifles from the Fraser, Trenholm & Co. warehouses. There, too, importers and exporters were offered the convenience of Fraser, Trenholm & Co.'s own private off-shore bank. CSS *Nashville* was to be one of the firm's better early acquisitions. The young officer made sure that the most reliable of his men were rewarded.

> *Upon my urgent request, Captain Gooding was given a command. All arrangements were made and I took a hurriedly collected crew to Georgetown. Coal was put on, my crew taken off, in the same day in broad daylight, with her flag proudly flying, the gallant ship steamed out before the blockading fleet returned to their posts.*

Nashville, no longer officially part of the Confederate navy, was renamed by Fraser, Trenholm & Co. and became the *Thomas L. Wragg*, the first of many names the privateer/smuggler would sail under. With a new crew, and freshly coaled, she skirted the blockade and shot south to Nassau for arms and supplies. She made several successful trips through the blockade; on one of them, she was said to have brought home 60,000 long rifles and a large amount of powder for the Confederate infantry. Gooding died of yellow fever on one of these trips, but his elevation is an early example of Whittle's judgment about the reliability of individuals at sea: "A more gallant, more truer spirit never existed."

Later still, amid the Egg Islands of Ossabaw Sound off the Georgia coast, and known at her last as *Rattlesnake*, Whittle's old ship was finally hemmed in by Federal blockaders. Attempting to break through into deep water, she ran aground near the mouth of the Ogeechee River and was destroyed by an ironclad monitor, the USS *Montauk*, brought in specifically for the task. A period engraving depicts her being blown up, as a Rebel fort in the background fired impotently at the Yankees.

After saving *Nashville* for the South, Whittle's fortunes took a downward turn for a time. He was sent to New Orleans to the CSS *Louisiana*, and during the overwhelming assault by Admiral Farragut's fleet he was captured, and held as a prisoner of war at Fort Warren, Massachusetts. He was soon exchanged, and was back on duty in a matter of months.

For the rest of his life, Whittle would recall with vast satisfaction how the U.S. Navy reacted to his single-handed flaunting of the vaunted blockade.

He wrote, almost fifty years later:

> *Her entry into Beaufort caused a howl among the federals. Her escape out, after they had taken so many precautions for her capture had made them wild.*

"The Federal Rebellion" war record contains a letter written on March 27, 1862, from Assistant Secretary of the United States Navy Fox, to flag officer I. L. N. Goldsborough, USN, commanding their North Atlantic Squadron. It reads:

"I have yours about the *Nashville.* It is a terrible blow to our naval prestige, and that will place us all nearly in the position we were at before our victories."

The successes of the CSS *Nashville,* as far as the U.S. Navy was concerned, were significant—even, one could say, *strategic*—defeats. For a naval blockade to be legal in the eyes of the world, it had to be enforced. It had to work. This one, as *Nashville* and Lieutenant Whittle had repeatedly demonstrated, did not. The secretary of the navy continued making this point emphatically in his letter to Goldsborough, commander of the fleet of the North Atlantic:

"You recollect Armstrong said, at daylight, he discovered the *Nashville* had anchored three miles inside of him." (The Armstrong referred to was the duped commander of the United States steamer *State of Georgia,* snookered when the *Nashville* ran into Beaufort.) "This is not a blockade."

He continued to berate the Admiral: "You can have no idea of the feeling here." "Here" was Washington, where even for a flag officer with as much power as Goldsborough, events like these are career-ending blunders.

Fox thundered on, "It is a Bull Run to the Navy."

As Whittle noted years later with evident satisfaction, it was worse even than the navy brass knew. Rightly claiming even more credit than his enemies were giving him in March of 1862, he also revealed the depth of his own humility when, by referring to his capture, imprisonment, and interrogation, he wrote:

> *I am persuaded that the Federals never knew that the* Nashville *ran [the blockade] into Georgetown, until it was revealed to them by my capture below New Orleans in April 1862. I had then among my private papers, the rough draft of my report to Secretary Mallory of our escape from Morehead City and going into Georgetown.*
>
> *The Federal officer assigned to examine these papers, seemed astonished and said:*
>
> *"This is a revelation. We thought* Nashville *went from Beaufort to Nassau, direct, where she was first heard of."*
>
> *He was surprised when I told him I myself had command of her.*

He savored the irony of his victory in the presence of his defeat.

Nashville was to be a lesson for life as he confronted the eternal fight/flight dilemma. He had indeed adhered to the period refrain, "He who fights and runs away, shall live to fight another day."

Two years before he stood on *Shenandoah*'s deck, he had doubtless already dwelt on his past choices to charge or surrender. He understood personal peril, had faced the enemy as cannonades tore toward him, and he knew how to survive.

Whittle summarized the effects that his captures, defeats, victories, and moments of traumatic personal peril had had upon his later life when he wrote in 1910:

> *The experience passed through taught me that even the youngest veteran should know when to run.*

It seems that *Nashville*'s escape and her suicidal attack also marked his final passage from boyhood to manhood: from that moment onward, he frequently signed himself, "Wm C. Whittle, Lieutenant and Lieutenant Commanding C. S. Steamer *Nashville*."

3

On CSS *Shenandoah*, the yearned-for action commenced at first light, Thursday, October 27, 1864.

Whittle had slept badly because of a severe twinge in his left side, his thanks for helping the crew move cargo and coal the previous day. Ignoring the pain, he arose at sunrise and hauled himself aloft, some ten stories above the deck, to the maintop for a look around the ocean. What he spotted healed his ache instantly: a ship on the horizon. His spyglass revealed the hallmark contours of a Yankee. *Shenandoah* turned to, her royals* billowing and her powerful steam engine at full throttle. The officers and crew aboard the unfortunate quarry could only stare helplessly at a sight that would absorb hundreds of seamen in the ensuing year: the living nightmare of a mysterious cruiser bearing down on them at a faster speed than most men thought possible. Faster, and more precisely, as well. *Shenandoah*'s sailing master, Bulloch, was among the most brilliant navigators on the world's seas. He had plotted Indian Ocean courses on CSS *Alabama*, had been with her when she sank over fifty Yankee merchantmen, and was on her when she was destroyed by USS *Kearsearge* in the English Channel. Blue-water combat, as he was about to demonstrate time and again on this new raider's odyssey, was as much in his blood as it was in Whittle's. Whittle knew Bulloch not only as a gifted global navigator, but also as a dear friend and a trusted warrior. They had been shipmates on *Nashville* years ago.

---

* Additional sails mounted to increase a ship's speed.

Now they steered *Shenandoah* unerringly toward an intersection point with her moving prey. Within a matter of a few hours, the Confederates had pulled alongside. A twelve-pound cartridge—a blank—fired across the bow inspired their quarry to heave to.

Upon boarding her, a party of ten men headed by Acting Master Bulloch and Assistant Paymaster Smith were confronted with a technicality that would frustrate *Shenandoah*'s hopes of conquest at intervals throughout her voyage. The ship—the *Mogul*, bound from London for Point de Gaul—was indeed a Yankee-built vessel. Unfortunately, her papers showed a legal transfer to British interests. The United States Merchant Marine, long since conditioned to live in terror of Confederate raiders (though the terror far exceeded the number of ships actually sunk), had begun selling off its fleet to foreign owners. By the war's end, eight times as many U.S. ships—more than 1,600, with an aggregate weight of 750,000 tons—had been sold as were sunk by raiders.

Whittle and Waddell sent *Mogul* on her way. And with her went firm news that *Shenandoah* was at war, and furthermore, where she was, how fast she was, and what she stood for. There would be no acts of piracy by *Shenandoah*, no impressing of sailors, from any neutral vessel. The most inflexible rule governing this Confederate raider was to be her code of conduct—a code reinforced as much by personal honor as by the prospect of the gallows.

"Better luck next time," Whittle jotted grimly in his log. Still, the chase, and euphoria over the ship's first artillery round fired in pursuit of the Confederate cause, revitalized the drastically shorthanded crew. Despite the delay involved in boarding *Mogul*, the raider covered 113 miles that day.

> *Gunners and gang* [the "gang" ran the artillery] *arranging ammunition. Altogether there is not an idle man in the ship. Oh that we had more men. We have a fine ship and the nucleus of a fine crew but we want men of all things . . . the truth is we will have to capture our crew and win their affections by firmness and kindness.*

"Firmness and kindness"—an odd prescription for a warship's officer. As odd, in its way, as Whittle's inflexible code of honor. And all these ideals were quickly tested. On four consecutive days, *Shenandoah* bypassed harbors where food, fresh water, ammunition, tobacco, and grog lay available—and where men might be recruited as sailors. But Whittle knew that harbors were potential death traps; once inside one, the raider could easily be pinned by hostile gunships. Best to keep moving and depend for sustenance on legitimate prey, and on the sea itself.

Of all commodities at sea, water was easily the most precious. Thirst could claim a life more quickly than anything save a round in the chest. Salt-filled seawater was undrinkable; but here, *Shenandoah* herself provided succor. Her steam engine both depended on and actually made fresh water. The seawater was rendered fresh when, over the coals in the engine's boiler, it heated past its liquid state and turned to steam—the steam that powered her pistons. But the steam had other uses. Raw steam, when cooled back below its gaseous state, will once more condense into a liquid, but one that has now desalinized itself by the transition, its salts and minerals left behind as scale. Collected and cooled inside carefully sealed tubes, the water was fit for human consumption.

The *Mogul* escapade, in itself futile, even dangerous, changed *Shenandoah*'s luck. More satisfying conquests lay just ahead. At first light the following day, *Mogul* was but a speck on the far horizon "although she had all studding sails on one side," Whittle noted with competitive glee. "Our ship must be fast as we were under topgallant sails and beat her easily."

Fresh prey soon hove into view, and the young commander all but licked his chops.

> *In the afternoon, we made a barque ahead under all sail. We commenced chase and at dusk were only about seven miles off and rapidly gaining on him. I am certain that she is a Yankee or a transfer.* After dark, we clewed up Royals* [took in sail] *to prevent running away from him during the night. Fortunately he suspects nothing or he would give us the slip as it is very dark. As it is, I am sure we will catch him bright and early.*

---

* A ship whose ownership, formerly Yankee, has been "transferred" to a flag of convenience.

Once again, the severe paucity of seamen took its wearying toll.

We have done an immense deal but we are too short handed and have so very much to do that our little makes but a small show. All hands are well and seem to be happy. In our young officers the Confederacy has a parcel of men of which any country could feel proud. We have done wonders.

As the Friday night of October 28 spread across the ocean, and he wrote by lamplight in the privacy of his cabin, the twenty-four-year-old allowed a deeper, more wistful strain of thought into his journal:

Notwithstanding my being so busy, I have much time to feel blue as I can't get my usual letters from own dear ones. Oh, how much would I give to know how they are. I leave them all to God. We have so much to be thankful for.

Whittle added, "We have fine weather and I'm preparing for bad," a thought that was perhaps meteorological, and perhaps metaphorical.

Morning of the fourth day revealed that the barque—whether by design or by whim—had worked itself around to the windward of *Shenandoah*.

She still had every appearance of being a Yankee and we hauled up for her. We sailed much faster than the chase and rapidly gained on him. Took in royals and topgallant sails [to slow down] *as we approached.*

Now came the moment for a blood-chilling ruse, one nearly as old as navigation—a ploy popular with pirates, and used by marauders of all sorts during the Napoleonic Wars.

We hoisted the English flag and he to our great joy hoisted a hated Yankee flag. We then ran up our flag and hove him to with a blank cartridge. We lowered and armed a boat and crew, and sent Act. Master Bulloch, Third Midshipman J. T. Mason, and Masters Mate Hunt to board her. Very soon we had the extreme satisfaction of seeing the flag which is now the emblem of tyranny hauled down.

Even within this deceptive stratagem, Whittle was keeping in concert with the rules of war. Showing false colors was accepted naval practice—as long as the attacking ship did not fire live rounds before hoisting its authentic flag.

The object of *Shenandoah*'s subterfuge was a mouth-watering piece of timber: the 573-ton *Alina*, of Searsport, Maine. Plump, freshly and beautifully built, *Alina* was hauling many tons of railroad iron from Newport, Wales, to Buenos Aires. She was also bursting with luxuries sorely lacking aboard the raider: good bedding, washbasins, soap dishes, rope, food, and other objects of seamen's dreams. Her total value was estimated at $90,000, a towering sum in the mid-nineteenth century.

Whittle and Waddell learned of these potential spoils after summoning the barque's captain, a Yankee from Maine named Staples, and his first mate Peters on board with their papers—their damned papers. As with *Mogul*, caution would be the watchword. Thus, "They were each sworn, put under oath and examined separately before the captain and myself, paymaster and surgeon." Staples lost no time making Whittle's flesh crawl with his Down East "I calculates" and "I guesses." ("Oh, how I do hate the whole race," the young lieutenant later scrawled, characteristically adding, "and still I can't help treating them kindly.")

Then, crushing frustration: as with *Mogul*, the examination appeared to spare the snared ship. Her papers, signed by the owner, now actually showed *Alina* to be British-owned, en route from one neutral port to another. The raider's officers steeled themselves to convey the maddening news to the crew. But then the shrewd Waddell, casting his gimlet eye over the bill of lading one final time, spotted a most interesting omission. The ship's owner had neglected to have the papers notarized.

The nonplussed Staples listened as his lovely barque "was condemned apprised to the Confederate states." Joyfully, the Confederate crewmen ransacked her. "We stripped her of everything we wanted," Whittle exulted, "which may well be imagined was an immense deal particularly as she was our first prize [the common term for a captured ship]" Even the austere Waddell got in on the fun, snatching away a coveted spring-bottomed mattress. Next came the evacuation of the crew via longboats—eight hands, a steward, two mates, and a captain, nearly all of them German.

And finally, the coup de grace: "We had her scuttled." Whittle

ordered holes bored in *Alina*'s hull. Then he stood on deck and enjoyed the aesthetics of this inaugural sinking.

> *At 4:45 p.m., she went down stern first under all plain sail and the*
> *sight was grand and awful. You might go to sea for many a day, and*
> *would not see a vessel sink.*

Alina took her time. Whittle described how finally the ocean swept
over her:

> *She settled aft. Her stern sank very rapidly and her bow went straight*
> *into the air and turned a regular somersault as she went down. [We]*
> *could distinctly hear the cracking and breaking of the spars of the sails*
> *and as the bow went under and a beautiful jet of water was thrown*
> *up high in the air.*
>   *This is our first prize and a good day's work we have had. The*
> Alina . . . *was a beautiful vessel and I'm told by all onboard that she*
> *was clean as a new pin. God grant that we may have many just such*
> *prizes.*

Here, in the center of the Atlantic, *Shenandoah* had begun to damage the enemy materially.

More important, she had begun the necessary expansion of her
crew. A seaman captured in wartime often faced grimly limited
choices—that is, if his captors were humane enough to let him live: he
could voluntarily "ship"—join ranks with his conquerors—or he could
remain "confined"—perhaps sitting immobilized on the deck with an
iron rod bolted across his ankles—perhaps belowdecks, in the dark,
with a shackle on his wrist, and a loop of chain cleated to a timber—
until he felt more comradely. One of the *Alina* crew shipped at once,
and became a coal tender. Another, refusing an order given by Whittle, was promptly shackled. Soon all except the officers were in irons.

The first victim quickly came to his senses and "shipped" aboard
the raider. "I trust we may get them all," Whittle noted blandly. "I
wish every one of them would ship except the Yankee. I would not
have him." Whittle's blazing categorical hatred for Yankees would
contend with his personal code of honor throughout the voyage.

The day's hard labors at an end, Conway Whittle ordered the "main brace spliced"—sea lingo for breaking out the grog. Soon the raider's men were in the state enjoyed by most men in most navies at the time—drunk. As normative as this condition might have been, drunkenness aboard *Shenandoah* would soon become a source of serious concern—and, eventually, a cause of crisis, with lives hanging in the balance.

On Sunday, Whittle chose to obey a rule from a higher source.

This is a day of rest. We have done nothing all day and unless it is absolutely necessary, we will always observe the Sabbath.

His piety perhaps paid off: of the eight *Alina* crewmen languishing belowdecks, six—two Frenchmen and four Dutchmen—shipped. Whittle saw exhilarating portents in their new allegiance.

These make seven out of twelve which, I think, is doing very well. It will be a very good accession to us. We now have fifty-three souls attached to the ship, of whom twenty-four are officers. I trust that at this rate we may soon increase our crew from our prizes to sixty exclusive of the officers. This would make us eighty-four all told. Even now we have enough to take care of her. This prize has given us a tremendous lift as we got from her men, ropes, blocks and every imaginable thing. Our men and officers are all well and cheerful. No set of men ever had more or greater blessings to thank their God for than the crew of the "Shenandoah." We have a fine ship and all will be well. We can run as fast as any can pursue.

Even the hated Yankee captive had reason to be grateful. Staples and his mate earned a measure of freedom about the deck by signing papers promising to pay fees for their eventual parole.

Our prisoners thank me for our kindness to them. What a contrast with the treatment of our noble veterans by their side. Looking at Captain Staples, who is as free as anyone on board, I can but think

what a difference this treatment presented with that meted to us
[when Whittle was imprisoned after the Battle of New Orleans;]
and I felt at the same time when I thought of the insults heaped by the
Yankees upon our women, an amount of hatred which strongly
tempted me to say, "Here master-of-arms, take this old scamp and trice
him up, gag & buck him." Oh! No! this must not be.

A dark bit of imagining indeed, but a well-earned one. The torture
that Whittle contemplated involved fastening a prisoner to an iron bar
by his wrists (sometimes behind his back), attaching the bar to a piece
of rope in a pulley and hoisting him in the air, his ankles fastened to
the deck. The "gag" in the mouth would be a piece of chain, fastened
by a rope.

Whittle had reason to be tempted toward this cruelty. Patriotic
loyalty to his Southern homeland formed only a partial motive for his
dedicated loathing of Yankees. The rest of it was visceral. The rest of it
sprang from searing memory.

Several months after his heroic escapades at the helm of *Nashville*,
Conway Whittle had found himself a combatant at one of the greatest
Southern debacles of the Civil War: New Orleans, in April 1862. He
was in charge of the bow battery as a second lieutenant aboard the
CSS *Louisiana*, by some accounts the largest of the ironclads built by
the Confederacy and rushed into the defense of the great port city
against a Union naval invasion—a defense commanded by Whittle's
commodore father. The Rebel ironclads were ships of desperation.
Financed largely by the liquidation of private wealth (sterling silverware, fine silks, precious heirlooms), they were hastily constructed,
badly designed, and disastrously ineffective. This overmatched contingent stood between the city and an ironbound Union armada of forty-
seven chain-draped warships steaming up the Mississippi from the
Gulf of Mexico: the combined fleets of Rear Admirals David G. Farragut and David D. Porter. The devastating naval battle that followed
and the loss of New Orleans badly damaged the Southern cause. The
Rebel ships were overwhelmed; New Orleans, the South's largest and
most vital city, fell under occupation by the land forces of the brutal
Benjamin "Beast" Butler; 15,000 bales of cotton were torched on the

wharves; a dozen Confederate ships and several other unfinished gun-boats and steamers were destroyed; the Mississippi was sealed off at its southernmost point.

In the early stages of the Federal assault, with his ship abandoned and on fire, immobolized by its dysfunctional engines, Conway Whittle was forced to destroy the CSS *Louisiana* to keep it from the Federals. The blast he touched off by igniting *Louisiana*'s ammunition was deemed one of the most violent explosions of the Civil War by Farragut's self-promoting second-in-command, Admiral Porter, a charge that Whittle, who was considerably closer to the blast than Porter, later energetically rebutted. Following the battle, Whittle was taken prisoner, transported to the North, and confined in a POW camp at Fort Warren in Massachusetts. Union prison camps were notorious for their squalor: overcrowded, their open latrines teeming with unremoved human waste that drew flies and other pests; rations that barely sustained life; filthy water; guards whose temperaments ranged from merely sadistic to homicidal. (Southern prison camps were seldom better and often worse.) The young lieutenant enjoyed but one satisfying moment during his confinement, and that moment all but made his suffering bearable: one of the Union officers debriefing him let it slip that the U.S. Navy considered the blockade-running *"Nashville* incident" their Bull Run.

By extension, this would make Whittle—the only officer aboard the ship at the time—the incident's Stonewall Jackson.

Otherwise, the treatment that Conway Whittle received in captivity shocked his sensibilities. It also annealed and personalized his hatred for Yankees, a hatred that stood in constant tension with his powerful moral restraint. When Captain Staples and his mate approached the young officer the following day to express appreciation for their kind treatment, Whittle was icy.

I simply replied that I treated them well for humanity's sake, and begged them not to think that my feeling was for them any other than hatred and that this hatred of the most intense kind and I told the captain that I hated them as I did the "Old Boy" [the Devil] himself. Notwithstanding, I will treat them kindly as long as they will allow

*me to do so, and when they do not conduct themselves properly they
will find me as severe as I am now kind.*

Later in the day, as they billowed southward toward the equator,
another blessing materialized—a new prey, standing to the northwest, crossed their track. *Shenandoah* lowered her propeller, turned,
and launched into pursuit, but the quarry ran rapidly, and it was
nearly dark when the Confederates drew within a mile. "She hoisted
the English flag when a squall separated us a little and the night was
so dark that we did not like to risk our boat." Captain Waddell argued for giving up the chase. Whittle concurred regretfully: "I am
strongly of the opinion that she was a Yankee for her actions and appearance and I am pretty sure that we left a fine prize when we gave
her up."

Now an enemy of another sort materialized: rough weather. Inter-
mittent rain squalls had been dogging the raider's progress, adding to
the hazard of routine tasks: fitting gun breeches, seeing to the rigging
aloft. On Tuesday evening the storm began to strike. The rain washed
down in torrents, but *Shenandoah* handled the churning seas with an
ease surprising for her size. Satisfied that all was well, Whittle "spliced
the main brace," and soon all hands were happily three sheets to the
wind. They covered eighty-five miles anyway.

They began sobering up at around four-thirty the next morning.
That was when the real squall hit, a serious mid-Atlantic hell-raiser.

*I went on deck and found it blowing very hard and told Lieutenant
Lee he had better reef down to it. He got two reefs in without any
damage being done. What a blessing it is that we have Cunningham's
self-reefing topsails.*

These sails were a new invention, among several that *Shenandoah*
boasted. They enabled a crew to draw in the sails from the deck, instead of laboring perhaps 120 feet up the mast, amid heavy winds and
a pitching ship, to take them in by hand. Whittle itemized the rough-
weather procedures: "I took a close reef in the topsails and a single reef
in the foresail." He was creating a written record in case the worst hap-

pened: the sails he was flying, the exact choices he made. These notes, if recovered, would benefit the next crew caught in an equatorial storm.

The shortened sail stabilized the ship—enough so that officers and crew turned their attention to washing their clothes in the freshwater downpour. Distinctions of rank evaporated. "It was a new sight to me, to see officers so employed that they can and will do anything to get along." Whittle filled his water casks with "nice water," and released the two mates and a sailor named Stinson from confinement. "I can't help being kind to the rascals and I often wonder at myself."

On the following day, Conway Whittle was obliged to show his steely side, and he did so without hesitation. In the midst of general hard labor—making sail, holystoning the decks—the lieutenant commander got word that a fireman named George Silvester had refused to take his turn cooking mess. Silvester was a simple-minded soul, hardly a candidate to lead a mutiny, yet no hand could be seen to flout discipline without paying a price for it. "I sent for him and he positively refused. This is the first piece of insubordination or anything approaching trouble, and I shall punish the offender severely and make an example of him. I had him put in irons and triced up and as he commenced to complain, I had him gagged."

Within an hour, this had worked. Silvester implored Whittle via the master-at-arms: he would do anything if the lieutenant would let him down.

I sent for him and told him that he was the first person I had to say a cross word or take a harsh step, and that this might make him feel ashamed of himself. I do not think I will have any more trouble with him. I am sure that by this prompt dealing, a lesson has been taught to all. I shall adopt prompt and just punishment to all offenders.

Whittle insisted on a positive view despite this confrontation—a trait that, over time, proved stronger than leg irons for the esteem it earned him: "Our men are a fine set of fellows and I only wish I had more of them."

To give the hapless Silvester his due, life aboard a nineteenth-century sailing vessel was never enlarging to the human spirit. Life, in fact, never changed—except in moments of extreme danger. Life was lived in watches; watches were lived in shifts. Four hours on, eight hours off. Or four on, four off. Or eight on, eight off. It didn't matter; it was all the same. The men took turns cooking and cleaning up after one another. Off-watch, they slept when they could. Then back to the shift. The watch could mean any number of things: standing ready to hoist a sail up a ten-story mast in the midst of a sleet storm; sitting out on the bow, looking for shallow water on a tropical afternoon. All the same thing, in the end. Life was lived in watches; watches were lived in shifts.

From time to time someone like Silvester decided he'd had all he could take. And then it was up to someone like Whittle to demonstrate how much more there was to take.

Small wonder that the slightest variations in the routine—a fresh wind, a shape on the horizon—could stir the senses to ecstasy, or terror, or both, indistinguishable.

I got up early and found a nice little breeze blowing.

Worth noting, even to a jaded warrior-mariner. The dour Waddell, oblivious to most pleasures, arose plumping for the steam engine; he wanted velocity. But Whittle prevailed, and *Shenandoah* slipped southward beneath the great arcs of white canvas in her mainsails: "The ship is very much more comfortable under sail than under steam and I am always glad to see her going steadily with her wings spread."

Another busy day, installing new main topsail halyard. These items ran Whittle short of a precious commodity: "All these were from prize rope (that taken from *Alina*) and as that is all cut, I will have to wait for another prize."

Another menacing interruption, another crisis of discipline:

A very disagreeable thing took place today. Mr. O'Shea, our carpenter, had a quarrel with Mr. Lynch, his assistant, and when spoken to, being clearly in the wrong, he was very insubordinate. [O'Shea] was clearly in the wrong and I reprimanded him very severely indeed. I had much trouble in bringing him to his bearings. I find that for a time that I will have to rule with an iron hand and by checking in the bud all offenses, I will get all straight.

On November 5, *Shenandoah* struck again.

Today has been a great one for us. Saturday, a week ago, we destroyed by sinking our first prize. And today we destroyed by burning, our second.

This was the schooner *Charter Oak* out of Boston, bound for San Francisco, and valued at $25,000. The Confederates spotted her the previous evening at a distance; by morning the distance had closed. At daylight, *Shenandoah* made its run under steam and overtook her in short order.

We hoisted the English flag, but . . . he paid no attention to us. At 7:30 we fired a blank cartridge when to our great joy he hoisted the hateful Yankee flag and we hove to. We ran up our flag and sent a boat to send off the papers and officers.

Soon *Charter Oak*'s captain, a curiously lighthearted fellow named Samuel Gilman, and his mate, Burgess, were presenting their papers. *Charter Oak* was transporting 168 tons of cargo: coal, for the most part; some tinned food; and the rest furniture: sofas, plows, chairs, and "bureaux." *Shenandoah*, as it happened, was a "bureaux"-deprived ship: the furniture would fill a pressing need. Whittle "appropriated" a piece of furniture for himself, an upright desk/bureau of Shaker design, closable into a cratelike form. Waddell helped himself to a sword.

Inconveniently, however, the captured schooner was also transporting two women: the captain's wife and her sister, who had brought along a small son. Either of the women, it was quietly and wincingly agreed among the sailors, was capable of sinking a ship on looks alone. Whittle and Waddell were faced with a decision. One choice was to "bond" the captured ship—that is, declare ownership in the name of the Confederacy, and enjoin her officers to sail her to the nearest port, auction off her assets and deliver the proceeds to a financial representative of the C.S.A. Needless to say, enforcing such a "bond" was out of the question.

The other choice was to burn her.

Whittle and Waddell talked it over.

The captain listened to me as to whether we should burn her and be burthened with two females and child or, simply, bond her and let all go. I concluded that whatever be the difficulties we should burn her and this was decided upon.

Burning her, of course, meant taking aboard her passengers—ten in all, including the first females to board *Shenandoah*. Whittle and Waddell watched the approaching longboats with their human cargo: "Captain Gilman, his wife, his sister-in-law Mrs. Gage, and her little son Frank."

Mrs. Gilman, Mrs. Gage, and Frank presented some obvious difficulties, which Whittle attended to with his characteristic courtesy. "I am very sorry to have females onboard but I will do all I can to make them comfortable. I was very busy in the cabin and with the master-at-arms made and arranged their beds with my own hands." But they offered some subtle opportunities as well—opportunities for a diplomatic gesture.

Shenandoah's status as a conquering warship permitted—and in a sense required—her commanders to demand any and all properties aboard her victim, including the personal wealth of the surrendering officers. The unflappable Captain Gilman admitted blithely that he carried some $200 on his person. But how might it look to the world, and especially to the proper Queen Victoria, whose support of the Cause was critical, if these Confederates looted their adversary of his cash assets, particularly in the presence of his family members? Mrs. Gage, as it developed, was a widow. Her husband had been killed while serving with Ulysses S. Grant's army in Virginia. "She does not seem to hate us as one would think she ought to," Whittle later mused.

It was Waddell who hit on the solution—a masterstroke of gallantry.

When the master came on board, the captain ordered him to give up his money. This he did at once. Then Captain Waddell, in the presence of Passed Midshipman Mason, gave it all to Mrs. Gilman. They all seemed to be thunderstruck and she was very grateful. We put the captain, the two females and the little boy in the starboard cabin, where they will be so much more comfortable than they have been in the schooner that I think they will like it.

Like *Alina*'s Captain Staples, whom he was soon to join in the wardroom, Captain Gilman was virtually giddy with gratitude.

I believe he was sincere. He said, 'Well sir, I cannot for the life of me see how you can be so kind.' I do not wonder at their being surprised for I am astonished at myself. When I consider how studiedly cruel they are to our dear women, now the noble act of Waddell today in giving the money to Mrs. Gilman, does anyone suppose that it was appreciated or that we will not be abused just as much as if we had kept the money?

Waddell's own journal certifies that his compassion was untinged by any thoughts of comparison with the evil Yankees. He'd given Mrs. Gilman the $200 only after making her promise not to turn a cent of it over to her husband. But,

The promise of course was a mere pretense. The fact was I felt a compassion for the women. They would be landed I did not know where and the thought of inflicting unnecessary severity on a female made my heart shrink within.[9]

Many and complex facets of character, it seemed, lay beneath James Waddell's glowering exterior.

Charter Oak's spoils—thankfully unspoiled, in this case—included more than 200 pounds of canned tomatoes and 600 pounds of canned lobster. "The former will come in very nicely, I think," Whittle noted with what might have been puckish humor.

Now came the firing-time.

Setting fire to a seagoing vessel in the late 1860s was not as easy as it might seem. Fire diversion and fire control were by then a part of shipbuilding technology. Whittle directed his men belowdecks to coat *Charter Oak* thoroughly with the pitch and turpentine found in her paint locker. Waddell, for his part, ordered *Shenandoah* to keep off the lee side of the doomed ship, so that no stray sparks would torch the raider. Whittle entered another dry log notation: "When this war ends, I am sure that we will all know how to make good fires."

Whittle mused afterward,

> *It is an awfully grand sight to see a vessel on fire at sea. I could but think how terrible it would be if any person had been onboard her.*
>
> *It is wonderful how quickly the fire spreads, and how rapidly the whole vessel seems to be enveloped in flames and still it takes a vessel a very long time to burn. It is to me a pitiful sight to see a fine vessel wantonly destroyed.*

And then the embattled officer eclipsed the sensitive young Virginian once again.

> *But I hope to witness an immense number of painful sights at the same time and I trust that the* Shenandoah *may be able to continue her present work until our foolish and inhuman foes sue for peace. God knows I pray that their deluded minds may soon be enlightened but until they are, I think that our present occupation will greatly tend to bring about the desired result.*

He paroled the captain and mates, and confined the crew. He admired the disintegrating remains of *Charter Oak* as the raider left her in its wake. "The burning wreck astern was looking very pretty. I saw both her masts go by the boards." Another fifty-five miles that day, patrolling the trade routes pinched between Africa and South America. *Shenandoah* was hunting squarely in the merchant lanes now, with yet another customer taking shape on the horizon. From Conway Whittle's vantage point, the War of Secession was suddenly going along very well.

4

⬥

At 10:30 a.m. on Sunday, November 6, two days before Lincoln's reelection as president of the United States, Whittle and Waddell mustered the *Shenandoah* crew on deck for a ritual of naval custom. All hands stood stiffly at attention under the semitropical sun, the officers sweltering in their fine Confederate gray dress uniforms—epaulettes, swords, looping gold French braid on the sleeves—while Whittle read them the rules of engagement as determined by Secretary Mallory, Master of the Confederate Navy in Richmond.

Aside from that ceremony, this Sunday was another day of rest. "We did none but necessary work. The men all looked very well and the ship quite well, but there is an immense amount yet to be done."

Later on in the seeming safety of that balmy Sabbath, in a flat sea empty of hostile gunships, Conway Whittle had a close encounter with the Grim Reaper.

Today at dinner I did a thing which has rendered me very unhappy as it is very dangerous. In eating a piece of rhubarb pie, I swallowed a piece of the glass bottle in which it was preserved. I found that the cook, instead of drawing the cork, had broken the neck off the bottle. I took three strong emetics and I trust that I got clear of it as the emetics were very strong and active. I feel very anxious but I know that my life is in God's hands.

"In God's hands" was something of a mantra for Whittle, whose personal code of conduct was undergirded by his strong Episcopal faith. He could not know it, but hundreds of miles northward, a threat far more menacing than a sliver of glass was in its formative stages. Not only Conway Whittle's, but the life of every officer and sailor aboard *Shenandoah* was sliding by slow, inexorable degrees into the crosshairs of Federal intelligence.

～～⊗⊙⊘～～

Thomas Dudley had never made peace with the fact that *Laurel*, loaded with cannon, powder and shot, had slipped down the Mersey past his eyes and those of his operatives, and into the open sea. The jug-eared American consul at Liverpool had spent most of the last three years working obsessively to thwart just such British-spawned threats to his government and nation: the endless undercover plots, dreamed up by the Southern agents swarming Liverpool under false identities, blueprints bankrolled by wealthy merchants with Southern sympathies and hammered into seagoing reality by shipbuilders who may or may not have known the purpose of the vessel under construc- tion. By all rights, Dudley's task was hopeless: he was a stranger on the far side of an ocean, cut off from home; a representative of a govern- ment hated even more by the great port city of his assignment than by official London. Not that official London sent him all that many floral bouquets; his diplomatic adversaries at Whitehall were experienced, coldly pragmatic creatures, at home in the corridors of European money and power, and utterly uninterested in America's fate. Only their grudging adherence to their country's Foreign Enlistment Act, forbidding the supply of war vessels or fighting men to the belligerents, prevented their open complicity with the Confederacy.

Alone (save for his staff), unarmed, inexperienced in British cul- ture, unversed in the nuances and secrets and power maneuverings of teeming, scheming Liverpool, Thomas Dudley might almost as well have been the United States consul at Richmond or Atlanta.

Against these obstacles, Dudley could mount only two assets: his intelligence and his steely nerve.

He was forty-five in 1864, a tough, canny Quaker farm boy who'd risen quickly in New Jersey law and in the upstart Republican party. A big-voiced six-footer, Dudley nonetheless projected refinement;

Washington politicos, who took penetrating intellect for granted, found him more than up to their standards. Dudley had already figured in the nation's destiny. In 1860 he'd helped sway the Republican convention at Chicago away from William Seward and toward Abraham Lincoln; the consulate at Liverpool was his reward, and the post of secretary of state was Seward's consolation. Their wartime duties threw them into close collaboration; it was a testament to Dudley's diplomatic skills that he earned the trust and respect of the fiercely ambitious Seward.

Dudley even proved more than a match for the mean-street intrigues of Liverpool. He lost no time, on his arrival in 1861, assembling a crack espionage team to subvert, expose, and dismantle almost every Confederate maneuver to extract ironclads and commerce-raiding steamships from the shipyards. He recruited detectives and put informers on his payroll. He prowled the docks and quays without rest and without fear, quizzing roustabouts and sailors about what they knew. He made himself an expert at combing British newspapers for telltale hints of activity. Several times a week he organized his findings into handwritten dispatches and sent them off to his patrician colleague, the Envoy Extraordinary and Minister Plenipotentiary at the Court of St. James, Charles Francis Adams. Adams reviewed them, confronted Palmerston and others with the evidence they contained, and sent the intelligence overseas to Seward's office in Washington. Federal blockading officers learned where best to concentrate their strength; even more important, dozens of schemes for Southern shipbuilding were intercepted and halted—including the plans to build that pair of giant ironclads at the Laird Shipyards.

And yet this damn raider *Shenandoah* had slipped through. Coal freighter! Quicksilver predator of unarmed merchantmen. This little game was not over. Thomas Dudley would have his day.

He'd learned at the end of October how he'd been fooled. On the twenty-first of that month, the *Laurel*—the ship that had supplied *Shenandoah* for war as it metamorphosed from the coal-bearing *Sea King*—put into port at the British-controlled island of Tenerife, off the coast of Morocco. On board were the forty-odd *Sea King* crewmen who had refused to sign on to Whittle and Waddell's adventure. The

British skipper, Peter Corbett, at first floated the fiction that *Sea King* had been wrecked off the Madeira Islands. The British consulate at Tenerife, Henry Grattan, demanded documentation, and waited several days for Corbett to come forward with the ship's papers. When Corbett did not appear after a week, Grattan had him arrested. Corbett's story compared unfavorably with the version of a pair of highly uncongenial former sailing companions who also wound up at the consulate: two of the defecting crewmen who were especially bitter that they'd been duped onto a raiding vessel in disguise. The depositions of these two men prompted the consul to seek charges against Corbett for violation of the Foreign Enlistment Act.

Now the true identity and purpose of *Sea King* was finally in the open. Now, unbeknownst to the hunter, she became the hunted.

Yet, aboard *Shenandoah,* on the day after Sabbath and now thousands of miles from Liverpool, it was drudgework that ruled the men's lives—"getting things in order."

The morning was windless, tedious, routine; until at noon, in a sea of dead calm, the lookout observed an intriguing shape in the distance. A target. With her propeller lowered, *Shenandoah* quickly surged to her top cruising speed, and overtook the craft within an hour. Again, the British-flag ruse; again, a Yankee flag fluttered upward in reply. Again, *Shenandoah* hoisted its bad news and fired a blank cartridge across the bow.

The trophy this time, *Shenandoah*'s third in ten days, was the ancient American barque *D. Godfrey,* thirty days out of Boston and bound for Valparaiso, Chile. The raider's usual "board of examiners" deposed the captain and his mate, and discovered that once again they'd made a lucky catch: her cargo included a store of lumber and "some very nice rope," of which a ship at sea could never have enough. Not to mention a contingent of ten fresh souls. Conway Whittle, referring to the raider's captives, generally accorded them the dignity of being "souls"—except, of course, when they were caught behaving like Yankees—or when they were other than Caucasian. These souls included the captain, two mates, six seamen, and a Negro steward. "They are all good young men and the darkie is the very man I want for ship's cook." If he boasted no other culinary skills, the "darkie" presumably knew how to draw a cork out of a bottle.

The Confederates looted her thoroughly, then fired the prize at 6:00 p.m., and set sail. Five of the seamen and the steward shipped at once. Two of these were Yankees, an ambiguous triumph for Whittle. (Toward Union officers, his loathing seemed insurmountable; as for common seamen—well, a deckhand was a deckhand.) Of the rest, three were English and one was from New Brunswick. All non-enlisting captives remained in the agony of irons. *Shenandoah* now carried fifty-seven seamen, two women, and the excited little boy Frank, for whom the whole thing was a great lark. The raider covered sixty-five miles that day, and Whittle, confident that his glass shard had settled somewhere at the bottom of the sea, was again feeling expansive.

> *Our men and officers all behave so very well when we take a prize. It makes me feel proud. Beyond any doubt this is the most demoralizing work any set of men were ever engaged in, and the strictest and most constant discipline will alone answer more particularly when we are actually capturing our crew. When in the world's history was a parallel ever known?*

Whittle supervised the emplacement of two forward eight-inch guns, the need for which he hoped would never arise: any U.S. Navy ship menacing enough to draw their fire would be a formidable foe for the lightly armed *Shenandoah*. He took far more delight in another Yankee-related phenomenon:

> *It amuses me to see our female prisoners. They really are so much more comfortable here than where we found them that they are quite in love with the ship and really seem to enjoy the capture as much as we do. As for the little boy, he gives three cheers for Jeff Davis every day.*

A hundred thirty miles southwestward the next day, under winds out of the east. As they sped, Whittle exhorted his men to their most productive workday of the voyage thus far. By the end of it, all the ship's guns were in fighting position ("But I trust it may not be necessary"). In addition, "I rove off much of the running gear and regulated all of the officers' messes."

These last were critically important accomplishments. "Roving" meant replacing the running gear, specifically the ship's rotting ropes, in this case, with cordage taken from *Alina, Charter Oak,* and *Godfrey.* A sailing ship required literally miles of high-strength rope in its rigging, and the strains were enormous: pivoting the huge yards, the timbers that supported the sails during a gale-force course change; bearing the heavy canvas sails themselves as strong winds applied constant pressure. Frequent drenching by salt-heavy seawater didn't help, either. Rope was an expensive commodity—but even if it were a bargain, putting into a port to acquire it would be tantamount to suicide for this fugitive raider. In the matter of rope, as with so many other necessities for survival, *Shenandoah* was as much seagoing scavenger as raider; she lived off her conquests, without which she might not survive.

As for getting the officers' mess in order, it resolved a lingering disciplinary crisis at the staff level. The ship's officers needed an ironclad schedule for cooking and eating. Lacking it, they wasted valuable time scraping up their meals, even cadging food from the seamen, stirring up resentment. It was just such a confrontation that had led to the shackling of Silvester.

His day's work at a satisfying end, Conway Whittle entered a favored thought in his logbook, one that he would enter again and again over the long voyage, through vast stretches of empty ocean, until it became a kind of refrain that brought peace and hope to his anxious, racing mind:

Tomorrow I think we will catch a Yankee.

He added:

I trust I may be correct, for nothing gives me more pleasure than to do as much harm as I can in a legitimate way to our inhuman foes. . . . I mean things which are legitimate between two civilized nations at war, which I do not at all grant to be the case here.

Again, Conway Whittle promised his bestial enemies that the Confederate gentlemen would treat them humanely. Whittle's conscience would prove his second-most-familiar adversary on this voyage. In certain ways, it was his most significant. Here, "legitimate way" wrestles on nearly equal footing with "our inhuman foes," an appraisal he had gained firsthand. He even refused to grant the North any claim as a "civilized nation." This dual allegiance to his honor and to his patriotism was soon to meet an agonizing test.

A line or so later, warrior passion gave way to a young man's melancholy:

> But how often do I think of my dear home and country. Oh, how they are all suffering. Oh, how often do I think of my own dear [ones] and wish that I could see them. Will we ever meet again? God grant that we may, and in the meantime I make the protection of God an . . .

Whittle made a late-night effort to complete this thought, but poignantly crossed out the words.

❦

A ship indeed appeared to leeward early the next day, as *Shenandoah* zigzagged south and east under variable winds. The raider gave chase, with the usual swift results. The stranger was a full-rigged brig; not the Yankee Whittle had wished for, but the Danish craft *Anna Jane* out of New York, skirting the east coast of Brazil, bound south for Rio de Janeiro. She proved useful still, but in a way that contained its share of peril.

James Waddell saw a handy solution to a shipboard nuisance. He wanted to petition the neutral ship to relieve *Shenandoah* of its prisoners and carry them to the South American port for release. Whittle opposed the idea, but this time Waddell prevailed. *Anna Jane*'s captain consented to the request, and the Confederates dispatched eight men to the Dane, along with a barrel of beef and a supply of bread, as well as a chronometer for the cooperative skipper, in recognition of his kindness. The transfers included Captains Staples and Hallock, their mates, and a few hard cases determined to remain in the torturous irons rather than "ship." Captain Gilman of *Charter Oak* chose to remain on board—perhaps after consulting his wife: "Our female prisoners asked if we were going to let them go," Whittle later noted, "and when we said no, they did not seem at all disappointed. But the fact is they are treated with more consideration than ever before in their lives and never are more of them contented."

For Captain Staples and his party, the charm of life aboard *Shenandoah* had worn thin. Their way of announcing it was not lost on Whittle.

> *When [they] left, they showed their regular Yankee character. He did not thank any one of us or say good-bye to anyone. What a miserable set of villains the enemy are. I hate them more than ever the more I see of them.*

Whittle brooded over the risk inherent in releasing the prisoners, a risk that Waddell had shrugged off as necessary, given that hostile men in irons, probably screaming at times in agony, were a shipboard distraction, and thus a liability. "I was opposed to the prisoners today being sent away," Whittle wrote, "as their release will certainly let all the Yankees know that we are near. I trust, however, that I may be wrong." That was unlikely. What could possibly dissuade these stubborn, aggrieved, and vengeful men from alerting the U.S. Navy to the raider's general whereabouts at the earliest opportunity? Less than two weeks into its desperate mission, the inevitable moment of *Shenandoah*'s reversal—predator becoming prey—would be greatly hastened.

Later that day, *Shenandoah* gave chase to another large ship to windward. This one proved Australian despite her Yankee lines, and to Whittle's great disappointment. He contented himself with reinforcing shipboard allegiance. He rewarded four men who'd recently shipped by rating them "captains of the top"—men charged with the critical chore of running the rigging. If the hunting remained productive, *Shenandoah*, still not at full strength, would soon have a crew composed mostly of sailors from captured vessels. The young lieutenant understood that getting these experienced seamen to identify with *Shenandoah* and its cause would make the difference between fulfilling the mission—and mutiny.

Thursday, November 10: "Another glorious day in our legitimate cause. At an early hour I was awakened by Mr. Brown who is Officer of the forecastle coming down and reporting to the captain that she was the brig *Susan* from New York."

This overheard conversation grated on Whittle: while he'd slept, this "she" had been spotted and pursued. The thrill of closing in on another Yankee ship—a recreation that gave Whittle the same pleasure that hooking and playing a trout afforded lesser men—had on this occasion been denied him. "I had no idea that any vessel was anywhere near us," he groused, perhaps a bit embarrassed that he had been sleeping with the enemy in sight, and that, even more vanity-damaging, Waddell now knew it. Whittle would have much preferred that Brown first notify him, as the executive officer, and allow Whittle to tell the captain. The comment reveals the subtle tension growing in *Shenandoah*'s chain of command. The executive officer was in charge of all operational decisions on a Civil War navy ship (and in subsequent wars as well). The captain was not directly responsible for small-scale decisions such as discipline, safety, supply, or even weaponry. He functioned more as an arbiter of last resort—remote from the daily life of the ship, but its ultimate authority. When a captain did focus on minutiae, it conveyed a perception that he, "the Old Man," could do the job better—even that he did not trust his subordinate. And when such trust vanishes, or appears to, it strains the chain of command to its limits.

Whittle continued,

> I jumped out of bed and going on deck found that Jack Grimball had a nice brigantine close on our weather bow. Grimball reported that she had been made during the mid-watch and that we had gained steadily on her.

He at least was in time to enjoy the sleight-of-flag trick that the raider's crew had by now perfected.

> We ran up the English flag and she to our great delight hoisted the detestable Yankee rag. We hoisted our true colors and fired a blank cartridge. She showed no sign of heaving-to and we gave him another

*which sent his head and yards all aback. Lt. Chew of Jack Grimball's
watch went onboard and we soon saw the emblem of tyranny come
down. The Captain, Hanson and mate came onboard with all of her
papers. The captain was put on oath and his deposition taken.*

(Conway Whittle—like many 19th-century mariners—used the
pronouns "he" and "she" interchangeably in reference to unfamiliar
ships. In this case the ambiguity fit: the vessel was the "Her. Brig.
Susan" of New York. "Her." was an abbreviation for "hermaphrodite,"
the nickname given ships that combined the two principal types of sail
construction: square-rigged sails on the foremast and, on the mainmast, a triangular topsail over a gaff mainsail.)

Susan was en route to Rio Grande del Sol, Brazil, with a load of
coal that she—or he—had picked up in Cardiff, Wales. Satisfied that
her bill of lading was not sworn before a notary as English property
(*Susan* was valued at $5,443), the raider's commanders informed the
captain that his ship was a prize of war, and sent him off to collect his
personal belongings. "This is our fourth prize," Whittle recorded, "and
the first catch which we have had no steam. There were seven souls
onboard; of these, three came up at once and desired to ship. These
three were all Englishmen. We have been extremely lucky in getting
men. I expect another [Yankee] tomorrow."

But then, of course, Conway Whittle *always* expected another
Yankee tomorrow.

Soon after the captives' boarding came *Shenandoah*'s signature
stroke. Whittle appraised it with his rapidly developing critical eye.

*As soon as we got all the useful articles from our prize . . . we scuttled
her and she went down bow first, her stern rising straight up into the
air. Oh, how I wish she had been a fine clipper ship. It is rarely the case
that a vessel will go down bow first. It is generally the reverse.*

That chore completed, Whittle turned into the wind and let the
230-foot *Shenandoah* show off her improving sailing abilities. With a
good breeze, and a growing crew, he worked the *Shenandoah* southward in the clear blue waters of the equatorial Atlantic.

Today we tacked the ship three times and each time the ship went around beautifully. I never saw a vessel work better. With even our few men we can tack her very easily and have enough to man our guns. I [hope I] will have just about 60 more good men.

These maneuvers were hardly a nautical joy ride. Scarcely more than two weeks into the mission, and with few chances to test her full capacities thus far, Whittle and Waddell were still at pains to know the vessel beneath their feet, not to mention the ever-changing crew that manned her. *Shenandoah*'s tacking prowess—her essential agility—was good news indeed. In violent seas, a ship slow to tack—shift her yards, and thus her sails, to change course abruptly—was a ship doomed to swamping, and sinking. In an engagement with a man-of-war, a ship slow to tack (especially a lightly armed vessel such as *Shenandoah*) was a sitting target.

But *Shenandoah* "went around beautifully." The crew was learning to play her ropes like strings on a violin. Of course, these were calm seas, and no batteries of cannon were hurling explosive shells her way. Still, the results put Whittle in a good mood. He had the decks holy-stoned, saw that more new ropes were rove—threaded—through the topsail braces and topgallant gear, and gave the still-confined prisoners from *Susan* a break by releasing them from their irons and assigning them watch shifts.

One who did not share the general high spirits was George Silvester, who'd had the dubious honor of being the first crewman—the prime example—put in irons, triced up, and gagged. On Friday, November 11, Captain Waddell ordered Silvester demoted from fireman back to coal passer—a job as lowly as it was self-descriptive. Rumors of Silvester's continued surliness had made their way upward from belowdecks to several noncommissioned officers. Now he was back at the very bottom of the chain. "This poor fellow," Whittle mused in his log, "is I think little better than a half-idiot, being very deficient."

Shenandoah skimmed rapidly along under heavy winds and squalls, en route to another near-100-mile day. A distant ship was spotted, then lost, as Whittle and Waddell concentrated on the ship's necessary maintenance: some of the coal—part of the original ruse—still required transferring from the berth deck to the main hold.

The next sighting proved irresistible—and touched off a skein of events that tested Conway Whittle's moral reasoning to the utmost.

> *This afternoon we saw a large ship to windward. We clewed every-thing and steered such a course as would bring us together. At mid-night, nearly all of us were in the lookout, even the two female prisoners. They say they hope she may be a Yankee as they want to catch a big one when they are with us.*

Shenandoah was bearing down on the equator as well. The seas swelled up as the winds increased and rain lashed the decks, making each step treacherous and muting the shouted commands and cries for assistance. No dress rehearsal now; *Shenandoah* was tacking for sur-vival. A little past midnight, the moon broke through to reveal a pale glimpse of the stranger's madly whipping sails to the windward. The raider, bobbing and pitching, lurched alongside her prey.

> *We passed very close to her and fired a gun and hailed her. She replied by heaving to and giving her name, which we did not understand. It was a very rainy, disagreeable night.*

The night was to prove disagreeable in more ways than one. The Ordeal of the Papers was about to be renewed.

> *We sent a boat onboard in charge of Lt. Lee. Very soon the captain and mates came onboard and we were congratulating ourselves upon hav-ing a fine prize, when examination of the papers put us in a stew.*

The "prize" was the *Kate Prince*. But—shades of *Mogul* and *Alina*—was she British or a Yankee? Neutral or fair game? As the At-lantic Ocean roiled and pitched beneath them, *Shenandoah*'s officers tried once again to solve this accursed puzzle.

The captain, a man named Libby, presented a sworn deposition that was not encouraging. It established that while his vessel was of Yankee origin, she carried an English cargo of coal bound for Bahia, Brazil. Her ownership papers were clear: she belonged to Hett, Lane & Company of Liverpool. Finally, the owner had sworn before a notary that he was a British subject.

That would have cinched the case in favor of *Kate Prince*, except for one small detail. That notarial oath existed only in the verbal assurances of Captain Libby. On the document itself it was suspiciously absent.

Here lay temptation. The coal cargo was of negligible value, but the ship herself reeked of wealth. To destroy her would be to inflict heavy loss on the enemy, which was the sum and substance of *Shenandoah*'s purpose. Did the missing document offer enough of a loophole for sinking *Kate Prince*, provided that the Confederates repay Hett Lane for the lost coal?

Lieutenant Whittle and Captain Waddell talked it over. In the end, it was the captain's distaste for carrying prisoners that sealed the decision.

> *We therefore bonded it for $4,000 and sent all our prisoners paroled onboard.*

The females and the little boy were of course not included in the parole, or ransom obligations. Unenforceable as they would surely be, these were not imposed upon women and children by the ever-chivalrous Rebels.

> *They were all exceedingly grateful for our kindness, particularly the women who I am quite certain would have preferred to have stayed. Therein we differ for I am very glad to get rid of them and I hope never to have a female prisoner onboard again.*

The transfer of prisoners by longboat was painstaking work in the rain and the high, dangerously pitching waves. It was not completed until 5:00 a.m., with young Frank begging the whole time to be allowed to stay. Captain Libby sent over a gift for the *Shenandoah* crew: two barrels of Irish potatoes. The sincerity of this "gift" remained ambiguous.

The *Kate Prince* ownership quandary paled before the ethical Gordian knot that presented itself the following day.

Shenandoah had just abandoned pursuit of yet another ship flying the Union Jack—"[she] really looked so English that we did not board her"—when "a clean-looking barque" hove into view. The raider leapt to the chase, and overtook her at noon. The stranger answered the customary shot across the bow by running up the flag of Buenos Aires. This time the Confederates were more suspicious, "but he looked so much like a Baltimore vessel that we boarded her."

Jack Grimball, the boarding officer, soon returned in bewilderment. He told James Waddell, "Well, Sir, it takes a better lawyer than I am to condemn this vessel, but I have brought off all the papers. I do not feel authorized to take the captain from under his flag."

Once again, Whittle and Waddell plunged into the thickets of registry, bill of sale, and other totems of identification. "She proved as we thought to be, a Baltimore built barque and bound from Baltimore to Rio de Janeiro." She even carried a Yankee cargo: flour, shipped by a New York merchant. Fair game, in short. Her captain, James T. Lynn of Virginia, protested. He argued that, yes, she *had been* a Baltimore vessel, but that she'd been sold to parties in Buenos Aires. The problem was—shades of *Kate Prince*—that the bill of sale was not aboard, "And everything was so mysterious that we decided to get the master on board and examine himself and his mate."

Captain Lynn again swore stoutly that the sale had indeed been legitimate; his ship was a bona fide Buenos Aires vessel. But her cargo was owned by Yankees, having been shipped to them by a businessman named Pendergrast, from Baltimore—the former owner of the vessel.

By now, Whittle's and Waddell's heads were churning like the Atlantic Ocean itself. Through it all, Whittle smelled a rat: "There was something very singular in the manner and bearing of the captain." He called for Lynn's mate—a man named Smith, a Baltimorean by the strangest coincidence—and put *him* under oath. Smith promptly muddled things further by undercutting his captain. The "sale," Smith opined, was bogus—a ruse to prevent Federal authorities from seizing the vessel, which, Smith maintained, was the property of Mr. Pendergrast—a gift from a friendly Southerner in Baltimore who had two sons in the army. "He said he believed that Mr. Pendergrast was the real element."

The salt air was now rank with the scent of foul play. Whittle and Waddell concluded that Smith was telling the truth: Mr. Pendergrast was the real, and covert, owner of the vessel. The course of action was clear: burn the ship.

Now Captain Lynn resorted to melodrama. "He was very much excited and said, 'Well, sir, Mr. Pendergrast will lose the whole value of the vessel, for she is not insured for a single cent.'" Sherlock Holmes himself could not have topped Whittle's quick riposte: "I caught him up at once and said, 'How is it, sir, that to save the vessel you said you knew the sale was a good sale and that she was a Buenos Aires vessel, and swore to this?—And now when you were told we were going to burn, you stated Mr. Pendergrast will lose the whole?'"

Lynn, apparently a stranger to shame, shifted tactics again—and dug himself a deeper hole.

"I put him on oath, and he testified that he would lose the whole value as she was not insured, and says it would break his heart as she was named for his wife. The captain perjured himself before all of us, and when I asked him how his two depositions could be so utterly and entirely incompatible, he had not a word to say." Now, in Whittle's cold appraisal, Captain Lynn was unmasked as the most contemptible of creatures: "And the poor wretch stood before us, a renegade Virginian and a perjured man." Which of these descriptions Whittle considered the more damning is hardly in doubt.

Yet neither did justice to the extent of James Lynn's craven instincts.

We stuck to our determination to burn her, and just as we sent the captain off to pack his traps, [Lynn] went to the captain and begged him not to burn, that he was a young man just married and all his little savings were invested in her. This was so disgusting that I could scarcely keep my hands off the perjurer. We recovered from him seven Spanish Brazilian prisoners and were busily engaged in shifting everything we needed from him. Dr. Lining came off with the [ship's] *letter bag. One of these was from Phipps Bros. N.Y. to the consignee at Rio telling him that the cargo was sent in their name and that the money must be remitted to Pendergrast. This letter threw open the mystery. It was evident that the name of Phipps Bros. was used to save the cargo* [from being identified as Southern] *which really belonged to Mr. Pendergrast. It was very late and much damage had been done but we could not burn the property of our friend* [ally] *and our only course was to undo what we had done and return everything to the vessel. This we did but great damage had been done as the preparation for firing, as made by us, did not leave any portion of the cabin whole.* [True enough: bulkheads, benches, partitions, everything inside the boat had been chopped into kindling.] *I am truly sorry this thing occurred and attribute the whole to the want of truth on the part of the Captain, or to the fact that he was not allowed in on the secret.*

A nice nautical irony here: Captain Lynn had kept the secret for Pendergrast, who never anticipated that the ship would be intercepted by the Rebels, but assumed he would need to be able to fool a blockading Yankee. In the event, it almost cost him his ship when stopped by the Confederates.

We did all we could to repair the damage and had the satisfaction of knowing that the vessel was perfectly seaworthy. [Fearing] *the fact that his vessel was let off* [by the Rebels] *might cause a confiscation of Mr. Pendergrast's property by the Yankees, we concluded to consider the* [bogus cover story] *sale good, and to* [issue a phony] *bond* [for] *the cargo.*

Imagining a world with a far different future than the one that awaited him, the honorable young Whittle appended a final thought to this bewildering escapade: "If ever I have a chance, I will explain to Mr. Pendergrast."

When he took up his pen again, in the evening, Conway Whittle wrote without reservations of any kind.

> *I wrote a few lines to my own dear Pattie and sent it by this opportunity. . . . There is no telling how long it will be before she gets it, but I am pretty certain that it will be received someday or other. Oh how much I would . . . give to know that my darlings were well. My thoughts are constantly of them. I console myself very often by reading over and over again their letters to me. Letters full of affection and love.*

By "this opportunity," Whittle referred to Pendergrast's mail bag. He also enclosed a letter from Waddell to his wife, an indication that the mysterious Pattie may well have been in England, where Mrs. Waddell was being harassed by Federal agents.

Once again he crossed out the few last lines that followed.

⁂

Shenandoah covered a prodigious 150 miles on November 12, and 62 on the restful Sunday after that, drawing within 1 degree 40 minutes of the equator. The crew went back to clearing coal from the berth deck on Monday. The drudgework ceased at 3:00 p.m., when the lookout made a schooner and the raider stood toward her. The good news was quickly apparent: a Yankee. *Shenandoah* closed on her like a cat leaping at its prey, and "to our great delight she ran up a Yankee rag."

This was the 140-foot *Lizzy M. Stacey,* as it turned out, from Boston, valued at $16,000 and headed for Honolulu with an assorted cargo and seven souls aboard. "The case was clear, and as soon as we got everything from her, we burned her." For once, Whittle felt a tinge of regret: "She was a fine little vessel and would have made a fine cruiser. And if we had the men, I would have applied for her."

This last sentence encoded a powerful wish that Conway Whittle nourished throughout *Shenandoah*'s voyage. He would have "applied" to James Waddell, and the application would have been for captaincy of *Lizzy.* Given his makeup, this was hardly surprising: along with his warrior's temperament came the warrior's wish to be free from the control of others—to *command*. Thus he had toyed with the idea of arming the 140-foot schooner, renaming her, and commissioning her in the C.S.A. Navy. Such a move was impractical, he quickly decided, and settled for the satisfaction of getting three of the *Lizzy* crew to join *Shenandoah*. They included a steward and a cook—specialties always welcome aboard a ship. The rest of them he clapped in irons.

But Whittle's fantasy of command would not be disposed of so easily. It would take hold of him again, as the long months aboard *Shenandoah* under Waddell's erratic command dragged by.

5

Southward. The officers and men of *Shenandoah* churned farther, ever farther from the Madeiras, and from their embattled native ground. They crossed the equator on November 15, alert and hungry for fresh prey, ever mindful, to a man, that this lonely vessel on which they sailed, this three-masted flyspeck at large on the planet's vast waters, represented the last best hope of reversing the tide of a great war in favor of their homeland. Of changing the course of history.

But . . . why *southward*?

In geographic terms, *Shenandoah* was sailing away from the action, not toward it. If crushing the Union's vital maritime economy were her mission, why was she putting more and more distance between herself and a northern oceanic hunting ground teeming with concentrated riches that seemed almost to beg for her plundering pleasure?

The answer lay in a geographic paradox, and the essence of *Shenandoah*'s mission. To reach its northern destination, the raider would have to go south—on a 17,000-mile detour around two continents, North and South America, before she could swoop down on the fat, rich, undefended Yankee ships that plied the far North Pacific, the killing fields of the New England whalers.

The architects of *Shenandoah*'s mission had realized this from the first, and realized the value that such an odyssey might yield.

In the early stages of the war, the South had secured the services of two of the most remarkable strategic thinkers in the American military: Lieutenants John Mercer Brooke and John L. Porter. Both men were career officers in the U.S. Navy; Porter was a specialist in naval construction. Navy Secretary Mallory, obsessed with schemes for breaking the Union blockade, ordered the two to collaborate on the design of an ironclad gunboat—a concept that just then dominated the fantasies of military utopians around the world. The result was the legendary *Virginia* (built from the remains of the USS *Merrimack*), scourge of the battle of Hampton Roads and prototype for the twenty-two Confederate ironclads built during the war.

But Brooke and Porter brought other precious resources to the South as well. As U.S. Navy officers before the war, the two had been sent on an expedition to survey the whaling grounds of the Arctic. Joining the Confederacy, the loyal Virginians brought with them their accumulated knowledge: their oceanic charts, their studies of the summer calving habits of the humpbacks and the minkes and the finbacks.

And of the fleet of Yankee whaling ships that hunted them.

This strategic knowledge was incalculably reinforced when Admiral James Bulloch thought to call upon an old friend of his. Mathew Fontaine Maury, yet another Virginian, had been among the preeminent explorers in the history of the U.S. Navy, where he'd gained fame as "the Pathfinder of the Seas." Now a commodore in the CSN, Maury offered his own great store of detailed charts that outlined the precise bearings of the whalers' destinations, and their preferred courses or "tracks," as well as their resupply points and favorite hunting grounds.

The Confederate vision of attacking the whaling fleet was no idle impulse. In the mid-nineteenth century, whale oil was one of the most valuable commodities in the world. As a lubricant it was unmatched. But most of it was burned in lamps. The light that it fueled—warm, clean, comforting, and slow-burning—was a staple of civilization. In 1855, its peak year of pricing, sperm whale oil sold for about $77 a barrel—or $1,500 in early-twenty-first-century dollars. It was a global industry that accounted for the great Yankee whaling fleets, each comprising dozens of ships and remaining at sea for years at a time, that plied the frigid waters of the northern Pacific. The whale ships bore only token armaments or none at all, relying for their safety on the strict international penalties for piracy. These penalties typically involved hanging.

In wartime, however, such ships would be legitimate targets for enemy conquest.

Brooke and Porter made it clear to Mallory that such conquest would require a long-range vessel, probably acting alone, and without much hope of resupply. It would take a strong vessel, capable of surviving fierce oceanic storms and the edges of the polar ice where the whalers worked the shallows.

And so Admiral Bulloch in England, in partnership with Commodore Barron in Paris and with the support of Secretary Mallory in Richmond, had set about to sink the whalers. And they settled upon *Shenandoah* as their weapon of choice.

※◎◇※

The straightest route from the Madeiras to the Aleutians, of course, was blocked by those two inconvenient continents. The raider had two unenviable options. The shortest route was to sail southward, then hook westward and brave the certain violence of Cape Horn, at South America's tip. From there, once into the Pacific, she could turn north again, and only then set her sights on her distant prey. But there were good reasons for a more indirect route. For one, nothing could be gained by arriving early in the northern Pacific: whaling could not commence before the thaw in the spring of 1865. However, a southern and then an eastward route, though longer, would take *Shenandoah* away from South America, under the tip of Africa and across the Indian Ocean, and finally to Australia, a country plentiful with Confederate sympathizers. This alone made Melbourne a potential haven for resupplying the ship and adding needed manpower.

And finally—as the raider had already learned to her satisfaction—these southern lanes were not entirely lacking in Yankee prey.

And so it had been decided, and the orders given in secret were soon to be carried out at sea. *Shenandoah* would swing east, angling far below Africa to avoid U.S. Navy patrols off Capetown; then hold her course due east, skirting the southern coast of Australia to the port at Melbourne; and, from there, set a course northward, at last, for the prodigious trek across the nearly endless Pacific. If all went well, the New Bedford whaling fleet would encounter a most vexatious visitor the following spring.

※◎◇※

Reaching zero latitude, the equator, gave Whittle and Waddell the opportunity to allow the men a bit of tomfoolery. "Crossing the line"

was an initiation ritual that awaited any sailor traversing the equator
for the first time. The traditional hazings dated back to the Vikings.
The ringleader was "King Neptune," a veteran salt decked out in a
fake beard and brandishing a trident. "Neptune" directed the adminis-
tering of various foul slatherings, emetics, and "elixirs" to the "polly-
wogs." Whittle, if not the stern Waddell, well understood the benefit
to shipboard morale of such ritualized roughhousing: with a crew as
diverse as theirs in nationality, and as conditional in their allegiance,
any bonding ceremony was worth its weight in grog. Whittle himself
was gobbed in the face with a blend of molasses, bearing grease, and
stewed apples, then soaked with the ship's pump. As Whittle recalled
it, "I pulled off to an undershirt and took it well and thoroughly." He
contrasted his good-natured participation with what happened moments later, as the hazing turned dark, presaging conflicts to come
months later with the hot-headed young doctor, Frederich J. McNulty
of Virginia.

> *All went on very well, and all took it very well except Mr. Codd one
> of the engineers who got mad and Dr. McNulty who when the bar-
> ber asked him where he was from, was not smart enough and replied
> very politely and had his mouth filled with shaving soap. This his
> Irish blood could not stand and he struck the barber and knocked
> him sprawling full length on deck. It was rare sport but I am very
> glad it comes but once. There was but one Lieut. (Lee) out of five
> who escaped.*

Morale, to be sure, was a precious commodity throughout the
Confederacy. Sherman's 62,000 troops were just then leaving the
ashes of Atlanta behind and commencing their March to the Sea,
their commander having gained the freshly reelected Lincoln's ap-
proval with the boast, "I can make Georgia howl!" It would be a tough,
wet winter for the half-starved Southern ground forces. Even Confederate sympathizers in London labored under unusually dense blankets of wet fog and persistent snow.

Aboard *Shenandoah*, though, all was balmy. Blown along by zephyrs
out of the southwest, the ship ate up 167 miles on November 16.

Whittle was satisfied, if watchful—and proud of his men's efforts, which he ruefully suspected would leave scarcely a trace on the world's memory.

> *This morning we can scarcely see the Englishman we beat so shamefully on yesterday.* [They had overtaken a fast British vessel the day before, impressing the hell out of all jack-tars aboard.] *All day hard at work getting the ship in order. It's very uphill work I can assure you. No one knows how much I go threw* [sic] *with and I am sure what we have done will never be appreciated, but I have one aim in this cruise, and that is to do my duty to the greatest advancement of my country's cause. I care neither for reputation or anything of the kind.*

An odd reflection, that last, jarringly personal: "I care neither for reputation or anything of the kind." An odd journal on the whole, for that matter, this notebook of Whittle's. Hardly a typical officer's log, it often ignored the minutiae of the ship's daily operation, dwelling instead, for great stretches, on personal observation, reflection, memory, musings of doubt, and complex moral reasoning: the most intimate workings of Lt. Conway Whittle's mind. Amid the tightly constrained, gruffly masculine "official" conventions of nineteenth-century military commanders' jottings, Whittle's journal was edging toward territory virtually uncharted: stream-of-consciousness. Confessional. A kind of literature.

But then, *Shenandoah* herself was plowing toward uncharted territory. In the surreal months to come, the ship would be "out of the world, and not of it," as Whittle himself would later observe—at sea almost constantly, cut off from communication with the continents, and thus separated from history—the ship a civilization unto itself, with Whittle its Homer.

As long, at least, as he survived. Something clawed anew at the insides of his stomach. Had the bottle shard, like an albatross, returned?

> *Today I felt wretchedly and am very uneasy for fear the piece of glass may have something to do with it. The doctors say it has been too long*

since it was swallowed for it not to have shown itself long since. It's either glass or tobacco, and I am not certain which. If the former, I will not long be in doubt, for it will prove fatal by day after tomorrow. I trust I may be better tomorrow for the anxiety makes me miserable.

Shenandoah raced 180 miles on Thursday, November 17, under steady trade winds, heading nearly due south, longitude 30 degrees 50 minutes west. "Our ship sails very well for the sail we have set, as we have been generally under short canvas." The short sail—particularly in heavy weather—was a necessity, not a choice. Whittle and Waddell still lacked enough crewmen to man all the lines, yet the ship sliced through the waves like a dolphin: 172 miles the following day, and under even shorter canvas.

Whittle turned his attention toward conquering another enemy: one familiar to countless "nicotine fiends" of his time, and after.

I feel today very much better, and came to the conclusion that it was the excessive use of tobacco which was injuring me. And I determined to stop both chewing and smoking. I took all of my best tobacco and gave it to my mess mates, and I'm going to do my best to break the chains of slavery to a habit which has done me so much damage. I may not have the power to quit it, but I'm going to make all the effort that I am capable of. God give me strength. This is by no means the first time that I have tried to rid myself of the habit, but heretofore I have made the attempt when I had very little to occupy my time, and I was therefore more tempted to recommence.

The erstwhile Confederate known by now as Mark Twain would put it more succinctly: "Giving up smoking is easy. I've done it myself a thousand times."

By Saturday—another 192 miles—*Shenandoah's* decks sparkled from days of cleaning by the crew—but a restlessness had set in, teased up by monotony. She had completed her first month at sea—Whittle counted her a "Confederate" ship from the day she'd been commissioned and received her munitions of war, October 19. After an exhilarating string of conquests, she had now gone six days without engaging a Yankee ship.

Whittle may have had more personal motives for dating *Shenandoah's* "birth" to October 19.

> *It is a little singular that this ship, I may say, was born on the birthday of my own dear Pattie. This will give me good luck, I am sure, and nothing is good luck to me, which is not good luck to all on board. Oh, what I would not give to see my darlings or to give, or to receive, one of their dear letters and how much would I not give to hear from home. I place my dear ones in God's hands, and only say, Thy will be done.*

Six days without action, running hard across miles of ocean and yet gazing out upon a seascape that never changed. Here lay a certain invitation to yet another fleet of enemies: Boredom. Melancholy. Homesickness. A hunger to recapture the details of a life before the war. Restlessness giving way to grievance, giving way to thoughts that test a sailor's discipline and loyalty to the ship. Above all else, a creeping torpor that can dull alertness, dull the sense of everyday duty. And they were now but a first, long month into a year-long voyage.

Whittle and Waddell did what they could to maintain a sense of mission. The Sunday ritual—inspection, a reading of the Articles of War—offered a useful occasion. On November 20, en route to a 190-mile day, all the ship's officers turned out in their finest dress-uniform trappings: gray braided jackets, short-billed kepis. James Waddell marched out as the flower of the company, a martinet-marvel of braid, crease, and polish. Whittle, on whom no detail was lost, regarded the finery in terms of the climate—and baleful symbolism.

> *The men were all dressed in uniform and looked very well, but gray will never stand the sea air. I have a suit which I never had on until I came on board, and now it looks as though I have been wearing it for a year. Oh no, the old Blue was the best. And I think the only color which will stand.*

Conway Whittle may have had a different kind of weather in mind here, or half in mind. "The old Blue" was his prewar uniform, the one he wore as an officer in the United States Navy. In judging it "the only color which will stand," he may have been slipping, not quite consciously, into a grim acceptance of what inevitably lay ahead for the South.

Another hundred miles on Monday, November 21. "Course, south by west a quarter. Winds east southeast, southeast. Hard at work, cleaning up the birth deck." Cleaning it up of coal. The coal still overwhelmed their living space. A form of camouflage at the outset, the coal had long since shifted its purpose. The coal now gave them fighting mobility and ballast. Still, its reek and cloying residue were oppressive and inescapable. Shovel it . . . sweep it . . . stack its black jagged anvil-lunks, hold it at bay; that was the best they could hope for. Coal and boredom contended for supremacy aboard *Shenandoah*.

Coal and boredom, and rigging. The ship's ropes and canvas formed another prime constant. The ropes, called lines, were omnipresent, unnumbered, endlessly complex, and literally held the ship together; they were its veins and arteries, their suppleness never to be taken for granted, their failings as perilous as a heart attack. Ropes, especially the traditional high-quality hemp ropes, were living organisms; they had life spans; they were susceptible to aging, disease, demise. They required replenishment; failing it, the ship sagged in the water like a spent human body. From the voyage's very outset—before *Sea King* had cleared the Thames—Whittle had been troubled by the state of her rigging. *Shenandoah* had already proven herself the fastest creature on the seas, but in the proving, she had taxed her original cordage to the limit. Months in drydock had further corrupted it. The ropes virtually groaned for replacement. Captain Waddell, who wrestled with various doubts throughout the voyage, almost certainly regarded the ropes as detriments to the ship's seaworthiness and combat capabilities. Fresh fibers had turned up with almost providential swiftness. From among the first ships she had conquered, *Shenandoah*'s boarding parties had returned with great stores of the new, golden, three-strand "manila" rope. Woven from the sturdy abaca plant, manila was rot-resistant, stronger, and easier to splice than hemp, and more reliable: hemp was notoriously given to contracting and swelling when wet, and sometimes a supply proved as soft as cotton. All rope had drawbacks—improperly stored, it could quickly rot—but sailors understood this, and knew how to prevent it. ("Knowing the ropes" was not an accidental phrase; many crewmen founded their reputations on it.)

In the early going, *Shenandoah*'s very success forestalled the process of rope replacement: chasing, capturing, and burning Yankee ships preempted most routine tasks. The turbulent seas between chases made the work too lethally dangerous.

Now, though, in the calm and lonely equatorial waters, *Shenandoah*'s crew faced the task of replacing the vessel's vascular system.

The job was immense, and consumed endless hours. The rigging was measured in miles, and every inch of every line demanded attention: each sail individually unanchored from its cleats and hauled down through vast pulley systems; old lines stripped, new ones spliced and threaded through. So many ropes: the footropes under each of the yards; the ladderlike "ratlines" that rose up on either side of the masts. The safety nettings, though few, like the essential cargo nets, were all made of rope. "We now have changed nearly all of our running gear from old hemp to new manila, all of which we have captured in our various prizes," Whittle recorded. He added a notation indicating that the "lonely" ocean was growing more crowded with each passing mile: "We pass, during the day, a great many vessels, but all showed a foreign flag, and all looked foreign." *Shenandoah* was some 1,000 miles off the eastern coast of Brazil now, bearing down on some of the best hunting grounds on the seven seas.

His unflagging attention to shipboard detail and to every distant shape on the sea did not distract Conway Whittle from noting, and honoring whenever possible, the humanity of his diverse crew.

Today I was a little amused by our captain of the hold, an Irishman named Moran, coming aft and saying to me, 'Mr. Whittle, Sir, would that you would take me on deck, Sir, I am not much of a scholar, Sir, and Mr. Smith, Sir, expects me to recollect where every package is, Sir. And I can't do it, Sir.

Whittle had been observing Moran. "He's a hardworking quiet man," he'd noted, "and I put him there [in the hold] because he would get more pay." Apprised of this boon, however, Moran held fast: he'd prefer to forfeit the pay advantage for the sake of getting out of the hold. Doubtless illiterate, the Irishman was clearly overwhelmed by the vast jumble of cargo and equipment—which the sneering Lt. (and paymaster) William Breedlove Smith demanded he commit to memory. Short of provoking open warfare with his junior-officer corps, Conway Whittle had little choice: "I rated Walter Madden captain of the hold in his place." He added, with what might have been a whistle in the dark, "We are getting along quietly and remarkably well."

Whittle might well have added, "Or so I pray." Getting along quietly and remarkably well was no mere luxury aboard *Shenandoah*. It was essential to the mission's survival.

> *The only fear I have is that when our six months men's time expires, they will not re-enlist. I trust however, that the nucleus will stay, and we can get another crew.*

Still only a month into the great raiding escapade, Conway Whittle knew all too well that both he and the crew tracked exactly how long it would be before military service aboard the ship, for most of them, would become strictly voluntary. *Shenandoah*'s cohesion was a near-miracle as it was: a polyglot collection of strangers culled from enemy ships. How many of these had "shipped" only because the alternative was unendurable confinement? Without more crewmen, a mass refusal by the short-timers to reenlist would essentially disable the ship. The process of locating, cajoling, recruiting, and training a new crew could stretch on for weeks, as the Confederacy's lifeblood continued to trickle away in Virginia and Georgia and Tennessee.

Conway Whittle needed to put away "the only fear I have"— because it simply was not an option. Typically of him, he looked to the brighter side of things:

> *But when I consider that when we started we had 5 men, including two quarter-masters in each watch, and now we have 12 [per watch] besides the quarter-masters, I say that if ever a set of men had*

cause to thank god, we are those men. We have enough to take care of
the ship in heavy weather, and we will get more in the course of time.

Still, the questionable loyalty of those men weighed on his mind
and colored his logbook entry for Tuesday, November 22, when the
raider covered 120 miles, on a southeasterly course under swirling
winds. "Today we have done a great deal," he admitted warily. "But really there remains so much undone, that to see what has been done is
very difficult. We can hardly tell we've done anything." The skies
promised little relief from anxiety. "We are having very unsettled
weather . . . passing squalls, which are sometimes very fresh."

"Fresh" was a technical term in Whittle's day, referring to the rising
levels of wave and gusting winds that—beyond "fresh"—would be
called a gale. A "full gale" would be more intense, prelude to a hurricane or typhoon.

⚓

The raider's next encounter prompted a devil-may-care defensive
subterfuge.

> *This morning, before we made sail, a large English ship crawled up*
> *on our lee quarter. But when we set on royals and topgallant sails, we*
> *dropped him very rapidly. He telegraphed* his name as the English*
> *ship* Harwich, *bound to Sydney, New South Wales. We telegraphed*
> *ours as the British gunboat "Hesper," bound on a cruise. He, no doubt,*
> *knew that such was not the case, as the "Hesper" is a very small craft.*
> *We tell any number of fibs, but all is fair in love and war.*

Running at top speed now, 200 miles on November 24, 1864, continuing on the southeasterly course—latitude 24 degrees south, longitude 31 degrees 28 minutes west. A new delectable-looking stranger,
tall in the water under her Douglas-fir masts: "This evening we made

---

* By "telegraphed," Whittle meant either a series of light-blinkered codes or flag sema-
phores. Although Samuel Morse's invention was a staple of Civil War communication,
it required transmission cables. Wireless telegraphy did not come into use until 1899.

a fine looking five-topsail-yards ship, and stood for her. I would have sworn she was a Yankee, and she had the appearance of one in every particular." Instead, another letdown: "To our disgust, she hoisted the Norwegian flag, and I suppose she is one of the many transfers in consequence of the war. We did not board."

Whittle probably guessed it right: in this brief time, *Shenandoah*'s earlier exploits had already sent shockwaves back through the U.S. maritime world. Since insurance rates were skyrocketing for cargo in U.S. flagged vessels, cargo owners booked space elsewhere, and the Yankee ship owners were watching helplessly as their profits shriveled. U.S. flagged vessels would ride at anchor in ports throughout the Atlantic and Indian Oceans. Whalers would leave the calving grounds and seek lagoons to hide in. Cargoes of tea would be left to swelter in Bombay warehouses, not set steeping in Beacon Hill sterling. Ships whose owners were willing, or desperate enough, to send them to sea could frequently find recruiting a crew as difficult as finding a cargo or an underwriter.

To be certain that the five-topsail craft now in view had actually been a New England–built and Yankee-owned ship would now require sending over a boarding party. Darkness was falling, and something about her led the Confederates to give her the benefit of the doubt. They let her sail on, a nice prize, perhaps one even reflagged as recently as its preceding voyage.

Conway Whittle may not have been fooled. But he did cling to his code of honor.

The "Norwegian" encounter triggered an incident that offered the young lieutenant further evidence—as if he needed it—of the thin membrane that separated an orderly ship from a floating Hobbesian jungle.

We've also got today, I am sorry to report, the second trouble with our men.

As *Shenandoah* made its run toward the tall unidentified craft, a troublesome second midshipman named Thomas Hall had begun a "discussion" with a captain of the top, a man named Raymond. As a senior noncom in charge of the sails on the upper masts, Raymond was a powerful overlord to the ordinary seamen on his watch. Hall's "discussion"—probably a wager, a punishable activity that Whittle chose to wink at—centered on whether the stranger was indeed Norwegian or American. It quickly progressed from words to fists. Whittle had walked past the men as they escalated their dialogue to the bloody-nose stage. As an officer witnessing a forbidden act, he had no choice: "It became my painful duty to punish them, which I did in a novel way."

Novel, to say the least: ". . . by putting them in single irons, <u>each one embracing the other, around an iron stanchion.</u> And then, taking their hands to a beam."

The manacled, embracing seamen thought at first that Whittle was joking. He was not. Shipboard justice in the 1860s had something in common with frontier justice of the same era: in a remote enclave, cut off from all civilizing norms and institutions—family, the church, the courts—an executive officer often had to style himself as a seagoing town marshal: a tough hombre, with whom you did not want to tangle.

They soon concluded that it was all on one side, and sent for me, please, to let them down. I did so after they had been long enough there to make an example of them.

No floggings here, no keelhauling, but pain and humiliation enough for any man. The lowly midshipman and the formidable captain of the top found themselves with their hands shackled around each other's chests—a forced intimacy that in itself must have galled them. But Whittle didn't stop there. In "taking their hands to a beam," he'd ordered them hoisted nearly off the deck via a pulley. Now pain overtook shame, as the men's arms were stretched over their heads at an agonizing angle, supporting their weight. The agony was all but unbearable. Little wonder that the polite word *please* quickly entered the brawlers' vocabulary. They begged to be let down.

I did so after they had been long enough there to make an example of them.

And long enough to trigger the second stage of Whittle's goal: gossip. In the tight shipboard community, gossip was a prime social commodity. Whittle well understood that news of this punishment would ripple through *Shenandoah*'s crew, until all the men had heard it. And were mesmerized. And would resolve never to replicate the action that had caused it. Conway Whittle may have been a gentleman, a civilized romantic, an adherent to his ironclad code of honor. But an aura of legitimate fear-based respect, as he well knew, was among the resources that made his ship safe for a code of honor.

Whittle's log would show no further incidence of men being forced to embrace in irons and lifted. Yet Thomas Hall remained untamed.

Still another incident arose on November 25, marring a 195-mile sprint by *Shenandoah*, now 1,500 miles below the shoulder of South America, where she turned east under winds that hauled to the north-northeast. The raider had made a barque at daybreak, on her lee, but disappointment reigned again: she proved to be British. "We hauled up to our course and stood on." Then Whittle was forced to play schoolmaster once again.

A first-class petty officer, the gunners mate William Crawford, was reported by master's mate John F. Minor, for insolence. Whittle recorded it with world-weary irony:

> The conduct was willful. And I have inclined that he was only trying an experiment to see how far he could go under the cover of being an old petty officer. The pretty little experiment worked perfectly, as he found out that he had gotten to the end of his line.

Another example of shipboard human nature: an experienced old seaman, a veteran from the line, trying to see how far he could push his younger yet now superior officer. "The end of his line" proved to be an interlude in irons, and trussed up. "I let him stay there until I thought he'd had enough to last him a year."

Defying a superior officer was a far more subversive act than a spontaneous fistfight. The first time it succeeded—or went unpunished—it sent a dangerous message through the ship that the officers were soft, susceptible to being ruled by the crew. Given that *Shenandoah*'s officers were almost all in their early twenties, and that their crew were grizzled, experienced men from around the Seven Seas, the danger of mutiny, either overtly or de facto, was constant. As always, Whittle, who'd seen this behavior in both the Union and Confederate navies, understood it and stood his ground with perfect aplomb.

> *When I let him down, [I told] him I would at any time repeat the dose when it was necessary. I hate to punish men, but if you do not rule them, they will rule you. Nearly all old man-of-war's men try these experiments, and if not punished, will go on. But if they are met properly, they behave beautifully.*

<hr />

A day later, in the blackness of early Saturday, November 26, *Shenandoah* found herself hurtling toward a different sort of calamity.

As the ship sliced southeastward, Conway Whittle was awakened by a tumult on deck: the thunder of many feet running about; the alarmed cries of men's voices; officers shouting desperate orders from the helm. Whittle, heading for the bow, raced the length of the deck in his slippers, and the gist of the shouts grew clear: Ship dead ahead! Change course! Or collide!

A set of ghostly images had pierced the darkness: a large sailing barque—identity and destination to be forever unknown—had materialized in the raider's path, its huge stern a wall of imminent collision. Only instant action could save the ship, and perhaps the Confederacy.

Merely spinning the ship's wheel was little use. A multi-masted sailing vessel scarcely noticed its rudder. The crew would have to steer by sail: seize control of the yards, which meant teams of men grabbing and hauling on line after line, straining against weight and the wind, to turn the wind into their savior.

But turn it where?

Still on the dead run, his soft sleeping slippers sliding on the spray-slick boards, Whittle peered into the oceanic dark toward the bow, trying to assess the looming menace's position, distance, and course.

. . . when I got forward I found we were close in on a bark on the opposite tack.

His judgment would have to be instantaneous.

I gave the order . . .

Whittle screamed:

HARD APORT!

It was a brazenly counterintuitive order. Instead of pulling off on a diagonal to starboard and away from the other ship, *Shenandoah* would attempt to lurch the other way and dive under the ship's stern, a dangerous crossing maneuver given that *Shenandoah*'s momentum could well hurl her into the barque's rear end. Winds and the ship's momentum told Whittle that this was the only chance.

The crew obeyed without hesitation. Seamen bent and strained to the task; pulleys groaned, timbers cried out in their rotation, and the great sails boomed and snapped in their shift against the wind. The invasive shape swelled as it grew closer. Seconds before impact, *Shenandoah* responded to her massive rudder. She pivoted, slanted to port, and slid miraculously just past the mystery barque's stern.

"If we had not kept away," Whittle recorded tersely, hours after the crisis was over, "we would have been into her." The two ships' swaying riggings would likely have entangled, and their hulls then would have collided.

As to the young duty officer whose responsibility it was to be vigilant for just such an emergency, Conway Whittle was singularly forgiving.

Scales, who was in charge of the deck, though without much experience, is very watchful and attentive, and will make an excellent officer.

This was Second Lt. Dabney Marion Scales, a valiant Mississippian whose record of heroism in the naval war nearly matched Whittle's. An Annapolis graduate like his superior, Scales had also served on an ironclad at New Orleans before signing on to *Shenandoah*. Scales's vessel, the CSS *Atlanta,* typified the desperate futility of the city's attempts to throw together a defense against Farragut's mighty armada: it was essentially a wooden-hulled, sail-and-steam-driven vessel festooned with iron plating and armed with a few insufficient cannon. Lieutenant Scales urged on his superiors the vainglorious plan of using this slapped-together tub-of-war to surprise the fast-forming Yankee assault fleet before it was fully assembled. Despite the heroic concept, the David-versus-Goliath upset was not to be, and the results were predictably disastrous. Under the command of a head-strong and inexperienced new captain, and pathetically underprepared for its mission, *Atlanta* puttered forth on an ill-timed, ill-directed, ill-considered attack, and the blockaders calmly blasted it to pieces. Dabney Scales, along with the rest of the survivors, was taken aboard a U.S. Navy vessel and sent to the Massachusetts prison camp that also confined Conway Whittle.

Now, after a brief crisis of decisiveness, if not alertness, on Scales's watch had placed *Shenandoah,* its crew, and its mission in mortal peril, the former prisoner of war was treated with quiet compassion by his former comrade in chains.

No such consideration lay in store the next day for the incorrigible Thomas Hall, who was caught in an unspeakable act.

Whittle had been feeling expansive as *Shenandoah* logged 120 miles under shifting winds and squalls that blew the ship nearly on its port side before the crew could get the sails tied back: "We have, I venture to say, as comfortable a ship as there is anywhere to be found." Whittle was particularly pleased with the tightness of the ship's decking, which ensured that the men belowdecks would not suffer from leaks during storms.

> *It is a treat to go down there in bad weather, and they are always dry, singing as happy as they can be. I am certain our gallant little crew is happy and if I had seventy more I would be satisfied.*

He had ventured too soon. Once again, the whiff of anarchy interrupted the lieutenant's serenity.

Today I was again forced to punish one of the men. I caught Hall, second midshipman, being guilty of a piece of scandalous conduct. And I confined him by tricing him up.

The exact nature of Hall's "scandalous conduct" went unspecified, but by inference it was sexual. While sodomy, as defined (without being precisely named) in the laws of Virginia, was "that act of which an upright man cannot give voice to," it perforce required a partner of some kind. Whittle made no mention of another sailor. *Shenandoah* frequently had livestock aboard, but again, no hint of such a liaison is given. Perhaps the offense was masturbation, or perhaps Hall "opportuned" (i.e., propositioned) a shipmate. Other offenses suggest themselves. The ship was still in warm waters, and living conditions were close for most of the crew, so the midshipman's transgression may well have revolved around some issue of common sanitation or personal hygiene.

Whatever Hall's offense, he did not suffer his punishment meekly.

He was afterwards very abusive, and I gagged him and triced him up higher. I kept him in this way until he said he would behave himself, when I took him down, and by recommendation he was disrated by the Captain.

The notion of a seaman screaming curses at an officer while hanging by his wrists suggests a powerful investment in whatever "scandalous conduct" got him into trouble. Yet Whittle remained hopeful, in a psychologically shrewd way, for Hall's prospects.

I think this will last Hall for a few days, at the end of which, I think he will try his hand again. Then, if I repeat the dose with a gradual increase, he will be made as good a man as any to be found. He's active, smart, energetic and all he wants to make him as good a man as you might want, is that he should be ruled into subjection. Never had I to deal with a man in nature whose case was more plainly understood by me than it is in this. And I will bet that the day is not far off when he will be as good a man as any in the ship.

Once again, Whittle had shown his intuitive genius for maintaining the hair-trigger balance between compassion and strict discipline on a ship at sea, and his understanding of why the balance was critical. He expressed it with terse precision that Sunday evening, in his log.

The ship can be made a happy one and I shall do all I can to bring about this state, but rely upon it, the first thing to be done is to show you are to rule and govern, and not be ruled and governed. Discipline is more necessary to the happiness of men than anything else. By discipline, I do not mean tyranny, but a thorough governing. . . . examine all reports . . . give the accused any doubt . . . [if] guilty punish him well. Let a man see that he is ruled by justice and he is ruled by you.

Whittle then turned once more to the private preoccupations of his heart:

This day I spent in reading my Bible and reading the letters from my darling Pattie, and from my dear ones at home. Reading letters from those I love always has a good effect on me. It is like reading some good book. In as much as it makes me think of God, and be grateful for his manifold and great mercies.

Squally winds followed *Shenandoah* southeastward the following day, and pushed her 104 miles. By day's end of November 28, 1864, the ship lay 26 degrees west of Greenwich, 30 degrees south of the equator. The ship's maintenance took precedence once again in Whittle's attention: he noted with disapproval that "our head casings had sagged down very much. And I set the boatswains to work getting them up in the yards." Yet the topsails made him brag like a shopkeeper. "We are blest. . . . We have Cunningham's Patented Self-Reefing Topsails, by which [only] three men can close reef a topsail, simply slacking the halyards and hauling on the brace." The Cunningham system made it unnecessary for a dozen or so storm-tossed seamen to draw in sails by climbing up into the rigging and pulling the giant sheets of wet canvas up against the yards and tying them up by hand. Cunningham's allowed them to roll the canvas up like a window shade. "I do not know what we should have done, shorthanded as we had been, had it not been for this rig. We can at any time in a very short time and without risking the safety of the men by sending them aloft, reef down to almost no sail and the sail rolls itself tightly around the yard." Safety in harsh weather was the paramount concern here, but this new edge of naval technology gave a combat officer a crucial further advantage. *Shenandoah's* enhanced ability to change sail rapidly, even while short-handed as the result of casualties, could well be decisive in battle.

All of this inspired Whittle to add a note of his cherished optimism: "We have been greatly blessed in every way, and if ever a set of men had cause to be thankful to God, we are those men."

A hundred thirty miles the next day, but the fresh northwesterly winds contained heavy squalls, making it necessary to put the ship under short sails toward evening, and also to resist the temptations of the chase: "At an early hour, we saw a large sail standing to the southward. And she had every appearance of being an English vessel." *Shenandoah* held back, its crew tending to the rigging instead. Whittle's predatory urges took hold of him again: "I wish we could catch another Yankee. The work becomes a little dull, unless broken up by an occasional capture."

No Yankee hove conveniently into view, but on a boggy, damp Wednesday, November 30, the ship's crew spotted something nearly as exciting—evidence on the ocean's surface that prey might well be in the vicinity.

We saw today a very favorable sign in passing what is called "Whales' food" [krill]. *This indicates that there are whales about here.*

Where there was whales' food, there were likely whales. And where there were whales, there were likely Yankee whaling ships.

Soon, Whittle knew, the chase would be on again. But in the excitement of the moment, the searching mind of the young mariner expanded from thoughts of blood spilled in warfare to an ocean made red by nature:

This "Whales' food" is a very singular thing. It is observable in spots and streaks in the water, and when it is thick the water is turned to a perfectly red color. I had a great desire to see what it was, and caught some in a bucket. I found the water alive with little red insects looking in form very much like lobster or shrimp. The water is more or less red as it contains more or less of these insects. They say that the whales eat this, but some say they do not, anyhow, it is a good sign of a whaling ground.

6

A hundred thirty miles under a shrouded sun, they tacked southward into the winds that blew December across the ocean. Hungry for letters, Whittle found himself overtaken once more by melancholy, and fought against it, as he always did, by willing himself to hopeful thoughts:

Oh what I would not give to receive a letter from my darlings. I miss their letters more than I can express. God grant that we may soon meet, and then what a jolly time we shall have chatting together. Whenever I am a little downcast, I have but to think of the happiness in store for me when I get home. Any little melancholy is at once changed to joy. God hasten our freedom.

Any such meeting would be impossible on this course. Whittle's ship was now below the tip of South Africa, but still well to the west of the Cape of Good Hope, and sailing directly away from his homeland. Moving into the far South Atlantic, *Shenandoah* was now almost equidistant from Africa, South America, and Antarctica. The temperatures of air and water were rising as the southern hemisphere tipped toward the sun, and the climate would adjust, and the growing seasons would reverse themselves, winter becoming spring. Exactly as the American South now hoped the fortunes of its beloved Confederacy would be reversed.

For Whittle, December would soon glow like June in these sub-equatorial latitudes. Sure enough, on the second day of the month, the sky abruptly brightened.

This has been as beautiful a day as I ever saw in my whole life. All day, we have had a nice warm sun, with a fine royal breeze. At first the wind was from such a direction that we could not hang on course, but the wind veered afterward.

Three hundred miles southeastward, as Whittle knew, and surrounded by savage seas, lay the islands of Tristan da Cunha. The five islands were discovered in 1506 by a Portuguese navigator who, after failing in his attempts to breach the waves and land on one of them, dubbed it after himself. Soon the whole archipelago bore his name. The first permanent settler, a Massachusetts man, arrived in 1810, renamed the group the Islands of Refreshment, and then drowned in a small boat that he'd foolishly taken out on these unrefreshing waters. In 1812 the British annexed the islands, restoring da Cunha's name. (Individually, they were called Tristan, Nightingale, Middle, Stoltenhoff, and Inaccessible.) Jules Verne used them among his settings for *In Search of the Castaways,* and commented on the extraordinary ugliness of the settlers there.

Good-looking people were not uppermost in Conway Whittle's mind. Prey was.

At, around, and about this Island is a great whaling ground, and the Island is their great resort, and I am a little disappointed that we have not caught a whaler or so. However, I suppose our time will come ere long.

The island group was also famous as a graveyard for sailing ships caught between its heaving, gale-blown waves and its rocks. By latitude it lay on the upper edges of the notorious "Roaring Forties" whose endless, global turbulence spawns the most dangerous wave conditions on the planet. Yet the area remained irresistible to whaling ships, given the bountiful pods of whales beneath the roiling surface. Thus it was irresistible to the *hunters* of the hunters, despite the hazards. *Shenandoah* turned her prow toward Tristan da Cunha. But not before a chronic shipboard predator, predictably, once again required Whittle's attention.

"Today I was forced to punish one of our men very severely." Thomas Hall had struck again—the same Thomas Hall who'd been forced to embrace his previous opponent around an iron stanchion, the same Hall accused of "Scandalous Conduct." "He has given more trouble than any man in the ship." Hall's current offense had been to torment a Frenchman named Louis Rowe with language so humiliating that Rowe could not restrain himself from lashing back with his fists.

As he had with Hall the first time, Conway Whittle made this miscreant suffer, both physically and psychologically. Tradition held that both men involved in a fight be punished equally. "But here was a peculiar case where one (Hall) used such language to the other, that if I had heard it, and the man had not resented it at once by knocking him down, I would have punished him very severely. I therefore triced Hall up, and let Louis Rowe go."

After two hours with his arms supporting his body above the deck, Whittle discovered that Thomas Hall required further reasoning. "I found that the devil had not left." So he ordered the seaman to remain triced for eight hours more. Now Hall began to come around to Whittle's way of thinking: "I found him as subdued as a lamb. He gave me his word that I would never have any more trouble with him."

In his log, Conway Whittle reiterated what for him had become a kind of mantra—or an innately gentle man's ongoing self-persuasion:

I hate to punish men but it must be done. You must either rule them or they will rule you. On a cruise of this kind particularly I consider discipline not only desirable but absolutely necessary to our very existence and when the men once see that you are determined and fair they will be better, happier and better contented.

And if they were not? If, for instance, the punishment had political ramifications aboard the tiny nation that was the ship?

Hall's being an Englishman, and Louis Rowe a Frenchman, punishing the former, might, with our English crew, produce a bad effect at first. But what I do in this way, I do with decision. And if they have any sense, they will acknowledge that I am right. However, it makes very little difference whether they do or not.

In this incremental, often personally repellent way—with each tricing, each de-rating, each use of the dreaded iron restraints, each carefully calibrated humiliation—William Conway Whittle built into the diverse crew of *Shenandoah* the moral value that, above all others, could save them from destruction, including self-destruction: a sense of unity. This strange, multilingual collection of strangers—men quite literally collected from vanquished ships—lacked the cohesion of common national purpose or, really, of any purpose whatsoever, beyond survival. Whittle knew, by instinct as well as experience, that only an unswervingly disciplined commitment to unity—as an absolute good, as synonymous with self-preservation and the preservation of one's fellow crewmen—could guarantee that when the moment arrived for him to issue orders under harrowing and deadly circumstances, the men would obey him.

Gone, now, were any delusions that "our men are a fine set of fellows and I only wish I had more of them." Gone, now, were Whittle's earlier daydreams about winning the crew's affections by firmness and kindness. No: "I consider discipline not only desirable but <u>absolutely necessary to our very existence.</u>" No overstatement here; no mere officer's bombast. Whittle expected his men to acknowledge in all circumstances that he, and he alone, was right. "However, it makes very little difference whether they do or not." As long, of course, as Whittle did not cross the subtly drawn line into tyranny.

The necessity for discipline seemed never to stop recurring in these early weeks of *Shenandoah*'s odyssey, as others joined the rogues' gallery inhabited by the likes of Silvester and Hall. The ship now seemed almost to be infested with slackers, intriguers, petty thieves, brawlers, and devious and insolent men.

I had also to report Mr. Hunt [Cornelius E. Hunt, a fellow Virginian, and one of the three master's mates] *for neglect of duty. He has given me an immense amount of trouble in this way: he is either very careless or utterly worthless. I put him on extra watch, and when he thinks he can tend to his duty, I will try him again.*

No sooner had Hunt been straightened out than a familiar name showed up on the miscreants' list again:

Mr. Minor today reported Silvester for insolence to him. Upon exam-
ination I found the report correct and I triced the offender up and kept
them there until he swore that he would never be guilty of the offence
again.

Promises, promises.

"It is only by punishing," Whittle ruminated in a thought that was
almost Zen-like, "that I will ever cease to punish."

And then things began to look better.

A bright omen on Friday, December 2:

Mr. O'Brien today finished scaling his boilers. They were very foul
and very much in need of overhauling. I am very glad that they have
finished, for I like at all times to be ready to run well.

By "run well," Whittle was not celebrating efficiency; he was celebrating *speed*. Speed for overtaking merchantmen, but also for outrun-
ning Yankee men-of-war. *Shenandoah* had thus far been lucky in that
respect, as no enemy fighting ship had shown herself. But the threat
was constant, and if the lightly armed raider were caught within range
of Federal cannon, without her speed, agility, and steam, her next port
of call would be the bottom of the ocean.

Shenandoah ran very well indeed on the following day, coursing 198
miles toward the sunrise, heeled over under strong northeasterly
winds, then streaking for the east as the wind swung astern and drove
them even faster. East, not south, but east. Toward the Indian Ocean,
toward the Pacific.

Here commenced the Rebel's epic eastward circuit, for here, at
15.29 degrees west, she set a course of east by south a quarter south, a
course they would steer almost without interruption for nearly two
months; one that would take the Confederate ship two-thirds of the
way around the globe on roughly a straight line; a course punctuated
by violent seas, and escapades and perils unimaginable.

Whittle seemed to sense the impending rush toward destiny. On Saturday the third, he rejoiced in the crew's success in securing the critical topgallant rigging—the outermost, uppermost sails—against heavy weather: men perched on wooden yardarms at heights equivalent to a twelve-story building, knotting and unknotting the ropes as the huge masts pitched them forward on terrifying downward arcs toward the bows, and then tried to launch them sideways into the ocean as they rolled from starboard to port and back. This was not work that men regularly performed at sea; it was done in the tranquillity of the docks. But the presence of dockside spies at London had made it too risky to draw attention with any conspicuous, and expensive, rerigging for a merchant ship. Further, more time spent in port meant less time in action. Little wonder that skeptical Waddell had doubted the undermanned, ill-fitted ship would be equal to her mission. Even Whittle had had his fears; and in fact the topriggings had remained a concern ever since *Shenandoah*'s hasty, disguised departure from the harbor and into open sea. But his bedrock optimism had carried the day, and now, topgallants secured, it was redeemed: "I can now with great joy say that we are ready for heavy weather. . . . I am greatly relieved."

That evening the lieutenant, along with Waddell and some other officers, allowed themselves a rare interlude of celebration. They drank to "sweethearts and wives" with liquor furnished by the ship's surgeon Charles Lining. Whittle's thoughts drifted once again into the melancholy chambers of his mind.

> *Whenever this [toast] is proposed, I think how dear she is to me and I always invoke God's blessing on my own dear Pattie. Oh how much do I want to see her. God speed our meeting.*

As *Shenandoah* broke through the high waves of the Roaring Forties, however, Whittle's thirst for conquest overtook all sentiment:

> *I have been longing all day for a Yankee but so far have been disappointed. We are now in the midst of a busy whaling grounds and I shall be very much disgruntled if tomorrow we have not better luck.*

He had longed, in fact, for longer than a day; three weeks had now plodded past since *Shenandoah* last struck, weeks of maintenance, of disciplining truculent crewmen, of sprinting virtually without incident across an endless sea.

His thirst for action was soon to be slaked. As Sunday, December 4, dawned under fog and heavy clouds, *Shenandoah* found herself in a veritable crossroads of ships.

At an early hour we saw a large double-top sail yard ship, standing as we were, and very much ahead of us, and under all sail.

The freshly rigged high canvases had their first test:

We rapidly gained on him under topgallant sails, and hove to under his lee quarter.

Once again, exhilaration gave way to frustration: the stranger, like so many others from the accursed North, had switched flags. Whittle recorded it with irritation:

But we saw her name on the quarter, which was the Dia del Mario, *showing a Sardinian flag. She looked so much like a Yankee, that we boarded . . . she had been a Yankee, but was transferred."*

Transferred from New York to Italian ownership, her papers showed. Once again the Confederates found themselves outmaneuvered by a piece of paper. Grimly, the boarding crew returned to the raider, but soon fresh prey appeared: not one, but two ships breaking through the fog—"one astern and one coming up aside the other to the leeward." The ship behind looked very like a Yankee, "but it was so misty that we could not tell certainly." The leeward ship was nearest, but something about its shape touched off an alarm bell in Whittle's memory—a memory imprinted with fire-belching shapes at the Battle of New Orleans. He relayed his misgivings to Waddell, but found the brooding captain primed for attack. The two officers compromised: *Shenandoah* gave chase, but cautiously. Whittle's caution probably saved the mission; the shape proved as menacing as it had seemed:

> *We kept away and made all plain sail then came up with her very rapidly and regarded her very closely. She looked so suspicious, that we decided not to go any nearer. This was a very wise conclusion, for if she was not a steam gunboat under sail, I never saw one. And she looked to me exactly like a Yankee steamer of war. We did not go so close as to endanger our safety, even had she chased us, as we had a splendid breeze and a smooth sea, and it would have taken a wonderful vessel to catch us.*

At 10:00 a.m., the enemy steamer well out of range, Whittle and Waddell mustered the crew for the Sunday ritual, the reading of the articles of war. "The men in the grey looked as well as is possible with the color, but I can't say much in its favor."

Yet again, as with the November 20 inspection, Conway Whittle found himself casting a cold eye on his men's dress grays. Perhaps gray was simply a disagreeable shade to him, or perhaps it preyed on deeper regions of his suggestible mind. Perhaps the foggy brush with the Yankee gunboat just hours earlier, a gray monster looming in the gray ocean, stood as another baleful foretokening. Waddell had ordered *Shenandoah* into a reckless contact with the enemy; only luck and adroit seamanship had spared all hands. Where would the captain's whims catapult them the next time?

And what of the vessel that had not been pursued? What fate might she have held? Whittle remained silent on the question of this second ship. In his log, he abruptly shifted the subject:

> *The breeze after muster was a little fresher, and . . . we had a fine chance to judge of our speed when by the wind. We were close to the wind with royals set and she went hour after hour 10 knots. I think that she is doing remarkably well and I never was in a vessel which could compare to her. We pass everything which comes near us and that too generally under reduced sail.*

At 11:00 a.m., through the spray of furious breakers, a hulking godhead of the sea loomed into view across the port beam: Inaccessible Island. Soon after that, Tristan da Cunha itself materialized.

Perhaps his gleeful preoccupation with what happened later on that day deterred Conway Whittle from expanding, in his log, on the visual impact of that sighting. After more than twenty days and thousands of sea miles without landfall, the dominating prospect of those great primitive shards (who else could survive there except denizens of elemental ugliness?) must have filled all *Shenandoah*'s crewmen with awe. Sailors across the centuries have exclaimed over them, yet Whittle's log bears no mention of his reaction to the islands. He was otherwise preoccupied.

A long afternoon set in, *Shenandoah* pitched by the wind and waves as she prowled the vicinity for prey. A heavy mist descended toward evening. And then, the day all but gone, Whittle's longing was gratified.

About five o'clock the man at the wheel saw a sail on the lee (starboard) beam, and we kept away from her. We soon made her to be a bark under single reef topsails, and we continued that she was a whaler, and if a whaler, a Yankee.

A cautious forty-five minutes ensued, and then,

we came down upon the sail, and all doubt was removed, as we found her to be under double reefed topsails and actually engaged in "trying out" as they call it, that is, boiling out the oil. We ran up the English flag and after some little delay she ran up the Yankee flag. This gave us great joy. . . .

With the Confederate colors now fluttering merrily above them, Whittle and Waddell sent a boarding party to the prize; they soon returned with the captain and mate.

We held our meeting, and I put Captain Charles Worth on oath and we took his deposition, and found his vessel to be the barque Edward

of New Bedford on a whaling cruise. He had on yesterday caught a
whale, and they had just finished cutting him up and commenced try-
ing. His vessel is very old, but she is a good prize, and we will lay by
her and get all her beef, pork and breads.

We of course condemned her and sent the Captain and his Mate
back to bring off their personal effects. We made all preparation to stay
by her all night. Placed Mr. Bulloch and Mr. Minor with the prize
crew to take charge of her. We brought on board Capt. Worth, three
mates, and twenty-two sailors as prisoners. These with our three from
the "Stacey" make twenty-nine. This is too many to have at one time.
We paroled the Captain [allowing him the freedom of the ship],
and confined all the others for safety.

Too many indeed. Most of the new arrivals were sullen Portuguese;
they spoke little or no English, and they appeared, to Whittle's eyes,
highly untrustworthy characters. Even in irons, they would disrupt the
raider's closely calibrated shipboard rhythms. They required space,
feeding, watering, some degree of personal maintenance. Nor did
manacles always guarantee an absence of menace. To that extent, the
captives exerted some captive force of their own.

It was a problem for another day. Just now, in the afterglow of
Shenandoah's drought-ending conquest, Conway Whittle's natural exuberance rose to the fore: his log entries that evening included an observation that one might not have expected him to concede even
under threat of tricing: "The Captain is the most manly looking Yankee I have ever seen."

The *Edward* presented a little captive power of her own. Foggy
night was drawing on; the stripping of her would have to wait until
the bright light of morning. The *Shenandoah* men would somehow
have to keep track of the whaler, make sure she remained in the vicinity. Whittle had decided to outfit her with a skeleton crew, and assigned his nonpareil navigator, Irvine S. Bulloch, to board the prize,
along with John Minor and a few others. It would be their job to keep
the *Edward* nearby during the fogbound night. If anyone could steer a
ship in near-blind conditions, it was the gifted Georgian. Certainly
Whittle was untroubled by doubt:

*Tonight we have heavy surf and fog. But Bulloch has such directions
and lights, that there is no danger of us getting out of sight.*

Daybreak revealed that *Edward* and *Shenandoah* had indeed
drifted a distance from each other, but the raider lost little time drawing near again. The Confederates lowered a large boat and commenced the happy task of shifting the whaler's huge stores to the
conquering vessel. The men soon discovered that their prize carried
five "perfectly new" longboats of her own, including two that Whittle
especially admired. "I shall induce the Captain to keep both of them
as they will be excellent for boarding in heavy weather." He had plans
for the remaining three as well, "for what reason tomorrow will develop."

All hands worked rapidly—or as rapidly as the roiling waters permitted. Whittle and Waddell sensed that another dangerous Yankee
might well be at large not too many miles away—specifically, the second ship from the previous day's encounter, the one left behind when
Shenandoah flirted with the leeward man-of-war. Should *Shenandoah*
be trapped, or surprised while offloading her prize, she would not
stand a chance against the Yankee guns. Taking a calculated risk,
Whittle threw the Portuguese prisoners into the task of shifting the
goods. Still, given the pitching waves, the hazardous labor consumed
the entire day—as the two ships covered a leisurely eighty-one miles
to the east-southeast, away from Tristan da Cunha—and even then
the task was far from finished. Again, Bulloch, Minor, and a few others pulled the lonely assignment of keeping the now-cavernous whaler
under control.

Back to the arduous work before daybreak the next morning. The
conditions were perfect now: a heavy mist that camouflaged the raider
from any enemy telescope, and glassy seas that had grown atypically
smooth. The two ships had slowed to a parallel crawl; they would
make only twenty miles on this day, and the risk of deadly surprise remained high. Still, Whittle and Waddell could not pass up the chance
to stock *Shenandoah*'s larders with excellent food. Whittle had ordered
the steam boiler fired up, so as to act at once on any need for sudden
movement. The boiler, now on standby, was the ever-reliable ticket
from "fast" to "faster still." But it took some time to deliver a full head

of steam. The normally prudent Whittle had come to take this piece of technology almost for granted—as an intrinsic element of *Shenandoah's* design. He was just days from a jarring lesson in the limits of that assumption.

In the midst of the morning's work, yet another tantalizing stranger showed her distant contours through the fog: a large, five-topsail ship. Greedily, Whittle and Waddell broke off the transferring from *Edward*—longboats filled with booty suddenly left idle between the ships—and gave chase. Fog soon enveloped the quarry, and *Shenandoah* groped about, shifting this way and that, hoping for good luck. When the clipper finally did reemerge, she answered the raider's decoy-colors with the Union Jack. Disappointed, the Confederates returned to their prize. Bulloch and his men had been efficient in their absence; they'd loaded all the remaining plunder into the longboats, and the harvesting was soon finished. The yield was spectacular, and *Shenandoah's* men were virtually assured of full bellies for a good stretch of the mission: 50 barrels of beef, 49 of pork, 46 of flour, 6,000 pounds of bread, 600 of coffee, 400 of butter, a barrel of hams, a barrel of pickles, and two barrels of black fish oil. The non-edibles included a large quantity of manila rope, 1,200 pounds of soap, and two half-barrels of sand.

Now anyone who would not be content with this is very unreasonable. We have more than enough provisions to last our cruise.

Now came the moment of flaming judgment: the ceremony that invested *Shenandoah's* mission with a biblical aura—and the spectacle that always evoked the boy in Conway Whittle, and unified that boy with the steely avenging angel of the South.

Bulloch, Mr. Minor, Mr. Harwood and I set her on fire fore and aft. She was so old that we were careful to do our work well and I am sure she will never go on another trip. She will burn well when warmed up.

That was the boy speaking. As the torched brew of whale oil, tar, and fatwood, laced with kerosene paint and turpentine, began its work, sending needles of orange flame skyward under growing plumes of thick black smoke, the steely angel's voice took over.

> *Our burning prize is distinctly in sight, and I have rarely seen any-thing which is more beautifully grand than a ship burning at sea. To see the rigging on fire, after it gets burnt in two and the burning ends swinging as the vessel rolls—oh it is a grand sight.*

And then *Shenandoah* reversed her course and stood back toward Tristan da Cunha.

Whittle's plan was brutally simple: he would deposit the twenty-eight prisoners on the island and leave them there. What effect they might have on the small population—about thirty-five fishing and cattle-farming people, sorted into seven families—was not his concern. Keeping the captives on board was unthinkable. They could not be allowed the freedom of the ship, and the alternative was what they now experienced, immobilized in close-packed rows behind iron bars secured by eyebolts, a condition that offended decency. Whittle and Waddell had extended only token invitations to these men to "ship"; they looked palpably hostile, and their numbers threatened a bloodily effective mutiny.

Besides, as Whittle noted in his log, the island group had been dis-covered by a Portuguese. In a sense, he was returning these men home.

Anchoring *Shenandoah* a safe distance from the shore, Whittle now put his plan for the three remaining longboats into play. His officers and crewmen herded the Portuguese into them—their lug-gage thoughtfully included—and gave them a good strong shove toward the shore. Whittle was not indifferent to the captured men's plight:

> *I must say I pity the poor devils, going to an island at least a thousand miles from any land, and with no chance of getting off until some vessel stops there. And this chance, ever so remote, that they may be here a year.*

He added a thought that may have hinted at certain wistfulness, even envy, beneath his pity. Perhaps an idyllic sort of peace beckoned these fellows from the steep, grassy mountains, a universe away from cannonfire and chains and the constant prospect of watery death: "However, if I come here two years hence, I shall confidently expect to find some of them still here."

Any such reveries were abruptly brushed away by reality, in the form of a shore boat that approached *Shenandoah* just as the captured Portuguese set off. Its lone occupant, paddling vigorously, tied up to the raider, heaved himself on deck, and commenced a sales pitch touting the island's goods: cattle, sheep, chickens, milk, butter, eggs. He neglected to give a name, but announced in a clenched Yankee accent that he hailed from New London, Connecticut. He opened up a glimpse of how Tristan da Cunha society worked.

> *We tried to arrange the prices, but he said he could not do it. It was not his turn. It seems, he told us, that there are 7 families on the island, and that they take regular turns in selling and trading. He said he would go off and bring off whose turn it was. We told him that we would exchange flour, at $8 per barrel, for beef at 18 cents. This is paying dearly for our whistle, but that makes little matter.*

Learning that this Connecticut Yankee had lived on the island for fifteen years, Whittle indulged a little private sarcasm.

> *He is the only Yankee here. One would very naturally suppose, that if there was any place in the world where a Yankee would not be found it would be such a place as this.*

And he could not resist adding that the Yankee "has evidently had enough to eat."

As the emissary's launch bobbed back toward the shoreline village—about ten stone houses—Whittle considered the man. A shrewd operator, the young lieutenant speculated:

> *I would willingly bet that this fellow not only has more money than any of the rest, but that he is a leading man among them.*

His judgment proved correct. Returning to the ship several hours later, the fellow now commanded one of the whaleboats the prisoners had used. He brought with him a kind of negotiating committee whose spokesman was a Dutchman named Peter Green. Green had been rooted on Tristan da Cunha about twenty-five years, but this had not dulled his own shrewdness. He understandably professed to be appalled at the prospect of twenty-eight hardened seamen suddenly set loose on his island, whose population of thirty-five consisted mostly of women.

He said to the Captain, in the way of a protest, that there was not provision enough upon the island to last the prisoners we landed until a vessel would probably take them off, and urged the absolute propriety of taking them back or sending provisions to serve them.

Green coupled this complaint with some subtle apple-polishing. The absence of Yankee whaling ships in the area? The *Shenandoah* raiders had themselves to thank for that. Before the war, it was common to count as many as seventy whalers in sight at a time. Now it was rare to spot a single one. The flattery worked. "It is wonderful that even here in this remote island, away entirely from our country, that people feel the effect of the war in our country," Whittle wrote. "This proves to us our importance."

But when Peter Green tried to push his sweet-talking a step further, into the area of intelligence-gathering, Conway Whittle came instantly alert:

Old Peter Green said to me, "Well, Sir, I see you are poorly off for men." "No," I said at once, "we work with quarter-watches." It was a fib, but it was a fib for the Cause.

Any rumor that *Shenandoah* remained undermanned, and therefore vulnerable, could motivate a focused search-and-destroy mission by the U.S. Navy, and required suppression at the outset.

Whittle and Waddell recognized the fairness of the islanders' basic complaint—the likely disruptions posed by the prisoners—and offloaded rations good for several months. Perhaps the two officers were assuaging their consciences as well. Green had explained to them the islanders' methods for preserving law and order:

If anyone did anything outraging the public, there was a meeting, and he was denounced as a dog.

For men accustomed to floggings and hanging by their wrists, this system could be imagined as unpersuasive.

As *Shenandoah*'s crew set her sails, triced up her propeller, and slipped away from Tristan da Cunha into open sea, James Waddell and Conway Whittle allowed themselves to swell a little over the news of their renown, as imparted by Peter Green. They'd become celebrities, of a sort.

Now if they could only find a way to turn the war around.

7

An absence of Yankees proved a blessing the next day.

This morning, bright and early we discovered a crack in our propeller. Which, if it had not been seen, might have proved fatal to us. To get the propeller up so it can be worked at was our trouble.

The crack was noticeable only because Whittle had thought to raise the propeller a little above the waterline on leaving the port of Tristan da Cunha to prevent its being ensnarled in the thick beds of kelp and also to keep it ready for rapid deployment. The fault line in the metal augured great peril. *Shenandoah* was not quite paralyzed—good sailing winds blew her ninety-nine miles eastward that day—but without her propeller she was just another sailing ship, days from a major landmass, lightly armed, easy prey for any hostile man-of-war. And with the debris from that burnt whaler bobbing in the ocean behind her, not to mention all those stranded Portuguese eager for conversation with any Yankee that happened into the island's harbor, *Shenandoah* was as good as a marked ship.

There was no question what must be done.

As our propeller is to us our life, we stopped all work to have it fixed.

This was hardly as easy as it sounded. Though hoisted—indeed "triced"—above the water's surface, free of its driveshaft, the great heavy blade remained beyond reach of Mathew O'Brien, the resourceful chief engineer. The blade, when not in use, rose by design into its own storage compartment—called the well—where it was virtually inaccessible. It would have to be raised considerably higher—a chore difficult enough in harbor, and fiendishly hazardous in a pitching, swelling sea. Shipboard routine ceased as the crew bent to the emergency. Their first task was to pry the roof off the pilothouse, which covered the top of the well and blocked the blade's vertical path. That done, climbers scrambled up the mizzenmast with thick ropes and pulleys slung over their shoulders. These they looped over the spanker-bolt, which anchored the great diagonal spanker boom that angled out above the ship's stern. Securing the bottom ends of the rope to the propeller blade, the men descended and hauled with all their might until the ponderous mass of metal, thirteen feet long and weighing many tons, rose from its wooden housing. A thick block of wood was wedged below it to give it some stability, and the blacksmith hurried to his surgical task.

O'Brien's first close look at the blade revealed a sobering fact. The crack—in a brass bearing—was not new.

"It is an old break, and has been done for a long time, as we saw where the screws had been put in to repair it," Whittle noted. They could also see that the crack had worked its way farther into the bearing since that repair.

This problem likely went unreported to the prospective purchaser, Bulloch, who had been eager to buy *Sea King* as quickly and quietly as possible. The ship, when Bulloch struck his deal, had just returned from her record-setting run and pushed her innovative design to its limits. The resulting cracks and strains demanded extensive repair, probably the result of a "design" that did not live up to its innovative theory. But Bulloch was hamstrung: the likelihood of Adams's spies growing even more interested in their work inhibited the prudent officer from getting any more repairs done in England.

⚜

Shenandoah, in other words, had been steaming on borrowed time. But at least the problem was now out in the open and available for repair.

Fixing the blade would require precision work—work normally done by metallurgists, machinists, and blacksmiths. Since few such specialists were on call in the South Atlantic, Mr. O'Brien would have to adapt as best he could: a sort of nautical family doctor called on to perform neurosurgery. Balancing himself halfway up the seesawing mizzenboom, leaning in to the giant shard of glistening metal precariously stabilized on its block of wood, the Louisianan undertook to perform a heroic feat of mechanical engineering thirty feet above *Shenandoah*'s stern.

The weather had grown rowdy, "disagreeable in the extreme, cloudy, overcast, foggy, damp and cold. A Yankee might be within six miles of us and he would be as safe as if he were a hundred."

As crewmen below shot him anxious glances, the daring engineer, assisted by two and sometimes three men, improvised the salvation of the propeller, heating the metal with bellows and coals, hammering it, tediously extracting the old screws. He was forced to abandon his perch at nightfall; but the next foggy morning, he was back in the rigging. As the hours dragged along, chimed by O'Brien's clanging and cursing in the rigging above, Lieutenant Whittle's hunger for engagement overtook him again. He seemed almost to assume that O'Brien would accomplish the impossible; in his mind, the propeller grew whole again, and the lieutenant seethed for the chase.

I wish it would clear off for I am very, very anxious to catch another fellow. I am always glad to catch them and very glad to get rid of them. The hitch is that I hate them so much that I find it hard to have my wants gratified. The more we catch the happier I will be.

Mr. O'Brien's wizardry in the rigging, when finally accomplished, earned him a brisk nod in Whittle's log on December 9:

This afternoon our Chief Engineer finished work on our propeller, and we lowered it in its place and unrigged all our purchases and commenced refitting the pilot house. I am delighted to know that we are again in running order.

But were they? Could the jury-rigged screws and brass plate meet the operational demands of an intact propeller? Or might it crack into fragments and go spinning to the ocean depths in the midst of a life-or-death encounter? No one knew for sure. Everyone wondered.

Perhaps this nagging dread ignited yet another crisis of shipboard discipline even as O'Brien hammered.

> *John Williams (colored), Ship's Cook, and George Flood, were brought to the mast for fighting. I found that the former had called the latter a violent and outrageous name. And I justified Flood, and triced up Williams. Here was a Negro against a Yankee. I had trouble in bringing him to his bearings but he finally came down.*

More questions, then: Would this crew of strays, misfits, and strangers never cohere? Would *Shenandoah* cannibalize herself before any Yankee could fire a shot at her? Whatever Williams called Flood—"son of a bitch" seems a likely candidate—had perhaps been inspired by some prior insult, some slur by a white man against a black—a black, moreover, whose presence aboard a Confederate warship was not entirely voluntary: the high-strung Williams was the "darkie" who had signed on from *D. Godfrey* in early November. (It could hardly have gladdened Whittle that the man Williams's insult had placed on the moral high ground was a Yankee.)

Yet none of this really mattered. Order, not personal preference—not even *justice*—was the highest value for any naval officer worth his salt. Whittle had listened to both parties in the fracas and made an instant decision, as he knew he must. Did Williams continue to scream out his violated honor even as he hung, muscles grotesquely distended, above the deck? ("I had trouble in bringing him to his bearings . . .") Then Williams would have to keep screaming as long as he could stand the pain (". . . but he finally came down"). Order before honor—at least the crewmen's honor. For Whittle, Waddell, and the other officers, order *was* honor. But when, oh when, would order aboard this ship be understood as the supreme honor for all?

⚜

A hundred forty miles on this ugly, fog-draped day—latitude 30 degrees 37–30 minutes south, longitude 7 degrees 7 minutes west. The next day, a Friday, Whittle called for a "general quarters drill." Jack

Grimball, a seasoned South Carolinian and Whittle's most reliable subordinate, whipped the crew through a thorough enactment of procedure under attack. The timing of the exercise was no accident: Whittle sensed the sailors' anxiety generated by the questionable propeller; a renewed sense of collective action—and risk—might refocus their energies.

The results, however, proved less than reassuring. The ship's two cannons remained ill-balanced and cumbersome, their weight abrading the forward "dumb-trucks" built to contain their recoil. "These I hope will soon wear up to their proper places."

Nor was that the extent of it:

> I do wish that our ports were in proper order, but as yet all we can boast of is that there is a round hole through which the muzzles of the guns point. If, however, we were to get in a fight, all "ginger bread" work would come down and we would do our best, however poor that might be, but I trust that we will have no fighting to do as we would fare very badly. I am very anxious to catch Yanks. But when Yanks are Tartars I want to let them alone.

On that happy note, *Shenandoah* slogged on.

A hundred fifty-three miles on Sunday under winds from the southwest. "Another day of rest," Whittle noted gratefully—a rest interrupted by only one tricing incident, this involving the Frenchman named Louis Rowe, the aggrieved party in the fight with Thomas Hall. This time it was Rowe who asked for trouble, by disobeying the orders from Acting Master's Mate Minor. Rowe went through the predictable stages of rage, denial, and acceptance.

> At first, with the usual excitability of a Frenchman, he became very angry, and commenced using very improper language when I had him gagged. He was very determined not to be subdued, but I brought him down by tricing him a little higher each time. When I took him down, he was like a lamb.

Tricing had become nearly as ingrained in the daily round as mess. It scarcely registered now as a break in the routine—it *was* routine.

Oh how rapidly does time fly. Summer seems to have just gone and here it is again. I've been somewhat disappointed today, as I had hoped that we would have caught a Yankee, as Sunday seems to be our lucky day. A nice breeze sprang up today, and we very easily glided along.

Whittle read his prayer book to himself, then succumbed to the deep yearning that was the constant mirror image of his lust for conquest. He foraged in his personal mailbag for letters from his Pattie: not new ones—fresh mail was among the simple pleasures sacrificed aboard a raiding ship—but well-worn ones whose contents he had no doubt virtually memorized.

Oh how much I would give to hear from her. If but to know that my darling is well. I read these letters as, next to later ones,* they are most dear. No wonder I should love her so profoundly. She has been at all times so devotedly attached to me. God grant her health and happiness.

By Monday, December 12, under light winds out of the southwest, *Shenandoah* had entered the eastern hemisphere, cruising across zero longitude in heavily rolling seas. Still southwest of Capetown and her infamous waves, Whittle kept his men busy at rigging repair—"We now have every piece of running gear with one or two exceptions of manila rope, and this, too, all captured from our prizes"—and drilling at the guns under Grimball. It was not just storms that concerned Whittle. The U.S. Navy was known to patrol the waters off Capetown routinely. "I sincerely wish we had our ports fixed as they ought to be, but I fear it will be a long, long time before I can so congratulate myself." The questionable propeller remained triced above the water.

The ship's rolling motion, its precarious metronoming between immense waves and breathtaking troughs, drew Whittle's attention—not because of seasickness, which affected only landlubbers, but for its effect on her progress. "And for rolling, I think, the *Shenandoah* goes ahead." This was testament to navigator Bulloch's prowess at converting the

---

* By "later," Whittle doubtless referred to letters he expected to accumulate at the end of the voyage.

high waves' perpendicular impact on the long ship into energy impelling her forward motion. The raider covered 142 miles that day.

She had a destination now, although it was not written in the log; no use confirming her mission to some Yankee visitor. She was headed for Australia.

Australia was a terrible risk. The likelihood of Federal gunships in the vast coastal waters and in the port at Melbourne was overwhelming. Indeed it was with misgivings that Bulloch had even sent a second supply ship, *John Frazer,* to meet them in Melbourne. Anticipating her need for an additional load of coal, Bulloch wanted her on hand in case the British were to deny *Shenandoah* even the right to refuel. Yet Whittle could see little choice. His men needed fresh produce for their health; the ship needed materials and repair work that could only be obtained at harbor. (The nagging question of prisoners of war—a new supply of which Whittle fully expected to harvest any day now—could be solved by lawfully depositing them on the continent.)

The most compelling reason, though, lay in *Shenandoah*'s irreducible mission: to seek out and destroy enemy ships. To "hunt where the ducks are" might not yet have entered the vernacular of his countrymen. But that is exactly what Conway Whittle intended on doing.

⁂

Well before sailing into those dangerous waters, however, Whittle would have to address a crisis nearer at hand, virtually at his elbow—a crisis that would beggar the repeated incidents of shipboard fighting and insubordination. This crisis posed a threat to the very legitimacy of the young lieutenant's leadership, and to his conception of honor as well. Its author was none other than Whittle's fellow commanding officer, James Iredell Waddell.

Waddell had remained a mostly silent but plainly discontented presence since the voyage began. A proud, principled, professional officer of the old school, he could not have welcomed the prospect of sharing command with an officer half his age, especially one who'd come equipped with his own halo, the legacy of the *Nashville* saga. The overlapping spheres of captain and executive had already generated disputes between the two, and Whittle had prevailed on at least his share of these—including the original disagreement concerning whether *Shenandoah* should take to the seas with such a drastic dearth of manpower. (Waddell, the staunch traditionalist, had argued strongly against the notion, but went along with it when the vote, proposed by Whittle, was finally taken.)

Since then, Waddell had mostly swallowed his pride; but with each new conflict of command, he'd grown more sullen, less able (or inclined) to mask his disdain for his fellow officer. No sailor could have failed to notice the icy atmosphere between the two men, yet Whittle, by refusing to engage the older captain, had managed to keep a semblance of unity at the command level.

All of that changed on Tuesday, December 13, a violent day of weather on seas that heaved so that the ship's rudder trembled against its fastenings and the cannon dipped underwater with each precarious roll.

I was very much provoked today by the uncalled for, and unnecessary, interference of the Captain with my duties. I told the Boatswain to fit the Mizzen Topgallant sheets in a particular way, and after it was done, without my knowledge, and though told it was on my order, he had all undone and figured another way. Now he has the power to give any order he chooses and to revoke any order of mine, but he should do it through me. If my orders are to be changed in this way in trifling matters, I may as well take a watch and give him the executive duties, for both of us cannot be Executive Officer. I showed by my manner that I did not like it and I hope he can, and will, profit by it.

Whittle's observation about duties cut to the heart of the confrontation—at least in organizational terms. Responsibility for rigging the ship lay quite explicitly with the Executive. But the deeper problem lay within James Waddell's dark, coiled temperament. Whittle's log reveals that his provocation was hardly a surprise.

I regard him a most unreasonable man in most things. It is a bit of a conceit to suppose that because he is the Commanding Officer he can perform the Executive duties and the duties of all his officers better than they can.

In setting down the reasons why he had not previously risen to Waddell's goading, Whittle took up an incident of almost fantastical poignancy.

I do not quarrel with him for two reasons, one is that it would injure the service. The other is that when I last walked with his little wife, she begged me to keep out of all quarrels on the cruise.

For Conway Whittle, undercover and under surveillance, even to risk being seen with the wife of a Confederate officer (their "walk" almost certainly occurred while Whittle was still in mufti) was remarkable in itself. For the wife—a Maryland woman of wealth and refinement—to have "begged" Whittle to avoid tangling with Waddell is a testament to the North Carolinian's capacity for destructive rage.

Whittle's attempt at quiet diplomacy—to "show by his manner" that he considered Waddell out of line—failed to smother this flickering fire. The following day, as *Shenandoah* rolled, pitched, and submerged her prow across 194 miles of turbulent seas, Waddell resumed his game of second-guessing the executive officer. He openly questioned Whittle's concern that the ship's rudder was working loose under the violent motion against the waves, which thrust it clear out of the water whenever the ship lurched over a crest, only to smash it back down as *Shenandoah* dove down into the next trough. Whittle believed that the pintles—the fasteners that connected the gigantic piece of teak and metal to the thousand-ton ship's stern—were losing their purchase on the huge mass of iron and wood. He joined the carpenter and they tried to examine the ship's stern, despite Waddell's disdain.

Waddell's petulant show of power was hideously timed. If ever *Shenandoah* needed clarifying unity, she needed it now. Ship and crew were unmistakably battling for survival in the thick of a powerful, worsening storm. The wind, Whittle observed, had intensified beyond half-gale force, "and now it is blowing a whole gale like blue light-ning." At one point,

> a gigantic wave passed over the vessel and it took a long time for the bow and the stern to come out of the ocean as this immense tonnage of ocean water drained out through whatever scuppers and gun holes it could get through. The noise of the rudder continues, and I cannot form any plan to correct it.

In fact, the raider had now been scooped up by an enormous sub-Atlantic north-Antarctic gale—part of the cyclical storm system that pinwheels continuously around the bottom of the globe. The impact of it was terrifying for the most hardened seaman: swells of ocean foamed up like the sides of mountains and broke across the decks with deafening crashes; stomach-churning tilts sent the fixed cannon underwater again and again. The wind was coming at the ship from directly astern, forcing Whittle to issue a dangerous order: he sent drenched crewmen aloft in their oilskins, picking their way out along the ship's rigging, groping for toeholds on loops of wet rope, to close-reef the fore main topsail, minimizing the wind's effect on velocity. Despite the storm the ship as a whole was performing well, "but the rudder makes a good deal of noise and I am anxious about it. We shipped a good deal of water. She is decidedly a wet ship."

And a divided ship—or would be, if Waddell had anything to say about it, which he did. On Friday, as the storm's intensity strained the nerves of the crew and the officer staff, and the racket of the great rudder's trembling rose above the wind, the commanding officer struck again.

> Tonight a thing was done by the Captain which seems to me can produce no good, but an immense amount of evil.

The evil deed was done at midnight, appropriately enough. Waddell, from his command post in the wheelhouse, had called for Whittle and some of the midshipmen whom Whittle had assigned to watch shifts. These men included some with substantial credentials. Besides

Lieutenant Sydney Smith Lee, the nephew of Robert E. Lee, there was Second Lt. Dabney Marion Scales, who had been an officer aboard the ironclad *Lantern*, and had served time in the Massachusetts prison camp with Whittle after the Battle of New Orleans. The well-respected Lt. Francis Thornton Chew of Missouri shared an ancestry with the proud Francis Thornton line of Virginia statesmen.

In the pitching, sprawling cacophony of the storm-lashed ship, James Waddell sarcastically questioned the competence of these seamen. Then, as all stood dumbfounded, he ordered two of them dismissed from their posts.

Whittle's log described the encounter in detail.

The Captain . . . commenced to talk about what a bad night we were going to have, and remarked that such weather required the best seamanship on deck, and that he would have to be up all the mid watch and all the morning as he did not consider Lieuts. Chew & Scales competent to take care of the ship in such weather. He is a regular self made martyr and thinks that the troubles, privations and evils of no man can be compared to his. I said, no, Captain, if you will keep Mr. Chew's watch with him I will do the same with Mr. Scales or vice versa. To this he replied, "No, you have enough to do in being on deck the whole day." I told him I would much prefer keeping one of the watches. He said no, I couldn't do more, and went below.

Here was a bewildering rebuke to Conway Whittle's judgment and authority, not to mention a bald humiliation of him in the presence of his men. More provocation soon followed. Having lurched and skidded across the roiling deck to his cabin, Whittle was abruptly summoned back to Waddell, who greeted the lieutenant by identifying the man he wished to replace Francis Chew.

He said, "I want you to send for Mr. Minor and tell him to keep [Chew's] mid-watch."

The young lieutenant was incredulous: Minor was but a master's mate, a noncommissioned sailor. Chew was a first lieutenant, appointed to his post by the president of the Confederate States, Jefferson Davis.

I saw at once that it was wrong, ruinously wrong, and said to the Captain that I would infinitely [prefer to] keep the watch myself. His reply was, "No, you have enough to do."

I urged no more. What more could I urge? I sent for Mr. Minor and gave him the order as coming from the Captain, and then, with the heavy heart of a man who saw evil ahead, started below . . .

But James Waddell had not finished rubbing it in.

. . . when the Captain said, "If Mr. Chew is not asleep you can tell him that I relieve him of his watch tonight."

Whittle had to be the messenger of the orders that preempted his own. As he had in all sorts of fraught moments in his brief naval career, the young lieutenant willed himself to remain under control. He did as he was told. He saved his vitriol for his log, and his response for the right moment, by the right means.

Now if Chew takes of this matter the same view that I do, why, there will be a row of consequence of it. I shall try and keep my skirts clear, but I know that everything like an esprit de corps *will be destroyed by such arbitrary and unwarrantable acts of authority.*

By Saturday evening the winds had moderated; the sea crests and troughs flattened out. The near-hurricane winds had hurled *Shenandoah* nearly a thousand miles eastward in four days—243 miles on that day alone. But the weather aboard *Shenandoah* remained stormy. Now, with the ship under control, the showdown between Waddell and Whittle would commence.

It began by proxy.

Mr. Chew feeling himself most improperly treated, went to the Captain and told him that he could not stand it. Whereupon the Captain told him that he did not consider him competent, and said furthermore that under such circumstances, he would respect neither person, nor commission.

As Whittle feared, Lt. Francis Thornton Chew blew up. He demanded to be relieved of duty altogether and sent home the first time *Shenandoah* made port. Waddell was only too happy to grant this. Whittle decided to make one last effort to salvage the situation—a decision that brought him face-to-face with his new opponent.

I went on deck and commenced to talk with the Captain and told him that if I were Chew I would not only do what he had done . . . but that I would report it to the Secretary of the Navy and that I considered that by his act a young man of fine spirit and sense was forced out of the ship.

Waddell feinted out of range. He'd acted only at Chew's request, he replied disdainfully. Whittle methodically bored in, and suddenly flashed a counterpunch.

My reply to that was that any man of spirit would pursue a similar course. . . . I asked him what right he had to say that Mr. Chew was not to be trusted with the deck when the wording of Mr. Chew's commission was identically the same as his own, and besides even if you consider him incompetent, I have volunteered to take the watch with him and your relieving him proves that you have no confidence in me.

Waddell chose again to bob and weave—to toy with the lieutenant. He sneered that Whittle had not volunteered "with the right spirit," and clearly had not meant what he'd said. The captain allowed that he was disappointed with his fellow officer.

Perhaps Waddell assumed that he could intimidate the younger aide with his condescension, his hulking presence, and his reputation as a duelist. Like so many other adversaries who lightly dismissed the slim young Virginian, Waddell badly underestimated his man.

I was astonished but replied, You, Sir, did not hear me, or else have a
very poor memory. . . . You not only know that I volunteered in the
proper spirit, but replied to my desire to keep the watch of Mr. Chew
by saying I had enough to do.

Then Whittle landed a flurry:

As to your second charge that I disappointed you, I must say that you
have no right to be disappointed. . . . you furthermore know that be-
sides my duties as Executive Officer, there is not an officer on this ves-
sel who has done as much watching as I have.

At this, Waddell's demeanor abruptly changed. Instead of lashing
back at Whittle, the captain gave vent to a startling cry of the heart—
a cry that issued all the way from the tortured chambers of his psyche
that he concealed under his brooding aura of menace. Whittle, on
whom little was lost, instantly realized that he'd glimpsed this side of
Waddell before.

He said, "Well, everyone is opposed to me." I marked well the remark.
He said several days ago that we were all his enemies.

This alertness echoed Whittle's earlier log entry that Waddell was
"a regular self made martyr and thinks that the troubles, privations
and evils of no man can be compared to his." The nerve-shattering
stress of the great storm seemed to have awakened some dark demons
in Waddell's soul. The haughty, patronizing veteran of the seas stood
revealed as a defenseless paranoid.

In the grip of his self-grievance, Waddell made a serious blunder:
he asked Whittle what he wanted. With that query, the captain ceded
a great measure of authority, and the power that came with it, to the
Virginian. Whittle grasped this at once.

"I said, 'Sir, I want to advise you to restore Chew to duty. You are
going to have an unhappy ship if you do not.'" Waddell was the picture of resigned compliance: "Well, if that is all that Mr. Chew wants,
I will agree if he will withdraw his application."

This mewling offer only consolidated Conway Whittle's private contempt: "I must say I was very much disgusted at the conversation, but determined to do all I could to bring matters straight."

Informed of this concession, Francis Chew sensed Waddell's collapse as acutely as had Whittle: "Chew said he would not withdraw his application unless the Captain promised him the deck, and that he should not be interfered with in the future." Upon learning of these conditions from Whittle after supper, Waddell retreated further inside his posture of pathos: "Well, Sir, I have no friends in the ship. You are all against me."

"No friends in the ship"? "You are all against me"? Conway Whittle bristled to full alert at these charges; he grasped their unspoken meaning at once. Waddell was implying mutiny.

No accusation could be more serious, and, if unproven, more reckless. Mutiny was an incendiary concept; its very suspicion—certainly if bruited about by the captain—could throw a ship's company into chaos. But Waddell's innuendo scratched against something even more precious to Whittle than stability. It abraded his honor.

What Whittle said in response to this went unrecorded, but it was hot enough to draw a snarling threat from the captain: "Whittle, be careful, you are speaking to me!"

Whittle brushed aside this bluster, and wrested control of the exchange from his Captain: "Sir, I am speaking when there is no such thing as silence. I demand to know what you mean!"

Hours after the event, the lieutenant was still seething—but quietly triumphant.

I can't write anymore of this extraordinary & plain conversation.

Conway Whittle refused to record the specifics of their exchange in his logbook that evening. The upshot of it, however, was gratifying to him, if painful to behold: Waddell agreed to humble himself by sending for Lieutenant Chew and restoring him to his watch. Then the once-imperious Waddell begged Whittle to forget what had happened—and thus invited the finishing touch to his reduction: "I told him my promise to his little wife, and said I had kept it as long as I could."

Whittle added in his log:

I trust now there will never be another disturbance. . . . I go only to preserve the peace of the ship. My aim is that of a friend, but he is so weak as to regard me in the light of an enemy. God knows I want peace for the good for the service.

Soon the sea beneath *Shenandoah*, now a thousand miles southeast of Cape Town, grew smooth again. The rudder and propeller, both having survived the storm without further apparent damage, were holding. A sprightly wind coursing down out of the Mozambique Channel ushered the raider 150 miles on Sunday, December 18. Whittle ordered the fore and main topgallants reset, the decks holystoned. Ship's carpenter O'Shea set to work building a permanent magazine to keep the gunpowder dry.

"I am getting heartily tired of not catching another Yankee," Whittle recorded three days later. "This is too much sailing without a prize." Yet his words sounded almost jaunty this time: the words of an executive officer, tested in crises of nature and human nature—triumphant, assured, and in control.

8

The Confederate raider's men had no means by which to comprehend it, but they had just been baptized into one of the earth's most demonic storm kingdoms: a nautical tundra where two oceans collide in a perpetual fury of mountainous waves, gale-force winds, and sorrow to the seamen in their midst. The liquid cliffs of saltwater washing over *Shenandoah* had been the infamous "Cape rollers," generated by the clashing currents of the Atlantic and the Indian oceans as they merge below the southern coast of Africa—there where the warmer waters pushing down from the equator collide violently with the frigid ocean waters blown up from Antarctica.

Viewed from above—higher by far than the perspective of the albatross circling disdainfully over Coleridge's Ancient Mariner—these waters can be seen as the spawning grounds of a vast, pinwheeling system of clockwise-streaming storms that rage endlessly above the deep seas between Capetown and Antarctica, and then circle the globe before spending their fury on the shores of the Antarctic coast, and upon the mariners unfortunate enough to find themselves sailing there. Compared to their magnitude, the armies of Lee and Grant were flecks on the landscape, tiny swatches of movement on the indifferent global surface.

Far tinier was the undermanned *Shenandoah*. Her freeboard—the distance between the surface of the water and the topmost edge of her hull—was barely fourteen feet. But her main weather deck—where her cannons were—was not enclosed by a typical chain railing, as on most clipper designs. Instead, a man-tall, wall-like wooden barrier called a bulwark or "coaming" enclosed her entire deck, running the length of the ship. The coaming protected the "mechanicals" on deck—the cannons and such—from the ocean, and gave her artillerymen protection from small-arms fire in combat. They made *Shenandoah* a beautiful ship, they made her a good fighting ship, and they usually kept the ocean at bay.

But this storm was no "usual" one. Swells, ranging in sets as high as twenty feet, pounded her for hours. "Rogue" waves went much higher. And *Shenandoah*'s sleek design, low decks, and high coaming meant the surface of the sea was less than nine feet below the open main deck of the ship.

Monster waves washed over both the coamings at the same time and into the enormous well created behind them. They flooded the main deck from the bow back to the officers' quarters below the wheelhouse. The seawater trapped on deck, probably 25,000 cubic feet of it, weighed well over half a million pounds.

Shenandoah struggled to shed this enormous load. She rolled to port, sending thousands of gallons over the side; then, trembling, she struggled back to the vertical, before shouldering downward again, this time to starboard, sloshing out another great load of foaming water. Just in time for the trough of the next oncoming twenty-five-foot swell.

Occasionally the wave-patterns thrust the raider's bow and rudder out of the water at the same time. In the ensuing steep dive, if she buried her bow in the sea, the waves racing aft could sweep spray up the mainmast most of the way to the first lubber's hole, over forty feet aloft. In such conditions, *Shenandoah* would be battened down: all hatches closed, all fires out, safety ropes on deck and below. Her helmsmen, both squinting forward into the gloom as she rode shuddering over the crest and porpoised down into a forty-foot trough, would behold the uphill side of the next wave as if it were the side of a mossy stone wall. *Horizon* was a word without meaning now.

The helmsmen would strain to bring the stern over a bit to soften the impact; the ship would vibrate with the weight shifts, a deep and disturbing resonance, and more water would come rushing over the bowsprit. And the next wave, a curling hedge of foam, breaking in a constant collapsing curve many miles wide, would slip over the forecastle, over the capstan, over the ship's bell, and then fall with a thunderous roar onto the gun deck. Like a tsunami, the cresting foam had no roller-form; it was simply an agitated mass of water that swept over the deckhouse, then exploded into collars of spray around the base of each mast, then submerged the hatches over the galley and engine room, then foamed over the poop deck's bulkhead, and finally rejoined the sea before the mizzenmast. In the wheelhouse at the stern, above the poop, the terrified helmsmen would watch, transfixed, as the wave passed—and did not pass. For the waves had often filled the gun deck from forecastle to stern, and it looked to the men in the wheelhouse as if the masts were growing up out of the open foaming sea. It looked indeed, as if the *Shenandoah* were underwater. Which, from all points objective, she was.

And yet *Shenandoah*—tiny, flyspeck *Shenandoah*—absorbed the rollers' onslaughts, and survived.

If *Shenandoah* was tiny, tinier still were the resentments, resistances, and designs of the human beings who slid about her decks and clung for dear life to her ropes. Yet upon the resolution of these little conflicts depended, perhaps, the fate of a great nation of the earth in bloody conflict with itself. At least this was what *Shenandoah*'s officers permitted themselves to believe, the conflicted conceits of men being larger—and often more destructive—than any storm system that nature could devise.

Nearly a week of tolerable weather following the storm gave Whittle the chance to order a flurry of repair work. O'Shea continued setting up a magazine for the dry storage of gunpowder. Crews holystoned the berth and spar decks. The gunnery crew under the British-born John L. Guy tested the cannon; the sailmaker Henry Alcott, also of England, restored the main topsail, which the storm had torn away. A detail of sailors re-raised the damaged topmast studdingsail. The lieutenant himself made repairs to shipboard esprit d' corps, re-rating Thomas Hall as quartermaster—"He has had the Old Boy taken out of him." As predictably as clockwork, Conway Whittle grew "heartily tired" for the want of a Yankee prize, and thought of home.

And then the storms unleashed themselves upon the raider once again—storms both natural and man-made.

The sea began to stir again on Friday, December 23. They were now well into the Southern Indian Ocean. Rain-bearing clouds welled up in the late afternoon, the storm's artillery. Behind the rain rushed the infantry, the wind. "As disagreeable as I ever saw anywhere," Whittle declared.

> *It is blowing a whole gale of wind and raining in torrents, the rain being a kind of sheet and as cold as hail. When you attempt to face the wind your breath is fairly taken away, and your face feels as if you had a number of prickers sticking in it. . . . Such a day as this makes the poor Mariner regret the day on which his destinies were linked with the sea.*

Chew stood the first watch; and Whittle, out of prudence and perhaps from solidarity as well, faced the rain-sheets with his embattled fellow officer. "Oh how much I would not give to be on shore," ran his thoughts as lightning turned the great rollers a spectral white, "with our dear country at peace, and a certain little angel sitting by me as my wife. I would certainly be the happiest man in the world."

Such happiness would have to wait. Shipboard strife—which now seemed to coincide with bad weather—arose yet again.

As to the weather, Whittle had done well to order the raider made seaworthy again during the lull. What attacked them now was not so much a new storm as a fresh section of the great, agitated atmospheric oval that spun around and above them. *Shenandoah* took on tremendous volumes of water. In the howling confusion, Whittle managed to notice, with a whiff of bravado, irony, and concern, that "she is a very peculiar ship: aft and forwards she is very dry and amidships she is flooded." Her fore and main topsails closely reefed, her foresails and fore topmast staysail reefed as well, *Shenandoah* ran hard before the wind and sea, like a scrap of wood and canvas on a wet, blustery street.

As to the strife, it involved yet a new culprit.

> *I may say that the first trouble we have had with any officer occurred today. While the ship was rolling very heavily, I found that the [fastenings] of the guns were not in their places under the trucks, and I asked Mr. Guy the Gunner for the reason. He replied in a most*

unsatisfactory manner, and then was so very insolent and insubordinate in his answer and language, that I ordered him to be silent, and sent him on the Quarter Deck and reported him to the captain who saw him and ordered me to put him off duty. I am very sorry the thing happened for he is a good man, but I will break these parties in or I will break their necks in the attempt.

Bad behavior seemed a kind of shipboard virus—it could erupt at any time from any unexpected source. In fact, the sailors aboard *Shenandoah* were little different from sailors anywhere: tough men, headstrong, fatalistic, for whom conflict and defiance were as routine as a spray of saltwater in the face. Added to this were the strained nerves resulting from seas violent enough to carry any one or several of them over the side or out of the rigging upon the slightest misjudgment. Whittle understood this. Typical of his unquenchable optimism, though, he decided that this would be a merry Christmas, despite all odds. In terms of Charles Dickens's already legendary Yuletide tale, he would take the role of Bob Cratchett.

Today I told the men that I had selected the largest pig in the pen for their Christmas dinner, and all they had to do was kill it. They were very much delighted.

Livestock, including geese, chickens, and sheep were carried on *Shenandoah* for food; and as on all ships the familiar presence of the ship's cat helped control the rats.

Whittle's benevolent gesture met with its usual success. On December 24, Christmas Eve,

Poor Mr. O'Shea came to me and reported Mr. Guy and Mr. Lynch for being drunk on the berth deck and abusing him. I at once sent for Mr. Guy and he said he was coming. He did not make his appearance for some time and I went to the Main hatch and called him. He still did not come. I then sent Mr. Mason to order him up. He replied that he had been put under arrest by the Captain and would only come on his order.

A hint of deep trouble here; a splintering of the crew's loyalties between Waddell and Whittle—just what the pitching, rolling *Shenandoah* needed as it heaved through the hurricane. If Waddell noticed such an opportunity, though, he did not exploit it.

I sent Mr. Mason to tell [Guy] that I, the Executive Officer, ordered him to come on deck. He positively refused, and then I reported the matter to the Captain and sent Lieut. Grimball with orders to bring him on deck and to use any force necessary, but hearing that he was too drunk to know what he was about the order was revoked.

Nonetheless, the besotted gunner soon lurched into view on his own. Once on deck—the ship's motion perhaps counterbalancing his own—Mr. Guy refused an order to step (or stagger) forward.

I repeated the order several times but as he showed no signs of obeying, I got down on the ladder and showed him forwards. He fell on deck and I picked him up and started him again when he caught a rope and held fast. Mr. Browne & Mr. Minor now came to my assistance and we landed him on the Berth Deck.

The Bob Cratchett inside Whittle gave way to Ebeneezer Scrooge.

I was never so tempted in my life to pitch in and thrash him as well. I next sent for Mr. Lynch and found him slightly tight. Just enough to make him look like a fool.

Where had the liquor come from? Whittle had an idea:

I conclude that they have been saving up their daily tots for a grand blowout Christmas. It is the last spree the worthies will have as I have had their grog stopped pour toujours.

The night before Christmas enveloped the raider and its men so far from their homes. As the seas worsened again, some crewmen managed to get a fire going belowdecks and impale the pig's 120-pound carcass on a spit. "I am anxious to see them enjoy themselves and would rather have a dull day myself than see them so," their lieutenant informed his log. As he wrote on in his cabin under a violently swinging oil lamp, the Ghost of Christmas Past seemed to cast his spell over Conway Whittle's mood, and he unburdened himself.

> *This is certainly a very miserable Christmas eve and it is a night upon which each one and all of us knows that at our far distant homes our dear ones are wondering where we, the absent spirits, are. God grant that they are all well, and give them his blessing and guidance. I am sure that my own dear Pattie has thought of me more than once tonight.*

And then the dark specter receded before a shaft of light.

> *Most sincerely do I, on the eve of the birth of Christ, invoke God's blessing and protection on my dear, dear country and all my dear ones.*

Only Tiny Tim himself could have improved on Conway Whittle's concluding thought:

> *God bless them all.*

Shenandoah's crew, and its struggling nation thousands of miles across the ocean, would need all the blessings they could get. Christmas 1864 found the South dazed, starving, grasping at hope and the rudiments of civilization. At Franklin, Tennessee, John Bell Hood's army had just been cut to ribbons in a freezing drizzle by the Federals under George H. Thomas, effectively ending the war in the West. Hood's dead and wounded lay along the muddy roadsides of his retreat. At Richmond, once-wealthy women pooled their scant remaining resources to distribute holiday dinners—or the pitiful semblance of holiday dinners—to Robert E. Lee's skeletal, maimed, diseased troops: the once-indomitable Army of Northern Virginia, the South's last remaining hope, an army that lay exhausted and virtually trapped in its trenches. Lee excused himself from his own family, with whom he had managed to reunite, to spend the holiday with his men. Sherman had completed his March to the Sea with the capture of Savannah, which he offered as a Yuletide present to his commander by telegraph. The recipient, Ulysses S. Grant, whose armies faced Lee's in a menacing arc around Richmond, replied that he wanted Sherman's 60,000 troops transported back north by sea to join his own legions and create an overwhelming strike force of 280,000 against the Confederate capital. Sherman had an even better idea. He would return north in the same fashion he'd come south: by land, bulling through the Carolinas and causing fresh devastation on a sixty-mile swath as he moved inexorably toward the Virginia front.

Christmas 1864 found the Confederacy effectively reduced to three states from its original eleven. Only Virginia and North and South Carolina could offer any resistance to the Northern juggernaut.

"This is indeed a Merry Christmas," Conway Whittle wrote with steel-plated good cheer on December 25, 1864. Perhaps he was trying to will it so with the words. The "very miserable Christmas eve" was only hours in the past; the storm had worsened again; the weather had all but spoiled the pig roast; and Whittle had felt it his duty to spend the midwatch once again with Chew. This storm would be memorable indeed.

> *At 7 a heavy sea came over the starb'd main chains and she toiled to the port and took it over the port side. It was so heavy as to fill our Spar Deck so that some of the men swam to catch over a rope to save themselves. The guns were actually covered entirely. I never saw a sea come aboard half as heavy. It rolled aft and went thru the wardroom filling several rooms, wetting several officers in their upper bunks. . . . The men were frightened but they soon recovered with water waist deep. It was very cold but I sang our Merry Christmas and indeed it looked very little like it for I never saw such weather.*

Or perhaps Whittle's sense of a "Merry Christmas" had been prompted by the near-miracle he had witnessed.

A thing occurred today which I suppose would take place once in a thousand times. When we shipped the two seas Wm. West, the Capt of our main top, was on the main hatch. The sea swept him overboard on the port side and the sea which came over to the port washed him onboard again. When the second sea took him he was well clear of the ship on the port side.

Whittle restored the gunner John L. Guy to duty.

A stranger—the first in many days—approached from the west on December 29, and *Shenandoah* thoughtfully waited for her to come up, cannon at the ready.

All hands thought she was a Frenchman. We ran up the English flag & she, to our great surprise, hoisted the Yankee colors.

As the stranger ran across *Shenandoah*'s stern, the raider reintroduced herself with a shot across the bow and the billowing Confederate flag. The Rebel boarding party found the intruder to be the American barque *Delphine,* en route from London to the Burmese seaport Akyab under the command of Captain Nichols.

She was a good prize, but the captain said that his sickly wife was on board and that to move her in such a sea might prove fatal. It was decided to leave the matter to the decision of the surgeon, who "took the Captain aside and upon hearing what Mr. Nichols complaint was considered *[decided]* that there would be no danger in making the transfer. Accordingly she was brought off and hoisted up in a chair without any trouble. We also brought off the Capt., two mates & 11 men as prisoners of war & the steward and stewardess."

Once again, *Shenandoah* found herself in the family-hospitality business: along with the Nicholses came their small son Phineas. (The family hailed from Searsport, Maine, as it turned out—the same hometown claimed by Captain Staples of *Alina.*) The captain's wife struck Whittle as in far better shape than the captain had indicated.

Mrs. Nichols really looks like anything but an invalid, being a large, fine-looking person, rather pretty. At first she is a little frightened but we can soon drive fear away by proving by kindness that we are gentlemen.

After estimating the barque's worth at $25,000, the Confederates torched the *Delphine,* and continued their eastward course through the steep swells.

Lost sight of our burning prize at 3 o'clock. This day has been very pleasant and we have had nice breezes. Mrs. Nichols is becoming quite sociable, and converses quite freely. We made sail to Royals and Staysails.

Her officers having clapped six of the captured seamen in irons, *Shenandoah* was now again a prison ship as well. Still, tranquillity reigned aboard her as 1864 slid into its final hours.

This has been a lovely day. We have been under all plain sail with a light breeze, nearly aft. Our lady passenger becoming more sociable and really seems to think that we are not all a parcel of piratical barbarians.

Conway Whittle decided to mark the passing of the old year.

I shall sit up, and bid it adieu, and welcome the new one in. Oh! may the incoming one be happy. God grant us freedom and peace, I humbly pray.

He thought again of his family back in Virginia, and of Pattie.

On Sunday, New Year's Day, "we hoisted the Confederate flag & kept it up all day to welcome in the new year."

Studdingsails on both sides added to the raider's eastward velocity: "It is the first time we have made sail with all sail set at one time."

At last Waddell had allowed Whittle to give *Shenandoah* her head. Whittle prayed once again, that night, that God would guard, protect, and cherish his country, "that he will open the eyes of our enemies to the cruelty of the war they are waging against us, and that He may teach them that they are wrong." The beautiful weather and fresh breezes prevailed through the week as the ship averaged well over a hundred miles each day. The crew resumed a task fundamental to the voyage's survival: the steam-powered condensing of seawater into fresh.

Passing St. Paul, one of the few small islands found scattered above Antarctica, the ship stopped briefly. St. Paul was unlike most Antarctic islands, which were virtually inaccessible, with their steep-sided mountain coastlines and forbidding surf. But at St. Paul, *Shenandoah* was able to enter the perfect circle of the island's sheltered interior harbor, an anchorage so choked with kelp that it once again threatened their propeller, its shore-side rocks crowded with penguins. Waddell and Whittle allowed a group of land-starved officers to go reconnoitering for a while. They brought back a penguin, some eggs, and a chicken, and news that they had conversed with a pair of Frenchmen who fished there for "a fish not unlike cod which is dried and very nice" and were used to seeing no one six to eight months of the year.

The idyll continued: clear and pleasant weather; 150, sometimes 200 miles a day. On January 8, Whittle ruminated,

Three months ago I sailed from England on the "Sea King" and here I am thousands and thousands of miles away. No one knowing outside of the ship where we are or where we will probably be at any time.

He'd triced up the truculent John Williams, the cook, for neglect of duty the day before—"he was as docile as a black sheep when I let him down"—and found it necessary to punish him again on the eighth for impertinence to the master-at-arms. "He is a sullen fellow and I have no doubt he will leave us in the first port we enter."

On Christmas Day, Whittle had begun adding barometer readings to his log entries—evidence of his growing alertness to threats of storms, or perhaps Whittle had begun using an instrument captured from *Delphine*. A high barometer indicates high atmospheric pressure, which has the effect of calming both the air and the ocean. When the barometer begins a downward move, some degree of trouble is generally on the way. In this southern sector of the world's waters, as the men of Shenandoah had discovered, the trouble was apt to be intense. *Shenandoah*'s barometer had been rising since Christmas. It would have to start falling eventually.

❦

Conway Whittle concluded his January 8 entries with an astonishing revelation, a glimpse into his own emotional barometer—and into a psyche that seemed constantly to ricochet between the warrior and the lover, the poet and the plain-speaker, the dreamer and the realist. The revelation involved "my dear Pattie." His repeated journal entries dedicated to her—"No one has any idea how I love that dear girl, and I humbly pray that God will soon ordain it that I may soon go to her"— had hinted at a deeply established romance that was broken off only by the exigencies of war. ("My love for her is as singular as it is pure," ran a typical declaration.) But on this day Whittle wrote, as if confessing to himself,

> *I never saw her but on one single occasion, and still my love for her is such as I never experienced for any person before.*

"Man is in love," William Butler Yeats would write half a century in the future, in a poem meditating on civil war in his own Ireland, "and loves what vanishes." On exactly such tides of chivalric passion were thousands upon thousands of Conway Whittles clinging, as 1865 began, to the love of a nation that never really quite was, that even then was in the process of vanishing, and that was never to be seen again.

❦

By now, *Shenandoah*, sailing at better than a 200-mile-a-day clip, had covered ninety degrees of the earth, a quarter the circumference of the globe. She would be more than halfway around it by the time she reached her interim destination. (Whittle noticed that day that he was in fact halfway around the world from his native Virginia, "and now we are getting nearer and nearer home in distance each day.")

Heading on a straight line to the east now, her hull and superstructure showing inevitable signs of leakage and strain, overloaded and undermanned, her rudder of unknown durability, mauled by storms that would tax twenty-first-century technology, the black raider continued to prove the value of her craftsmanship. Her powerful stern, raised high to provide stability, her steam engine, her superbly conceived rigging system—in these and other details, Shenandoah was the analogue of that later masterpiece of wartime design, the B-17 bomber of World War II, so vulnerable-looking on its surface, yet impervious to the elements, and so difficult to bring down.

Her crew was likewise fragile on the surface, yet strong and resilient underneath. These men, these fugitives and strangers culled from the captives of her conquered "prizes," these brawlers and drunks and chronic insubordinates, were beginning to coalesce. They had survived some of the most hellish weather on the seas; they had witnessed potentially disabling power struggles; some of them had directly challenged their superiors and discovered—painfully—the limits of their rebellious instincts. The ship and her crew were now ready for anything. Or so Conway Whittle hoped. He'd made that assumption several times before.

❧❧❧

On Monday, January 9, his ship sailing smoothly, Whittle lapsed into idle self-regard.

> *Today for curiosity's sake I got weighed. My weight astonishes me beyond measure. It is 140 pounds, and two months ago when I stopped the use of tobacco, I weighed only 118 pounds. I have thus gained 22 pounds in two months. This is one of the proofs of how ruinous tobacco was to me. I do not think I will ever re-commence its use.*

❧❧❧

The January days rolled on as Shenandoah raced ever closer to Australia: light winds, a reasonably smooth sea, routine duties, small alarums. On the tenth, Whittle encouraged the gifted navigator, Irvine Bulloch, to leave his post temporarily and give his sorely over-exposed eyes a rest. "I am very sorry for Bulloch but he will soon get well now. His eyes have been damaged taking sights."

That was putting it mildly. Irvine Bulloch was in a cycle of agony over a magnified assault from the sun's rays on his unprotected reti-nas—a cruel, often blinding occupational hazard for every navigator of that time. The damage resulted from an obligation as necessary as it was inhumane: to "take the bearings" of a ship, in order to establish its position in an ocean with no visible land.

The bearings were taken via the sun, at its highest and brightest point, noon. "Shooting the sun," as it was also called, required a small, precision-ground, partially mirrored telescope with a pivoting arm at-tached. The navigator peered through the telescope toward the hori-zon, trying to align it with a horizontal line inscribed on its lens. Maddening as this task could be on a rolling ship, it was the easy part. Once these two lines were in synch, the punishment began: the naviga-tor pivoted the spoke-shaped arm, which carried a second mirror in its tip. This mirror relayed the image of the sun onto the mirror in the navigator's lens—and from there, searingly, into the navigator's retinas. When the bottom edge of the sun just touched the horizon line in the telescope, the degree of the arm's angle in the arc was noted. Then chronometers, keyed to the British Royal Observatory at Greenwich, could be used to calculate the number of degrees that separated the sun above the ship and the sun above Greenwich (the sun moves through 15 degrees an hour), and thus the ship's longitude and latitude.

Damage to the eyes was inevitable. The navigator might as well have been training a magnifying glass on the sun. No compromises were possible: not the micro-slitted openings in sliced walrus tusks that Eskimos used to combat snow blindness, not smoked lenses—which could not filter out the damaging ultraviolet solar rays. It was not even allowable to perform this ritual in haste, because even a small miscal-culation could set the ship wandering on a false course with no end in sight. Patience—and prolonged exposure—were essential to the task.

Irvine Bulloch had been sailing master, a ship's navigator, for nearly the entire war, first on *Nashville,* then on *Alabama,* and now on

Shenandoah. His skills were legendary, and so was the personal risk he took every day with the most important navigational tools of all: his eyes.

The symptoms were progressive: first the pain, then the loss of depth perception. Darkness was the only remedy—a temporary one at that, because tolerating the damage was part of his job. Irvine Bulloch would take sightings until the pain overwhelmed him. Then he would lie blindfolded in his cabin until the worst of it wore away. This might entail several days. When the pain was endurable, Bulloch would set aside his blindfold and try to withstand the brightness of the deck. If he could "shoot the sun" without screaming, he was fit for duty.

They had smooth sailing for days, and peace, or a most convincing il-lusion of it, now enveloped the commanding and executive officers.

> *The Captain asked me if I would let him have a boat to take a run around the ship. I had the gig cleared away, lowered and manned, and had him piped over the side. This is the first time the ceremony of pip-ing over has ever been done in the "Shenandoah." He came back very much pleased with her appearance.*

The mutual geniality extended to evening recreation: "Tonight the Captain & Dr. McNulty and Bulloch & I played four games of whist. B. & I beat three out of four."

In this interlude between storms and crises of command, *Shenan-doah* seemed almost to exhale, to restore herself. The crew returned to the almost endless task of shifting coal from the fore hold to the bunkers. The valve to the air pump gave way, and Mr. O'Brien re-paired it. Even the war seemed somehow a bit less threatening. On the seventeenth, a stranger hove into view, a large ship with double topsail yards. She bore evidence of Yankee lineage, but the boarding party found her British papers in good order, and the captain's sworn oath persuasive. The captain, a jolly fellow named Finlayter, sent over half a dozen bottles of brandy as a goodwill gesture. Whittle turned twenty-five on Monday, January 16, and Waddell presented him with "a nice book marker." He wrote a letter to Pattie.

The chief form of aggression remained cards, and Whittle remained the chief aggressor: "Tonight the Captain & Dr. McNulty, Lee and I played three games of whist. Lee and I beat the rubber."

One familiar shipboard figure disturbed the general tranquillity. His repeated acts of provocation could not have passed without effect on the superstitious sailors. On the 12th, "I caught Williams in a piece of rascality, i.e., stealing the ward room steward's shirts. I have stopped his grog until further orders and triced him up when he is not at work. I fear he is a great scamp." Two days later, Whittle had to do it all over again. Less than a week after that, Williams came complaining to the lieutenant that the steerage steward, William Jones, had called him a "black scamp."

I had an idea of letting Williams know that I agreed with Jones; but upon examination by questioning witnesses I found that Williams had called him by some outrageous epithet, and not being able to tell who was most wrong I . . . punished both worthies.

And, perhaps once again betraying a certain set of received attitudes: "Williams is a great villain."

But a far more troubling source of anxiety had by then emerged. O'Brien had ordered the propeller triced up to give him access to the air-pump valve. On examination, "we found that all the bolts which we had put on the coupling strap had broken and that it was as bad as ever. Mr. O'Brien got to work on it and I hope I will soon have it in fine order."

⁂

Melbourne grew ever closer, and with it the prospect of dry land, wet tavern nights, and willing women. Beyond Melbourne, as most of the crew well understood, lay untold dangers for *Shenandoah*. But for now, a mood of giddy good spirits swept the ship. Even the black-tempered Captain Waddell was caught up in it—enjoying a huge laugh at Whittle's expense: the straitlaced lieutenant had been caught flirting—with the wife of a Yankee prisoner! Or at least so spread the rumor.

Whittle dutifully recorded it, in his honest and detail-conscious way:

*This morning I was staying by the wardroom door and Mrs. Nichols
came up and commenced talking to me. She said, "Well Mr. Whittle, I
trust we may soon have peace." I concurred in the hope. She then said,
"Do you think we can ever be friends?" Said I, "No madam, never."
"But Mr. Whittle, if after peace was made and you were to meet me,
would you speak to me?" "Certainly madam, I would speak at any
time to a female." "But would you not speak to my husband?" "I might
do so as he has never served against us."*

As if peevish that she had not made a dent in the lieutenant's
façade, Mrs. Nichols abruptly switched tactics.

*She was admiring the uniform cap of our men and wondered if she
could make one. I replied no as it was woven. She said she would like
of all things to have one. She said this in such a way that I was forced
to yield and said that I thought I could get one for her. She thanked me
a little but when she gets it, she will thank me more. The truth is I can
at all times know how to deal with men, but not always with women.
If proper, I can always say no to a man, but not so with a woman.*

Outmaneuvered! The fire-eating hero of the *Nashville* escapade,
sinker of Union ships, Rebel scourge of the South Atlantic, found he
had just promised to give a Yankee woman a Confederate naval
officer's cap! There had to be a rational explanation for this. Yes!
Whittle had been victimized by Yankee bad manners!

*Now I contend that before one of our Southern women would have
done such a thing as this, she would have cut her hand off. Such is the
marked difference. If I had given her a cap I have no doubt she would
have handed it over to her husband and he would probably have sold
it and considered his wife what they call a "smart 'un."*

This would have ended it—nothing more than a little Yankee sab-
otage, which Whittle absorbed with manly silence, and no one the
wiser—except that someone *was* the wiser: Jack Grimball, who had
soaked up the entire exchange from his room. Grimball lost no time

dishing the dirt to his whist partner, Captain Waddell. The captain, Whittle gamely set down in his log,

> *tells it as a very good joke on me. . . . He says he will tell all in An-*
> *napolis how I flirt with Yankee prisoners and says that he would ad-*
> *vise me to write to my sweetheart and made a clean acknowledgment*
> *as she will certainly hear of it. I contend that with any woman who*
> *has so little delicacy as to place a gentleman in the fix I am in, he has*
> *the perfect right to consider the promise as not made and on this prin-*
> *ciple I will let the cap alone.*

On this note of edgy masculine bonhomie—a rare note, and all too soon to grow virtually extinct—*Shenandoah* parted the famously troubled waters of the Great Australian Bight, her prow set for the approach waters of Melbourne Harbor.

9

<hr>

The continent rose up at them from the early-morning darkness of January 25: a great, far-stretching interruption of the void they'd been sailing through, the anti-world to the infinity of ocean. A silhouette, one that took on color and texture as the light broke. A continent: solid earth, trees, rocks; the old lost sound of waves breaking against rocks. As they neared, they could see green hills above the cliffs. The long curve of shoreline shimmered with life: penguins and seals, and birds, suddenly a universe of birds—shrieking gulls, albatross with their twelve-foot wingspans. Even closer to port, they stared at houses and church steeples, and the wonder of smoke from chimneys. Ships. People. Civilization.

At 5:00 a.m. saw Cape Otway . . . beautiful land fall.

An oddly terse entry, given the moment. Otway commanded the arrowhead-tip of Victoria that pointed southward into the ocean. Rounding this point, sails hauled, *Shenandoah* would steam another seventy miles northeastward along Victoria's coastal cliffs toward the narrow entrance to the stomach-shaped Port Phillip Bay, and then thirty-five more miles across the bay into Melbourne Harbor, at last, at the inlet's northern rim. Whittle's bleak notation showed no interest in latitude or longitude. It made no mention of Otway's great elegant lighthouse that towered above the surf of the narrow Eye of the Needle. The facts and evidence of landfall hardly interested him. Neither did the excitement of the raider's crew as they drank in the coastline that yielded its full textures under the clear skies. For once the lieutenant's natural exuberance was muted. He believed this stop to be a mistake—the crew's yearnings be damned. This stop was a mistake. He had believed it from the first.

"As long as we have had to go to port, I do not care how soon we get there," he'd written four days earlier. "But I had much rather not go at all. Except to hear some news, ports have no attraction for me . . ." Whittle well knew that there would be no news for him; certainly not any personal news. ". . . as there is no chance of hearing from my darling or from home," he'd continued. Nor from his father, who could well have been languishing in a Yankee prison camp.

Why should there be? His ship, *Sea King,* had been lost—sunk. That at least was the story as the world understood it—as his father and sweetheart understood it. It was the story the raiders themselves had been at pains to establish. If the operatives tracking the ship from London knew otherwise, it was not in their interests to tip this knowledge.

Whittle's thoughts had then turned to the war; to the maddening absence of information about its progress; and he'd dreamed a scenario he probably knew to be impossible:

> *Oh! how much joy it would afford us all to hear that Peace had been made. We would then take our noble ship into port in Dixie. Then where would I go? I would strike a "bee line" for her whom I love. She knows who.*

In the following entry, however, Whittle got to the practical heart of the Melbourne matter:

> *I sincerely wish that we were not going there for I think that our cruise will be greatly injured by it as from that place there are little vessels carrying regular mails to different fishing depots at which the Yankee whalers congregate, and as soon as they hear that we are in the neighborhood, they will all run into port and we will catch very few.*

He did not add the obvious corollary: as the Yankee whalers ran into their ports, the Yankee warships would run out. Port Phillip Bay was a classic bottleneck: *Shenandoah* might outrun a warship south-ward across its wide expanse, only to confront the narrow, violent strip of water known as "the Rip," which separated the bay from open sea. Slowed by the surging waves, she might have to turn and fight. In which case she would be destroyed.

Nonetheless, he wrote, "Waddell has his mind made up about get-ting a mail."

And that settled that. To be fair, the captain was merely following the original operating orders from Richmond: Sail to Melbourne and connect with a British mail steamer that was scheduled to leave the port on January 26. "If we missed her," Waddell later noted, "we would not have another opportunity to send letters to England for some time."[10] Perhaps the steamer would have delivered further orders to him from his superiors. Conway Whittle may have stripped Waddell of his moral legitimacy, yet rank was rank, and this was not the time for another test of personalities. Or so Whittle decided. And lapsed into glumness.

His mood hadn't been improved, either, by yet another con-tretemps with Waddell—this one two days earlier, on Monday, Janu-ary 23, in the crowded sea lanes approaching the Bass Strait. As *Shenandoah*'s crew stopped engines for a quick repair, four ships be-came visible at a distance. One of these was a six-topsail craft—"which I took to be a Yankee," Whittle recorded. But the Captain spurned Whittle's urgings to make chase; he believed the ship to be nothing more than *Nimrod,* the suspicious Britisher whose jolly cap-tain had sent over the brandy. Waddell was convinced that making the London-bound mail steamer from Melbourne was more important than a capture. He was determined to press on for the harbor, regard-less of lost opportunities. Whittle, holding himself in, had once again deferred. "The weather is beautiful," he appended to that entry—a likely sarcasm, aimed at Waddell for letting a potential prize go free under ideal pursuit conditions.

As events made clear, Waddell's assumption about the stranger was wrong.

By midday, the raider having breached the Rip and headed northward through the Bay's calm waters, Whittle's detachment blossomed into pride. His beautiful dagger of a ship, her 230-foot sides gleaming with fresh black paint, the Confederate colors aloft, was strutting into port undisguised—a visible, powerful, manifestation of the Confederacy as a Nation—and the whole of Melbourne, it seemed, had turned out to cheer. *Shenandoah* was receiving a hero's welcome.

> *Passed on with our flag flying. Numerous steamers, tugs and sailing craft saluted by dipping their ensigns and in some instances by cheering. All these greetings were cheering, and were returned cheerfully.*

Even Waddell noticed the excitement. "Cheer after cheer greeted us from the generous, brave hearted Englishmen and Australians, who believed in the justice of our cause," he wrote.[11]

Captain Waddell chose to anchor in a serene part of the great harbor just a few miles to the west of Melbourne, a sector known as Hobson's Bay. Shortly after noon, all hands commenced the elaborate task of preparing the anchor for dropping. The great, double-bladed iron hook had not been dropped since Deserta in the Madeira Islands, when it took the whole undermanned crew, and all the officers, to haul it up again. The lowering began around 6:45 p.m., and reached a depth of forty-five fathoms.

Immediately a miniature flotilla—steam launches, sailboats, tourist craft—converged on *Shenandoah,* their decks swarming with passengers who cheered and craned their necks to get a glimpse of the warriors high above them. The Rebel sailors, lean and toughened and tested in combat with the world's most tumultuous seas, gaped back down into their own godlike stature, mirrored in the townspeople's eyes.

Conway Whittle immediately saw the moment for what it was, and for what it might mean to his nation.

> *If we judge from outward signs, we are likely to find a good deal of sympathy here among the people. It is the first time these people have ever seen our flag or any of our people and as we have, as it were, the*

reputation of the Confederacy to make and maintain, it is very incumbent that every man and officer should be very circumspect.

Before dropping anchor the ship had paused twice—at midday—after passing through the Rip: once to take on a harbor pilot named Nichols—the name was suddenly everywhere—and once to pass contagious-disease inspection by the port surgeon. For the first time since the previous October, the raider's crew learned news of the world beyond the void. Not all of it was entirely accurate. Lincoln, as all had expected, had been reelected president in a landslide; that was true enough. Less credible was the word that "Lee had gained a great victory near Petersburg." This feat, if it happened, remains among the best-kept secrets in the annals of warfare.

The siege at Petersburg—Grant's Army of the Potomac in its forty-mile arc facing Lee's entrenched Army of Northern Virginia twenty miles south of Richmond—had begun the previous June, well before *Sea King/Shenandoah* sailed. After a series of Federal attacks had cost the bluecoats 70,000 dead, wounded, and captured, the armies had settled into the standoff that would grind on for nearly ten months. Lee's men had repulsed an assault on his works at Hatcher's Run on October 27—the day *Shenandoah* sailed out of the Madeiras toward the equator—but nothing significant had happened since, except for the disease and starvation that crept through the Southern lines.

Nor was this the extent of it. The raider's officers would have been shattered to learn that they now had no way of reentering their homeland from the sea: on January 15 the Yankees had seized the harbor at Wilmington, North Carolina, the last remaining active Confederate port. Thus CSS *Shenandoah*, even as she basked triumphantly in the cheering hospitality of Australia, a respected emissary of a noble land, was now unknowingly and forever cut off from her home.

Not that many illusions remained. "This all looks like no end to the war," Whittle wrote. "God alone can tell when or how it will end."

Meanwhile, *Shenandoah* would abide by the rules of wartime diplomacy. ("I shall observe the neutrality," Waddell assured the local officials in a letter.) Her initial warm welcome was hardly a complete

surprise, given that Australia was under Queen Victoria's sovereignty—the Deep South of the British Empire, so to speak. Yet
Britain remained officially neutral; niceties must be observed. As twilight descended over the town and harbor, Captain Waddell dispatched Second Lt. John Grimball of South Carolina, the ship's
third-ranking officer, to the chambers of Sir Charles Henry Darling,
governor of the Province of Victoria. Grimball carried formal papers
requesting permission to remain long enough to make repairs, take on
coal, and unload the *Delphine* prisoners (this would include Captain
and Mrs. Nichols and young Phineas).

This request skirted the edges of international law. Neutrality
agreements prohibited noncombatant countries from aiding and supporting any belligerent's wartime activities. Thus any maintenance
work aboard *Shenandoah* would have to be performed without the
help or materials of the port city—the official city, at least. There
would be no resupplying of powder, ammunition, propeller screws, or
tackle for the cannon. Not officially. Offloading prisoners was allowable under law, yet the ship's officers were careful to frame this right as
a courtesy of the Melbourne government. There would be no recruiting whatsoever.

Darling sent back word that he would make a decision on Waddell's request the next morning. The governor found himself caught
between powerful conflicting pressures. A major international port,
Melbourne harbored—literally—a large contingent of U.S. sympathizers, official and unofficial. Yet the British Crown, which ruled over
his city, province, and nation, commanded neutrality. Whatever Darling decided, it was certain to provoke outrage.

Shenandoah's men prepared for the night. Reluctant to retain the
captured seamen aboard their ship a minute longer than necessary, but
unable legally to order them to shore, the two commanders approached the confined men and let them know, without suggesting
anything, "that there were plenty of boats alongside and they could
[all] remain until we got permission to land them or avail themselves
of the boats. They decided (sensibly) as it was late to remain all night."
Waddell reported in his memoirs that the prisoners had subsequently
"deserted," but was honest enough to add, "much to my comfort."[12]

The governor called together his executive council on the morning of January 26, and, after two hours of intense debate, sent word to Hobson's Bay that he would grant Waddell the courtesies that a neutral nation would extend any belligerent. The Rebel captain could offload his prisoners, and could resupply and repair his ship. News of this decision spread quickly through the city, and soon a celebratory flotilla of small boats drew alongside the anchored cruiser, the crowds aboard them avid to see and touch the storied raider and her men. "Before the permission was given we had to wave a good many off," Whittle recorded, but now the ship was surrounded by steam tugs, sailboats, and other small launches that overflowed with visitors. Whittle and Waddell yielded to the clamor and, incredibly, actually opened *Shenandoah*'s decks to visitors.

The locals—like the hordes of a later century milling about the decks of a decommissioned aircraft carrier or squeezing into the cockpit of a rebuilt B-29—were thrilled to set foot aboard this beautiful scourge of the South Seas. Some of the smitten Aussies invited crewmen from the raider to be guests in their homes, or to go crawling with them through Melbourne's pubs. Some certainly even offered more carnal refreshment. Nichols, the port pilot, eagerly volunteered his own small launch, the *Modesty*, to ferry officers and men to shore and back, and to procure whatever delicacies and comforts the Confederates desired. "Invitation after invitation has been already extended to us and the hospitality of the people is apparently only surpassed by their immeasurable curiosity," Whittle observed. He could not resist adding, with a warrior's satisfaction, "They look at us with apparent surprise that we have not tails. If this is what we are to expect, the sooner we get to sea, the less chance I will have of going deranged."

Somewhat less innocuous were a pair of British naval officers who came aboard for an informal visit, at Waddell's wary invitation. One of these later reported that the ship was in good order and her officers gentlemen in handsome gray-and-gold uniforms. The other sniffed that the decks and engine room seemed slovenly, and the crewmen as well.[13]

The next day, Thursday, January 26, Paymaster William Breedlove Smith went chugging from the ship to the city aboard Mr. Nichols's *Modesty*. He bore with him a bulging leather bag, sealed carefully, and marked for shipment to England. Its fragile contents were Hope incarnate: letters.

Whittle described them in the log:

> *It contained, of mine, one to Commodore [Samuel] Barron [in Paris], giving him in detail a full account of our cruise, one to my dear father enclosed in a short note to Mr. Moses R., and one to my darling Pattie. I trust they may all reach their destinations to relieve the anxiety produced by the report of the wreck of the ship. Under how many trials we have done our duty.*

Captain Waddell also sent a letter to Commodore Barron, and enclosed his own (upbeat) report on *Shenandoah*'s exploits thus far, addressed to Navy Secretary Stephen Mallory. Other correspondence included letters from crewmen and officers, such as Lieutenant Grimball, that sought to assure relatives back home that they were still alive and the ship still sailing, contrary to the published reports of some four months earlier.

Whittle's "trust" faced long odds. Where his father was, he had no idea. Was he even alive? Did the Whittle home city of Norfolk still stand, or had it been burned to the ground by the Yankees? The same uncertainty, of course, held true for Pattie. Conway Whittle really had no clue to the whereabouts of his chimerical sweetheart, the love he had met but once. Nor could Pattie possibly have guessed the whereabouts of Whittle, or whether he still existed—if indeed she still remembered him, or cared. Perhaps the false news of *Sea King*'s destruction had broken her heart. Perhaps she had steeled her heart against him. Perhaps she merely suffered through the days, racked by anxiety. His understanding of this likely distress, this distress he'd been forced to inflict on his sweetheart, undoubtedly gnawed at Whittle's highly tuned conscience, assailing him on those oil-lit late nights in his cabin when he made his journal entries, struggling to maintain his officer's official voice, and so often failing.

None of the Southern Americans among the officers and crew were likely to have dwelt on the most desolate possibility of all: the likelihood that none of their laboriously calligraphed letters would even reach their homeland. Mail service in the South, especially international mail service, was effectively destroyed. Commodore Barron, who likely was in Paris, might receive his dispatch. As for the rest . . .

Under how many trials we have done our duty.

Or, in the case of some, failed to do their duty. It was in his cabin, that first day, while poring through the stacks of Australian newspapers brought aboard by the harbor pilot, that Conway Whittle made an astonishing discovery—one that bore on "duty" as perceived by James Waddell.

Whittle's interest in the local press was more than casual. The papers of this major port city were filled with news about the comings and goings of merchant ships. They offered tabular data as well: harbormaster's reports, dockage reports, sailing schedules, ship names. Just the sort of boring compost that might yield up a bright nugget or two: news of a Yankee clipper, say, preparing to haul its fat defenseless carcass out upon the dangerous high seas . . .

Whittle snapped to full focus when he came across the listing of a certain arrival at Adelaide, a port city some 600 miles up the Victorian coast northwest of Melbourne. The vessel's description—it was a six-topsailer—matched Whittle's memory of the ship he'd urged Waddell to chase back on the twenty-third—the ship Waddell had shrugged off as *Nimrod.* The entry under his eye listed no *Nimrod*; the name attached to the six-topsailer was *David Brown.* Whittle frowned at the item for a few moments. Then he arose and left his cabin and strode off in search of Captain William Nichols of the captured *Delphine,* who had not yet left the ship. Could Nichols identify the barque in question? Nichols could—and his identification all but floored the young lieutenant.

The . . . David Brown, bound to Adelaide . . . was commanded, and in great part owned, by Mrs. Nichols' Brother. I learned this by the

arrival of that ship at Adelaide about that time. Capt. Nichols when
he saw the arrival [notice] said she was the ship we passed at this time
and he was certain of it at the time and was very uneasy for fear we
would give chase.

Whittle's decision to ask Captain Nichols to identify this particular barque—owned by his wife's brother—seems almost to smack of psychic intervention. More likely, it was pure coincidence. The lieutenant was being his characteristically thorough self, checking out any and all possible sources of information on the enemy (and, in this case, all sources that would confirm his harsh judgment of Waddell). Nichols, for his part, no doubt rejoiced at being able to shock the lieutenant with the provenance of this prey, now that it was safely out of sight.

In any case, Whittle backdated this bit of information, appending it to his January 23 log after an asterisk. His point was as unmistakable as it was subtle: his commanding officer, Captain James I. Waddell, had made a serious error in judgment, and in doing so had let a lucrative Yankee prize escape unchallenged. His asterisk referred to the line he'd entered on the twenty-third—"Which I took to be a Yankee."

Later, as the Nichols family at last took its leave from the anchored ship, Mrs. Nichols hissed a few choice words at Conway Whittle. The would-be seductress had somehow lost her interest in flirtation. "Mrs. Nichols, on leaving the ship, said she was very much obliged by our kindness," wrote Whittle with obvious bewilderment, "but hoped that we would sink at sea in six months. She said she liked all the officers except Dr. Lining and myself." Ruefully, he confessed, "I thought I was a piece of chicken for her. Anyway, I was very kind to her."

What Whittle did not know was that the Nicholses made straight for the office of the U.S. consul, William Blanchard, in the company of some dozen other souls from *Delphine*. Captain Nichols summarized their status as *Shenandoah* prisoners and told Blanchard of the parole documents they'd all signed: documents that bound them not to reveal information about the Confederates. The captain struggled to remain true to the letter of his parole terms; but Mrs. Nichols, seldom at a loss for conversation, disgorged everything she had seen, heard, and experienced. Soon the other former prisoners loosened up as well, giving detailed information about *Shenandoah*'s weaponry, the number and makeup of her crew—even the inscriptions on her silverware. Blanchard jotted it all down, and then quickly wrote a pair of letters. The first, dashed off in time to make the departing mail packet, was to Charles Francis Adams in London, recounting everything he'd learned in the depositions. A copy of this letter went to the U.S. consul in Hong Kong, 4,600 miles to the north-northwest, pleading for a Yankee gunboat to come and reduce the raider.

Blanchard wrote a separate letter to Governor Darling, asking him to seize the ship for "piratical acts."[14]

❦

For *Shenandoah*'s crew, the day brightened immediately with the arrival of fresh fruits and vegetables. Boatloads of produce converged on the ship. The *Shenandoah* men had not bitten into anything but hardtack that crunched under their teeth, or squirted juice down their chins, for four months. Whittle seemed in some danger of gaining a few more pounds.

> *Oh how I did enjoy my first fresh meal. I am no epicure but that is not necessary to make one after four months at sea, enjoy something fresh.*

A few days later, an emboldened Waddell sent a letter to the Commissioner of Trade and Customs requesting even more: he wanted fresh meat, vegetables, bread, brandy, rum, champagne, port, sherry, beer, porter, molasses, lime juice—and "light material for summer wear for my men." He added, with elegant counterfeit remorse, "I have to communicate that all those persons whom, on the high seas, I considered my prisoners . . . left the ship without my knowledge, in shore boats."[15]

Their bellies sated (along with God knew what else, during shore leave), the crew received its orders to commence the ship's repairs. Chief among these tasks was the caulking. The wooden sides of nineteenth-century ships absorbed tremendous battering from ocean

waves and the warping effects of rain followed by bright sunshine. The
Cape rollers alone had torqued many of *Shenandoah*'s decking boards
out of alignment. Small rows of kneeling crewmen, carefully spaced,
now crept along the decks, fore and aft, performing the rhythmic yet
potentially dangerous task. The first row of men, wielding short mauls,
sharpened bevel gouges, and cleaning hooks, teased out the weakened
tar-and-sisal caulk tucked between the great slats of teak decking. The
second line, also on their knees in the sun, played out the fibrous new
caulk from warm forty-pound rolls. Twisting over the strands of pun-
gent, greasy brown hemp, basically flattened strands of untwisted rope
called "oakum" that had steeped in congealed preservative, the sailors
drove the new caulk in using wide, flat-faced chisels and strange, short-
handled caulker's hammers with huge iron-bound wooden heads the
size of rolling pins. Behind the kneeling men then came the hot-tar
crew. Using a portable brazier and kettle, one crewman would tend and
dispense a steady supply of molten tar, which greatly increased the
task's hazards. The whole process involved a rapid, coordinated system
of scooping, chiseling, and hammering. The fresh caulk was driven into
the spaces opened up by the removal of the old stuff. Everything, indeed their very lives, depended on how expertly the new oakum-
soaked rope was folded and then lined up precisely just within the
cavity between boards to await the tamping-in knocks of hammer and
chisel. Once the caulk depth was precisely set, it was the tar man's task
to "pay in" the near-boiling liquid to the remaining cavity, filling over
the caulk, and waterproofing the joint. He used a big blackened
witch's-hat funnel with a spout just the size of the crack, and he had to
work with his head down, not stopping until he ran empty. Before the
tar had set, stepping on it was worse than stepping in fresh cement.

The caulkers were well used to the demands and the dangers of
their job. They were not so used to an audience and being appraised by
hundreds of pairs of wondering eyes. By this day, *Shenandoah* had become a tourist attraction, a kind of working model of itself. The
throngs of visitors were so thick, Conway Whittle noted, that "the
caulkers had to give their mallets a good swing as the only means of
getting on with their work." This "good swing," he was too polite to
add, was a means of clearing out the vicinity.

No doubt a hammer or two found its fleshy mark. Whittle estimated that a thousand gawkers roamed the raider at a given moment. They came and went on little steamers that advertised one shilling for a ride out to the ship—and another shilling for the ride back. "These crowds are composed of all sorts—men, women, children, the lame and deaf all bound to see the ship," he wrote. "If I had said once that 'it's the 32 pounder of 5700 weight; this is a rifle gun,' I have said it 50 times. I am polite to all but as often as possible I excuse myself from showing them around as the Captain is ashore."

This last may have been entered as a muted complaint. James Waddell had vamoosed the ship early in the day, when the vamoosing was good, and left his lieutenant to play the tour guide. He'd hitched a ride in Nichols's launch to pay an official visit on Governor Darling in his mansion. The governor proved to be not at home. He had perhaps misunderstood the time of the meeting—or perhaps he had not. Almost certainly, Captain James Waddell, CSN, was the last person he wanted to see in his office.

Tensions between the two men were soon to grow worse.

⚜

The following day, Saturday, the twenty-eighth, the mania over *Shenandoah*'s arrival worsened as well.

During the whole day the ship has been thronged with visitors of all ages, sexes and conditions of life. The ship is entirely in their possession as they roam all over in and about her. I am thoroughly disgusted and tired and wish we were out of this place. I thought the crowding could not continue without some accident. Today a boat with three men and one woman in it capsized. They were all fished out with no damage except a cold dunking. I never saw anything like the sensation which our ship has created. People have come from points at various distances from one mile to 300 hundred miles in the country to see the ship. All these people have the same questions to ask and receive the same answers. And when I told several that I did not expect to see so many visitors, they consoled me saying, "This is nothing to what you can expect tomorrow."

Many of the Melbourne men who clambered aboard the ship had more than sightseeing on their minds. Like small boys plotting to run away and join the circus, these citizens flattered themselves that for merely volunteering, they might soon be setting sail and braving the salt spray alongside the glamorous raiders. "We could get here 5,000 men as there is not a day passes that we have not application after application," Whittle noted. He added sternly, "We will not and cannot violate the neutrality of the port and the same answer, that is, we cannot ship them, is given to all."

As the numbers of prospective crewmen soared, however, the number of actual crewmen began a slight but suspicious decline. Whittle noticed that not all hands were reporting back from their shore liberty on time. They could hardly be blamed. The city of 180,000 had thrown itself into an uproar of adulation over these men—these nameless, hard-laboring tars of the world's great vacant seas, who suddenly found themselves lionized as living legends. Those who could muster up a gray dress uniform trimmed in gold allowed themselves an extra measure of prance. "Our stay in Melbourne was one round of pleasure and honors," one hand later recalled. They were showered with free railroad passes to any point in the country. The most exclusive club in the city, the Melbourne Club, elected them members, and transformed itself into a kind of Rick's Café to the southerners. The great curly-haired Shakespearean actor Barry Sullivan, then performing in *Othello,* honored the men with a special performance heralded by banners that read, UNDER THE DISTINGUISHED PATRONAGE OF THE OFFICERS OF THE CONFEDERATE STEAMSHIP SHENANDOAH. "There we looked down upon an auditorium packed to suffocation as we sat in the royal box," the seaman recalled.[16]

Whittle knew that Melbourne's orgy of hospitality for the Confederates was far from unanimous. Sprinkled through the crowded pubs and streets and train stations, and perhaps even on *Shenandoah's* teeming decks, lurked dangerous enemies. "Yankee sympathizers and Consul are using every inducement to strip us of men," he wrote.

The highest rewards are offered to any and all who will defect. The general underhanded rascality which characterizes them as a nation is

showing itself here in the individuals who reside here and who come
from the U.S. The Consul is now said to have some of our men at
boarding houses defraying all their expenses.

This was true. Employing instincts that in a later century would be associated with powerhouse football coaches and corporate head-hunters, the U.S. consul had turned himself into a recruiter in reverse: Blanchard had been seeking out crewmen from the Rebel ship as they roistered through the city, and putting them up in hotels and guest rooms at his expense—even offering them inducement money. His aim was to "liberate" these men, as he explained in a letter to the American secretary of state, William Seward, and coax them away from the ship, thus reducing her already understaffed crew.[17]

James Waddell was seethingly aware of this effort—a travesty of honor, by his lights—and the memory of it rankled him for the rest of his life. He fumed in his memoirs that "the abortive efforts to discredit the character and officers and crew of the ship . . . had, as was openly asserted, been followed by the still more unworthy course of tamper-ing with the allegiance of the crew."[18]

By Saturday the fragile goodwill between *Shenandoah* and official Melbourne had begun to crumble. Governor Darling had made it clear, in giving his permission for the ship to remain in port, that he wanted the repairs and resupplying done as quickly as possible. But now the officers had gauged the full extent of the nec-essary work. The damaged rudder, the worn-out sails and ropes, the rattle-prone pintle, the weak places in the hull that caulking could not restore—it was shaping up to be a month's worth of labor. Not only that: *Shenandoah* might well have to be dry-docked. And the only dry docks available for such work belonged to Her Majesties government.

Diplomatic tensions. Shrieking hordes of visitors running riot on his decks. A ship badly in need of overhauling. And once again the hidden menace of enemy agents, as sinister as any on the docks of Liv-erpool or London. Little wonder that Whittle's nerves were stretched to the limit by Sunday, a day in which the visitors had all but turned his ship into a nautical theme park.

All I can say today is that I have been harassed almost to death. The ship has been a perfect mass of human beings. The rail, rigging and masts have been crowded and filled. There were so many that steamer load after steamer load had to shove off as they could not find an inch to land on. I really feared the ship would burst.

On top of that, rumors circulated of a breakdown in discipline.

I learned that two of our men were ashore in jail for debt and sent Mr. Alcott with a note for the Chief of Police asking for their release and a bill for their debts.

The report of the jailed sailors proved false. It also proved that the rumor mill in the city was running at full power. How to sort the truth from the fiction?

As for the calming, motivating presence of the commanding officer:

The Captain is out of the ship and has been all day. Everything falls on me and the officers whose duties keep them here. Oh how I wish we were once more at sea.

And then Whittle added a chilling entry, a confirmation of his earlier anxieties:

We have received warning that the Yanks are determined to destroy our ship by some means. These may be boastful and empty threats, but they are of such a dangerous nature that we are all on the alert.

With that entry, Conway Whittle's journal falls silent for twenty-one days—days that saw *Shenandoah*'s presence in Melbourne grow ever more imperiled by hostility official and otherwise; days of violence between crewmen and townsfolk; days that carried the Rebels to the brink of a shooting war with the city's police and soldiers.

A guided inspection of the province's new Parliament buildings, still scaffolded by their builders; a widely noted visit to the Legislative Assembly; a formal dinner in their honor at the Melbourne Club on January 27—these events marked the peak of the warm feelings between Melbourne society and the *Shenandoah* officers. But anti-Southern sentiment in the city was growing bolder by the day in its repudiation of the Confederates: a Melbourne newspaper derided as "soft-headed flunkeys" the members who'd opened the Melbourne Club's doors to them.[19] Things began to fall apart rather quickly after that.

Even amid the balls, tours, and dinners that continued to pamper them, the officers encountered moments of jarring hostility. Midshipman John Mason and Lieutenant Scales endured angry glares from several worshipers at a Church of England service on the twenty-ninth. The hostility got physical. At dinner at Scott's Hotel, a group of the officers was interrupted by a wild-eyed local citizen, who pushed his way to the table and commenced an abusive denunciation of the Confederacy. Rebuttal came in the form of a hard punch to the jaw thrown by *Shenandoah*'s hot-tempered assistant surgeon, Frederich J. McNulty—a punch that ignited a general crockery-cracking brawl. Mason, who was among those present, later blamed the entire episode on McNulty, who in fact was a vicious man when drunk. The Irish-born assistant surgeon, Mason wrote in his diary, exemplified the glut of "good for nothing fellows that we were compelled to make officers for want of others."[20]

The tension surrounding the Confederates increased as repairs to *Shenandoah* dragged slowly on. Waddell had initially led the nervous Darling to believe that the raider would be at sea again after only a few days in port, but an underwater inspection of the ship, performed by divers, revealed deep structural damage that could not be ignored. The propeller was on the verge of separating from the ship; its casings, which kept the shaft in place, were gone, and its wooden bracings showed serious rot. Beyond that, worn-out rigging begged for replacement, and the hull revealed problems that routine maintenance could not restore. The only option available to allow the necessary repairs was the government-owned dry dock.

Great Britain herself would now be wielding the hammers and bolts.

Unless, that is, a paper-thin technicality proved enough cover. A private marine engineering firm called Langland Brothers & Co. leased the dock that the government owned. Perhaps this would satisfy the rules of neutrality. On February 4, workers began offloading *Shenandoah*'s stores. The work stretched over five days. Not until the ninth was the crippled raider floated to the dry dock so that the repair work could begin.

Now the Rebels were without any means of escape should once-adoring Melbourne or any of its denizens, public or private, decide to move against them. And in fact, Whittle's suspicions were more accurate than he knew. Such a move had already been made. The Confederates never saw it coming.

10

The plan had taken shape aboard a Union merchant ship, *Mustang*, out of New York. *Mustang* was anchored in Hobson's Bay when *Shenandoah* arrived, and its captain and crew took an instant loathing to the cruiser flying its Confederate colors. After a few days of staring across the water at the Rebels with helpless hatred, the Yankee ship's captain and a few of his crewmen decided to take action of a decidedly unmerchantlike nature. They rigged up a torpedo containing 250 pounds of gunpowder. A cocked pistol was fitted onto the bomb's exterior, with a long line connecting the trigger to the hand of a *Mustang* crewman.

Late on a January night, Yankee crewmen gingerly lowered the torpedo into a longboat. A small crew rowed softly and slowly in *Shenandoah*'s direction. They escaped the notice of the three guards that Waddell had posted. They laid the device in the calm water alongside the raider's hull and slipped back to their own ship.

The line broke; the torpedo never exploded. No one aboard *Shenandoah* ever learned how close their ship had come to destruction.[21]

After that, no one sought to attack the ship again; yet by mid-February a bomb of a different sort was set to explode. Constant prodding by the infuriated Consul Blanchard began to take its effect on Governor Darling, who initiated an official procedure that would compel the raider back to sea. Blanchard's detestation of Captain Waddell and his Confederate crew had increased after the arrival in his office of yet another disaffected *Shenandoah* refugee. This was, once again, John Williams, the defiant Negro cook who'd come aboard from *Godfrey,* and whom Whittle had repeatedly punished for insolence and neglect of duty.

Williams had been punished most recently just a few days earlier—clapped in irons—by Lt. Sidney Smith Lee, for drunkenness. Upon being released, Williams boldly stole away to the ship's railing, jumped over, and swam to shore. He asked directions to the U.S. consulate, and shocked Blanchard with detailed descriptions of the punishments he'd endured. When he added the information that some twenty Melbourne men had lately joined the Rebel crew, Blanchard launched a flurry of letters at Darling, demanding action.

The governor in turn urged the Melbourne police to board *Shenandoah* and search for the Australian men—who, Darling charged, had violated the Foreign Enlistment Act by signing on. The police twice approached the drydocked ship. They were turned away, first by Lieutenant Grimball, and then by Captain Waddell himself. Darling then escalated the stakes by moving to revoke *Shenandoah's* privilege of remaining in port.

On February 14, two hundred Melbourne policemen descended on the Langland Brothers dockyards. They were accompanied by fifty soldiers. Guns drawn, they surrounded the gangway and the timbers that braced the ship, held now out of the water entirely by wooden supports. They immediately shut down all work—which was by now virtually finished. The police renewed the governor's demand that the raider be searched. Waddell was livid. His ship was a vessel of war, and was "part of the territory" of the country to which she belonged. No civil authority had a right to breach this territory.

"Having abided strictly by the terms of neutrality imposed during my visit," he later wrote, "I asserted that the privileges of a vessel of war should remain intact."[22] He offered to order his own ship's police—"viz., the master-at-arms and his posse"—to make a search. The Melbourne officials brushed that offer aside. Waddell ordered the search anyway: "The [men] reported to me they had looked throughout the vessel and found no strangers. They had examined even the coal bunker."

Waddell conferred with Lieutenants Lee, Grimball, and Whittle, and several hours later issued a letter that repeated his refusal to allow an outside search. He ordered the crew to take up positions to repel boarders.

Though his ship's police had taken up defensive positions onboard, Waddell understood that *Shenandoah*'s plight was dire, as she sat helplessly high and dry. "If an attack was made, the attacking party would have knocked away the props, and the vessel would have fallen from the slip and been rendered a hopeless ruin."[23]

A tense night passed with no action. But Rebel crewmen had by now quietly completed all the details of repair that the Aussie workman had been obliged to abandon. *Shenandoah* was ready to sail.

The following day, Waddell surprised Governor Darling with a brilliant, if all-or-nothing, gambit: the Melbourne police presence, he informed the official, constituted a de facto seizure of the ship. If seizure was Governor Darling's intention—why, then, he, Captain Waddell, would surrender ship and crew. And the Melbourne governor would be left with a belligerent nation's ship on his hands—and a likely diplomatic confrontation with the Confederate States of America.

Darling wanted nothing of the kind. He wanted only to see the damned Rebel raider out of his docks, out of his harbor, out of his life. He revoked his orders to block the ship's departure. At 5:30 p.m. on February 15, the repaired, refitted, and rejuvenated *Shenandoah* floated out of dry dock on a high tide and anchored in the bay. She was resupplied with coal and provisions the day after that, and three days later *Shenandoah*'s uneven Australian idyll was behind her, as she steamed once more into the global sea.

⚜

"I trust that the dull monotony of beating to windward will be relieved by catching a Yank," Whittle wrote with his customary chops-licking brio as his log resumed on February 20—at sea once again.

Life was back to normal at last—better than normal, actually. The crew was looking robust and fleshed-out after a month's dining on Melbourne's finest produce and cuisine, and the raider herself had been restored to her maiden-voyage seaworthiness: renewed copper hull firmly in place, boards recaulked, rudder and prop in good repair, her storehouses bulging with quantities of food, water, medicines, and ammunition.

A neatly carpentered new galley now graced the berth deck beneath the main deck, sealed off from the weather. The change made it possible to dismantle an awkwardly nailed-together pile of boards that had offended Whittle's eye for order since the beginning. The ugly shack had stood on the spar deck forward, and had served as a cook's galley and miniature mess hall. As Whittle well knew, the structure could serve as something else entirely in combat: as shrapnel, if an enemy ball hit and splintered it. Ordering it cleared from the decks may have been a sign that Whittle believed the chances were increasing for such an encounter.

Shenandoah was presently bounding along off the headlands of Cape Howe at the southern tip of Australia, at latitude 38.15 south, longitude 149.37 east—smack in the Yankee merchant-freight lanes. She was at last turning her prow northward, and ultimately toward the great whaling fields near the Arctic Circle.

Her globe-circling mission would now entail three additional legs, each one alone roughly the distance she'd covered from the London docks to Melbourne. It would consume ten more months, virtually all of it out of contact with the world.

The cause for which she sailed would be lost within six weeks.

Half a world from that onrushing debacle, the revitalized *Shenandoah* enjoyed a new beginning, filled with hopeful portents. For the first time, James Waddell and Conway Whittle enjoyed the luxury of a full crew—ninety-six hands, more than the raider had held at any time since she ran up her colors, even with prisoners. Many of these men had seemingly materialized out of thin air once the ship had crossed the Rip and put Port Phillip Bay behind her. Actually, they'd crept into the sunlight from assorted dark corners below decks: the irreducible hard core of the many Melbourne men who'd begged to sign on with the Confederates. These new hands seemed equal to their tasks, Whittle noted, but "they have been stowed away so long it is hard to give them enough to eat. After we get them well filled up we will be all right."

The strangest and most enigmatic newcomer to *Shenandoah*'s

company had not stowed away; he had volunteered to join the crew as a marine at Melbourne, and Waddell accepted him on board—along with his personal servant, a Negro named Edward Weeks—and granted him the rank of sergeant. This gothic figure called himself George P. Canning, and claimed to have served on the staff of the Confederate general Leonidas Polk. He'd been wounded at Shiloh, Canning maintained—shot through the right lung.

Exactly how George Canning had made it to Australia, he preferred not to say. He was cryptic about nearly all the details of his life, in fact. He'd hinted that he had traveled to Europe after suffering his wound, in the company of his wife, and then to Australia without her; but he refused to give any details. Few of his new shipmates liked him. "He was an ungrateful man," the surgeon Lining later wrote, "never thinking that any one did him a favor by doing any thing for him, but rather that all things should be done for him, no matter what it might cost others. He quarreled with every one who had much to do with him, & was generally very abusive in his epithets." His manservant Weeks came in for particular browbeating, but remained quietly loyal to his master. Canning suffered a relapse several days into the voyage, and remained bedridden thereafter.

On February 22, Lieutenant Whittle marked a date already enshrined in American history. In so doing, he gave voice once again to the painful division in his heart, and in the hearts of so many of his fellow Confederates—the division of loyalty between his beloved America and his embattled South. On February 22, he wrote:

This is the 130th anniversary of the birth of George Washington, Virginia's Washington. And how sad is the thought that the very spot where 130 years ago this "father of our country was born" is now flooded with blood of his countrymen fighting against hordes of the North for principles and rights, for the protection of which he is this day hailed by these very hordes . . . and his birthday celebrated as no doubt that [of] old Abe will be if the vandals are successful. These miserable Yankees are fighting against the very rights which they thought so sacred in the Revolution. Nothing but a desire to gain wealth induces them to do it. They will sacrifice everything for money. Principle, life and honor. I regard them individually and collectively as a pack of scoundrels consummated in every variety to rascality.

On a happier note, he added,

This day is another great national one in that our dear President [Jefferson Davis] was inaugurated the 22nd of February, 1862. I can only celebrate it by drinking a glass of sherry, doing my duty, and praying for the triumph of the cause which our noble Jefferson Davis represents.

And finally,

This day is also one of private importance as it is the birthday of my dear Jennie [his sister] who is on this day 21 years of age. I can scarcely realize that such is the case. Only a short time since and I thought and looked upon her as a little child.

God grant me many happy returns of this the anniversary of our first father's birth and of the inauguration of our first President and second father.

The mundane trials of shipboard life once again dragged him down from these lofty musings. The troublesome drunk this time was the officers' cook, James Marlowe, who'd perhaps over-sampled the cooking sherry. "Got the devil in him and then came neglect of duty and then oh dear, the severest punishments he ever heard of." As usual, doling out the penalty hurt Whittle as much as it hurt the offender to receive it—nearly as much, anyway. "I punish myself when I punish one of the men who I know would stand by me at any time. But I rule or he; both cannot. And I take the shortest, severest, and surest way of proving to him that I and not he must govern."

A far darker threat to *Shenandoah*'s governance resurfaced on the following day. James Waddell, his fragile personality unraveling again, unleashed a series of open assaults on Whittle's executive authority.

I do not like at all the way in which things are being conducted. Of all men I ever saw, Waddell has the most provoking way of meddling. I do not know half the time what is being done in the ship as he gives orders which should either emanate from or pass through me. This way of doing business does not suit me and it must be stopped.

But this time Waddell was not simply wreaking havoc with the chain of command. The older officer had in effect sneered at Conway Whittle's manhood.

I will not allow myself to be treated as though I was a boy. I am no boy and claim that I am quite as qualified to perform my duty as he is to perform his.

A more reckless provocation could hardly be imagined. Perhaps still seething over being stared down by Whittle during the December 13 storm, the erratic captain now stalked *Shenandoah's* deck spewing random orders that impugned Whittle's competence as an officer. The ship's crew, a virtual millwheel of rumor and intrigue in the best of times, and teeming with the new, inquisitive hands from Melbourne, now carried an overload of grist for seditious speculation. On a voyage that had already eluded several perils and currently faced several more, Waddell was bidding fair to do the Yankees' work for them.

What to do about it? The lieutenant wrestled with the question. *Treated as though he were a boy?!* Any other officer of his youth and stature—daredevil hero of the *Nashville's* escapades, distinguished combatant aboard CSS *Louisiana* at the Battle of New Orleans, icy-nerved survivor of the lethal Union spy network in Paris, Liverpool, and London—might have lashed back. Perhaps he might have demanded satisfaction for this besmirching of his honor—and, in so doing, risked anarchy aboard ship and a likely court-martial.

Whittle held his fury in check. As he had in past crises, the lieutenant placed the interests of his ship above his personal interests. He searched for a rationale for his restraint, and found one, under the rubric of gallantry.

Nothing but my remembrance of his sweet little wife's last request has prevented my having had an open rupture with him.

Then Whittle added a thought that seemed rooted in the essence of his Christian faith, specifically in the matter of "charity."

I know his good points as well as his bad and I know that few persons can understand him better than I. He is impulsive, weak and vacillating, going always by extremes. I will wait and try to let him come to without a break. I feel the importance of our being on perfectly good terms. But if he throws up the gauntlet, what can I do. I humbly pray that he may see his error.

This particular prayer went unanswered. Waddell's erratic behavior continued unabated. If hope for shipboard order remained, it lay in the fact that James Waddell was growing increasingly isolated. On Saturday, February 25, as the ship raced 240 miles northeast in front of a perfect wind, Whittle ruefully, but with impressive psychological acuity, noted:

The cloud which on yesterday I represented as hanging over the harmony of the ship still remains. The captain all day has had the appearance of a man who had lost all his friends and was all day as dignified as weak men become when dignity ceases to be a good quality.

He went on,

Poor W. I pity him with all my heart but I will never feel the kindly friendship for him which he knows I have felt. He has treated me in a manner which he knows is unworthy of him and he knows it but he has not the moral force to come to or send for me and say, Whittle I have been wrong. I am very, very sorry for him.

Whittle then paraphrased Goldsmith: "With all his faults I love him still." He reaffirmed his promise to Mrs. Waddell, and lamented that because of it, "I am a great sufferer." Still, "with him is the fault and <u>with him the cure</u>. I trust he will come to his better self."

Some shrewdness lay alongside the simple humanity in these lines. Conway Whittle never lost sight of the fact that his log was not just a personal document: its primary function was official. As such, it would likely be presented as evidence into any naval hearing, should matters escalate into an open test of power. Whittle knew, as well, that Waddell had now lost the support of the other lieutenants—the cream of the junior officers, and the most distinguished veterans of combat, save for Whittle himself.

James Waddell, in short, had painted himself into a corner. The only remaining question was this: How dangerous was a cornered James Waddell?

Shenandoah turned more sharply toward the north now, leaving the Tasman Sea, and making for the sea lanes of the South Pacific. Her velocity slowed a bit in the face of a strong wind from the north and a powerful current running against her. She managed 122 miles on February 26, but her reduced progress was offset by refreshing tropical temperatures—refreshing, tending toward hot. "This has been as lovely a day as I have ever beheld," Whittle wrote on February 26. He conceded that "the middle portion was terribly hot, so much so that the pitch boiled out of our deck." Despite the long ribbons of syrupy tar oozing out of the freshly caulked joints, Whittle was still pleased by the weekly inspection and general muster: "We have a fine crew, all able bodied men and good seamen."

Yet that tropical sun had its lingering impediments: "There is a dark cloud which overhangs us and she is not the happy ship she might to be. Our C is still in the dumps. His conversation unless absolutely on duty is with his clerk. Why, what is the matter with him?"

Whittle answered himself—again, with some diagnostic acuity: "Alas! I fear it is irrational. I did not know him before."

The young lieutenant consoled himself that evening as he so often did—by reading the now well-worn letters of his sweetheart, Pattie. But before turning in, he made one final entry, and damned James

Waddell with an appraisal whose insulting power only a true Southerner might have understood. "As long as the war lasts, I . . . will put
up with anything and will sacrifice everything for my country's cause,"
he began, and then struck: "My great fear is that W's foolishness will
impair the service of the ship."

Conway Whittle had called James Waddell a fool. A worse condemnation scarcely existed. But "toxic fool," had the term existed,
might have applied.

February 27 found a grumpy, exhausted Whittle mired in drudgework, supervising the straightening up of tons of barrels, crates, kegs,
and bundles that lay helter-skelter about the fore and aft holds.
"I never saw a ship stowed as badly as this one was at Melbourne," he
groused. "The things were simply dumped in without any kind of
care." Casualties included the rum barrels, which had leaked most of
their contents. Whittle understood the severity of this loss. "There is
nothing which conduces more to the contentment of the crew than
the ration of grog." His familiar frustrated craving for action with the
enemy grew again in him. "We have not seen a single sail since we
have been out and it is becoming very dull. How anxious I am to catch
a Yankee."

Still, the largest source of anxiety remained the Captain.

*W is still in the dumps. He is the weakest man I ever saw in my life.
He goes from pity, to concern for fear of irrationality, to disdain—the
weakest man I ever saw in my life. I begin to think that he is under
the foolish impression that in order to retain the respect of the officers,
he must cease to have anything to say to them except absolutely on
duty. He has gone so far with me that all his orders are even written.*

Then Whittle added a little tit-for-tat dig:

This is a childish foolishness that a boy of ten would be ashamed of.

The name-calling probably provided little satisfaction. It certainly
was no answer for the awful suspicion that was growing in Whittle's
mind: that James Iredell Waddell was going insane.

The situation deteriorated almost by the hour. An entry for Tuesday, February 28, the fifth day of the captain's deep-freeze: "W's dumps continue. I am entirely at a loss to understand this man who I once thought I knew." And then, cryptically: "I will not put any two opinions on paper but his conduct proves to me that he is one of two things. What these things are I withhold."

Whittle did not withhold his concern for the effects of such "things":

> *I am fearful that his conduct to me will not go unnoticed by the crew,*
> *upon whom it could have no other than a bad effect. I trust it will*
> *[change], for I consider that it is more incumbent on the Captain and*
> *First Lieutenant to keep upon good terms than everyone else. These*
> *two as a nucleus is all, but without them we will I fear be adrift. The*
> *Captain now not only does not speak to me privately but does not <u>even*
> *speak</u> to me officially. I am fearful that the efficiency of the ship will*
> *suffer. For our country's sake I hope not.*

That was Conway Whittle the Southern patriot and professional naval officer speaking. But always, within this exceedingly complex young man, several other versions of himself constantly vied for expression. The death-defying blockade runner, the vengeful prison-camp survivor, the gleeful torcher of enemy merchant ships, jostled with the strict moralist who respected human life, and gave ships of questionable nationality the benefit of the doubt. The icy-hearted Yankee-hater gave way to the humane steward of Yankee prisoners, especially their womenfolk. The unhesitant tricer of troublesome crewmen agonized over the need for inflicting pain. The committed paladin of the seas melded into the nighttime romantic, pining for pastoral Virginia, his family, the half-dreamed affections of the sweetheart he had met only once.

And always, within this absent commodore's son, who had been thrust into military manhood at age fourteen, and who bridled at his captain's taunts of immaturity, there yet beat the heart of the eternal Boy.

Now, on an ocean blank of enemy ships and nearly blank of weather, aboard a ship subdued by the emerging blankness of James

Waddell's affect—into this atmosphere of torpor and lost passion, the Boy crept out of Conway Whittle's depths and dreamed a bold, none-such escapade. On March 1, Whittle set in words a daring idea—one almost unimaginable in the thoughts of the dutiful lieutenant. He'd talked it over already with his best shipboard friends: they would escape *Shenandoah* and Waddell together, and go roving the seas with Whittle in command of his own raider!

The notion began out of exasperation. "We are still jogging along in what is said to be the track of the Yankee whalers and we have not seen a single sail," he wrote on that day. "I think it looks very much as though we were out of the regular track. One thing is certain, either we are out of the track or they are. I am getting tired of so much sailing to no purpose . . ."

And then the full pipe dream emerged:

. . . but I feel that tomorrow we will make our first prize. I would like it to be a fast barque of about 400 tons [about a third *Shenandoah's* size] *with double topsail yards, and I would make application to take charge of her. A vessel of that description fitted out here would do quite as much damage as the* Shenandoah *and the probability of capture would be very remote as we could pass right through a Yankee fleet without suspicion. Oh how I would glory in such a chance. I would either call her the Dixie, the Norfolk, or the Tudor. God grant me this blessing. Lee, Scales and Bulloch are all applicants for any vessel that I am placed in command of. In fact, I could take any of them as all would like to go.*

These three battle-tested lieutenants, the cream of the officers' corps, were as aware as Whittle of the giant clock ticking away the Confederacy's survival hopes, as avid as he to renew the assault on the powerful enemy, and as out of patience with Captain Waddell's zombie-like condition.

Whittle would return to this far-fetched fantasy many times in ensuing weeks. He seemed to find a psychic renewal in its dashing concept: a means of vaulting over inertia, a growing despair for his nation, and the growing strangeness of his co-commanding officer. He kept the idea alive even after it appeared that James Iredell Waddell was edging back into the world.

"The Captain has come out in new colors," Whittle wrote on that same day, "and has spoken to all but me. I should have been first but I suppose he will try me [further]. His treatment of me has been very outrageous and he has lost in me as good a friend as he ever had or will have."

Refocused (for the time) on the raider's mission, Whittle directed a test of the pair of rifled guns, likely operational now, thanks to parts acquired as part of the refitting at Melbourne. "They behaved splendidly." *Shenandoah* was thus assured of a potent new level of response to a hostile warship. Rifled guns ranked near the top of the many upgrades in weaponry generated by the Civil War. Far superior to the old ball-lobbing capacities of earlier smooth-bore cannon, these pieces propelled a spinning, pointed, exploding, projectile at lightning velocity on an almost flat trajectory, taking accuracy and destructive power to new orders of magnitude.

All the raider needed now was an enemy to shoot at.

But no enemy appeared in the ocean around her. No warship, no merchantman. Not even a neutral sail. The days passed. The weeks. The weather remained balmy, the northeasterly sailing smooth. Whittle ordered the spar deck recaulked and pitched. Then he looked for other tasks to order. The days lengthened. Latitude and longitude shifted. No sail. A third assistant engineer named McGuffney and a fireman named Rawlinson got drunk. Mr. O'Brien investigated, and found that the bulkhead in one of the storage rooms had been forced back. "Through this, they had bored a hole in the cask and had a regular spree." A gunner's mate named Crawford was insolent to Whittle, and Whittle triced him. After two hours, Crawford could not guarantee he would keep a civil tongue; politeness did not set in for another five. Was a certain defiance taking hold among the shipboard miscreants? Were the crewmen testing Whittle's limits? His manhood? There was no real way of telling. The days passed. The ocean surface remained empty of sails. "I cannot tell why, but I do not like it."

James Waddell's return to semi-civil behavior proved short-lived. "W's dumps continue. I do not understand them." Few people would until 1886, when a German psychiatrist named Emil Kraepelin began to classify patterns of such behavior under the rubric "bipolar disorder." Meanwhile, more-commonplace afflictions beset Whittle: "I have been quite sick all day."

The ocean itself began to turn moody. On March 4—Lincoln's Inauguration Day—the waves roiled up at latitude 25.08 south, longitude 170 east; the propeller was hoisted. "I think that we will have a heavy gale out of this fellow." The gale arrived with nightfall; a sea abreast the fore-rigging stove in some of the bulwark and capsized one of the new rifle guns. The gale worsened over the next few days, but by Thursday, March 9, the sun was out again. "Oh what a joyous thing is a pleasant day after a heavy gale." Then the sun itself became a problem. "The heat of the day has been terrible and the pitch from our seams would scarcely allow you to walk on deck. Oh, how I wish we could catch a Yankee."

Well over 1,500 miles off the Australian coast now, but still far south of the equator. Windless. Under steam again. Days spent repairing damage from the gale; bulwarks, rigging, sails. Tedium. On March 11, engaged in the delicate chore of reaming out the damp fuse-holes of the shells and refilling them with dry powder, Whittle let his thoughts drift back to his fantasy ship:

I am quite in love with chances of getting a little vessel on my own hook. I do not care how soon my time comes for I am very anxious to have a second craft in these seas. I care not for distinction or anything except such as is to be won by doing my duty in my country's call. I am sure that with one gun a vessel such as I desire could do fine work before her existence was known. As soon as it became at all likely that a Yankee cruiser was informed of my approximate whereabouts, I would take a long cruise to distant parts.

Parts unfrequented by Yankees, or, say, the likes of James Waddell. Whittle had grown so invested in the idea by now that he risked letting Waddell in on it. Waddell (perhaps not surprisingly) signaled his eagerness to wish the breakaway lieutenants bon voyage. "I would prefer a smart little barque of about 600 or 500 tons," Whittle jotted on March 12, with the dreamy wistfulness of a boy composing a letter to Saint Nicholas; then added, revealingly, "as the captain has promised to give me the command of any vessel which would suit."

The Boy in him dreamed how it would be:

> *If I get such a command I shall be very circumspect. I will form all of my plans and will confide in none but my executive officer. This would be not because I would not trust [the other officers]—but people will talk and speculate among themselves. And as soon as they talk among themselves they will be less and less cautious and any prisoners we might have would get hold of information as to our movements and we would find a Yankee cruiser on the "qui vive."*

How these prisoners would communicate this information to a distant Yankee ship, the Boy did not say. Perhaps it was all a way, a Boy's way, of coping with the chilly withdrawal of his shipboard father-figure. The Boy would, by God, give his fellow renegades a dose of this same medicine!

However, as *Shenandoah* ventured farther into the warm equatorial climates—temperatures in the high eighties by March 13, at a latitude of only 18 degrees south—it was a man's work, rather than a boy's fantasies, that regained Conway Whittle's attention. "I never knew what work was when I came in this ship," he wrote on that day, as he pitched in on restoring the fore and after holds and filling more shells with fresh powder.

> *When I consider how much devolves on me, and how unsatisfactory to myself my best endeavors are, I feel blue. But with the steady, stern re- solve to do my best I drive ahead, and it is only when I look back and see how much I have done, that I feel at all content.*

And then concerns of a far weightier nature descended on him. The realization struck on March 14 that within weeks, *Shenandoah* stood to lose most of her original crewmen, the most skilled and reliable of all hands—petty officers, most of them, the hands-on men who made the ship run. And there was not a thing that Whittle or Waddell could do about it.

Some of our old men are shipped for six months only. In fact, above 16 out of 21. Their terms expire the 18th of next month and I fear that nearly all of them will want their discharges.

If every eligible hand chose to leave the ship, *Shenandoah* would still be left with eighty men, of whom twenty-five were officers. The remaining fifty-five seamen still represented three times the ship's original number. But raw numbers hardly expressed the threat such a loss would pose to *Shenandoah* and her mission. Here were the sailors who knew the ropes—literally. Here were the men who could be counted on to show the younger, less experienced hands what it meant to be responsible for, say, a specific subset of sails. Teamwork was utterly critical to a ship's survival prospects. Five or six men who had worked the foretop together since shipping out—the foretop with its gigantic array of canvas and rope and wire—knew those inanimate objects as though they were living things. Such experience-based knowledge simply could not be transferred to other men by mere words. The veteran sailors recruited from *Shenandoah*'s early captures could be counted on to compensate to some degree. But more than half the crew now consisted of the Melbourne stowaways: adequate hands when working in tandem with the veterans, but hardly seasoned enough to be reliable in a gale, or in pursuit of a stranger, or in a gunfight with a Federal cruiser.

Characteristically, Whittle searched for the bright side.

Goodness knows they will be great fools for desiring such a thing way out here, when by sticking to the ship, they get better pay, grub and treatment than they ever did before. . . .

And was obliged to add, glumly,

But sailors are singular animals.

The prospects of a vitiated crew. An unbalanced fellow officer. A sick list larger than it had ever been—Second Lieutenant Grimball, for example, the number-three officer in command, incapacitated with inflamed eyes. Not a single sail visible since departing Australia, some two thousand miles ago. ("This is disgustingly remarkable.")

An ache for his lost Pattie ("Oh if I could have three words, 'I am well,' how happy I would be"), an ache made even more acute by a staggering awareness of planetary isolation: as they headed toward the Fiji Islands, ship and crew were now almost exactly on the other side of the globe from Greenwich, England—longitudinal zero.

Did anyone on the other side still remember or care for them? Did their Southern nation still exist? Or were they a kind of living ghost ship, damned to an eternity of sailing blank oceans, seeking solace from indifferent strangers on unwelcoming shores?

It was with thoughts such as these burdening his mind, thoughts that had chased the audacious Boy back into the dark recesses, that Conway Whittle entered perhaps the most doleful sentence of *Shenandoah*'s saga:

I may say that we are almost out of the world.

11

They had rolled into the deep tropics now, wending northward through the great constellations of Pacific islands clustered above and below the equator. Fiji lay somewhere to the east, Tonga and Samoa farther beyond; northward lay the Solomons, the Gilberts, and the Marshalls. Jagged landmasses large and small cluttered the ocean now, mounts formed by long-extinct volcanoes and accumulated centuries of bird droppings. Irvine Bulloch, bereft of reliable charts, called on all his instinctual skills as he twisted and turned *Shenandoah's* course to keep her in deep water, clear of the treacherous fast currents and the many beautiful, deadly reefs submerged at the islands' edges. It was another "world" indeed for most of the crew: an island world of whistling tree ducks and sandalwood trees, of bolo snakes and giant pigeons and huge clams and cloud forests, of orange doves and massive bats and stump-toed geckoes, of perfume trees and breadfruit trees and orchid trees, of curlews and godwits.

Of cannibals, or rumors of cannibals.

Yet it remained a world apart from the ship, its many venues of enchantment and danger separated by miles of sheet-metal ocean surface. More than seventy-five years into the future, mighty navies of a reunited America would deliver thousands of men onto the shores of these islands—islands named Guadalcanal and Tarawa and Eniwetok—to face an enemy far more lethal than cannibals, with the fate of the world in the balance.

The temperature climbed—wet heat washed with frequent squalls. "The thermometer was 92 in my room," Whittle wrote. He sought out the tormented Waddell, who haunted the decks now, unable to return to his cabin for rest.

> He has had the blues all day. He gives way too much in trouble to suit such service. He told me that he felt his having to be on deck so much was beginning to bear on his health and he felt himself breaking.

With no diagnostic insights available to him, Conway Whittle could not recognize Waddell's paranoia for what it was. Yet he intuited that the captain was suddenly ready to talk to him; and in spite of his revulsion at Waddell's symptoms, Whittle listened.

> He takes an exaggerated view of his troubles which are far fewer than ours. He has not sufficient confidence in the ability of his officers, in which he is wrong, for I never saw a better set and one who trained so rapidly. He complains that with [Dabney Marian Scales, whose competence Waddell especially distrusted], he has to be on deck all the time. . . . He was so blue and melancholy that I pitied him and told him he was very much mistaken as to C's qualification [Francis Thornton Chew, also on Waddell's black list] and that I considered his being on deck unnecessary.

Waddell was in no condition to believe this. And so Conway Whittle, who only days earlier had written off the captain as irredeemable—"he has lost in me as good a friend as he ever had or will have"—reached out once again.

> He insisted to the contrary and I volunteered to keep all of Scales' watches with him in addition to my duties as Executive Officer, which God knows are far more trying than of any man I ever saw. My legitimate duties keep me on deck from 7 in the morning until 8 at night, and then to keep one of the watches (for Jack Grimball is sick) is very trying and will tell on me. But if one is to break it had better be me than him and I shall stand it as long as I can walk.

The young lieutenant thus committed himself to an open-ended stretch of sixteen-hour days on duty. With all Waddell's faults, it seemed, Whittle protected him still.

Whittle's compassion was tested immediately. On that very night, already exhausted, he joined Scales on the first watch. He would have to will himself awake and alert until midnight. The stakes, as he well knew, were life and death. Death, perhaps, by being eaten alive.

> *Surrounded as we are by rocks, islands and doubtful shoals, the navigation is intricate. There is in this connection another thought, not at all consoling. That is, if by misfortune we should run ashore and be wrecked, we would probably be thrown on the Fiji's or New Hebrides and we might be eaten by cannibals. This would be a terrible fate.*

He essayed a little gallows humor of the sort that even in his native South would one day draw a cringe:

> *I am decided that in such a case, I will cover myself all over with coal tar, turn my hair and I might pass as an inedible Negro. With this dark bright idea, I will say* bon soir *and bad luck to the Yanks.*

⁂

Eighty miles on Thursday, March 16, zigging and zagging through the opaque shapes in the solitary sea. Eighty degrees Fahrenheit, the wind baffling: now from the north, now west, now north, then east. Monotony. Monotony and exhaustion and hot sun and then rain. And monotony. And exhaustion. On Thursday, March 16, Whittle, bleary-eyed from days of double duty that had reduced his sleep to five hours a night, scrawled wearily in his log, "Oh for a cot in some vast wilderness."

A fascinating choice, that line: a slight paraphrase of a stanza from a 1782 poem by William Cowper (who'd yearned for a full "lodge," not just a sailorly "cot"). The stanza probably expressed the wishes of most hands on the ship:

. . . Some boundless contiguity of shade,
Where rumor of oppression and deceit,
Of unsuccessful or successful war,
Might never reach me more.

It is unclear just how familiar Conway Whittle was with Cowper's works—whether, for example, he knew that the poem from which he'd drawn the line was called "Charity," and was a centerpiece of the British poet's vast "Anti-Slavery" cycle of verse. Cowper wrote the cycle after forming a friendship with John Newton, the British curate who had commanded a slave ship until 1748. After a violent storm off the African coast threatened Newton's ship with disaster, he'd called out to God. His ship survived the storm, he became a passionate Christian, and, in the 1760s, composed the words for what became the enduring hymn to redemption and brotherhood, "Amazing Grace."

Cowper's "Charity" concludes:

But slavery!—Virtue dreads it as her grave:
Patience itself is meanness in a slave;
Or, if the will and sovereignty of God
Bid suffer it a while, and kiss the rod,
Wait for the dawning of a brighter day,
And snap the chain the moment when you may.
Nature imprints upon whate'er we see,
That has a heart and life in it, Be free!

Perhaps, indeed, the world wasn't so far away after all.

Monotony, Oh! Monotony. No Yanks in sight! No sails in sight! No anything in sight!

A shadow more brooding than Cowper's had overtaken Whittle: Coleridge's Ancient Mariner, with his primal wail, "Alone, alone, all, all alone, alone on a wide, wide sea . . ."

Charles Lining had joined Grimball now with a disabling attack of damaged eyes; Lining, the surgeon. Squalls formed up, and rain lashed *Shenandoah* in torrents—"I never saw such rain"—and headwinds slowed her progress to a crawl. And always the invisible reefs threatened, and the cannibals waiting on the shores beyond them. No albatross was needed to underscore this ship's plight.

Whittle, exhausted, ransacked his mind for activity, structure, hope—for anything to keep alive a sense of purpose in the restive crew. "Today we had a short drill. The men did very well. They are a good set."

He resolutely found restoration in the smallest things, the most ordinary pleasures. "This morning I got up at 4 o'clock to keep the morning watch with S," he wrote on March 18. "I must say I did feel very tired, but after a nice cup of coffee, I felt very much refreshed." He found glum humor in his own battered faith. "Oh! the dull monotony of being at sea in such a cruise and not to see a single sail. When I first got up, I, the prophet scholar, said we would have one today. But the same unbroken monotony reigns."

Sunday, March 19: inspection at quarters. "All feel better, cheerfully passing the time." Yet—"Had to trice up James Fegan, able bodied seaman, for refusing to obey the Master at Arms. This is his first offense and I will nip it in the bud."

Thoughts of Pattie. Her letters.

Another tricing on Tuesday, of a fireman, for insolence—again, toward the master-at-arms. Exhaustion was turning him physically ill, "but I will soon rally." On the evening of March 20, a view of what the young lieutenant wistfully called "the Southerner's Cross" hung in the heavens, as if to rebuke the discord below. "All is beautiful," he managed to write.

A hundred degrees in the shade the next day, *Shenandoah* laboring under steam at eight knots. Eighteen degrees hotter in the sun. And hellishly hotter still belowdecks, where the coal heavers, in an almost unimaginably brutish ballet, shoveled the relentlessly heavy, glistening black coal into the open mouths of the steam engine's fireboxes.

And as ever, Whittle faced a kind of starvation for news of the faroff world.

Oh! if I could know that all was well with those dear to me. In God's hands I leave them.

Sleeplessness now ravaged him; he savored the occasional small respite.

After the morning watch I felt tired until between 12 and 1, while the men were at dinner, I took a sly nap.

None of this nearly superhuman resoluteness earned him the slightest sympathy from Scales, the officer on whose behalf he'd extended himself.

S [Scales, whose watch he's sharing]—*protested with the captain against my keeping watch with him. But it was productive of no change, by which I may expect to keep for an indefinite time, one of four watches at night besides being up all day attending to my duties as Executive Officer. It is hard, but as long as a merciful God gives me the health, I will do all I can.*

Men around him began to crack under the oppressive blankness—most notably the men charged with safeguarding the others. The surgeon Lining, who'd been feverish from his throbbing eyes, stared and stared toward the horizon, obsessively seeking a sail. The normally volatile McNulty, Lining's assistant, took refuge in rum from the heat and boredom, and fell into a stupor. "He looks very much reduced. He is a high-minded and noble fellow, and has that I know of but one fault & that is an infirmity by which he can't help from occasionally imbibing too freely. He is now on a stool of repentance and I trust his good sense will take him clear of all temptation."

On March 23, *Shenandoah*'s officers, in the grip of wishful thinking, identified a distant landmass hugging the horizon and steamed for it.

This was Drummond Island, the largest of the Bishop group in the Gilbert Archipelago, thirty miles long and four wide. Its native name was Taputeouea. Surely Taputeouea and its sunlit coves—surely it had sunlit coves—attracted specimens of what they were looking for. "I think we may be repaid for the recent monotony by finding several unsuspecting Yanks hovering around," Whittle wrote—sounding a little like a parched man expecting to see an oasis in the desert.

Toward nightfall, *Shenandoah* closed within twenty miles of Drummond Island, picking her way gingerly against a strong westerly current. "Very little is known of its extent," Whittle noted, referring to its underwater dangers. Four hours steaming early the next morning brought the ship as close as she dared by 8:00 a.m.

We did not deem it safe to approach within less than six or eight miles. The land is low and at the distance seems to be thickly wooded with coconut trees. There is no harbor, port or light.

There were, however, Taputeoueans, and they streamed out to meet the stranger. "We saw several boats coming off under sail and waited for one hoping to get some information of value." New human faces, the first in more than a month. A hungry anticipation swept the ship. Whittle made a sketch of one canoe, and avidly described its ribbing and framing—"of a small bush twisted in the proper shape," under a coating of bark. The anticipation was soon dampened. The canoe bore three of the natives.

They were the most miserable looking set. They were perfectly naked and head bare. They had straight black coarse hair, were of copper color and looked very like the American Indian except that in the face they had few signs of intelligence. They had in their boat nothing but a few fish, some of which we bought giving them tobacco.

A sailmaker's mate named Glover,

who spoke the gibberish, tried his best to get them to come onboard, but they were too much afraid and said they would come when the other boats got alongside. Their language is peculiar to them, being like that of no one else. They said they had not seen a ship for a long time and none had been near the island. They were very much frightened of the guns.

And so the fantasy of engagement dissipated into the hot wet air.

We soon got clear of them, and without waiting for any other boats, stood off under sail, letting the chain go down and hoisting our propeller, and soon left the island out of sight.

Whittle could not contain a cry of sheer agony. "Oh the terrible, terrible monotony!!!" But he instantly regained control: "N'importante. 'Let us live with a hope,' for our time will come. I am as certain that a merciful God has our holy cause in his own hands as that I am here and I most devoutedly say, 'Thy will, oh Lord, not mine, be done.'"

More of the Lord's demanding will lay just ahead.

Today our Gunner's mate, Wm. Crawford, one of the Alabama's *crew, was guilty of insolent conduct at the mast and the Captain disrated him to seaman. He is one of those whose term expires on [April] 7th and no doubt the shortness of his time influenced him. I wish he was out of the ship.*

I think these men will leave, but thank God we can be independent as we have enough without them. . . . They will have a nice time getting home.

At about 8:00 p.m. on Saturday, March 25, *Shenandoah* recrossed the equator into the Northern hemisphere. No festivities this time as with the mid-November crossing; no ritual horseplay, no King Neptune, no emetics or sacks of stewed apples. A grim fatalism had long since overtaken most of the officers and crew, seasoned equator-crossers anyway, nearly every one. Whittle, among the very few who still "lived with a hope," continued to find that hope mocked by the fates. "We were all very much excited and elated this evening by the

report 'Sail ho!' " he wrote on Monday, March 27, "but found it only
to be clouds."

⁂

From the southern Gilberts, *Shenandoah* shifted her course to the
west-northwest and commenced a straight six-day, 930-mile sprint
toward the outer edge of the Carolines, an enormous archipelago
pinned like a tiara above the length of New Guinea. Their destination
was the rudimentary anchorage that passed for a port at Ponape, then
known also as Ascension Island, one of the larger islands in the eastern Carolines. Propeller lifted, topsails out, they ran along through extremes of weather; searing heat alternating with fierce brief squalls
that could readily, violently, and unpredictably burst into gale-force,
crisis-level storms. The winds lacerated the sail canvas; the crew reefed
and repaired the sails on the run. Soon the raider slipped into the
northeast trades, and the steady free wind blew her along at nine
knots. Still: "No sails in sight! Oh! the monotony!" Heat and squalls
took turns assaulting them on March 28—"Dull monotony reigns
and really it is painful." The next day, "I never saw it rain harder and
more continuously. . . . Really, in this region 'it never rains but it
pours.' " Whittle being Whittle, he turned this weather "lemon" into
lemonade: he rigged up clean canvas funnels from sailcloth to catch
the rain and channel it into the ship's tanks—fresh drinking water.

The thrill of action, finally, on that day—the first in a month—
even though the quarry proved hardly worth it:

> *At 4:45 p.m., just as it lightened up, the joyous sound of 'Sail ho!'*
> *roused us all up. Sure enough, there was a little schooner on our port or*
> *lead beam. We stood in chase. At 6:00 p.m. we came down to her and*
> *hove her to.*

She proved to be only a small Hawaiian trading schooner, and
Shenandoah let her be—threw her back, in fishermen's terms. Still, it
had been fun while it lasted—and the skipper had tantalized all hands
by reporting four vessels at Ponape.

A quick speculative detour into Charbrol Harbor on Strong's

Island on Tuesday, March 30—no prey there. "Made all sail, worked off steam, hoisted the propeller, and went booming along." Whittle's homesickness, perhaps, or the lush green tropic hillsides, played some tricks on his mind: "The scenery is fine. We were very close in and it looked like the portion of my dear old Virginia on the Virginia & Tennessee Railroad above Liberty."

On, then, to Ponape. "Oh I trust we will make some prizes here."

And then, more than two thousand miles south-southeast of Japan, three thousand miles from Melbourne, on the far western edge of the Pacific, after weeks of lashing squalls, psychological tension, tedium, illness, and concern for the social cohesion of the crew itself—after all this, on April 1, 1865, Lieutenant Whittle's indomitable trust was finally, spectacularly, rewarded.

⚓︎

A night of sitting tight in the darkness, twelve miles from the reefs of Ponape, the invisible black ship poised like a beast about to pounce. No prey was yet visible, but the beast sensed something. At 2:00 a.m., before first light, the beast unfurled her topgallants, fired her mighty steam engine, and made her sprint for the harbor.

Sure enough.

Four ships, fat and complacent, lolled at anchor in the middle harbor, zebras at the watering hole, "All but one with the detested Yankee flag hoisted." The raider dropped anchor at an unthreatening distance, offshore from the village, under British colors. A fifth ship now became visible. Toward noon, the officers hired a local pilot to steer them across the harbor toward the small herd.

> *Fearing some treachery on [his] part, we warned him that if he got us aground, death would be his instant portion. He was an Englishman named Thomas Horreicks. We had the English flag up, and he supposed us to be the English surveying ship.*

Not really, as all in the vicinity were soon to learn.

> *The entrance is narrow, but very deep. We steamed in and moored ship in 15 fathoms water. We were delighted. There we were, safely*

moored, close to five prizes and they, thinking we were an English
vessel. Some [locals] tried to come along side, but we beckoned
them off.

Now the rebels acted with swift, disciplined military precision.
Four longboats were lowered and filled with armed men: sailors now
acting as Confederate marines, equipped with rifles. In charge were
Shenandoah's junior-officer elite: Lieutenant Grimball in the first,
Lieutenant Lee in the second, Lieutenant Chew in the third, and
Lieutenant Scales in the fourth. They would be looking to round up
captains, mates, and papers of registry.

Oh what an April fool to the poor Yanks. There were no Captains on
board as they were in the lead harbor "on a bust." The boats shoved off.
We fired a gun and ran up our flag. What a time.

One of the ships showed a Hawaiian flag. The remaining four were
fair game: the Yankee whale ships *Edward Carey* and *Hector,* and barques *Pearl* and *Harvest.*

The helpless shock of the merchantmen aboard these ships must
have echoed that of the Union army as it tended its evening campfires
at Chancellorsville, when 30,000 of Stonewall Jackson's foot soldiers
and cavalry came bursting out of the Wilderness and spoiled everyone's dinner. Conway Whittle recorded the unfolding adventure with
the gleeful pacing and detail of a novelist.

The [Harvest] was the only one about which there was any doubt,
but she had no bill of sale, a Yankee Captain and mates. She, with the
rest, was condemned as a prize. The mates were all put in irons.

Now the rebel gunmen under Grimball sat in their armed boat
under *Harvest's* gangway and awaited the return of the carousing Yankee captains. They didn't have to wait long.

Their whale boat came through a short cut. They, not suspecting any-
thing as our flag was down, pulled leisurely, looking at our ship. All
were a little tight. They were singing, laughing and talking when our

*boat, in charge of Lieutenant Grimball, pulled ahead of them. He
hailed, "Boat ahoy? Haloo! Go along side of that ship." "We don't be-
long there"* [responded the drunken captains]. *"I don't care, go
alongside." Seeing him armed, they obeyed, and over our gangway
came Captain Eldridge of the* Harvest, *Captain Edwin P. Thompson
of the* Hector, *Captain Chase of the* Pearl, *and Captain Baker of the*
Edward Carey. *What a perfectly April fooled party. When they
learned what we were, they were astounded. They were all put in
irons except the Captain of the* Harvest. *His deposition was taken,
and the sale of the vessel was, as she had the same Captain and mates,
all Yankees and the same name, and no bill of sale, considered bogus,
and he was out in limbo with the rest.*

This was great fun. Lucrative, too.

*Having the Captains, first and second mates on board, and not know-
ing the feeling of the natives, we withdrew our men, after having
taken out all navigating instruments and we all had a great rejoicing.
This amply repays us for our monotony, and is not a bad haul, as the
cargo alone of one, i.e. 300 gallons of oil, is worth $4,000. These raised
our prize list to 11 and two bonded, making 13.*

The "feeling of the natives" soon became apparent. As in Melbourne, the *Shenandoah* raiders were greeted as heroes.

*Of course we were soon surrounded with boats, all the natives in ca-
noes, naked except a grass covering around the waist. The pilot was
delighted when he saw our flag and knew who we were and said we
would be heartily received by the natives. This is an island under none
but local authority and protection with no civilization, and everything is under our guns. The Yanks were certainly caught napping this
time. I only wish there were 50 instead of 4.*

But the joyful tone in Conway Whittle's "novel" abruptly gave way
to deep dismay. The captured captains had some bad news for their
captors.

They say Hood has met with a terrible defeat at Nashville. Sheridan has taken Savannah, and Porter Fort Fisher at Wilmington. All this, if true, is very, very bad.

To which Whittle added the familiar thought from the part of himself that must have explained his remarkable equilibrium:

Thy will be done oh Lord.

The bad news was several weeks old, but substantially true, and its import dire beyond measure.

John Bell Hood had met with disaster after deciding to invade Tennessee in November 1864 as a tactic for drawing Sherman's army away from Atlanta. (Sherman had bludgeoned Hood's forces when they'd ventured out of that besieged city to attack him.) His withered arm and stump of a leg apt symbols for the South's mangled state, Hood led his ragged army of 37,000 men across the Tennessee River from Georgia in mud and rain. After executing a brilliant flanking maneuver against Union defenses, Hood moved toward Nashville. At Spring Hill, outside the city, confusion in the Confederate chain of command resulted in a pullback order in the midst of a battle that the Rebels seemed likely to win. Compounding this error, the distracted generals allowed a Union division to march in the black of night through the teeth of Hood's trap as his soldiers slept. Angry and confused, the Confederates pursued the Federals, who managed to set up strong defenses at Franklin, south of Nashville, before their pursuers caught up with them. Hood launched an impetuous attack against the Union center; thousands of his men were slaughtered; and Hood, his chances of a great victory wiped out, sat on his horse and wept. His 25,000 survivors stumbled on to Nashville anyway, where a force of 70,000 drove them into exhausted, hysterical retreat. The West was now lost to the Confederacy.

It had been Sherman, of course, and not Sheridan, who'd capped the rout of Hood at Atlanta by commencing the March to the Sea. At Savannah on December 20, Sherman had sent his famous telegraph to

Lincoln offering the city as a Christmas present. As for Admiral David D. Porter, he had reduced the vital Confederate Fort Fisher with a withering two-day bombardment that ended on January 14. The fort, a mile-long series of earthwork constructions about thirty miles south of Wilmington, North Carolina, had guarded one of the few remaining ports open to Confederate blockade runners off the Atlantic. Here, as at Nashville, the Confederates squandered several chances to defeat the Federals before they were fully prepared for battle.

On the day the *Shenandoah* crew learned of these disasters, the Confederacy was a week from collapsing.

⟆⟨❀⟩⟅

On Sunday, April 2, *Shenandoah* opened herself to a state visit from the local royalty.

> *At 10 we set the pilot in the longboat with an officer, to bring off the King of the tribe of this portion of the island. He came with some half dozen of his chiefs. The whole affair was very ludicrous. Each of the dignitaries was naked, and covered with coconut oil. Each, upon getting up the side in the gangway like monkeys, would not come aboard until some officer gave them the hand of friendship. Each had a covering about the waist made of grass or coconut bark, and each with a slit cut in the lower part of the ear, through which they stuck the stem of a common clay pipe, which, after they took a turn* [twisted it once around], *was secure.*

The King's name—Whittle was scrupulous about the spelling—was Nananierikie. He was short and fat, and was escorted by about fifty canoes, and he brought with him a few attendants and his grown son. "They expressed astonishment at the size and general appearance of the ship. . . . The Captain took him in the cabin and gave the party something to drink. And then told him at length the object of our visit."

When Nananierikie learned the object, "He was much delighted and begged that the prizes might be destroyed in the harbor so that [the locals] might get the copper" that lined the ships' hulls. "This was, of course, readily acceded to by us, and as it obviated the necessity of our taking them out and applying the torch."

Nananierikie became the latest landlubber to receive a grand tour of the ship. The guns in particular impressed him. Before the king left, the officers struck a deal with him:

> We promised to let him have a great many of the things from our prizes if he saw that no harm was done to our stern fasts, or no thievery was permitted before we burned our prizes. [If anyone was going to help themselves to the captured ships' stores, it would be the Confederates!] We made him a present of 22 old prize muskets, and an old sword. This last, we made him buckle around his naked waist, the blade dangling about his legs, much to the injury of his shins.
>
> He left us the best of friends, inviting all of us ashore, and claiming that we all had his hearty welcome. During the whole day we got quantities of coconuts, pineapples, pigs, chickens, bananas, plantain, etc, giving tobacco in payment. We got some few articles from our prizes.

Before disposing of these "prizes," Whittle and Waddell allowed the crew a little shore leave—a low risk, in that no liquor existed on the island—and oversaw some maintenance chores aboard ship, such as reconfiguring the ballast of coal—the stubbornly problematic coal—toward the stern, so as to lighten the bow in anticipation of heavy weather. As the men worked, they digested the bad news they'd received, and brooded on the fate of their homeland.

Sherman's sweep through Georgia, Whittle knew, had left Charleston, South Carolina, open to an attack from the rear—"which will, I fear, ensure its fall." Hood's defeat in Tennessee "shows that we are weak and will, I fear, cause an evacuation of the ground gained." As for the fall of Fort Fisher: "This, if true, closes our last port of Wilmington, and closes all doors to the world."

Typically, Whittle could not allow himself to close off all hope. "Much allowance is to be made of this news coming via California, which it is well known is very unreliable." Honesty compelled him to add:

But I fear that there must be much truth in some of these reports. If they are all true, it is terrible. In God's honor, I resign all, and in his divine will is my trust. I can never think that an almighty and merciful, and all powerful God will allow such a people as ours to suffer such subjugation. God grant us his blessing I pray.

The next day the Confederates commenced consolidating what now must have seemed an infinitesimal victory, measured against the larger war. Whittle's accounting of it lacked the poetry that had infused his earlier descriptions of enemy ships destroyed.

One boat employed transferring stores from our prizes. In the evening, sent an officer with a boat, got the prize barque Pearl *underway. Ran [her] aground on a reef high up and destroyed her by fire. She's the 8th vessel burnt.*

The day after that, "Having taken the prize ships *Hector* and *Ed. Carey*" to the places pointed out by the King, we fired them. . . . We brought the barque *Harvest* nearer the ship in order to be more convenient for shifting stores of which we will want a good deal." Eight days later they got around to firing her, too.

Whittle and Waddell were more than happy to honor the king's wishes and situate the doomed ships so that their charred skeletons would be left visible high above the water. This would allow the islanders easier access to their copper hulls; and it would also serve as a calling card from *Shenandoah.* No longer were her officers concerned with stealth and subterfuge. They were here, in this part of the watery world, and they did not care who knew it—Yankee skippers, Ambassador Adams, Consul Dudley, Abe Lincoln himself. Their business, after all, was to destroy those who might object. And there was little left to lose.

On Friday, April 7, "Shifting coal and stores. Weather pleasant. The officers making many purchases of curios, paying for them with tobacco, cloth, etc."

On April 8, "Employed stowing fore hold with provisions from our prize. The times of Simpson, Reid, Fox, Brosnan & Crawford expired. Brosnan reshipped for 12 months. Weather very pleasant."

On April 9, the day that the Cause died on the other side of the world:

A day of rest. Let the port watch go on liberty in the forenoon & the starboard watch in the afternoon, each carried two plugs of tobaccos. Pleasant.

The next day, *Harvest* was stripped of her stores and fired. Whittle estimated the total value of the four Yankee ships at $107,759. On Thursday, April 13, he and Waddell pardoned all prisoners, put them ashore to tell what tales they would to the next visitors, stowed anchors and chains, hoisted the great propeller, and made sail. "I am rejoiced to be once more at sea," Whittle wrote.

Despite this joy, Whittle and the rest of the men with him were almost infinitely alone now. And in one sense, despite a growing kernel of denial, their mission was actually over.

His Southern nation existed no more, but the voyage of *Shenandoah* was just now truly under way.

12

Two unusual pages immediately following the routine one dated
"April 9" in the logbook of Lt. William Conway Whittle, Executive Officer, CSS *Shenandoah*, show time out of joint.

They shift abruptly to the future, with material that the lieutenant
in fact wrote more than two months later, on June 22 and June 28,
1865, in the soul-dampening fog shrouding the Bering Sea. It was on
the twenty-second that the raider's officers listened as the captain of a
captured New Bedford whaling ship told them that, weeks earlier, on
April ninth, Robert E. Lee had surrendered his army to General
Grant after abandoning Richmond. Six days later this news was repeated by the skipper of a Hawaiian barque.

Clearly, Whittle removed these pages from their chronological
place in the log, late June, and inserted them after his April 9 entries.

One of these entries is coldly factual: a businesslike tabular list of
Yankee ships captured and sunk or burned by *Shenandoah*, and the
total estimated worth of those ships and their cargoes. The other
burns with emotion: a poem, a psalm, composed—disgorged—by
Whittle in four ten-line stanzas and a coda of four lines. Not so much
polished verse as chant, and not so much chant as a heart's cry of intertwined grief and Christian acceptance, this untitled poem reads almost as a knight's epitaph.

> *Oh mighty God, hast thou decreed*
> *That our land shall not be freed?*
> *That we shall be o'er run by foes*
> *Whose deeds of shame each homestead shows?*

Foes cruel, relentless and barbarous; seeking gain.
Shall our efforts, oh God, be vain?
If not, oh Lord, I humbly pray
That thou will change this night to day.
Look down in this, our time of need,
And with thy hands our rulers lead.

Our battles are with a savage foe,
Our deeds and valor all do know;
Sometimes driving, and others driven,
Trusting in ourselves and Heaven,
Fighting for everything that's dear,
Ever hoping that Thou art near.
Ah! many a Southern man we miss
Who died alone for a Freeman's bliss!
And many a helpless woman's wail
Rings out like a death knell on the gale!!

Let every southern knee be bent,
And up to heaven the prayer be sent,
That God will aid us in the Strife
For Freedom far more dear than life,
So he will soften the hearts of cruel foes
Who would such a fate on us impose
That if their anger he can't appease
He will in justice our banner seize,
And carry it with his own just hand
Till every foe has left our land!

Convinced of the justness of his cause
Let not a single Southron pause,
But leave his fireside, his home, his all
In answer to the righteous call,
And rush to battle with the cry,
"We will be free, or we will die!"
Let not his strong arm be staid

And let him not once sheathe his blade,
Till every Yankee invading foe
Feels the weight of its revengeful blow.

But if indeed our race is run,
Our every effort is outdone,
Then grant, Oh! God! that everyone
May cry, "Oh Lord, Thy will be done"!!

Beneath the poem is the notation:

C. S. Str. [steamer] *"Shenandoah,"*
At sea, June 22
W. C. Whittle, Jr.
Written after we heard of the surrender of a portion of Lee's army
and the fall of Richmond.

The reasons for the shuffled entries are self-evidently symbolic in one sense—to punctuate the end of the Civil War, and thus of *Shenandoah*'s mission—and somewhat mystifying in another.

As of April 10, the raider's attacks had garnered a dozen ships and about $300,000 in Yankee dollars. But by the end of June those figures would skyrocket to thirty-seven ships and just shy of $1,400,000—or more than $16,500,000 in 2007 dollars. Why would the lieutenant enter the ship's postwar conquests (complete with accurate dates, to be sure) with those achieved before Lee's surrender?

Perhaps the switch in chronology reflected Conway Whittle's concerns about the legitimacy of *Shenandoah*'s exploits after the war ended. To capture and sink an enemy ship during wartime is a recognized military action. To do the same after the war has ceased, however, is something else entirely: it is an act of piracy, and it is punishable by death.

Would *Shenandoah*'s crew be held accountable for an illegal campaign of serial destruction even though, to the best of their knowledge, they were acting under the rules of warfare? Even Lee's surrender, in and of itself, did not officially end the Civil War. Jefferson Davis remained at large until May 10, and resistance by scattered Confederate remnants continued until the end of May. Not until June 2, when the Confederate general Edmund Kirby Smith signed surrender documents presented by Federal representatives, did the South formally acknowledge its defeat. Months more would pass before word of this reached *Shenandoah*.

There remains one further strong possibility:

April 9 was the day, as Whittle realized only in retrospect, that the world began to learn that the Civil War was over—yet of course it was only later that he learned it. By repositioning the prize list to this date, Whittle may have been boldly underlining the inescapable fact that he and the others aboard *Shenandoah* were "criminals" under conventional rules of war, while at the same time insisting on their innocence on moral grounds. Here, Whittle may have begun laying the framework for defending his honor in the event of a military tribunal.

Conway Whittle may or may not have been absorbed by these themes when he tucked his June tabulation and his June poem back into the April pages of his log. The two documents are probably more significant for another reason entirely: taken together, they form a near-perfect, if inadvertent, snapshot of the two halves of Whittle's nature.

By 2:00 p.m. on Thursday, April 13, *Shenandoah*, having dispatched her prisoners in small boats to an uncertain fate on the tropical shore, surged outward from the Island of Ponape (which Whittle again calls Ascension) under full sail. The ship, by afternoon, was some twenty miles from the island's shoreline; the earth's curve had rendered it mostly invisible, all but a smudge of gray-green mountaintops and their bright white cloud cap. It was to be a long time before her officers and crew set their eyes on substantial land again.

The next day, Abraham and Mary Lincoln, having been turned down by fifteen other invitees, finally coaxed young Henry Rathbone and his fiancée Clara Harris to come see a play with them at Ford's Theater in Washington.

⚜

On April 14th, *Shenandoah* made 210 miles to the northwest under brisk winds off her starboard beam. "She is like a duck in the water,"

Whittle exulted, "steers beautifully, and under short sail has averaged about 9 knots. This is splendid, and I consider that she is now in better trim and order than she has ever been." Their black-faced labors to carefully reposition the bunker coal had paid off handsomely: by settling her ballast they had significantly enhanced her sea-keeping strengths. It would prove vital quite soon.

Adversity was never completely absent: Whittle's ailing right-hand man and trusted ally had now worsened.

> *Jack Grimball is still very sick, having had a continuous fever all day. He is at times delirious and talking all the time. Poor fellow, he suffers very much, and he's very impatient, thereby rendering his condition more painful. I have the greatest affection for him, and will nurse him, as I know he would nurse me.*

In fact, a number of men voiced health complaints. Yet no real crises threatened—such as cholera, for example, the bane of ships at sea in that time. Even Captain Waddell seemed to have his psychic ailments under control. Thus Whittle writes optimistically, "I am delighted to be once more at sea, and hope to remain so until our work is done. I am a hater of port."

Another 195 miles the next day, and Grimball's fever broke; 186 miles the day after that; then 203. The brisk trades were hustling *Shenandoah* along toward a coveted expanse of ocean: the east-west shipping routes on a line between San Francisco and China. Whittle's irrepressible optimism overtook him once more. He could almost scent the herds of unsuspecting merchantmen meandering back and forth beyond the horizon—or so he thought—and the aroma made him giddy:

> *Here we are ripping along at 8 and 9 knots under double reef topsails. Our noble ship is in splendid trim. Tomorrow we will be in a great track for prizes. I trust we may see something, and I hope that something will be a fine Yankee clipper. . . . Jack is nearly well, and all are happy.*

By Tuesday, April 18, they had reached a latitude of 19.41 north. Whittle sensed that these helpful winds could turn with little warning into heavy weather, and ordered the crew to re-rig the stays for the masts. On that same day, the timetable he dreaded reasserted itself: "Five men's time expired today." Yet three of them immediately re-shipped; the specter of mass desertion remained at bay. Grimball turned twenty-five, and the officers drank to his health in sherry.

But no prize. Perhaps restlessly, *Shenandoah* commenced a course change the next day, shifting northward from her dash to the northwest, and then, on the twentieth, east by north. *Where were the Yankee merchantmen?!* Whittle piled task upon task, to quell the crew's impatience and also to fortify the ship against the storm he now felt sure was approaching. They rove fresh manila for the lower rigging; they made fresh water; they drilled at the great guns. Warm nights made sleep refreshing. But the breezes bore an undercurrent of danger.

Our wind from the northeast is growing much fresher, and I fear that the change of the trades to the southward and eastward will be attended with a gale. We are in all respects better prepared for it than at any previous time. But still, I would rather not see it. I am not so romantic as to see the grandeur of a gale. If I ever was. I have seen so many as to drive all such foolish admiration out of my head. Oh, if only I knew that all was well in our dear country. That God with his mercy will look upon us is my constant prayer.

Impatience now began to wear down Whittle's good humor, as it often had on this voyage of long, frustrating intervals between brief, intense engagements. "The same old routine," he allowed himself to grouse on April 21, "standing across the track of the California & China clippers. Not a sign of anything but constantly expecting to have better luck." And then he brooded about the underside of that good luck.

Any vessel we might take would in all probability bring us news, later, by two to three months than any we have heard. I shall receive it with fear and trembling. It may be bad, it may be good, just as God wills it.

He did his stubborn best to dismiss the dire news received from
the captured captains at Ponape:

> . . . *if true, which I very much doubt, it is very bad. Let it be ever so*
> *bad, our course & duty is clear and every new disaster . . . should*
> *nerve us to do our duty like men.*

❧

By this time *Shenandoah* had interrupted her rapid run up the western
Pacific. Chagrin and bewilderment at the absence of the expected
Yankee traffic prompted her officers to shorten her sails and throw her
into a holding pattern: ten miles in one direction, nineteen in another,
thirty-one in another. She was "standing-station" pacing, not sailing; a
predator off the scent, snooping around the sea lanes, or "tracks," in
hopes her prey would stumble onto her. "I may say that we are almost
out of the world," Whittle had written a month earlier, a thousand
miles off the Australian coast. Now the world seemed to have vanished entirely, and, with it, any sense that *Shenandoah* was guided by
purpose. "Not a sail have we seen since we left Ascension," Whittle
wrote on the twenty-second, "and the last vessel seen was the wreck of
the destroyed *Harvest*. Oh, I wish we could catch something." And
then, from the core of his sustaining resolution: " 'Have patience,' says
a little whispering bird."

He found reason for hope in the very shimmering fact of the
cruiser beneath his feet, and above his head. "I consider that the ship
never before was as clean, as seaworthy, and in as good condition." He
saw that maintenance intensified and took on a near-liturgical form
and significance: the decks kept constantly smooth via squads of crewmen on their hands and knees at close quarters with one another, rubbing their abrasive blocks of Bible-sized stone back and forth across
the sand-sprinkled decking planks in unison, as their mates stooped in
front of them, scattering water and sand in their path. "The decks all
looked cleaner, and everything in better order [after inspection], than
at any previous time. What an immense amount of good results from
frequent use of sand and 'holy stones.' "

He finished reading Thackeray's *Adventures of Philip*, "gaining
therefrom much useful information." The novel, published a year be-

fore the British author's death in 1863, is a rambling narrative focusing on Philip Firmkin, the loutish son of a seducer from a previous novel, as he lumbers through an unsympathetic society before a chance discovery leads him to wealth. Its full title is *The Adventures of Philip on His Way Through the World Shewing Who Robbed Him, Who Helped Him and Who Passed Him By*. Such a character would seem to offer little in the way of "useful information" for an upstanding fellow such as *Shenandoah*'s executive officer. But perhaps Conway Whittle felt a growing affinity with Frimkin's alienation from the world. On April 23 he set down one of the darkest entries of his entire log:

> *How very long it will be before anyone in the world knows where we are. Only think that since we left Melbourne for parts unknown more than two months ago, we have seen nothing which could report us for months. No doubt our ship will be reported as having been taken to Father Neptune's bosom. I trust that they may not get any such report at home, and if they do, I trust that they may only say that we are in God's hands.*

And again, the following day:

> *Today's routine has been the same as that of the past week, with the same results. I do not know when I have felt worse than I have since I got up this morning. I, for some reason or other, slept very little last night, but took a little medicine today, and ate no dinner, and now feel well. We've had squalls of wind and rain all day. I have felt awfully homesick, but . . .*

Indomitably . . .

> *. . . tomorrow may bring us a prize.*

Not exactly.

> *Not a sign of a sail. If this be "the track," I think we had better be making some tracks ourselves. I feel tonight as tho . . .*

Inevitably . . .

. . . we would catch something tomorrow.

However . . .

Well here is another day gone and no sign of any prize. We are now, I fear, to the Northward of the track, but our time will come. . . .

He based this fear on a mariner's way of knowing. He could feel the altered quality of the wind against his skin.

The next day, nothing relieved the monotony except a fight between two drunken marines, "the grog of both being stopped in consequence."

The following day's excitement involved condensing saltwater with the steam engine.

As to that issue of "being reported": Whittle clearly expected that Union sympathizers had long since circulated the information regarding *Shenandoah*'s visit to Melbourne. Federal warships were doubtless under orders to scour the Pacific for the raider. They would be clueless, of course, as to the ship's direction—until, say, King Nananierikie at Ponape disclosed to a Federal skipper just how he'd come into possession of those muskets and that beautiful sword. Weeks would have passed, of course; but inevitably the great Union net, cast over the entire Pacific, would begin to tighten. At which time only one hope would remain:

. . . that we are in God's hands.

On Friday morning, April 28, after 11 days of fruitless course-reversals across the trade lanes, *Shenandoah* "made sail to royals on our course." That is, she accelerated northward under extra sails laid on by her crew. She followed a zigzag route for several hours, still hoping to nab a merchantman that had strayed from the tracks, making only eighty-six miles; but the next day she changed tactics and raced 192 miles on a northerly straight line. Whittle's exhilaration at being on the move again was tempered somewhat by the prospective loss of two good seamen. Louis Rowe and Peter Raymond, a pair of Frenchmen from *Alina*, the raider's first prize, announced their desire to leave the ship at the first opportunity. "They are excellent men," Whittle lamented, "and have been as hard as steel." This brought to nine the number of crewmen resolved to leave the ship. How many more harbored similar intentions?

The barometer plunged the next day, and Whittle found a fresh reason for anxiety: "I trust we are not going to have a gale." Nonetheless, "We prepared for it by reefing the main topsail and close reefing the fore main." The skies cleared for a time, but the month of May rushed in on a moderate gale and a high sea. As the ship pitched and the crew laid on extra safety rigging, Whittle's thoughts turned to a worse storm far from the western Pacific: "I wonder how our dear country is getting along." The dear country no longer existed, as the lieutenant probably suspected.

<hr />

Fickle elements toyed with the raider for several hours as she struggled toward latitude 35 north. The winds moderated, only to pick up again. Little hope remained for a capture in gale conditions; simply fighting for control of *Shenandoah* was often the helmsman's only concern. But the waters yielded evidence that ships of some sort had been in the vicinity—chilling evidence. On May 3, during a break that followed a two-day gale, the ship knifed through great swatches of "whale food," but they saw no whales. What they did see would draw the somber notice of any mariner in a wooden ship in these storm-ridden seas. Whittle's notation of it was terse:

> . . . *we passed some driftwood which looks like a portion of a wreck.*

The omens darkened considerably a short time later.

> *I saw what I have heard was never seen north of the line; i.e., a large albatross.*

The albatross's hour quickly arrived. Near midnight strong winds blew in a rain storm that assaulted the ship like artillery, and the seas ran wild.

Scales had the night watch. At first light, in the teeth of a rising storm and in need of backup, he sent for Whittle.

> *I was called at 6:30, the quartermaster informed me that it was windy, rainy, and squally weather. I went up to let Scales fix his toilet and found the ship under double-reefed topsails & reefed foresails, with a fresh breeze and a high sea a little abaft the starboard beam and going 9¹/₂ knots.*

Shenandoah was ripping along, taking every advantage of the tempest behind her. She sailed northwest, on course, with the gale at her back, and just enough sails, pinched tight to the wind to drive the ship among the great Pacific swells at a rapid, controlled rate. Young Scales had chosen a fine balance between speed, risk, and performance, and Whittle was pleased. The captain would not be.

Whittle was about to be irritated not only by Waddell's denigration of the absent Scales, but also by his less-than-aggressive approach to outsailing the oncoming storm, the strategy Scales had chosen to good advantage.

James Waddell, whose darkest demons seemed to find release in storms, now limped into view along the heaving deck and immediately countermanded his executive officer.

Shouting through the torrents, Waddell ordered Whittle to take in virtually all the sails and turn the ship into the wind. He essentially told Whittle to slow *Shenandoah* down and turn her off.

Glistening crewmen now labored aloft to tie back soaking, gale-driven canvas. The helmsman turned the wheel to starboard, and, rolling dangerously as the force of the gale broadsided her, *Shenandoah* slowly lurched about to face the seas that tormented her. In Whittle's jargon, the ship was "laying to."

Now she was no longer a sleek, fluid sailing ship making her way before the wind. Now she was at the mercy of the Pacific Ocean: a teak-and-iron container, filled with terrified men all wondering if they would ever see their loved ones again.

The ship, "brought by the wind, and laid to," would now ride up and over each set of waves as they marched toward her. Keeping the rudder amidships gave the ship's direction entirely over to the winds, waves, and currents. It also took control away from the helmsman. This struck Whittle as basically sound—so far as it went. *Shenandoah* was still riding the storm safely, but as darkness fell and the gale lashed the ship up and down, Waddell pushed the tactic beyond good sense.

> *This ship, under our present sail, with the helm half down, will lay to and ride the waves like a duck. But the Captain orders that the helm must be kept amidships. This throws her in the "trough of the sea", which is very high, and she is laboring very much more than is safe, comfortable, or necessary. On these things he's as stubborn as a mule, and I fear that his stubbornness will some day do us harm. Oh, how I do detest a gale of winds!!!*

Whittle understood that running with little in the way of sails (which, in wind this fierce, could actually destabilize the ship), and using the rudder to help control the ship's roll, they might survive by simply letting the gale slip past. Abandoning most attempts to control the ship became about the only way to save it.

But on this Waddell disagreed as well.

Waddell's orders put ship and elements in opposition. Now the wind shoved and bullied the ship, converting it from an agile sailing vessel to a 230-foot barge. Now the raider bounced roughly, clumsily, through the high waves, taking them side-on, lifting to their crest as they drove in, with her spars nearly touching the water, then tilting to the opposite side, like a giant metronome, and sliding helplessly down the back trough, as men clung to ropes with one hand and their stomachs with the other. Only to be met at the bottom by another blind-siding wave. And another. And another.

Perhaps it was the very seaworthiness that Whittle had so recently admired that kept *Shenandoah* from being swamped, swallowed up. Lost. Father Neptune could not claim her as a prize through that long, torturous night. By midmorning of May 4, the winds were swirling, but much calmer; the sea still high, but less lethal. The sun actually came out. "This has been to all appearances a fine day,"

Whittle was able to record. Yet the barometer remained low (29.4–29.3), and all hands understood the implications of that. Either they were in the eye of an enormous typhoon, or the post-equatorial shift in the trade winds he had looked for earlier now had them up against a conveyor belt of eastbound seasonal storms.

At ten-thirty that night, Whittle labored to keep his hand steady as he scrawled his log entry; the ship rocked and pitched as a new gale blew in from the southwest. And a new natural enemy arrived to reinforce the angry ocean: cold. Officers and crew shivered helplessly under the frigid torrential rains. Whittle imagined that the icy air emanated now "from the snowclad clifts [*sic*] of Japan." His armor-plated *duende*, however, remained undiminished: "Going as we are from extreme warm to extreme cold weather & back, must make us suffer. But what care we in such a cause."

By the end of the following afternoon, *Shenandoah* had clawed and stumbled her way across 122 wave-smashed miles. The storm seemed almost to be circling her, drifting away for a while, only to come rampaging back, like wave upon wave of icy, blue-clad infantry. Whittle's equanimity grew almost surreal: "The weather is quite cold. Our time passes monotonously. But there are so many of us, and all so cheerful, that we manage to drive a good deal of care away." And then the inevitable mantra: "I expect that when we shape our course for our cruise grounds, having given the ice time to drift clear, we will catch a good many Yanks. I trust it may be so, but patience!"

The "cheerful" crew turned out splendidly clad for inspection on Sunday, May 7, but as for "so many of us," Whittle received more glum news that the ship's numbers would soon shrink some more. "The times of three men were expired today and none desired to renew their engagement. This makes 12 who are only waiting an opportunity to get clear. These are, thank goodness, the last of the "six months men," and I am heartily glad of it." He made some calculations: "These taken from our 104, leaves 92 souls all told belonging to the ship. From these, after deducting 25 officers and 12 boys, stewards, and cooks, making 37, leaves us 55 all told, including firemen and marines." Again, the silver lining: "This seems small, but when it be compared to the 46 all told with which we started, it will be seen that we are well off."

Somewhat better news the next day: four of the ship's best men, whose terms of service had expired, came forward to announce that they would like to reship "upon condition that they would be discharged at the first European port we got to. The Captain consented. . . . This raises the number of 92 souls attached to the ship as enumerated yesterday, to 96. Thank God for this."

The weather lifted now—or seemed to—allowing *Shenandoah* a couple days of sailing at something like her accustomed cruising speed. Then, on the tenth, another gale struck her, "which nearly took us aback." Did take them aback, in fact; caught unprepared by the violence of the winds out of the northwest—winds that threatened to blow men from the rigging—the crew had no time to adjust the sails or change course. The steersman managed to swing the bow around so that the ship, rather than being swamped, was merely blown backward out of control. And, struggling as she was to survive, let alone sail, she covered some seventy miles on a course entirely of the storm's choosing, fighting heavy seas and winds so strong as to blow the sailors' breath from their lungs.

I am sick and tired of gales. I have seen enough.

But gales had not seen enough of *Shenandoah*. It was springtime in the western Pacific, when storms bloomed like magnolias in Virginia. Gales, it seemed, would be the raider's curse until she cleared a latitude of 45 or 50 degrees north. She was presently at 39.54. At 2:00 p.m. the next day, a sudden wind shift to the northward prompted an emergency close-reefing of the fore and main topsails and forestaysail. Too little, too late. Two hours later the wind, gusting furiously, blew the lead main topsail to pieces. Among the most important stabilizing pieces of canvas on the ship, it was suddenly nothing but scrap. Now it became a fight for control. The crew performed heroically.

[We] unbent the remnants letting all but the patent [furling device] blow overboard. Not being able to bend another topsail while by the wind, we goose-winged the foresail, and got the ship before the wind and ran before a furious gale & terrific sea. Got up and bent another main topsail and set it close reefed, gale blowing furiously.

Each of these tasks entailed terrifying, life-threatening risks. Crewmen edged their way across the rain-slick deck to the coaming, their eyes nearly shut against the torrents and their bodies leaning into the wind. They climbed up the wildly whipsawing ratlines, knowing that any false purchase on the ropes would mean a plunge to the death. Once aloft, they hacked away at the remaining debris, then sheathed their knives and rigged the replacement sails with their bare hands, keeping an elbow hooked around the boom to prevent the wind from whisking them out to sea like kites.

Somehow they succeeded, and *Shenandoah* rode out the hellish Saturday night of May 13. At around 3:00 a.m.—"gale moderating but a terrible sea"—they hung on as the ship rolled nearly on her side; then, surviving that, they set the main staysail. All hands labored virtually without letup until nightfall and another blast of bone-chilling cold.

❧

By Tuesday—exhaustion rampant throughout the ship—the worst of it was over. The raider made eighty-three miles and sat at latitude 43.29 north, nearly out of the danger zone. "This has been a good relief after the bad weather for the last few days," Whittle wrote in an understatement. "The temperature getting mild and pleasant with a fine sun to dry our sails and decks. I trust we will be taken to the northward of the 45th parallel without any more bad weather." His trust was augmented by what he took to be a kind of anti-albatross vision. "I witnessed today a peculiar sign of something. There was a very bright and distinct ring around the sun. I hope it indicates good weather."

Whittle trusted too well and too soon; the ring indicated the opposite. Wednesday, May 17—the day Shenandoah crossed the long-anticipated 45th parallel—brought a new heavy swelling of the seas. The temperature dipped below freezing, and the latest maelstrom was accompanied by another unwelcome traveling companion, whose damp blankets would shroud the ship for the next several dismal weeks.

"A heavy fog superseding the rain," Whittle described it. The fog betokened yet another menace peculiar to these arctic latitudes: it "made us think that an iceberg was near."

The wind abated the next day, but freezing rain pelted the ship. The fog thickened. The ship lay to. The thermometer continued to drop. Ice coated the deck. The crew was depleted—one more northeast gale could be a disaster.

There seemed but one option left for the Confederate ship and crew that had sailed out of the world.

Today we celebrated Bulloch's 30th birthday.

13

❖

The world into which the storms had thrown them was now a cold gray world, a motionless world, a world devoid of shapes or sounds beyond the murmurings of the ship herself. The fog, when it descended, blotted out everything. Even the rain, which alternated with light snow, was invisible until it struck some man-made surface. As long as the fog lay upon them, they would have warnings of neither weather nor icebergs nor rocks. The fog seemed to obliterate time itself, and every moment became a moment of fear. Blinded, they worried north.

At last a westerly wind on Saturday morning, May 20, blew some of the fog away, and the men of *Shenandoah* were able to comprehend how far they'd wandered from Dixie—or even from Australia. They had reached latitude 49.04 north, longitude 155.40 west. They were now north of Seattle, albeit over 3,000 miles due west. In the fog they had been sailing toward a dangerously narrow gap, one of the North Pacific's most inhospitable passages. Finally a landfall some thirty-five miles to the northeast revealed its low, smudgy contours to the lookouts high in the masts, and navigator Bulloch identified it as Ounkatan.

Ounkatan: an island near the top of the Kuril archipelago—thirty-one volcanic islands that stretch like a tripwire in a 600-mile southwesterly line from tip of the vast Kamchatka Peninsula down to the island of Hokkaido. Far beyond them lay the whaling grounds in the Sea of Okhotsk, and before them were the Kurils, a picket line of semi-submerged, semi-active cones that gave rise to the deep tectonic vents of the "Ring of Fire."

Kamchatka was a part of Russia. Hokkaido was one of the Japanese home islands. The Confederates were looking at Asia.

To their north, for nearly 2,000 miles, the Bering Sea washed against Kamchatka's long eastern coast. Far to the east across the Bering Sea lay Alaska. And beyond, even farther north, the Bering Strait, the narrow passage between Alaska and Russia, gave entry into the Arctic Ocean. It was to be somewhere within this remote, wintry region, universes removed from the Potomac, the Mississippi, the sunlit killing fields of Antietam and Shiloh and Gettysburg, that *Shenandoah* would fire the last shot of the American Civil War.

All of the island was covered with snow, and as we got the wind from it, it was as cold as anything. We commenced to steam, and as we could not carry our square sails, we furled them and set all fore and aft sail. We found it fresh through the Amphitrite passage blowing too much, and never would have gotten through but for our steam.

By noon, they were safely in the Sea of Okhotsk, the enormous bay that separates Kamchatka from Russia's Siberian coast. Okhotsk, an arm of the North Pacific, was nearly half the size of the Gulf of Mexico. Whittle's resilient spirits soon rebounded again. "This has been a delightful day," he wrote on May 22, as Shenandoah at last crossed the 50th parallel, "and most charming weather. It is a great relief after the weather which we have had."

The raider loafed northward across the great bay for a couple of days, its lookouts scanning the horizon for Yankees. Okhotsk was famous for its whaling grounds; but *Shenandoah* was as much prey as predator now, and her enemy was not gunships, but Neptune. His most terrifying weapons were the ice floes that laced this shallow sea, and the blizzards that came roaring across the frigid water to toss the ship toward them. Southeasterly winds, up from Japan, and westerlies out of Siberia, pushed the raider eastward almost against its will, toward Kamchatka. A vicious snowstorm struck her on May 24, and another followed in its wake on the next day. Yet the calming of winds and sea brought no relief, only peril of another kind. The dense fog returned, setting nerves on edge as visibility receded; and paralyzing ice claimed great reaches of the placid waters' surface.

The bay's depth increased abruptly as the ship picked its way northward, and now to the west. "Cast the lead finding no bottom at 100 fathoms [600 feet]," Whittle wrote on May 25. "Very foggy." "Very foggy and disagreeable," he added the following night, at latitude 54.55 north.

The fog pursued *Shenandoah* stubbornly as she turned away from Kamchatka and felt her way ninety-six miles to the northwest, into open sea and toward Siberia—and toward God knew what mortal hazards of ice and rocks. And then, on Saturday, May 27, after fifty-six storm-ridden days of futility, a strike.

Course north northeast, a quarter east. Barometer 29.5–29.54. Winds southwest and calm. Filled away under close-reefed topsails. As soon as the fog cleared up, we saw a large quantity of floating ice in the port beam. Very soon we saw a sail on the other side of the ice. Made sail standing around the ice for the sail. Made her out to be a barque standing for us. No doubt to "yarn."

Instead of a friendly chaw and a chat, the stranger found herself greeted by cannon fire.

[We] *Hove to and she came right for us. Fired a gun. She hove to, hoisting the Yankee flag. Sent a boat, bringing aboard the Captain (Nye) Ebenezer, and all his mates.*

This proved to be the barque *Abigail*, out of New Bedford. The Confederates set briskly to work on their latest victim: "We soon condemned the vessel, put a prize crew on board, and commenced to transfer the personal effects of the officers and crew, and remained by her all night." Lieutenant Scales was placed in charge.

Abigail's cargo featured a disturbing quantity of liquor, which proved an insurmountable temptation for the raider's parched crew, and a grave distraction from the mission. "This has been a terrible day for me," Whittle moaned the next day. "We brought off a great deal of liquor, and many of our men and two officers got drunk. Put all [not officers] in irons, gagged and triced up right and left. I never had such a time." Among the party-boys was the esteemed Lieutenant Scales himself. Whittle suspended him from his rank. Less fortunate was Mr. Lynch, the second carpenter, who made the combined mistake of drunkenness (not for the first time) and insolence to the lieutenant. Whittle clapped him in irons and muzzled him.

"Our men have heretofore been so clear of any such thing," Whittle mused—drawing on a somewhat selective memory—"that it comes as something new. . . . But I am determined that they shall not repeat it." On the brighter side, the prize crew transferred five hogs "and many valuables" to *Shenandoah,* along with thirty-five prisoners, whom they paroled. Then, matter-of-factly, they set *Abigail* on fire. Whittle put the quarry's value at $22,000. "Saturday is our lucky day," he noted tersely.

And then the drab gray world closed about the Confederates again. Another gale hit them on Monday, with fierce winds and swirling snow. They were now high up in the Okhotsk, forbidding Kamchatka on the starboard bow, and the snowy Siberian peaks visible off the port bow. A kind of sickly daylight filtered through the fog for most of every day: "It is never dark and you can read on deck all night. The sun rises at 3:00 a.m. and sets at 9:00 p.m." Prospects for further prizes seemed imminent. "We learn from one of the prisoners whose sympathies are with us that all the whalers are out at Saint Iona's Islands in the ice and we will remain here until they come up to enter the NE bay and pick them up there." Whittle had slightly misidentified Iony Island, a tiny heap of rock near the middle of Okhotsk, where thousands of whales gathered to feed.

But no whalers came along to be picked up. The taking of *Abigail* proved a fluke. Routine took hold of *Shenandoah* once more, chill-laden routine—the long, empty days made to seem even longer by the near-constant presence of the arctic sun. Lieutenant Scales was restored to duty. The crew chopped up one of the longboats taken from the New Bedford prize; concern had arisen about the stability of a deck now crowded with plunder.

Clear skies, balmy temperatures, and calm winds ushered in the month of June; *Shenandoah* now sat at latitude 58.28 north, just off Tausk Bay. "I never saw a more beautiful day than the last day of May and I trust it will continue." It didn't. Tausk Bay, another reputed haven for whalers, proved to be entirely closed by ice. Skunked again. Now *Shenandoah* began a course change; she attempted what amounted to a sweeping portside U-turn, trying to make her way back over 700 miles southwest, and quit the Okhotsk altogether. Her goal, if the hunting stayed poor, was to round the tip of Kamchatka and then head north once more, even farther north this time. This time into the Bering Sea, and across it, and even farther thereafter. They were heading for the Arctic Ocean.

The elements massed against her. The barometer, subject of Whittle's frequent nervous attention, plunged from 29.48 to 29.20 in a few hours on June 3, and freezing rain laced with hailstones pelted the becalmed *Shenandoah*. Ice coated her sails, ropes, masts, deck, yards, and rigging, "and the ship had the appearance of being made of glass." Her braces and gear were immobilized. "The sight was certainly beautiful & grand but was most severe [dangerous]."

With the crew shivering and trying to protect their extremities against frostbite, *Shenandoah* managed to crunch through the ice-crusted waters for thirty-five miles that day. Then trouble: with her sails frozen in place, the wind freshened. Frozen pulleys and ice-caked rope prevented crewmen from hauling in the foretopsail, and on Saturday night, June 3, *Shenandoah*, her propeller now useless in the ice-clotted water, was suddenly being blown helplessly toward an immense floe, "which without our knowledge was on the lee bow."

The men of *Shenandoah*, an isolated wooden speck on a frigid alien sea near the top of the planet, now struggled for survival against prehistoric forces of inexorable power. The arctic ice around them had carved the edges of continents across the eons, had stripped Siberia of its great coastal rocks. Now it was pressing in on the teak hull and copper plating of the raider. The jagged margins of the ice were relentlessly mobile, colliding with one another, then pulling apart in the wind, and closing again, creating phantom channels and lethal cul-de-sacs. Against this leviathan, the crew's weapons were primitive, puny, pathetic. Lt. Sidney Smith Lee Jr., the officer of the deck, ordered all hands on deck to beat the ice clear of the pulleys—with belaying pins, capstan bars, anything available. The men swung into the task, climbing 40, 60, 80, 120 feet above the decks on frozen ropes, in the dark, their faces and hands exposed to sheets of freezing rain, and pounding, and pounding, and pounding again. The brutal work continued into the next watch, under the relief officer, Chew, until, at last, the pulleys began to creak and turn, and the sail-bearing ropes moved through them, responsive once more to the desperate hands of the mariners. Whittle recorded the drama.

> We then braced aback, to force her out stern first, but this brought such a strain on the rudder, that we were afraid of splitting it. We filled away and forged ahead.

The goal now was to get out of the floe ice, fast, before it crushed them. To do this, they needed to turn the ship around, so they could maneuver, rudder-last, through the constantly shifting shards of ice— "Some pieces thirty feet deep and fifteen yards square," Whittle noted. Once the rudder was engaged, of course, another peril immediately arose: its blade could easily become jammed in the ice, and fail.

Before she could even face that peril, however, *Shenandoah* needed to get turned around, and this was not proving easy.

> Her head was southwest, and we knew we were getting further & further in. The ice, tho rotten, was very large, and but for some punch on the fore post and bows, we might have ripped off our stern copper, or stove our bows. The ship was so ticked up in the ice, that we scarcely thought it possible [to escape].

Then, toward 6:00 a.m. on June 4, a chance at salvation.

> But thank God, just ahead, we saw a clear, or comparatively clear spot of about 40 feet square. This was our only chance.

The "spot" was a minuscule stretch of soft, mushy ice—a sort of nautical quicksand; but good for the rudder's purchase. If the ship was going to turn, she would have to turn here. If she failed, her great quest would end here, or a hundred fathoms below here: ship, officers, and crew forever united under an icy shroud. Or perhaps on the frozen rocks of the Siberian coast, as food for polar bears.

We hoisted with great difficulty the fore topmast stay sail and very slowly wore to the northwest and north, and then, just using sail enough to work very slowly ahead, we finally pushed our way back the way we came. At 8 o'clock, we were out of the heavy ice, and made sail to get well clear.

"I was very uneasy," Whittle was able to admit to his journal when the terrifying, exhausting ordeal was over, "and feared the stoving in of our bow." His explanation for survival was his usual, simple, undeviating, utterly serene explanation for everything:

God favored us.

⊱⊰

The narrow escape had sobered Conway Whittle, but it had done nothing to diminish his zeal for the mission. Nor had the likely fall of his South (at least not so long as he did not know officially that his South had fallen). For him, if not for the others, *Shenandoah* was on more than a mission now; she was on a crusade—a crusade on behalf of the Cause. Nor was it simply "the Cause" any longer. He had lately expanded and sanctified the reference in his log; he now called it the Just Cause. He, and the ship, would persevere in behalf of the Just Cause for as long as "God favored us." If and when God ceased to favor "us," they would accept death, however desolate, however wintry, however pointless, however far from home. The Just Cause now defined Whittle as much as his reflection in the mirror. Whether those capitalized initials had a dual significance—whether they were meant to merge this "J.C." with the J.C. of his biblical faith—only Whittle knew.

Meeting ice here at some 200 miles [east of] *St. Jonas Island proves to us that we can't go near there for whalers, and must con-*

*tent ourselves in plucking them up as they go north into the bays
after the ice is broken away. The sides of our ship are thin, and are
in no way suited, like the bluff-bowed & sheathed whalers, to go
into ice. I give my vote to keeping out of all ice, as necessary to the
safety of the ship. I trust we will catch a great many before they get
into the bays.*

His attitude toward the ice, then, was one of calculating respect—
not fear. The perilous turnaround amid the ice floes had been merely a
tactical maneuver—not a retreat.

But where did his fellow officer stand on this matter?

On June 5:

*At midnight I was again aroused by thumping and hurried on deck. I
found the ship in heavy ice. Grimball had relieved Scales and got her
clear without damage.*

Was this new near-catastrophe a result of a capricious order by
James Waddell? The issue of braving the ice once more—whether it
was "proper and safe"—had been vigorously debated that afternoon.
Whittle had advocated for prudence. He was sure, he'd told the others, "that without any sheathing or fixings, we are entirely unfit for it,
and if we did not materially endanger the safety of the ship (and all
hands) we would lose our copper, thereby ruining our sailing qualities
and our more important work hereafter."

Not everyone had agreed with him. Waddell had been inclined in
his direction,

*but to additionally arm & secure himself against any future censure,
he determined to call a consultation with Lieutenants & Master.
Lieuts. Lee, Chew, Scales and I were of the same opinion, i.e., that we
ought to keep out. Lieut. Grimball & Master Bulloch thought we
ought to go in.*

Seeking to forge a consensus, Whittle had offered up a plan both
daring and contingent on the capture of a prize.

My idea was to catch one vessel, put a crew on her and let her go in the ice, fitted as she will be for the purpose, keeping our vessel out which can catch them as they come up to go into the Bays. If this vessel be fitted out as I most earnestly do and will recommend, I will try and command her.

Whittle's offer drew on the same knightly reserves as had his legend-establishing escapade aboard *Nashville*. He would once again risk his life for the greater good of the mission—for the Just Cause.

The others had agreed. *Shenandoah* would not tempt fate by plunging into the ice floes again. The thumping that awakened Whittle at midnight had signaled a miscalculation: the ice had caught up with the ship. Luckily, she escaped damage.

God favored us.

❧❧❧❧

The Siberian Arctic now stalked *Shenandoah* across the sea: the ice, hundreds of square miles of it, breaking loose from its solid winter freeze in the June warmth, calving scores of huge, swirling chunks, most all large and heavy enough to bat the ship into oblivion. Often the ice was joined by its own brooding confederate, the fog. A third potential predator—the gale, whose force could hurl these ice chunks as if they were snowflakes—remained a constant source of anxiety; the barometer was seldom ignored for long.

"This morning, we ran along the land between the Tauck & Babushkin Bays," Whittle noted on June 7. "We made ice as far as we could see. This we made out to be very high and very thick. . . . To enter it would be folly & we determined to skirt along it."

Shenandoah had reversed course again. Abandoning her southwesterly route toward Siberia, she was heading northeastward again, toward Kamchatka. She remained in the Sea of Okhotsk, inside the vast embrace of Russia, disdaining the thought of swinging down around the peninsula's tip and out into the Bering Sea. Bulloch was now steering toward the enormous cul-de-sac of the sea's northwest coast, bordered by the narrow neck that connected Kamchatka to Siberia. The water was shallow there, good whaling grounds.

Yet the ice remained a barrier. "Our only hope lies in the possibility of picking up some vessel off the entrance [to the bay] and sending her in the ice after the rest," he wrote again. He added, "The Capt. and a majority of our officers are of my opinion, and this will be our plan."

Once again, Whittle had assumed too much from James Iredell Waddell. The lure of the Bering Sea would not be ignored after all.

On Thursday, June 9, he wrote with tightly controlled frustration:

> *The Captain came to a somewhat sudden conclusion in deciding to quit the Sea [of Okhotsk] and accordingly changed the course at noon for the Amphitrite, or 50th passage. When the main object of our cruise was to do work in this sea, I can but deeply regret coming so far and destroying but one vessel. I was utterly opposed to taking this vessel into the ice. . . . I was, however, in favor of remaining a short time, and trying to pick up a vessel off the northeast gulf, and sending her, fitted as she would be, into the ice after the rest.*

He entered the reasoning of his fellow officer and adversary:

> *The Captain however, thinks that this, even if successful, would cause too great a loss of time. He says he has found out, upon good authority, that while there are about twelve whalers here, there are some sixty to eighty in the Arctic and Bering seas, and by remaining here he would lose so much time as to prevent his going there.*

The source of Waddell's "good authority" was unclear. Had he learned it in Australia? The Carolines? Did a prisoner from *Abigail* disclose it? Was his claim of a source merely a cover to legitimize a hunch of his own? Conway Whittle, the loyal team player whenever it was remotely feasible, gave his fellow commanding officer the benefit of the doubt:

If these facts are correct he is right in going on. Whatever he decides upon, I will do all I can to assist in carrying out. So here we go for the Bering Sea, I trust with good luck ahead.

The fog, once more dense and blinding, followed them southward for the first hundred miles. The vapors were accompanied by some bad personal news that seemed to worm its way into Whittle's soul, reminding him of loss and mortality—of family, and of nation.

I have been very sad all day. It is only now, when I have little to do, that my troubles come more heavily upon me. The sad fate of my dear uncle, Captain Arthur Sinclair [reported drowned in the Lelia near Liverpool], renders me sadder than I can express. The loss of so noble and affectionate an uncle is, of itself bad enough. But when I consider the state of poverty and grief of his dear wife and children, I am thrown into a sad state of gloom. My constant prayer is that God will be merciful to my country and dear ones. Into his hands and to him, as a just God, I am happy to trust all.

How Conway Whittle learned this, he did not say. The most likely source would have been a report in a newspaper, of uncertain vintage, brought on board by one of the captured seamen from *Abigail.* Such a paper could well have been circulated for several days among the prisoners, and only gradually worked its way out of the hold and through the ship's officers before reaching the lieutenant.

Arthur Sinclair's fate dovetailed with the fates of his nation; the paper brought more bad tidings:

The latest news, representing the taking of Savannah and Wilmington, is calculated to distress us. But at the same time, it is an incentive to me to make a greater exertion to do my full, whole, and highest duty. Our cruise thus far has been commenced & vigorously executed amid unprecedented difficulties, and we are certain, with a proper degree of energy, to come out with flying colors. God aid us I pray.

The raider, blinded again, was steering by compass, chronometer, and dead reckoning as she picked her way slowly southward through perfectly calm seas blanketed by dense fog on June 10. She made only fifty-two cautious miles. Adding a note of unwelcome irony were the abundant whales that leaped and spouted around the ship—whales, but no whalers.

And no shortage of shipboard distractions.

> *Today it was reported to me that Capt. Nye, late of the prize "Abigail," had been using every argument in his power to prevent some of the "dagoes" of his crew from shipping, telling them that a Yankee man-of-war would catch us and hang them. We want men and as they are not Yanks and can haul ropes we would like to get some of them. Besides, such talk would discourage any of our men who were at all weak nerved.*

Whittle dealt with Captain Nye's loose tongue by using the same persuasion that had helped so many *Shenandoah* crewmen see the error of their ways.

> *I sent for him and told him that if he continued to talk in this way, I would put him in double irons.*

Whittle enjoyed some satisfaction at Nye's expense when a prisoner named Thomas S. Manning, Nye's second mate, came forward to join the Confederates. Waddell rated him ship's corporal. "I was glad to have him," Whittle wrote, "as the more Southerners we have the better. Besides, he is an old active whaler and may prove a valuable man to us. . . . He is a fine looking fellow."

The damned whales continued to frolic about the ship as breezes brushed the fog away on Trinity Sunday, June 11. "I had no idea we could see them so far. . . . I thought at first they were sails. The 'spouts' looked like volumes of smoke or steam."

He added, "I trust we will see a sail, but I scarcely think we will catch any until we get to the Behring [*sic*] Sea. I trust we will succeed, and I am sure we will do our best."

As Whittle knew well, the Bering Sea still lay more than 1,600 miles north of the Amphitrite Strait—named for the Greek sea goddess and wife of Poseidon. The Amphitrite separated Okhotsk from the North Pacific at the 50th parallel, toward the far reaches of the Kuril archipelago. Still sailing in near-zero visibility, *Shenandoah*, trusting herself to the skills of Bulloch, plunged through its dangerous twenty-mile gap in heavy fog on June 13, and set sail on the final leg of her epic northward journey—a leg that would take her near the top of the world. And into conquest on an epic scale.

Whittle's mood had brightened with the "shipping," the day before, of a dozen *Abigail* men—"nearly all Sandwich Islanders or 'Kanakas.'" Their names gave him as much pleasure as did their badly needed manpower.

> *Among them were Jim California, John Boy &c. One's name was from his being so tall, "Long Joe," but someone suggested that he had better revise it, so he just put himself down as Joe Long. They are a poor looking set but they can haul on the ropes.*

Whittle took quick advantage of this increase by organizing another gun crew, "which gave us four guns on a side with full crews." That night he shipped a Prussian named Burueth, whom he made a marine. And then a final stroke of good fortune: "Also our two Frenchmen, Peter Raymond & Louis Rowe, whose terms expired on the 29th of April, re-signed. This gives us upwards of 110 men exclusive of officers."

Nine days of quiet, fogbound sailing ensued, the lull before the storm. On June 14, Whittle—perhaps intuiting the victories to come—ordered the clearing out of the after "tween decks," "which I shall use for prisoners." A good breeze the following day carried them 188 miles under billowing topgallant sails. The rain soon returned, and a low barometer kept all hands braced for a deadly, ice-strewing gale. By the sixteenth, *Shenandoah* had run three days without observation, on dead reckoning. The fog dissipated at midafternoon that day, "and had it not lifted when it did . . . our ship's ribs would most certainly have been on an uninhabitable island. Surely, God is with us." So were two more men from *Abigail*, who shipped on that day.

The tension of virtually blind sailing gripped Whittle as he arose groggily at 6:30 a.m. the next day. "What with the noise of the propeller and the anxiety felt as to the true position of the ship, I slept very little and awoke feeling fatigued rather than refreshed by my last night's restlessness." On the other hand, *Shenandoah* had finally crossed into the Bering Sea, "standing," as the lieutenant wryly noted "with a gentle southerly breeze for the fishing ground with nothing to look out for [but] about 400 miles of ice." Fog and rain the day after that, and more anxiety: "I only feel apprehensions about ice, but *"on dit"* [*French for "conventional wisdom holds"*] that we will not see any so far South. . . . I am growing impatient to have our work up here finished. I want to go where we can see more of the sun and the enemy's property."

His overwrought state revealed itself in a logbook entry nearly inconceivable given his nearly constant affirmations of his unshakable faith in the will of God.

> *The day I have spent in reading my prayer book given me by my own dear Pattie. Oh! how much I do wish I was a Christian.*

By June 19, *Shenandoah*, still northbound, was carefully sailing. Caution soon mixed with dread. She had reached eleven and a half knots:

> *We were going too fast for this icy region and we shortened sail to single-reefed topsails. We are now in a region which will not allow us to run too fast as we might be roused up at midnight by striking floe-ice. This ship should never go into ice, she is too frail.*

By now, Whittle had internalized James Waddell's "good authority" prediction of a sea thick with Yankee whaling ships. "Tonight is calm," he wrote on the twentieth, as *Shenandoah* breached a latitude of 60 degrees north,

> *and if, as is highly probable, we make some of the whalers, a calm is the very thing we would desire. There are some sixty vessels up here,*

*and we ... might see ten at one time and if there was a calm, we
could, with our steam, catch the party, but if there was a breeze ...
two-thirds might escape.*

June 21, as the ship stood toward Cape Thaddeous at the southern
end of Anadyr Bay, found Whittle tangled up in trying to explain
what day it was. His nerves frayed from a second sleepless night, and,
no doubt from excitement over the approaching rampage, the young
lieutenant threw off all thoughts military, logistical, romantic, and rev-
erential, and abandoned himself, in his log, to a rare burst of pure
wackiness.

The occasion was the ship's crossing of the imaginary line on the
globe that had provoked head-scratching cogitation among sailors,
philosophers, scientists, Magellan's navigator, Edgar Allan Poe, and
countless others and since its "discovery" in the fourteenth century:
the International Date Line.

Now it was Conway Whittle's turn to dilate. He began with his
usual seriousness:

*If you sail from England to the Eastwards and go around the world,
returning to England say on the 21st of June, you will find that if you
have not kept up the necessary correcting for change of longitude, your
21st is their 20th so that you have gained a day.*

From there, he careered into near-slapstick.

*We today crossed the 180th meridian from Greenwich and are there-
fore 12 h. ahead of them or tomorrow being by our account is regularly
Thursday June 22nd, it is with them Wednesday, June 21st, or in
other words we will have a week with two Wednesdays, a month with
two 21sts and a June with 32 days. We will also for tomorrow have to
take out the same declination equation of nine &c &c as we did today.
This will puzzle some of our old sailors when Sunday comes to find the
day on which they expected Sunday, Saturday's work will be done.*

Presumably allowing a few moments for his head to stop spinning,
he added, in a more serious vein:

We expected to see some prizes today but are disappointed and expect them further to the eastward near St. Lawrence Island. We passed a great deal of whale "blubber" showing that the whalers are not far off. I trust that tomorrow will bring them.

For once, Conway Whittle's unquenchable trust was fulfilled. Tomorrow did bring them. The greatest spree of nautical conquest in the history of the North Pacific, if not the world, was about to commence.

14

Conway Whittle was a not a man inclined to distract himself for long from his mission: destroying the United States maritime economy. Thus he began his logbook entries for June 22, 1865, with a brief but fussy little clarification.

Yesterday I was too soon in saying that we would have two 21sts & two Wednesdays as we did not cross the 180th meridian as today we were but 14 miles from it. We will have two Thursdays instead.

That cleared up, Whittle got down to detailing the serious business transacted on the "first" Thursday. It had proved a day of exhilarating triumph, but the triumph had been undercut by heartbreaking news, and soon he detailed his poignant thoughts on that, too.

At 9 o'c A.M. we made two sails on our port quarter. Furled sails and stood for them under [steam]. At 11 o'c hove to and boarded the six topsail yards whale ship Wm. Thompson *of New Bedford, Mass., Capt. Smith. Put a prize crew on board & brought the captain and mates onboard our vessel and stood in chase of the other vessel.*

Six topsail yards indicated a substantial vessel indeed, at 495 tons. *Wm. Thompson* stood as the second-largest ship taken by Shenandoah.* But the action was only beginning; there were many more whalers ghosting about in the fog.

---

* *Delphine* was the largest, at 705 tons.

At 12:00 boarded the whale ship Euphrates *of New Bedford, Mass. Brought the crew with their personal effects onboard and fired the prize.*

They were laboring in the typical Bering pea-soup, a fog now streaked with flickers of flame, and tinged with the unmistakable smell of smoke. With the first fire set, the Confederate boarding crew was busily stripping *Wm. Thompson* of her rich stores—beef, pork, and other welcome provisions—when a third sail grew hazily visible to the northwestward. "We gave chase." This time the prey was a neutral vessel, the whaling barque *Robert Fowades* of Sydney, Australia. Groping their way back through the thickening fog, the raiders relocated *Wm. Thompson* and finished the job of stripping her.

These early conquests raised all spirits aboard the raider. It seemed as though Captain Waddell's "good authority" might prove very good indeed.

But for Whittle, at least, the exuberance was crushed by news on "good authority" of a far darker nature. The young officer, who had willed himself to hope and optimism through all the voyage's crises and frustrations, and the long weeks of fruitless searching for prey, had learned information that compelled him to conclude his entries for the first June 22 with a long lamentation bordering on despair.

I will now say something of the news which has this day come to us. Capt. Smith gave us all he seemed to know. We heard first of the assassination of Mr. President Lincoln and a similar attempt upon the life of Mr. Seward. I only fear that these attempts will be put to the credit of some confederate, but I am certain that it was not done by any from our side.

His belief in the chivalric nature of the Just Cause thus remained unshaken. But his determination to believe in the South's capacity to fight on, already weakened by earlier news, now ebbed toward rock-bottom.

I am very much cast down by the news, which if true, is very bad. Charleston, Savannah and Richmond taken. How awful this is. The [capture of the] two first I looked for and was certain that upon the fall of Wilmington, Richmond would be evacuated, but General Lee is reported to have surrendered after his evacuation of Richmond at Appomattox with his whole army and rumors of General Lee's negotiating for peace, &c., &c.

Yet Whittle still clung stubbornly to a scrap of hope. It was centered upon the conviction he'd shared with nearly every one of his Southern countrymen that Robert E. Lee was, if not invincible, at least incapable of surrender. He dismissed the report as propaganda—they would have to capture Lee by himself; he would never surrender his army.

All this last I put down as false. General Lee may have left a portion of his force to protest the retreat of his army and even he might have been taken with this position, but as to his surrender of his whole army and his treating with General Grant for peace, I do not believe one single word. There is no doubting the fact that the confederacy has received in prestige a heavy blow, but further I do not believe.

In clinging to this desperate conviction, and doubtless without being aware of it, Conway Whittle echoed a great voice from literature—that of Edgar in *King Lear*: "The worst is not, as long as we can say, 'This is the worst.'" He continued:

With Richmond we might lose for a time, if not permanently, Virginia, my own dear state, which to me as a Virginian, and to every true Confederate is a great blow. One would think [by reading] some of the papers that the Confederate states were subjugated but I know too well the falsehood telling propensities of our enemies to place too much confidence in their statements.

And with this, his black thoughts began a long, anguished refocusing from his nation to his family.

This news is bad, very bad, and it is calculated to make a person feel blues. My heart is heavy! heavy!! heavy!!! but my prayers to an almighty God give me great relief. God alone knows what will become of my darling little sisters, if our dear old state should be given up to our cruel and relentless foes. They are with no means of support in a country already devastated by invasion. . . . Virginia must be evacuated and I fear it will never be ours again. God protect us, I pray.

Such forebodings, in fact, had eaten at him throughout this foggy day.

During the day my thoughts have been running on my home and dear ones and really I have almost gone mad over the helpless and destitute condition in which they must be placed. In my anguish, I sought consolation in reading my little prayer book which my dear Pattie gave me, when my eyes fell on these words: "I have been young and now am old; and yet saw I never the righteous forsaken nor his seed begging their bread." God help us I pray. Oh! God protect us.

By the following day—the "second" Thursday, June 22—the lieutenant had regained his military composure. It had, after all, been a most productive day.

At 1 we made nine sails, stood for one which proved to be the whale ship Milo *of New Bedford; bonded her for $46,000.*

The Confederates did not even pause to torch this prize; more game was afoot.

Sent all prisoners onboard [Milo] *and keeping her papers, ordered her to follow us. Chased the next vessel, a ship which put on all sail, running into the ice. We gave her two shots which hove her to.*

Yet another New Bedford whaler: *Sophia Thornton.* Again, there was scarcely time to secure her. The ocean now teemed with targets: four sails on the far side of an ice floe to windward, and three on the near side. The Rebels gleefully repeated their new tactic. "Threw a prize crew onboard, keeping as prisoners the captain and mates and ordered her to follow."

They picked out a fast one for their next victim, a clipper-rigged whaling barque. She tried to escape, but *Shenandoah* was far faster. She raced after her quarry, *Jireh Swift*, for an hour; then, inevitably, "hove to and boarded. Taking off the officers and crew with their effects we fired her and stood for our prizes."

The panic on board the other whalers in the area can only be imagined. The chilling crack of *Shenandoah*'s cannon fire would have carried clearly over these calm waters; the fires on the burning ships would have been visible through the mists.

The frantic New Englanders, assuming they had guessed what was happening to their countrymen's ships, would only be able to wonder if their friends were still alive. And wonder whether they would be next. The steam-powered Confederate raider must have struck terror into many Yankee hearts as she prowled that day through the Bering Sea with *Sophia Thornton* and *Milo*, now nothing more than prison ships, bobbing helplessly behind her, and every other whaler she'd met going down in flames in her wake. She made only forty-two miles; but speed was hardly the point now.

Nightfall—or what passed for nightfall at latitude 62 north— ended the fun; but by early the next day, Whittle and Waddell had the crew working briskly to solve a paradox: the sapping of *Shenandoah*'s effectiveness caused by the very successes of the past two days. The crews of captured *Sophia Thornton* and *Milo*, et al., threatened to create a shift in the balance of power. There would soon to be far more prisoners than Rebels. Some new operating tactics were called for.

Whittle and Waddell improvised an action plan. Before the captive crewmen started stripping *Sophia Thornton* of her stores, food, and water, they were ordered to hack down her masts—effectively disabling her so there would be no chance of escape while *Shenandoah* left them unguarded. Then Waddell instructed the captain of *Milo* to tie up alongside *Sophia Thornton*, and had her crew comb her for useful provisions. Everything they could carry was transferred to *Milo*. While this was going on, *Shenandoah* began a transfer of her own. The raider had been encumbered with some two hundred paroled and hungry prisoners, men collected from *Abigail, Wm. Thompson, Euphrates, Sophia Thornton,* and *Jireh Swift.* These men the Rebels now dumped onboard *Milo,* whose captain, a man named Hawes, suddenly found himself with an entirely different cargo from what he'd anticipated back in New Bedford.

Milo, of course, had hardly been designed to hold two hundred human beings, much less two hundred captives. But that problem would have to wait. *Shenandoah* had a few immediate chores to take care of, so it was going to be up to Hawes to take the bonded *Milo* and her human cargo back to civilization.

Shenandoah steamed off after more victims, leaving the captain of *Milo* with orders to finish stripping *Sophia Thornton* and then administer the coup de grace himself, "After which he had orders to fire her."

> *Made a sail to the south and west, stood for her. She proved to be the American brigantine* Susan Abigail, *a fur trader from San Francisco. Taking off the crew and officers with their effects, we fired her. Standing to the north and east, past the* Sophia Thornton *burning. We shipped several men from our various prizes.*

If Captain Hawes, from his vantage on nearby *Milo,* had harbored any thoughts of defying the Confederate's instructions to burn *Sophia Thornton,* he suppressed them after witnessing this textbook display of the raider's lightning prowess. In the space of a few hours, *Shenandoah* had darted southward to the horizon, pulled over another ship, set it afire, come about, and headed directly back toward him. If ever a whaling skipper was overcome by the need to bum a light, it was surely Hawes.

June 23 ended much as had the "first" Thursday, with fresh triumph born of bold action—and more bad news; or, rather, the confirmation of bad news. Captain Smith of *Wm. Thompson* had known what he was talking about regarding the South's plight, as *Susan Abigail*'s skipper confirmed.

> *Toward night, stopped steaming for fear of getting into ice as it is very foggy. The vessel which we captured today is one of the late arrivals from San Francisco and brings the confirmation of the assassination of*

Lincoln, the fall of Charleston, Savannah, Wilmington, Richmond
and the surrender of General Lee with 16,000 men.

Once again, Conway Whittle groped wildly for hope, like a drowning man thrashing for some slender reed. He grasped the strand that had always been available to him: a belief in belief itself.

The news is, if true, very bad, but, "there is life in the old land yet."
"Let us live with a hope." "The God of Jacob is our refuge." Oh, let us
trust in Him.

What justification, what possible pretext, now remained for continuing on with the mission?

There was this: the news from San Francisco had confirmed only military losses. There was no pronouncement that Jefferson Davis had been captured, or that the South had formally surrendered. Besides, propaganda was rife in the Northern press; everyone knew that. It pulsed through the telegraph lines to San Francisco. One could not believe what one read in the papers.

Shenandoah would fight on.

"This has been a bad day," Whittle recorded on Saturday, June 24, but this time his reference was to the weather: a high barometer, indicating easterly winds that would sweep in more heavy fog. "It was certainly so today for the fog was like rain." The raider picked her way carefully, moving under steam and only when "we could see any distance"; the constant fear of ice slowed her pace, but still she made eighty miles. A steady trickle of captured crewmen had been offering allegiance to the Confederates, and on that day two more stepped forward. They were from *Susan Abigail*, bearer of the hard news from San Francisco, and their enlisting heartened Whittle; it gave him new reason to resist conscious acceptance of what he must have known, at some depth of his being, was the inevitable.

The fact of their joining shows how much faith they had put in the
news. They all agreed in saying that there is very little confidence to be
put in it and that very little of it was to be believed.

Whittle stopped short of asking himself, *How much of what these* men say is to be believed? Proclaiming allegiance with the Confederates was their only way of escaping the fetid dankness of the hold. What rational man would not humor his captors in such a situation?

Instead, Whittle feverishly chose to build hope on the foundation of another scrap of unconfirmed news:

> *They say that there are riots all through the North and that the public mind is most feverish. God grant us his aid I pray.*

❧

St. Lawrence Island revealed its seventy-mile length off the port bow late that evening. At 2:00 a.m. in the eerie light of the Arctic night, *Shenandoah* set her course in its direction, wary of the shifting currents and vast ice fields that stood in the way. St. Lawrence, forty miles off the Siberian coast and 230 miles west of Nome, Alaska, put them but a two-day sail south of the Bering Strait—the pinch-point between North America and Asia. The portal to the Arctic Ocean.

Sails soon appeared in the raider's path. Two ships. She gave chase, but one turned out to be French and the other Hawaiian. No cause for frustration, though, in these waters: "Soon after saw a sail on the starboard bow. Stood in chase." Closing with the stranger just below St. Lawrence Island, the Rebels found themselves observing Yankee whalers at work harvesting their own prey, wielding their giant flensing knives upon the carcass of a whale tied up alongside. These crewmen were filleting the beast's blubber for boiling down into whale oil—but they would never finish the job: "She proved to be the whale ship *Gen'l Williams*. Capt. Benjamin of New London, Connecticut. We got the prisoners with their effects off and burnt the prize."

Hard upon this conquest, *Shenandoah*'s crewmen found themselves obliged to switch personas, once again, from warriors to genial hosts. However improbably in this remote ocean, an ocean strewn with ice and storms, they found themselves surrounded by a flotilla of primitive small craft. Envoys from the island now heralded a new invasion by curious natives. Whittle and Waddell welcomed them cordially, but the lieutenant's appraisal of them was not burdened with tact:

> *Several Esquimaux from St. Lawrence Island visited the ship in their canoes made of skins of Walrus, stretched over a wood frame-work. A miserable looking race of people of a light copper color with straight black hair, but well formed and muscular. They were dressed from head to foot in skins of the thickest kind. They live on fish and whale blubber and are said to be no more choice in their diet than are buzzards.*

The "Esquimaux" had their look around, reboarded their canoes and paddled away. For a few hours the ocean remained vacant of sails, and some semblance of routine returned to the ship: "Placed Master's Mate C. E. Hunt and Capt's Clerk I. C. Blacker under arrest for fighting. Upon investigation the former was restored to duty." Whittle then paroled the roughly two hundred new prisoners, allowing them freedom from confinement in leg irons, but keeping them under guard. This was a combination of the lieutenant's humaneness and the fact that there weren't nearly enough leg irons to go around.

Around midnight, the sun's weak light shone dimly on three new strangers, and a few hours later, *Shenandoah*'s great spree resumed. "Steamed for them, passing several fields of ice." The chase was brief, and brought the usual results:

> *Came up with the three vessels, which proved to be barques* Wm. C. Nye, Catherine *and* Nimrod, *all of New Bedford, Massachusetts. Took off all the prisoners with their effects, paroled them and took them in tow with their baggage in their own boats and set fire to all three of them.*

That early red dawn, June 27, 1865, revealed as bizarre a procession as any ever undertaken in naval warfare: a sleek three-masted cruiser winding her way carefully among the great slabs of ice, and being towed along behind her, like obedient ducklings, a dozen longboats packed tightly with men and tied together, bow-to-stern. Prisoners of war in a war long past.

This was James Waddell's makeshift solution to the burgeoning number of prisoners his Confederates had taken from the destroyed whalers. Fearing an insurrection if the captives were herded aboard *Shenandoah,* the captain had ordered them aboard their own longboats and had them towed.

Luckily for those passengers, the wind and seas were calm, if foggy. Luckily, as well, their captors were scrupulous in regard to human life. Conducting a sightseeing excursion through the Bering ice fields was not exactly part of the Confederates' assigned mission, but they had no civilized choice. The raider chugged ahead at reduced speed to minimize the chance of swamping her victims; but she remained on full alert for quarry. The pickings would never be this good again.

Shenandoah steamed on through the maze of ice. Behind her, the calm ocean surface glowed orange with the reflections of flames from three burning ships.

And the day was just beginning. Still in the early morning, "Five sails in sight to the south. Stood in chase of the four closest together. At 8:00 a.m. came up with them in succession and took possession of the barques *Gen'l Pike, Gipsey,* and *Isabella.*"

It was probably from one of those three captures that the raiders heard a ghastly rumor concerning the fourth ship, *Robt. Cummings:* its crew was infected with smallpox. Here was a horror unlike any *Shenandoah* had encountered. Little was known about this terrifying viral disease in the nineteenth century except that it was untreatable. Vaccines derived from the cowpox virus had existed since 1796, but inoculations were not yet routinely performed. While not always as lethal as the dreaded cholera, smallpox could be devastating within small, enclosed populations. Populations of fleas, of rats, of men. The crewmen of *Robt. Cummings* were trapped with the disease. No doubt many if not most were in the throes of fever, covered in lesions, and vomiting in pain.

Shenandoah sent a longboat close enough for its party to observe and verify the truth of the rumor; then they quickly backed away from the stricken ship, to the dismay of the suffering men aboard. This withdrawal carried an excruciating moral implication, one left unexamined in Whittle's diary. It likely amounted to a mass death sentence. Isolated now from their captured sister ships, which were about to burn, and with no port in easy reach, *Robt. Cummings*'s decimated crew (certainly there would only be a few hapless survivors) would not be enough to sail a ship, and would almost certainly perish, slowly and agonizingly, on a frigid, blank ocean thousands of miles from their families.

Yet there was nothing the southerners could do. Any contact with these men would risk dooming them all. As for towing her to some port, where medical care would in any case be futile—that was simply not an option. As scrupulous as *Shenandoah*'s officers had been about preserving the lives of their captives, they were not on a humanitarian mission. And they were not suicidal. Death was a component of warfare; in some ways it was the point. Death—by hanging—might well be the fate of every *Shenandoah* officer and sailor at the end of her voyage. But to invite smallpox on board now would be both suicidal and pointless.

Robt. Cummings disappeared over the Bering horizon, and from the living world.

Shenandoah quickly resumed the business of war. "The *Gen'l Pike* being the slowest," Whittle wrote on the twenty-sixth, "we decided to bond her and send all prisoners on board." "All" meant the captives from *Susan Abigail*, *Gen'l Williams*, *Nimrod*, *Catherine*, and *Wm. C. Nye*, as well as from *Isabella*, *Gipsey*, and *Gen'l Pike*. These latest captures added to the Confederates' prisoner count by some three hundred additional souls. *Gipsey* was fired immediately. *Isabella* carried the most provisions. The Rebels cut her masts away and spent the rest of the calm, foggy day relieving her of stores of food and water. Water now became at least as precious a commodity as food. *Shenandoah* would head back south before long, and not even her vaunted steam-condensing capacities could convert sea water to the fresh spring waters collected in the whaler's casks:

water from the clear springs of Hawaii, water from the sparkling falls of Ponape.

Whittle's crisp entry at the end of that day suggested an officer almost too wrapped up in action to set words to paper: "We have finished at midnight and set her on fire, and stood in chase of two sails to the south and east."

He could hardly have imagined what the next two days would bring: the first, a day of sly stalking; the second, a day of pouncing.

In the short Arctic darkness, *Shenandoah* had lost sight of the "two sails" spotted shortly after midnight, and turned back to the northeast; but she did not wait long for fresh opportunity: five new sails to the windward set her into attack mode once again.

> *The wind being fairly fresh, we knew that if it came up fog, we would certainly lose our prizes or at least some, so that we stopped steaming, hoisted the propeller, and made sail and commenced to beat up the straits in company with, but a good way off from, what we knew to be a fleet of Yanks.*

Ravenous at the prospect of all this booty, and reluctant to risk letting any of it get away, the Rebel officers cloaked their wolf of a ship in some sheep's clothing.

> *We passed and re-passed several times . . . they saw that we were a steamer but were as unsuspecting as babes, so we will wait until it falls calm and then pounce upon them.*

For the entire windy day the Rebels tacked along beside her prey, to reinforce the illusion that she was harmless. The imbalance of what was to come—fat, helpless Yankee merchantmen; lean, fast, armed, implacable Confederate raider—tempted the kindhearted Whittle to pity. Almost. His deep rage at the violation of his nation—as he saw it—rose in him once more, and came spilling onto the page like lava.

It does make me feel sorry for them, but when I reflect that they have burnt the houses over the heads of our women, stolen their clothes, and all kind of property, and inflicted hardships and perpetrated outrages which [make] me blush with shame for them, and maddens me to a degree which I never thought myself capable of reaching, when I think of this, I say, everything like compassion gives place to intense hatred and a determination in this cruel and relentless war to fight the devil with fire.

The heavy scratching of Whittle's pen, the grinding of his clenched teeth, all but ring out from his concluding vengeful thought:

The laws of nations in war respect private property on shore, but not in the sea, and all I can say is that I will burn as many as is my good fortune to catch.

And so *Shenandoah* tacked, pacing back and forth like the hungry wolf she'd become, shadowing her unsuspecting prey—watching, waiting, waiting, watching—tensed for just the moment of perfect deadly calm.

She waited all night, but commencing the next morning—Wednesday, June 28th, 1865—*Shenandoah* all but set the Bering Sea on fire.

"What a day's work we have had today," Whittle wrote at the end of it, in one of the great understatements of naval history. It began at 6:30 a.m., twelve miles southwest of the Diomede Islands, two rocky landmarks near the center of the Bering Strait between Alaska and Siberia, one of them on either side of the international dateline. At that hour, the raider's lookouts spotted ten sails. The officers knew at once that they had these ships cornered. "The sails to windward cannot get away as the wind is too light." Confident that this covey of Yankees would remain available through the day, *Shenandoah* fired up her steam engine and gave chase to a closer ship sailing to the southward. The pursuit lasted only a little more than ninety minutes. The prize proved to be the whale barque *Waverly* of—where else?—New Bedford.

The raider's crew allowed their captives time to round up personal effects before ushering them off their decks—a courtesy that also allowed the Confederates to ransack *Waverly* for chronometers, navigational charts, journals, anything that would provide intelligence regarding these whaling grounds and who was fishing them, and where. Then they burned her.

The flames and smoke of course alerted every Yankee inside the horizon that a very bad day might be at hand. Time was now of the essence. Within an hour after closing with *Waverly*, the Rebels were hightailing it back toward the hapless onlookers. Standing first to the westward to avoid the ever-menacing ice, *Shenandoah* wheeled toward the north. Ten crews on ten ships watched in mesmerized horror as the raider knifed ever nearer. Their agony was mercifully brief.

"At 1:30 p.m. came up with the fleet of ten sails, all at anchor. All hoisting the Yankee flag." Nine of the ships, as it turned out, had converged to help the tenth, the barque *Brunswick*, whose hull had been ripped open by ice on the previous night. Their good deed did not go unpunished. They sat cringing like livestock in a pen while *Shenandoah* methodically gathered in the biggest single strike of her entire mission.

We hauled away and manned all boats and boarded in succession the following vessels, all Yank whalers. Ships Hillman, Jas. Maury, Nassau, Brunswick, Isaac Howland, *Barks* Martha II, *and* Congress *of New Bedford, Mass., Barks* Nile *of New London, Connecticut,* Favorite *of Fair Haven, Connecticut, and* Covington *of Warren, Rhode Island, capturing all ten which we made prizes.*

In the midst of their exuberant rounds, the Confederates came upon another story of human tragedy. The captain of the *Jas. Maury* was dead, having expired at sea. His widow was on board. Whittle and Waddell had been helpless to assist the crew of the contaminated *Robt. Cummings*, but here they had an opportunity for a humane gesture, and they acted on it.

[We] bonded her for $37,000 and sent half the prisoners paroled on-board to be taken to San Francisco. We picked up the next slowest vessel, the barque Nile *of New London, and bonded her for $41,000 and sent the rest of the prisoners paroled on her for a similar passage. We then towed the rest clear of those bonded, anchored them and burned the whole party.*

For the first time in months, Conway Whittle could feel a sense of awe in the Confederates' handiwork.

We could still see the Waverly *burning so that there were nine in sight in flames at one time.*

Whittle might have been pardoned for spreading his arms, throwing back his head, and bellowing his satisfaction for this billowing bonfire and all that it represented. Here, in these orange, ship-eating flames, coating the sky with the black smoke of Yankee whale oil, Yankee tar, the Yankee-hewn timbers of these Yankee-built ships—here burned the consummation of all the vengeance Whittle and his comrades had sought in their desperate quest. Vengeance for a mauled, slaughtered, starving nation. Vengeance for his lost Pattie, consigned to God knew what fate. Vengeance for his proud, defeated, imprisoned generation—for his imprisoned self. The heat of the blaze, radiating out across the waters to *Shenandoah*'s decks and quickening the skin on his face, could hardly have approximated this inner heat of Whittle's, this hatred of the alien North, so often expressed and re-expressed in his journal:

. . . but when I reflect that they have burnt the houses over the heads of our women, stolen their clothes . . . and perpetrated outrages . . . maddens me . . . everything like compassion gives place to intense hatred and a determination in this cruel and relentless war to fight the devil with fire.

He'd been born into a military culture; it had been all he'd known since before he'd attained the age of reason. He had fired his cannon

point-blank against the return fire of a Mexican gunboat for hours.
He'd been annealed in the flames of *Nashville* as it blazed its way unarmed through the fire of the Yankee gunboats in Georgetown harbor.
He had just sailed 25,000 miles across barren and stormy seas; he'd
survived the net of Northern spies at London; he'd survived gales that
laid his ship flat against the great waves; he'd survived treacherous
plots at Melbourne; he'd survived the menace of James Waddell in his
gale-tossed derangements. He had sailed here, nearly to the top of the
world, to the north of the North; and now he was searing the Bering
Sea with flames of plundered Northern wealth.

> *. . . I will burn as many as is my good fortune to catch.*

Now the ships were burning. Now, if ever, was the moment for an
avenging god's bellow of triumph.

But that was not Conway Whittle.

"It is a gloomy sight," he confessed in his log that evening, at the
onset of a typically Hamlet-like meditation:

> *To see these magnificent and valuable works of man so summarily de-*
> *stroyed, but do our enemies in their hellish acts of barbarity of burning*
> *the houses over the heads of helpless, defenseless and unoffending women*
> *and children, consider this? No. [The ships' conflagration] is an awful*
> *sight. But suffering as we have suffered from the ruthlessness of an in-*
> *human foe, we can but consider that we are doing our duty in punishing*
> *them as the only hope of bringing them to their proper senses, for if you*
> *touch a Yankee pocket, you wound him in his sensitive and vital part.*

He'd totaled up how much his day's work had touched the Yankee
pocket, and entered it in the log.

> *This day, we have destroyed property to the amount of $400,563 and*
> *bonded property to the amount of $78,600.*

These were astonishing figures. In early-twenty-first-century dollars, they would have amounted to more than $4.8 million.

With his inextinguishable optimism, Whittle concluded:

This will create an excitement. I trust it will do our hearts good by encouraging our noble people.

Here, Whittle had calculated wrong. By now no amount of money in the world could save the Southern Cause.

15

⤞✦⤝

Conway Whittle could not have realized it, but his own cause—*Shenandoah*'s mission—had now expired as well.

Covington, the latest ship taken by the raider, would bring the estimated aggregate value of these prizes to $1,399,080—or $16,500,000 in modern dollars. Many more months of lonely patrolling lay ahead for the black raider, but *Covington,* burned on June 28, was to be *Shenandoah*'s final prize.

The last two times her gunners had fired—at the fleeing *Sophia Thornton* on June 22, less than a week earlier—were the final shots of the Civil War. *Sophia Thornton,* the second-most-valuable of all the raider's prizes, had tried to make a break for it as *Shenandoah* faced down the nine whalers. She didn't try for very long. As soon as the raider started firing, *Sophia Thornton* stopped running. In all, there would be twenty-three others that surrendered without trying to run. But in Whittle's log, she was the last to draw fire.

They had been near the northern edge of the Bering Sea, latitude 62.40 north, longitude 178.50 west, closer to Asia than to North America.

Whittle had written up the *Sophia Thornton* action with no fanfare—he had no way of realizing that his gunners had fired the Rebels' final rounds in pursuit of an enemy.

> *Chased the vessel, a ship which put on all sail, running into the ice. We gave her two shots which hove her to. We boarded her, she proved to be the ship "Sophia Thornton" a New Bedford whaler. Threw a prize crew onboard keeping as prisoners the Capt. & Mates and ordered her to follow.*

Shenandoah would take a total of more than one thousand Yankee prisoners, many of whom had just recently been bobbing along behind her in longboats. Her rampage so far had decimated the New England whaling fleet and driven it to near extinction. And she was not done hunting. But it had all come too late.

She would continue to scan the horizon, not looking just for prey, but for any ship at all that might have West Coast papers with more-current news. Indeed, from her last prize, *Covington,* the raider had continued to move the hunt aggressively, if fruitlessly, northward. But her officers doubtless understood by now—though no one dared voice the thought—that it was almost time to go home.

But where was home? *What* was home?

All they felt about the war's outcome now was doubt and fear, but these they put aside. For the officers of the *Shenandoah,* both emotions were incompatible with honor and duty.

By the end of June, the last and greatest fire of *Shenandoah*'s mission burned itself out on the Bering Sea, and she edged deeper into the kingdom that now ruled her once more—the kingdom of ice.

In the evening of the conflagration, the raider pushed slowly northward through the treacherous Bering Strait toward the Arctic Circle. Two lonely landmarks let them set their position as the morning mists burned off a bit. The Diomedes, the small, grim set of islands that form the storm-swept western boundary of North America, now lay off to the east on *Shenandoah*'s starboard side, and off her port bow they could make out the headlands of Cape Dezhnev, or the East Cape—the northeasternmost point of Asia. Beyond, in the Arctic Ocean itself, they hoped to find more open water, and even more whalers. Then the fog swept in again, limiting visibility to a ship's length, and a treacherous current soon made each increasing knot a test of nerves. The next morning, as the fog gradually blew away, "we saw ahead and all around heavy ice, floe and pack." Further penetration would surely bring on a collision, a gash in the hull, frigid deaths for all hands. And with nothing but ice ahead, unbroken beyond the northern horizon, *Shenandoah* could expect no more whalers. It would be madness to go on.

At latitude 66.14 north, on June 29, 1865, *Shenandoah* reversed direction at last, and headed back south toward the Pacific, which lay nearly 1,000 miles below her on the far side of the Bering Sea. *Shenandoah* was about to travel 10,000 miles southward, then arc round again and sail another 9,000 miles north, back into the world.

"We went inside the Arctic Circle as was shown by our bearings," Whittle noted proudly. "I suppose Yankeedom will be astonished at our coming away here after them." He might have added that, with apologies to Gen. George Armstrong Pickett, *Shenandoah* had just reached the true "high water mark" of the Confederacy.

Fog and ice—familiar baleful companions—curtained the ship and dominated her crew's concerns for the next several days. They were in a realm envisioned by Edgar Allan Poe, a macabre phantomland where unseen danger threatened annihilation. On Thursday the twenty-ninth, shapes materialized, the dark contours of ships. "We hove to a French ship and the Hawaiian brig *Kohola*, who told us that the northern president had been killed and General Lee had surrendered," Whittle wrote. "News anticipated."

The sea was calm, but for once this was not a good sign; it was exactly the opposite. A calm sea in these waters meant that the normal swells were being muted by ice.

The terrifying ice worked its way deeply into the Confederates' consciousness. At times the fog grew so dense that a sailor could not see his hands, much less the surface of the sea. In these intervals *Shenandoah* sailed on pure faith, and at horrible risk: "At 12 [noon], a very thick fog, but it being a little rough, we took it for granted that we were not near any heavy ice." The ship's propeller was raised out of the water as a precaution, her smokestack lowered, her topgallant sails unfurled. "I went to bed feeling very uneasy for fear of ice."

The ice followed Whittle to bed and entered his nightmares. "At 1 o'clock in the midwatch I got up having dreamt that we were in ice," he wrote on July 1. Neglecting his overcoat, he dashed on deck and found Lieutenant Lee in charge of the watch, "the ship going very smooth and a dense fog." These were danger signs, as Whittle instantly grasped; but Sidney Smith Lee, true to his family name, tended to laugh at danger. "I asked Lee how long it had been so smooth, and he said for all his watch and two hours of Grimbell's. I told him my dream and said we were very near ice. He said he did not think so."

Whittle ordered Lee to slow the ship. Less than a minute remained before his nightmare came true.

I went to my room for my overcoat and had not gotten to the door before the startling report of "land dead ahead!" was given. It was soon reported to be high ice. We were within a ship's length of it before it was seen as there was a very heavy fog.

The calamity dreaded by everyone was at hand. Scrambling and hauling like madmen, the crew managed to swing the ship's sails, and a southwesterly wind filled them in time to slow her down before the impact. Yet impact there was.

Everything was thrown aback but before she stopped her headway, she struck very heavy ice hard enough to wake everyone up. The shock was very heavy and those below thought she had knocked a hole in her bow.

The concussion of hitting a solid wall head-on, even at a crawl, was enough to send shock waves through the heavy ship. As she trembled and bounced backward, crewmen spilled from their hammocks and scrambled on deck to see whether they were about to drown. They were not; no gash opened up in the ship's hull. *Shenandoah's* teak-and-iron hull had held. But the crisis was just beginning. Whittle, still coatless in the gelid Arctic wind, fought to keep his mind clear, to focus on what needed to be done, instant to instant. A loss of focus would mean panic, and destruction. Leaving the overcoat behind, he dashed back onto the freezing deck, into action.

"I went forward, lowered the mats, while Lee took in all sail. Before he did this, she was well in the ice and going rapidly astern." (The "mats" were thick, ice-buffering manila-rope blankets taken from the captured whalers.) A new fear suddenly seized him: the rudder. He sprinted for the stern to investigate, and arrived at the last possible moment.

> *Went aft and found it aport. Just had time to put amidships and put three men to hold it when it struck with great violence against a heavy piece of ice. Holding it amidships alone saved it. When it received the shock, the rudder chain was broken and the relieving tackles were broken in time to save it. The ship was in great peril. The ice was high, hard and heavy, and the fog very dense so that we did not know which way to go.*

This second blow—at the stern—might have caused far more damage than the first, delivered to the bow, had not Whittle's lightning analysis and instant orders, and the crewmen's prodigious strength, prevented the worst. "Aport" meant that earlier, in a futile attempt to miss the iceberg, the giant flap of a rudder had been fixed "hard aport" at a 90-degree angle to the ship's stern—an angle of maximum stress. The oncoming ice floe probably would have sheared the rudder away and left the raider unable to control her direction. By turning the great blade edge-on to the ice, and then holding it there, the three crewmen had acted like toreadors, with the rudder as the sword and the ice as the charging bull.

Yet the ship remained essentially out of control. Her rebound off the ice wall, reinforced by the wind, was now driving *Shenandoah* backward; and, as was the case with her forward motion, she had no real braking system. The next collision could smash her into splinters.

Only drastic action now could save the ship. No protocol in these Southern seamen's experience provided for this profoundly Arctic predicament. As the frigid masses around them closed in—as the seconds ticked away their chances for survival—*Shenandoah*'s officers groped feverishly for an idea. And then inspiration struck: they would gain salvation by harnessing that which threatened to destroy them. They would use the ice floes themselves, first as an anchor to slow the ship, and then for leverage to propel them out of the closing ice-prison, and into a channel that would set them free.

We lowered a boat and ran out a grapnel to the west of north, hooked it to a heavy cake and winded her head in that direction. Ran it to another and hauled her ahead. Got up steam, lowered the propeller and by means of oars and poles, kept the ice clear of the propeller while we steamed very slowly. Hoisted our boat. At 4:30 got out of the heavy ice but during the early part of the day, up to 9:30 a.m., we were passing through heavy floes. At 9:30, got clear and I trust we may never see any more.

Open sea—befogged and featureless though it was—had never looked so good. It was Sunday morning of July 2, 1865, the day of the week on which Whittle customarily mustered the crew and read the Articles of War. On this Sunday morning, any such ceremony might have seemed superfluous, even a cruel joke. Most of the crewmen were leaden with the fatigue of their ice-floe exertions; moreover, evidence had mounted that *Shenandoah's* war no longer existed. At 7:00 a.m., a sail had emerged briefly through the dense fog, but was enveloped again—it would be the last evidence of other human presence on the planet for a month. Yet Whittle commanded the Sunday ritual anyway. If *Shenandoah* was truly "out of the world," and if the world as her officers knew it had been obliterated, then the world on her decks would have to suffice. And ritual would continue, affirming that civilization endured.

A depleted Conway Whittle spent most of the rest of the day in his cabin, absorbed in the Bible—the Old Testament, judging from an entry two days later. He concluded his journal entries that evening with an entreaty to God, on behalf of his family and his beloved (provided they still existed), that expressed a dread he had not expressed before. It was a dread inspired perhaps by his experiences in the Yankee prison camp, and by his awareness, even back in 1864, of the South's depleted resources.

God protect and feed them I pray.

It was the dread of famine.
Fog and drizzling rain dogged *Shenandoah* the following day, but

exhilaration ruled her decks. She had put the Bering Strait and its icy teeth behind her and was running southward before the wind under full topgallants, with her fires banked and her propeller hoisted—a classic creature of the nineteenth-century seas, lean and elegant and assured. She was hardly out of danger yet—the currents beneath her were uncharted and wildly eccentric; the Aleutians lay ahead, where the lingering mists disguised the danger of a rocky island looming up. But the Confederates were racing for latitudes more congenial to them—the fat, sunny part of the globe—and besides, they had survived perils unknown to most seamen. God only knew what had become of their nation, but at this moment they felt unconquerable, invincible. The ship made 198 miles that day, running well, and by nightfall had reached latitude 56.56 north. "We are beginning now to have night, as in days of yore," Whittle exulted. But then his anticipation of the fearful passage between the Aleutians resurfaced, and he hinted at it: "I shall be very much rejoiced when we get out in the broad Pacific once more. I shall hail it with joy."

Two days later, Conway Whittle's joyful mood tumbled down into pitch-darkness. He reached into his soul and ripped apart the lining that normally constrained the deep well of rage that he harbored toward the nation—the alien civilization—that had destroyed his homeland. The occasion was July 4, observed as Independence Day in America since 1777—a holiday, he well knew, that the North would celebrate with special vigor this year.

The South had once celebrated the Fourth with equal vigor. But the war had contaminated the day for Dixie. It had been on the Fourth of July two years ago that besieged Vicksburg surrendered to Grant's army, while at Gettysburg, Meade had just decimated Lee's legions: the beginning of the end.

And so, on an evening of smooth seas and light winds, *Shenandoah* having covered 185 miles, Conway Whittle ensconced himself in his cabin, raked his pen through pure venom, and unleashed into his journal a torrent of invective that a century and a half later remains a remarkable document, as pure an expression of the Southern patriot's take on the Civil War as is likely to be found anywhere.

This is the 4th of July. Who can celebrate it? Can the northern people, who now are, and for years have been, waging an unjust, cruel, relentless, and inhumane war upon us, to take from us the very independence, the declaration of which 90 years ago made this day to be gloried in? Can they glory in the day? Have they the bare-faced audacity, when five of the original thirteen are now battling against more grievous wrongs from the others than they could ever urge as a support to their cause? Should they not rather blush with shame at their present course and relent?

He angrily answered his own rhetorical question.

Yes. They have the audacity. Their honor, honesty, Christianity, civilization is all gone. They blush at nothing except that which may be honest & honorable, and in their own acts they rarely blush for even these causes. Oh God mete out confusion and discord to their councils.

"Independence"?! The North had corrupted its very entitlement to the word! As Whittle scrawled on, he found himself disgorging a thought that might have shocked at least some of his fellow officers.

If any people can celebrate the day, the Southerners are the ones, for they are now battling the same right aggravated by causes ten times as strong as those for which in 1775 they fought. But if such a thing is possible and these wicked men be successful, I for one would regret from the depth of my heart that we ever knew a 4th of July for tomorrow I would rather be ruled over by the President of Liberia than by the Yankees.

Liberia, of course, was the west African coastal settlement occupied since 1820 by "free men of color" who emigrated there from America under the auspices of the American Colonization Society. It had declared itself a republic in 1847, and now was home to nearly 13,000 citizens.

In his next sentence, Whittle defiantly reaffirmed his cultural blasphemy, in language that in a later century would be denounced as arrant racism.

Yes, I would rather see the most worthless Negro in the whole world rule over us than the Yankees, who I consider a race of cruel, fanatical scoundrels, lost alike to honor, decency, honesty & Christianity. Any but those cruel, inhuman brutes, baser than the basest.

The greatest iniquity, to the men of Whittle's time and place, was not Southern racial subjugation, but Northern hypocrisy:

They will celebrate the day with even more enthusiasm than before. To the world they say they are fighting to free the slave, because they have in such a war the sympathy of the world; to their soldiers, they cry Union and the old flag, as the cry best calculated to make them rally. Whereas in their own cruel, cowardly, dishonest, and inhuman hearts, their sole object is gain, and not a single one exists but that has his eye on the rich spoils of land & property to be had in the south.

The Yankees tell the world they are fighting to free the slave? Very well, then! Let Dixie's last stand reveal to the world the corruption of this claim, affirm the true cause of this war, and show the true affinity that united the two races in the Southland!

Let us free and arm our slaves, let every old man, every young woman in the south be armed. Let their principal practice and cry be to shoot dead the invader, whenever and wherever he be found, putting their trust in the justice of an Almighty, all powerful and all just GOD. The God of Jacob be our refuge.

The God of Jacob!—it was a biblical reference not lightly chosen by the anguished young Southern Episcopalian. Perhaps his recent nights of combing the Bible had drawn him to it. The God of Jacob was the Old Testament God of the elect, the God who chose some men and spurned others not in response to their intrinsic merits, but out of the mysteries of His own sovereign will. God chose flawed Jacob (the "cheater," the owner of slaves, later a slave himself, and an exile) to become the patriarch of the Twelve Tribes of Israel.

Upon such suggestive myths rested a philosophy that Whittle surely knew well: the "Bible defense of Slavery." This tradition, refined in Southern churches across two hundred years, pointed to the Scriptures for evidence of slaveholding as divinely sanctioned. The devout Whittle would have heard many sermons invoking—insisting upon—the righteousness of this view.

Now, at the height of his fury and anguish at the subjugation of his distant homeland, Conway Whittle turned to Scripture to reinforce a wishful thought of almost magical proportions: the notion of the Southland's slaves rising up in the hour of gravest peril to become God's instruments in hurling back the heathen invaders and restoring Dixie to the harmonious kingdom it once had been. He'd witnessed one hopeful portent aboard *Shenandoah,* when John Williams, the pugnacious cook, and a free black man, had elected to ship with the Confederates.

The larger unreality of this hope was hardly unique to Whittle. Nor were the limitations in his feel for the greatest, most fundamental and tragic of America's contradictions.

Calls for the enlistment (or conscription) of Negroes had swept through Southern legislatures almost from the war's outset, although seldom, in the early years, as armed troops. Black units, such as the First Louisiana Native Guards, were rare exceptions, and functioned mainly as provost guards. Male slaves more typically served—many of them quite willingly, many others with impassive fatalism—behind the lines, as teamsters, cooks, laborers, nurses, musicians in military bands—even, in a few instances, as chaplains. Only in the third year of the war, as reckless charge upon reckless charge decimated Confederate ranks, and the replacement pool of young Southern white men grew shockingly thin, did generals and politicians begin to think the unthinkable: slaves must be armed and, if necessary, freed, to fill the gaping holes in the Southern lines. Reports of this panacea would have pulsed across the ocean to Rebel operatives in Europe, and caught the attention of Conway Whittle in Paris and London.

In truth, nearly 200,000 black men saw front-line combat in the Civil War; but most of them—some 180,000—fought in the Union cause. Following Lincoln's Emancipation Proclamation in September 1862, free black men from the North and escaped slaves from the South rushed to enlistment, forming 163 units. Such regiments as the First Kansas Colored Volunteers fought with astonishing ferocity in battles such as Island Mound, Missouri; Honey Springs in what is now Oklahoma; Port Hudson, Louisiana; and the fabled doomed assault on Fort Wagner, South Carolina.

Whittle's dream of Negro solidarity with the Cause proved largely baseless, irrational, an impoverished reading of racial and cultural psychology. Ironically, so did the dreams of most black men who fought for the Northern cause. So did just about everyone's on that subject, on that continent, in that time.

Whittle's charge of "hypocrisy" had merit: the Union's same Negro regiments that proved their bravery time and again on the battlefield (a third of them lost their lives) faced daily disdain, exclusion, even outright animosity from their white comrades in arms.

Lincoln himself seems equivocal about the institution of slavery in the months leading up to the war, and later promoted the state of Liberia as another magical sort of solution to the American Dilemma. The corrupt cynicism of the Federals who oversaw Reconstruction dashed whatever illusions of brotherhood might have survived among black veterans.

A final indication of these Faulknerian complexities lay in the fact that Conway Whittle's dream was not *entirely* baseless. Within the slaveholding system, inherently cruel and dehumanizing, bonds of loyalty did develop between master and slave, bonds that some captive African Americans were willing to fight and die for. As one scholar has written, "It should be noted . . . that in almost every instance where a slave served loyally with his soldier-master, there was a long-standing close relationship between the two. Slave and master had often grown up together, and the emotional ties between the two were strong."*

Shenandoah ran on southward, at speed, through heavy mists that blotted out the light and made the complex and deadly prospects ahead impossible to imagine.

* Charles Rice, "America's Civil War," http://www.civilwarhistory.com/slavetrade/blacksoldiersCSA.htmNovember, 1995.

16

Nine days of rapid sailing under gradually clearing skies brought *Shenandoah* on latitude with the new state of Oregon and a small settlement known then by its thousand lumber-jack citizens as Stumptown, and now as Portland. Her destination, and her mission, remained basically unclear, even to her officers—except for her commanding officer, James Waddell. Waddell had a plan in mind, a bizarre and desperate plan that he shared with no one. It was the reason, though, that he had recently ordered a rehearsal of the ship's cannon by the gunnery crew.

Everything depended on whether the South and the North were still at war. Nearly all hands on board had their opinion about this, but since no conclusive proof of the Confederacy's surrender had reached them, duty trumped doubt as always. This was, they all believed, likely to change as soon as they met another ship, perhaps in a day or two. Warily the Rebels drew southward, still well offshore of San Francisco, a cosmopolitan center of shipping trade with Asia and the terminus of transcontinental American commerce. The telegraph had reached San Francisco in 1861. Whatever the news that awaited them, it would thus almost certainly be delivered by a ship out of San Francisco. And it would have to be considered definitive.

Meanwhile, *Shenandoah* was traveling ahead of her own news, moving as fast as possible, and moving incognito. Ponderous *Milo*, with her cache of two hundred prisoners, had set sail from the Bering Sea a full week before the Confederates, but had almost certainly been becalmed for several days; the raider had switched to steam and hurried down into the Pacific. The other ships were doubtless even farther behind.

All of which suited James Waddell's plans perfectly. *Shenandoah*'s captain had been nursing his secret bold idea ever since the ship broke free from the Bering ice floes and raced southward, a plan that—so it seems he had come to believe—depended on utter secrecy for its execution. He apparently had not shared this idea with Conway Whittle; at least, Whittle's log made no mention of it, nor did that of any other officer or crewman. Yet the notion had deep roots, in Waddell's mind and in the minds of some of the Confederacy's more imaginative naval strategists. In fact, it had fueled part of the Confederacy's hunger for those giant Liverpool-built ironclads, frustrated by the British embargo of 1863. James Bulloch, the man who singlehandedly created the Confederate navy's blue-water cruiser force, and his superior, Navy Secretary Stephen Mallory, had dreamed of uses for these behemoths that went far beyond blockade-running and storming America's inland waterways. The two envisioned dispatching them around Cape Horn—their great trapezoidal hulks somehow neutralizing those powerful waves—and northward through the Pacific to shell and level the coastal cities of the West. Now James Waddell found himself in a position to carry out at least a version of that dream, however reduced, however fanciful.

His plan was to attack San Francisco.

In his memoirs, Waddell pinpointed the resurrection of that plan. "It was the 5th of July when the Aleutian Islands were lost to view," he wrote, "and the craft made for the parallel where west winds would hasten her over to the coast of California, for I had matured plans for entering the harbor of San Francisco and laying that city under contribution.[24]

Incredibly enough, the captain counted on a handy ironclad, lying at anchor in that harbor, to aid him in this assault. The fact that it was a Union ironclad made little difference.

He had learned about this vessel (the USS *Camanche*, built in Passaic, New Jersey, and shipped around the Horn in pieces) from the Union newspapers captured in the Aleutians: "In the harbor . . . was an ironclad commanded by Charles McDougal, an old and familiar shipmate of mine. We had been together in the *Saginaw* and McDougal was fond of his ease. I did not feel that he would be in our way, any officer of the *Shenandoah* was more than a match for [him] in activity and will." Given that no other Federal warship was in the vicinity, another tidbit from the San Francisco papers that may well have been false, Waddell envisioned an easy takeover. "[T]o enter the port after night and collide with the iron ram was easy enough, and with our force thrown upon the ironclad's deck and in possession of her hatches, no life need have been lost. [McDougal] could have been with the officers secured, and e'er daylight came, both batteries could have been sprung on the city and my demands enforced."[25]

But Waddell knew that to attack the city without definitive assurance that the Union and the Confederacy were still at war would be to risk the lives of all aboard: "Prudence dictated communicating with a vessel recently from San Francisco before attempting the enterprise." If the South had already surrendered, no court in the land would refrain from executing the captain and every member of his crew.

Ironically enough, information of the South's surrender had been addressed to James Waddell several weeks earlier, by Bulloch himself in London, along with precise instructions on what to do, or at least *not* do: "Desist from any further destruction of United States property upon the high seas and from all offensive operations against the citizens of that country."[26] The problem, of course, was that delivery of this letter was fundamentally impossible. The accommodating British distributed it to several ports that *Shenandoah* might visit. She visited none of them. She simply advanced cautiously southward, in open sea, no land remotely in sight. Her mission now—the cruelest irony—was to discover from a passing ship some news of the war.

James Waddell had been absent from Conway Whittle's journal, and therefore almost certainly from his thoughts, for many days. (So also had Whittle's daydream of arming a captured ship, rounding up some junior officers from *Shenandoah* and commanding a parallel operation. The whalers captured en masse on June 28 had presented a golden opportunity, but the lieutenant had let it pass.) But on Thursday, July 13, Waddell celebrated his forty-first birthday. And Whittle let pass another golden opportunity, this one for a thorough fence-mending with the troubled captain. All the other junior officers pooled their limited resources and treated Waddell to a festive dinner in the wardroom. Lieutenant Grimball presided, flourishing a white tablecloth and covering it with meat, vegetables, and several varieties of wine—"great luxuries at sea," as Lieutenant Chew noted.[27] But Whittle, playing a bit of tit-for-tat, bowed out, offering a somewhat far-fetched excuse— especially given that he was Waddell's second-in-command—for keeping his distance.

> [B]y invitation he took a nice dinner with us in the wardroom. As it was blowing a gale, I only was present to drink his health, and then went on deck.

The gale had come up suddenly, from the east, at four-thirty in the afternoon. The wind's movement all day had been peculiar, Whittle noticed. Now its force was such that navigator Bulloch turned the ship about so she could run with the wind behind her. Soon it was necessary to furl the foretopsail and close-reef the main topsail and fore staysail. But Bulloch's turn only placed the ship at a precarious angle for swells. "There was a heavy sea and she rolled fearfully. Everything was playing Isaac and Jonahs." (Whittle meant that the ship was rolling over so far to one side, and then the other, that a classic watery death threatened all hands in either direction.)

Where had this monster storm come from, and why had it struck so suddenly? It seemed almost supernatural. And so it proved!

> No one could account for the gale until it was reported that the cat was overboard. As soon as this was known, there was no doubt of the cause.

The gale was the ship's cat's fault. The cat, having slipped—or, far worse, having been pitched—overboard, had placed the ship under a curse.

More than a few crewmen would have taken this theory at face value. Ships have been hothouses of superstition from time immemorial. Sailors attached ancient significance to all sorts of things. A woman aboard a ship would roil the waters (but a naked woman would calm them; there being a shortage of available naked women through most of maritime history, carved topless figureheads became popular). If the rim of a glass rang and was not stopped, a shipwreck would ensue. A halo around a seaman's head—the fabled "St. Elmo's fire"—signaled that he would die within a day. It was bad luck to kill an albatross, or even a seagull, because such birds contained the souls of dead sailors. Pouring wine onto the deck would guarantee good luck, but throwing stones into the sea would bring on storms. Flat-footed people should be avoided at the outset of a voyage, and likewise red-haired people. If such contact could not be avoided, speaking to them before they spoke to you would be of some help.

Cats comprised an ocean of superstitions unto themselves. Cats could forecast the weather; a yowling cat meant the voyage would be a rough one (but a playful cat indicated smooth sailing). If a cat licked its fur against the grain, a hailstorm was on the way. And if a cat was thrown overboard—well, that was the most reckless cat-related augury of all. Bad luck of all kinds would plague the ship. The most common and immediate form of bad luck was the sudden gale.

Now, as *Shenandoah* rolled from side to side in the suddenly ferocious seas, the rumor of "cat overboard" raced from crewman to crewman. And few of the sailors harbored a doubt as to the culprit. The culprit was Lieutenant Conway Whittle.

He'd brought on the speculation himself, to be fair, via a spectacularly careless remark. "I thought the cat was overboard," he later admitted, in rather arch language, to his journal, "as I had intimated to the Master at Arms that such an expenditure would be agreeable to me." He added, "I was by no means one of the superstitious ones."

The problem was that "the superstitious ones" constituted a huge majority, and now this majority was focusing its indignant attention on Whittle—or at least as much of its attention that could be spared from hanging on to the ship for dear life. "All were scolding me as the Jonas," he lamented to his journal, perhaps intending to write, "as the Judas." It was starting to look like a tough spot for the lieutenant, tougher in its way than his ordeal by fire aboard *Nashville* . . .

. . . when up walked the cat.

This put a slightly different spin on the situation.

"No one was more surprised than I," he allowed in the privacy of his cabin, "for I thought poor pussy gone. I gave orders to let the cat live."

The cat apparently appreciated the gesture: "The ship is rolling fearfully but easily, being in fine trim." But perhaps not: the next day, Jack Grimball was felled by a bout of high fever, and one of the Kanaka transfers, John Boy, suffered a mangled right hand when it was caught in a block on the main topsail halyard.

⚜

Conway Whittle may have disdained superstition, but religion was a far different matter with him. His relationship to Christian faith was at once ardent and—as he occasionally let slip in his journals—tortured. On the balmy, uneventful Sunday of July 16, as *Shenandoah* covered 189 miles under favorable winds, Whittle led two devotional services on the raider's deck, "and many consoling passages cheered my poor heart." In the early evening he repaired to his cabin to reread, for perhaps the hundredth time, his tattered letters from Pattie, and "commune with my God." Excruciating worries followed him: worries about his brother and sisters, about the specter of his nation's subjugation. He imagined himself penniless and thus without means to consummate "my fondest hope," marriage to his dream girl. All of it teased up the curious, lacerating self-doubt he harbored about his worthiness as a follower of Christ.

> *Oh! how I wish I was a Christian! And why am I not? Why can I not be? Most honestly I pray God to assist me in my desire and attempt to become one.*

Whatever qualities Whittle felt were missing from his qualifications as a Christian, devoutness was not among them.

> *Were it not for my belief in his almighty justice, my reflections about the condition of my dear sisters and country would run me mad. I paced the deck and my thoughts all revert to them and are gloomy, sad*

and distracting almost to insanity. But then I think of the blessed as-
surance from God and oh, how consoling. Oh! God teach me to trust in
thee!!

Well south of San Francisco on July 17, as Waddell remained discreetly on the prowl for a stranger bearing war news, Whittle let his
thoughts drift to more satisfying fancies. The dedicated naval officer
again replaced the seeker of faith. How shocked the Californians
would be, upon *Milo*'s docking, to learn of *Shenandoah*'s great fiery
rampage in the Arctic! The outside world had not heard of the raider
and her crew since Melbourne, nearly six months earlier. "I have no
doubt," he assured himself, "that we have been reported and rejoiced
over as wrecked." They were about to learn differently. Of course the
news, telegraphed across the continent to Washington, would galva-
nize the entire Federal fleet—but in the wrong direction! Whittle
imagined the Yankee ships converging in the northern seas, "when we
will be booming along some 800 miles from San Francisco, and some
thousands of miles from where their whole fleet will be looking for us."

If anything, Whittle underestimated the effect of *Milo*'s news. The
whaling ship did in fact dock in San Francisco three days later, and its
crew's accounting of *Shenandoah*'s fiery rampage in the Bering radiated like shock waves through the city and up and down the coast.
Californians had been in a state of near terror for months, as news
from Melbourne had warned of the raider's approach to the continental coast. A chilling rumor had it that a sister ship of *Shenandoah* had
already stolen into port, incognito, and its crew had rounded up supplies for the approaching monster. Even as far north as Puget Sound,
residents were regularly scared silly by reports that *Shenandoah* was on
her way, intent on spewing fire and destruction.

That evening, still far out in the Pacific, the heavens themselves
cheered Whittle's thoughts, and he found a new reason to let gratitude
replace his fugitive gloom: "Tonight we see a great many stars which
increase in number. In the Arctic region, we never saw one. Again we,
too, have night and day." Stars were important to a mariner for many
reasons. Psychologically reassuring—old friends in the night sky—
their patterns offered a welcome contrast to the featureless ocean.

These same fixed patterns, of course, provided essential reference points for navigation. Whatever else may have changed, vanished, been transformed beyond recognition, the stars at least would always be where they had been on the previous night.

Whittle was not likely a reader of that archetypal Yankee, Emerson, and it was just as well. In 1860, the last year in which all was as it had been in America, Emerson had written a brooding poem about illusions that contained the lines "Know, the stars yonder / The stars everlasting / Are fugitive also."

On Tuesday, July 18, at latitude 36.03 north, Whittle remained hopeful of another conquest. He noted the strong southwesterly breeze, and commented, "I trust it may last until we get the regular northwest breezes which are to run us down to where we catch the regular trades."

His optimism, perhaps willful by now, had begun to isolate him from his fellow officers, including James Waddell, and thus from Waddell's intentions. His journal entries revealed his lack of access to the captain's mind.

> *I trust we may be so fortunate as to pick up a vessel from San Francisco to China which will give us late news. God grant that it may be good and that the views of some of our officers may not be consummated.*

Those darker views found expression the following day, when Waddell ordered an artillery drill: "We . . . fired two blank cartridges from each of our starboard guns, firing by broadside." The presumed targets of these guns would not likely be merchantmen. The assumption had swept the ship that soon *Shenandoah* would be confronted by Federal men-of-war. Whittle, clinging stubbornly to his pose of optimism, made no mention of this; instead he accentuated the positive:

> *Considering that it was our first time, we did remarkably well, but we need practice and without it, we cannot expect to be perfect. I was much gratified by the working of the guns.*

Waddell ordered the drill repeated the following day, July 20, 1865, "and the men did much better than on yesterday showing that they only need practice to become proficient." Proficient under what conditions, Whittle chose not to say. The shipboard sense of impending combat was by now all but inescapable. Yet by Sunday—July 23— Whittle was still in his studiedly serene frame of mind. It was almost as though his sanity depended on it.

All hail another day of rest. I feel that I enjoy the holy day more and more as they come. I feel that now I would like to be a good man, a Christian. I feel more in earnest when I commune with my God and I feel more faith in my prayers being heard, listened to and answered than formerly.

But his Christian charity was growing as strained as the prevailing mood. Henry Canning, who despite his infirmities struck Whittle as "the greatest pest of the ship," abraded Whittle's taut nerves the next day, and paid the price. This time Whittle betrayed no regret about punishment, and offered no homilies about the essential goodness of the crew, writing only that "I triced him up for three hours. He is more trouble than he is worth. I wish he was out of the ship."

Two days later the façade began to crack—at least in the privacy of his cabin.

All day I have been thinking about my dear ones at home, and taking the report about the occupation of Virginia as true, my thoughts are sad! sad!! sad!!!

On the last day of July, a clearly restless Whittle moaned that "we have traversed three tracks of vessels to China, Japan and the Sandwich Islands and have not seen a single sail." And then he made the mistake of expressing a wish: that "we could see a vessel if but to get some news. We have none since we heard of the death of President Lincoln."

Two days after that, Whittle's wish horribly came true.

On August 2, *Shenandoah* had completed a wide, sweeping course change, in search of wind. She had lost her northeast trades, as Whittle had noted on July 25, and faced "the doldrums," as the lieutenant put it. She'd completed a turn to starboard that took her to the northwest, and now had shifted back to the east-southeast. And into the path of a stranger out of San Francisco, which brought the news that Waddell had grimly sought and that Whittle had so hopefully yearned for—news that broke the young man's heart.

At sea, August 2 . . .

The darkest day of my life. The past is gone for naught, the future as dark as the blackest night. Oh! God protect and comfort us I pray.

In a few words I will say why we are plunged into the deepest distress that ever men were threw [sic]. *At 12:30 made a sail bearing NW and made chase. Overhauled the chase which hoisted the English colors, an iron bark. Boarded her; she proved to be the Bark* Barracouta *from San Francisco 13 days ago, bound for Liverpool. She brought us our death knell. Our dear country has been overrun, our President captured, our armies & navy surrendered, our people Subjugated. Oh! God aid us to stand up under this, thy visitation.*

There is no doubting the truth of this news. We now have no country, no flag, no home. We have lost all but our honor & self respect and, I hope, our trust in God Almighty. Were men ever so situated? The Captain gave me an order to dismount & strike our battery, turn in all arms except the private items, and disarm the vessel as no more depredations upon the United States shipping will be done. We went sorrowfully to work making preparations but night coming on, we will await tomorrow to finish our work. Hoisted propeller and made all plain sail.

I feel that were it not for my dear ones at home, I would rather die than live. Nearly all our work in the Arctic must have been done after this terrible visitation but God knows we were ignorant.

When I think of my darlings at home and all our dear ones, my heart bleeds in anguish. From my father's position I can form no idea what they will do with him. He is excluded from the amnesty proclamation, and God's intervention alone can induce them to spare his life. Beverley [his younger brother who had gone to war at sixteen] *was in the army, but I pray God that he may be spared. What is then to become of my five sisters and two little Brothers. They have no means, no property and God alone knows what is to prevent them from starving.*

The anguished Whittle consulted his Bible again. Revealingly, he moved from the fiery Old Testament to the New, with its messages of peace, hope, and redemption. And thoughts of famine forestalled. He quoted again from Psalm 37:25:

Trust in the Lord. "I have been young, and now am old, but never have I seen the righteous forsaken, or his children begging bread." Let this be my motto until I can get safely into some port. Oh! God protect them for Christ's sake. I am almost mad and will lay down my pen.

He wasn't the only one—though few of the others came near to expressing their grief with anything like Conway Whittle's customary soulfulness.

James Waddell's egocentric recollection years later of how he received the news, for example, took refuge in ornately worded self-exoneration:

My life had been checkered from the dawn of my naval career and I had believed myself schooled to every sort of disappointment, but the dreadful issue of that sanguinary struggle was the bitterest blow, because unexpected, I had yet encountered. It cast a gloom over the whole ship and did occupy my thoughts.[28]

To his credit, and by his own accounting, Waddell instantly cast aside his personal distress and tried to focus his thoughts like the by-the-book officer he was, and the intrepid mariner he believed he was.

I had, however, a responsibility of the highest nature resting upon me in deciding the course we should pursue, which involved not only our personal honor, but the honor of the flag entrusted to us which had walked the waters fearlessly and in triumph.[29]

In this telling, Waddell had hit upon the proper course instantly: "At the first blush of surrender of the *Shenandoah* I saw the propriety of running her for a European port which, although it involved a voyage of seventeen thousand miles, it was the right thing to do." He added, as if turning from some high drama enacted upon a stage to address the audience directly: "A long gauntlet to be run, to be sure, but why not succeed in baffling observation or pursuit. The enemy had gloated over his success and would, like a gorged serpent, lie down to rest."[30]

Some of those in the front-row seats, however—officers and crewmen who observed Waddell closely over the ensuing days—did not join in any ovation. They later recalled him reading from a different script altogether.

Conway Whittle continued his own passionate dirge the following day:

> [We] *have been going slowly & mournfully along with a light breeze. In obedience to the order which I received from the Captain upon the receipt of the melancholy news which reached us on yesterday, I struck all our battery below, dismounting the guns and striking down also the carriages, also fired off all the pistols and muskets and boxed them up, disarming the ship. This will prove to any but the most prejudiced enemy that we are no longer a vessel having any intention of making any captures.*
>
> *When I think that all our privations, trials, loss of life & blood since the war* [began] *have such an end, I scarce know what to think or do. We are certainly a pitiable people. To think of our fair country being overrun, and our people subjugated, conquered and reduced to a state of slavery which is worse than death. This, of course, is enough to distract one, but what of my dear ones? Who will protect them? There is but one who can. He who afflicts can comfort. God!!! All powerful!! All mighty!! Oh! God give me the Christian life to see threw* [sic] *all this darkness thy power to save! Teach me to resign my all to thee!!*

The officers and crew of *Shenandoah* now grappled with a chilling new reality: they were no longer combatants in a declared war. Their

war had ended in April. Their exhilarating spree of capture and burning in the Arctic thus had no sanction under rules of military engagement. In the eyes of international law, they were pirates. And so they
were subject to the criminal penalties handed out to pirates, which included death by hanging.

17

With grim prospects clinging about her like a permanent fog, *Shenandoah* wandered on vaguely south, parallel to the American continental coastline. Less raider than hobo now, she careered about, scavenging for the wind that had gone out of her sails. She dragged herself barely a hundred miles to the southwest on August 4. Whittle's logbook probably caught the mood of every officer on board:

All day my mind has been distracted by the most painful thoughts.

How ancient the exhilarations of the previous October must have seemed—if anyone on board bothered to think about them at all. How foreign the language of Whittle's exultant entries ten months back: "We hoisted the English flag and he to our great joy hoisted a hated Yankee flag. We then ran up our flag and hove him to with a blank cartridge. We lowered and armed a boat and crew. . . . Very soon we had the extreme satisfaction of seeing the flag which is now the emblem of tyranny hauled down. . . ."

No more.

At one o'clock in the afternoon—Friday, August 4, 1865—a resigned Captain Waddell ordered all of *Shenandoah*'s officers and crew onto the main deck. There he spoke directly to them, for the first time, about the crisis looming over all of them. "It was my duty as a man and a commanding officer," Waddell later wrote, continuing the pose of heroic resolve in his memoirs, "to be careful of the honor as well as the welfare of the one hundred and thirty-two men placed in my hands."[31]

Fine words and true—yet the unapproachable Waddell likely called the assemblage only because he had no other choice. He felt himself hounded down, chased into a corner—first by the Federal ships he believed to be scouring the seas for *Shenandoah,* and, even more tragically, by his own junior officers. Several of them had approached Waddell sometime within the last day or two with a "petition" that they probably intended him to understand as a subtle ultimatum: they wanted to know exactly where the captain proposed to take the ship. No mention of either the petition or of the shipboard meeting appears in Conway Whittle's journal; his notations for August 4 are limited to a note or two about the weather and his own tortured thoughts about fate and faith. But he clearly understood the ship's direction, and the implications of that direction. *Shenandoah's* course was designed to loop southwestward, not eastward; obviously, then, the plan was to swing well below Polynesia, then make for Melbourne. Whittle saw little need to debate, and left the meeting to the junior officers. Accounts of the event were dutifully recorded in the journals of Lieutenants Lining and Chew, and a midshipman named John Mason.[32] They were worried.

In the hours following the news from *Barracouta,* Waddell's pose of forbidding hauteur had begun to dissolve. Any scheme of attacking San Francisco now was obviously moot; but contrary to his later declaration that he "saw the propriety of running her for a European port," Waddell had neither found nor voiced any clear-headed decision on where *Shenandoah* was headed. He'd appeared to accept a majority view of the officers that they return to Melbourne, which lingered in their memories as a haven of friendship and good times. There they would surrender to whatever British or American authorities presented themselves. Only on the morning after he'd instructed Irvine Bulloch to chart a course for Australia did the captain change his mind. Australia, he decided, was too far from home for most of his officers. Instead they would head for some English port, which he did not specify. Then he decided that the port would be Liverpool. Then he had said that, no, it would be a Yankee port instead, unspecified.

Waddell began the meeting on the fourth, as Lining remembered it, by thanking all hands for their service. He insisted that he had no hard feelings for the officers' petition. Then he pointed out that he and his fellow officers faced consequences far more dire than the non-commissioned crewmen; they were almost certain to be prosecuted as criminals, very likely imprisoned, perhaps even hanged.

Then, in Lining's version, Waddell reconsidered yet again and announced the latest course on which he and the officers had agreed: "I shall take the ship into the nearest English port and all I have to ask of you men, is to stand by me to the last." He added, "As for this cruise, it is a record which stands for itself & all you have to do is be proud of it."[33] As Lieutenant Mason remembered it, the crew responded with cries of "We are" and "We will stand by you." Several were in tears.[34]

Even so, Waddell's phrasing—"the nearest English port"—left room for nervous speculation. Did he mean Liverpool? Or Melbourne, which was nearer, and part of the British Empire? Or Capetown, South Africa? Or was he intent on being purposely vague?

"Applications were here made to take the ship to Cape Town, and I declined to do so, keeping to the east of the 30th meridian," he wrote, but that would come later. What seems true in this moment of deep cosmic unknowing was that no one, not even the captain, knew with any certainty at all where *Shenandoah* was headed.

Dismantling the armaments was hard, slow-moving work, and to complete it would require several days. The task of arming her at Deserta had been arduous, too, with seamen working around the clock to transfer these same arms from *Laurel*; but then the labor had been buoyed by the sense of high adventure, the romance of the last desperate chance to save a nation. Now the nation lay, starving, subjugated, no longer a nation. And the hauling of the iron weapons was merely a backbreaking strain.

Firing off the pistols and muskets was the only effective way to disarm the muzzle loaders. In these weapons lay a gauge to the ferocity that had launched *Shenandoah*'s mission. Pistols and muskets were small arms, the weaponry of the Confederate marines aboard ship, useful only in combat at close quarters. The Southern raider had put to sea prepared to fight to the last man. Any Yankee warship bursting from the fog at close quarters would face a death struggle, a hand-to-hand fight, blood and thunder.

But now—discharged into thin air. Into the fog.

"I never undertook a more painful piece of work," Whittle recorded.

South of Mexico now, under balmy skies, less than two weeks above the equator. "It is deemed proper that we should cross the Equator to the 'Eastwards of 115W' in order to clear with the southeast trades the Tahita group of islands," Whittle jotted on the fourth, his handwriting lax. "We are making a poor [job] out of our attempt. I trust that we may soon have a chance for the better."

It was common lore among mariners that certain locations in certain oceans would offer predictably favorable winds during certain seasons. Thus, south of the equator and "Eastwards of 115W," a ship would find trade winds coming reliably from the southeast. Such beliefs drew on experience, primitive meteorology, rudimentary oceanography—and luck.

More central to Whittle's doubt was the very salvation of his soul: "All day my mind has been distracted by the most painful thoughts. Oh that I was a good Christian and that I might with true faith resign myself to my fate."

The crew dismounted two signal twelve-pounders and stowed them below on the following day, "but having limited room for the [heavy] guns, we secured them on deck." The wind remained anemic, and *Shenandoah* fired up her steam engines.

But—steaming for where? Whittle's log still offered few clues. Perhaps he intended to keep any capturers in the dark. Perhaps Waddell himself had not yet disclosed his destination to his executive officer, or even decided on it. Would he order the raider to Tahiti for a hiatus while he thought of a final plan? Could he persuade anybody on board to follow him whatever he decided? Would he bite the bullet and sail her back to England? Did he simply wish to take her out of the now-dangerous shipping lanes? No one knew. Or at least no one was recording any such knowledge. A kind of lethargic indifference reigned as *Shenandoah* continued on her meandering course for the next ten-odd days, a course to nowhere: southeast generally, tacking back and forth in search of wind, headed as if for Colombia or

Ecuador, or perhaps Panama, but not aiming at any of those countries really. A ship still out of the world; a ship without a country; a ship hunted now by an enormous, triumphant navy—a ship, perhaps, of dead men, or men soon to die.

More lamentations for Pattie on Sunday the sixth—lamentations giving way to near despair: "Oh! the first wish of my heart was to call her mine. All is blasted! All is gone save honor, self respect and love. . . ."

Practical concerns took over the next day. Whittle double-reefed the fore and main topsails under winds that suddenly had turned to squalls. "I rove off a new full set of braces," he noted that evening, putting to good use the beginning of the end of his stores from the New Bedford whalers. Whittle was starting to rig for heavy weather. *Shenandoah* had sailed nearly 6,000 miles since leaving the Aleutians, and had logged over 35,000 miles since leaving Deserta. The wear and tear on the rigging was by now tremendous; fraying and overwrought braces likely had caught Whittle's eye. The same strong winds the Confederates were seeking thus became a hazard and a boon.

No amount of make-work, however, could relieve Whittle of his overwhelming sense of calamity.

How difficult it is to act when you can't feel.

And the next day:

Oh! God how cast down I feel. When my thoughts revert to my country and dear ones and they rarely stray therefrom, I feel that God alone can give us strength to bear such adversity.

And the day after that:

To know how I feel would give anyone the blues. How my position is altered. No country, no home, no profession, and alas: to think the fondest wish of my heart, i.e., to marry, must be abandoned. Oh! my darling Pattie, how can I give thee up?!!

And the day after that—August 10 now, the ship reeling to windward, east by north, in another squall, under all plain sail:

What is to keep them from starving I cannot imagine. And my poor dear father, what will be his fate? I dread to dwell upon it but I am prepared to hear the worst. I fear that they will deal but harshly.

Whittle could not bring himself to write down what he meant by "harshly," but his fear, clearly, was that his father, the commodore and director of the naval defense of New Orleans, would be hanged as a traitor. Or that he had already been hanged. And that the survivors in the family would be turned out to starve.

Whittle's dark imagination, vivid enough when applied to his family, could never have embraced the scope of devastation on the continent beyond the horizon on *Shenandoah*'s port side. An estimated 200,000 men, Union and Confederate, had been killed in action during the war—but that was only the start of it. More than 64,000 would eventually die of their wounds. The greatest killer of all, disease, claimed an additional 400,000 lives. Most of the diseases had germinated in the miasma of poor sanitation: diarrhea, which claimed 35,000; typhoid, which killed 29,000; and dysentery, responsible for another 9,500 slow, agonizing deaths as well as measles, mumps, smallpox, tuberculosis, malaria, and the lethal effects of drinking from streams where dead bodies lay. All these and other horrors—24,000 died in prison—contributed to the toll: over 600,000 dead.

Tacking to southward on Friday, August 11, latitude 6.19 north, longitude 107.45 west, winds southward variable, thermometer 80 to 77, cooling down. Then a tack eastward. Then a tack to the southward and westward. Then to the southward and eastward. "We are literally beating to the southward when we should have the northeast trades. These have entirely failed us. We are all wonderfully blue. All will be adrift as soon as we get home."

And so "home" remained alive as a concept in Conway Whittle's consciousness. But then, so did loss: "adrift" meant nothing if not "without mooring." Homelessness.

Some variety—if only a change in the type of setback—at last on Monday, August 14: "Started to get up steam but broke one of the screws on a guide rod and had to delay until 8:20 p.m. for repairs."

Another day of tacking west by southwest, then a 90-degree right turn, an enormous dogleg the next day, under steam. A goal had formed, though hazy enough to qualify as fantasy: "to get safely to some neutral port without capture." But two days later, Conway Whittle had essentially lost all interest in his safety, his future: "I would just as willingly die as live."

Shenandoah accomplished 146 miles on August 17, traveling by steam, trusting the repaired screw, and crossed the equator sometime during the morning watch. No one celebrated anything this time. But Whittle made a faintly optimistic note of the event. "Again we are in the southern hemisphere and its numerous stars are brightly lighting our weary way. The Southern Cross, Antares, and the Sickle are looking brightly on us." The Southern Cross—one of the most vivid constellations that a sailor could wish for, perfectly proportioned, commanded a prominent swatch of the night sky. Many seamen, looking at it, had been seized with the impression that it was beckoning them. But Whittle, God-obsessed though he now was, seemed unable to respond to its transcendent glow: "Oh, how I wish we were just going in the Northern Hemisphere on the Atlantic side. All will be well if God so wills it. Trust in Him."

And there, finally, thirteen days after meeting *Barracouta*, Whittle had revealed a course. Or, if not a course, a goal: the Atlantic, "North of the Line."

Shenandoah was now about a week into her southwest course, a deviation of perhaps 100 degrees from the due-south trajectory she had been following. Strong winds had returned at last, and Waddell ordered the topsails unfurled and the steam shut down. She raced 225 miles on the nineteenth; but a key factor in her increased speed became a matter of concern as well. "Our ship is getting light and we have to watch her carefully," Whittle wrote. In the months since leaving Melbourne, *Shenandoah*'s coal supply had dwindled—and, for that matter, the food supply as well: "our diet is regularly slim, regularly salt, and I would be ashamed to look a salted pig or cow in the face." A lighter ship was a less stable ship. The only significant ballast that remained—the cast-iron cannons—threatened to roll about with the seas, adding to the instability.

And yet she sped on, though to what destiny none aboard knew. She still headed south by west, and she still moved more toward Australia than Africa. She made 188 miles the next day, paymaster Breedlove Smith's twenty-fourth birthday. ("We celebrated it without any extra show.") and 205 the day afterward; then 214, then 227, then 214 again. By August 24, Lieutenant Chew's twenty-fourth birthday (again, noted without fanfare), she had reached latitude 22.26 south, longitude 127.15 west: the middle of the South Pacific. *Shenandoah* and her crew of youthful Rebels were now only a few hundred miles from Pitcairn Island, a spot any mariner afloat that day could well recognize. For Pitcairn Island was the destination of Fletcher Christian, leader of the most famous mutiny of all time. Shenandoah was probably less than a day's sail from the resting place of HMS *Bounty*.

"We are, I expect, the youngest set of officers whoever went to sea," Whittle reflected dully that evening. "The oldest member of our mess (Dr. Lining) is but 31 and the others range from 28 to 21. There are but four older than I and I am not 26."

Far from *Shenandoah*'s lonely location, and unbeknownst to her crew, America had commenced an uncertain voyage of her own: the rough, fraught passage toward a healing that would tack just as fitfully, searching for its own strong winds, for more than a century to come. On August 17, Clara Barton, the "angel" of dead and wounded Union men and founder of the American Red Cross, raised a flag over the newly consecrated Andersonville National Cemetery in Georgia, on the grounds of the largest and most hideous of all Civil War prison camps. Nearly one-third of the 45,000 Federals imprisoned there had died of starvation, disease, exposure, and their own wounds since the camp opened in early 1864. In Washington, President Andrew Johnson ordered that all charges of treason against former Confederate generals and politicians be dropped. The brutal commander of Andersonville, Captain Henry Wirz, was among the exceptions; he was hanged at the same Washington gallows as those accused of plotting Lincoln's assassination.

The failed healing—the horrors—of Reconstruction lay ahead.

❧❧❧

Still hunting the trades—and a purpose—on August 23, *Shenandoah* found herself far out in the central Pacific, more than 3,000 miles west of the South American coast and her ideal trajectory. (But then, what meaning could "ideal" have, absent a destination?) She had all that day continued to hold a course that could indicate Australia: south by west. But toward evening she began to hook southward again, and the winds, like an omen of her fate, remained swirling, capricious, "baffling." They crossed the Tropic of Capricorn on August 24, and their westering ended. They were now some 3,000 miles off the coast of Chile. The next day they would make their final turn east.

August ended with the raider at latitude 19.18 south, longitude 120.02 west. The nearest land would be Easter Island. Whittle was not sorry to see the calendar turn: "Looking at what I have gone threw [sic] during the month, I will always recall it as the most trying time of my life."

September began with plunging temperatures, and shipboard morale headed in the same direction. Whittle sent a seaman named Vanavery to the masthead for nine hours for insolence, without food or water. "When he came down he was like a lamb. A good thrashing would do him great good."

Seamen Peter Raymond and Thomas Evans occupied the place of honor the following day, for fighting. Whittle may have had things other than meteorology in mind when he scrawled, "It is getting cold."

The inner weather worsened as well. "I am weary, weary, weary," Whittle wrote on September 6, more than 1,000 miles from Cape Horn. "No language can express my brokenhearted feelings."

❧❧❧

Days of desultory winds had pushed them slowly southeastward and out of the South Pacific Basin into the waters west of the Horn—"into the thoroughfare," as Whittle called it. This was the east-west trade route for merchantmen headed toward the Drake Passage, the tortuous 400-mile stretch between Antarctica and Cape Horn on the southern tip of South America, where the Atlantic and the Pacific collide. The waters ahead were among the most violent in the world.

The strong winds so maddeningly absent during *Shenandoah*'s mournful creep southward seemed to appear at last as they approached the tip of South America. For five uninterrupted days there had been favorable weather with near-perfect winds: she covered over 262 miles on the ninth of September, her record for the cruise. The almost uncanny conditions continued to improve, and on September 11, roughly where the Pacific Ocean starts to funnel down into the mouth of Drake Passage, Whittle chose to write, with prescience:

> *Ship under all sail. Crossed the Royal Yard. Here when we have been led to believe that we might expect the most terrible weather, we are having as fine weather as I ever want to see. It is a little odd that it is nothing. I suppose the weather off the pitch of Cape Horn will make up for this. Nous verons.* ['We will see.']

And so they did see.

Surprisingly, during the actual passage under Cape Horn itself, the weather still remained virtually perfect. That afternoon, however, and true to their reputation, the winds picked up, but still the skies remained clear. On the twelfth, the crew spotted their first sail since *Barracouta* had crossed their path with the bad news. They had been out of touch with humanity for forty-two days, while covering 6,000 miles. "Kept in company," Whittle wrote. Here was a different motive for pursuing a stranger: loneliness.

It was no good. The stranger proved—perish the thought!—faster. On the following day, she hoisted an English flag, "& signalized, but we did not reply. She walked right away from us most shamefully. Got up the port fore topmast studding sail but she still beat us."

Shenandoah had not "signalized" because she really did not want to get too close to any ship, even for the sake of human contact. She was incognito now, and she struggled along like a furtive shadow-creature, head down, features concealed. And, as feared, the weather worsened.

"Beautifully clear weather, but blowing like scissors with a heavy sea . . . I suppose we will have it heavy." Here, probably, was one of the laconic Whittle's most understated predictions.

The gale that finally smashed at her would last nearly six days.

The cyclonic winds whipsawed her, now coming down from the

mountains of Tierra del Fuego, now churning up from the South Shetland Islands, off the tip of Antarctica. The winds brought heavy seas from the north that seemed intent on pushing the ship back, in a savage, nature-spawned reprise of the late war. At moments *Shenandoah* seemed once again to be trapped in an endless gale.

The crew fought to maintain control night and day as mountainous seas and a powerful northerly wind pushed her far off course to the eastward. By the fifth night of the storm, Bulloch and Whittle, indeed all the men, worried about being blown into the notorious Shag Rock in the dark. That danger passed, but hundreds of miles of rocks lay in their path, an unnerving archipelago starting with the South Shetlands and the South Orkneys.

It was a storm that made men think about one single thing: their own mortality. And it was about this storm that Waddell later expressed a memory of wishing that the gale would take both the *Shenandoah* and himself beneath its waves and end their torment.

An inner desolation, even darker and colder than the moonless South Atlantic, took hold of the captain, and his thoughts turned toward the welcoming peace of oblivion:

> *The struggles of our ship were but typical of the struggles that filled our breasts upon learning that we were alone on that friendless deep without a home or country, our little crew all that were left of the thousands who had sworn to defend that country or die with her, and there were moments when we would have deemed that a friendly gale which would have buried our sorrowful hearts and the beautiful* Shenandoah *in those dark waters.*

18

❧——⬥——☙

B y September 19, the gale was behind them. But not the icebergs. Even larger than many of the rocks, the bergs now demanded a reckoning.

"Today our enemy, ice, made its appearance," Whittle wrote on September 20. "At first we saw a small piece and then several large icebergs, some of which were very close. Heavy fog occasionally. Doubled the watch to look out for the ice." The ice was not hard to spot: some of the bergs rose to heights of 300 feet, and the ex-raider tiptoed gingerly among them. The great frozen masses inspired Captain Waddell to take a plunge, once more, into the unfamiliar waters of lyricism. "Day after day icebergs and savage blocks of ice came near us," he wrote in his memoirs. "We were without a moon to shed her cheerful light upon our desolate path. Some of the icebergs were castellated and resembled fortifications with sentinels on guard, but although the nights were dark we escaped injury."[35]

And so *Shenandoah* was spared a reprise of her Arctic misadventures: she avoided contact with these monsters. By Friday, September 21, Whittle's log showed a new dominant course: north. In fact the course would slant to the northeast; but with the turning of the Horn, *Shenandoah* and her crew now entered their endgame. For better or for worse, after nearly a year of conquest, on a cruise without equal in the history of the world's navies, they were headed back to where they'd started. Toward a new world, or the next world.

❧✦☙

When the gale-force winds finally calmed, they had been pushed far southeastward, not north. With lookouts aloft for sails and ice, *Shenandoah* finally swung out into the far South Atlantic, clearing the unforgiving Scotia Sea and seeking waters off the main trade routes.

At roughly the same time, the heavily armed Yankee cruiser USS *Wachusett* left Rio on an intersecting course with *Shenandoah*. Her mission: find and capture or sink the hated raider. She cruised eastward, searching the South Atlantic for weeks but reached Capetown without success. *Shenandoah*'s luck would hold. *Wachusett* passed within a few dozen miles of her prey, but failed to sight her.

Meanwhile, the restless crew was again wondering: north toward where? At this point, *Shenandoah* could plausibly be sailing for either Cape Town or Liverpool. But no one save the captain knew which.

Waddell's air of secrecy strained shipboard tensions, already at crisis levels. Anger, anxiety, and paranoia, even black despair, had infected the 132 officers and crewmen since the encounter with *Barracouta*. The raiders now had sailed 40,000 miles since leaving Deserta nearly a year earlier, and every mile now weighed on them. Laughter had grown extinct. Small annoyances exploded into grim confrontations, even fistfights. Factions formed, one of them in favor of heading for Cape Town (the "Longitudes"); the other (the "Latitudes") advocating for Liverpool. As of September 26, *Shenandoah* remained on a course that still left her captain time to choose either.

No relief from the fraught atmosphere came from their commanding officer. Here was the figure most responsible for demonstrating the ideals of discipline and morale. This captain was not up to it. Scowling, stalking the decks in imperious silence, erupting suddenly into bewildering tirades and issuing punitive commands, James Iredell Waddell could not contain his capacity for making matters worse.

Discovering Irvine Bulloch and the assistant surgeon Charles E. Lining engaged in conversation near the propeller house, James Waddell branded both of them—for reasons unclear—"a couple of croakers."[36] Worse was shortly to come. Informed that the exhausted Lieutenant Dabney Scales had overslept one morning, the thickset captain flew into a rage. He summoned Scales and lashed out at him for willfully violating the rules of the ship. This marked at least the second time that Waddell had singled out Scales for abuse: in the midst of the terrible mid-December gale, he'd relieved Scales and Francis Chew of their watches, declaring them incompetent, as an incredulous Whittle had looked on in private disgust.

Scales, veteran of the same Yankee prison that had held Whittle, chose the high road here; he gracefully pleaded guilty and tried to convince Waddell that he'd had no disrespectful intent. This only served to incense Waddell further: he threatened to "give Scales passage to the nearest port."[37]

Waddell was only beginning. A few hours afterward, his self-possession veering once again out of control, he summoned the young midshipman John Thompson Mason and told him he'd assigned the fourth watch to his own clerk, Mr. Blacker, "and that if [midshipman Oris] Browne and myself had any objections to make he would relieve us from duty."[38] This was utter nonsense, a tacit slander against the experienced midshipman's competence. Mason held his composure and acceded to the move. The master's mate, Cornelius Hunt, was more candid. Hunt did not want to share a watch with Blacker, an administrative officer untrained in naval duties, and told Waddell so. Waddell banished him from duty. That night, clearly in the grip of his monomania, the captain took the watch himself.

Scales and Hunt were restored to duty a few days later. But the raging Waddell remained a loose cannon. His next discharge was directed at none other than Sidney Smith Lee Jr.—the nephew of the Confederacy's vanquished godhead. Charles Lining was among the witnesses. "Old Lee got into trouble this morning for the first time since he has been in the navy," Lining recorded with acid humor, using "Old" as a term of affection for his comrade. "It riles the old fellow a good deal." Lee's crime involved taking a few puffs of his pipe during his morning watch. Conway Whittle observed him and reported the infraction to the Captain. Waddell summoned Lee—Waddell was doing a lot of summoning these days—and tried to make him promise not to do such a thing again. Lee refused, and was stripped of duty. "I think that Lee is perfectly right in not letting any promises be extorted from him," opined Lining.[39]

It was Waddell's own bumbling that halted this particular spree.

"The Captain put his foot in it again," was the way Lining character-ized it.[40] Still in a manic mood the day after his crackdown on Lee, he ordered all the watch officers to his cabin and explained to them that because of Lee's insubordination and removal, everyone's duty time would have to be increased. Whatever reaction he was hoping for, he did not get it. Instead, Lieutenant Grimball spoke up, saying that he himself had smoked while on watch. Then Scales—perhaps savoring the chance to repay his tormentor—joined in: he'd smoked as well. Waddell, in Lining's memory, was speechless. He threw the junior officers out of the cabin, wrote out a meaningless command restating his prohibition, and restored Lee to his post.[41]

Waddell's shortsighted petulance defied comprehension. No one more than he should have recognized the blatant perils implied by this crisis of unity, and done everything in his power to heal them. He cer-tainly could not count on deep-seated bonds of nationality to hold the *Shenandoah* crew together, no allegiance to common purpose. She was a ship of strangers, of tough seamen-of-fortune who'd been scav-enged—enticed to ship—from this conquered whaler or that. Men from all over the world, speaking all languages, each of them spurred by his own motives, his own degree of commitment to the ship's mis-sion. Now, their mission abolished, death by hanging a distinct prospect for one and all, what was to prevent these hard, tough, de-feated men from turning against *Shenandoah* and her captain? What were the guarantees against mutiny? Only loyalty, and Captain Wad-dell seemed intent on destroying anything left of that.

Conway Whittle's logbooks are silent on the captain's self-inflicted predicament. Despite having sparked the affair by reporting Lee in the first place, Whittle confined his observations during all this turbu-lence largely to remarks about the weather. Months, even weeks ear-lier, he would have jotted down and pored over every detail of Waddell's mismanagement of his command, of the petitions, of the dissension. But now he resisted such temptations. Larger obligations loomed. Everything had changed. The mission as he had understood it—*civilization,* as he had understood it—these no longer obtained. The known universe had shrunk to *Shenandoah* and her crew. With all else lost, these must survive. Survival would depend on the crew's unity, its sense of common cause. To that end, an officer must display rationality, and self-discipline must prevail over any other impulse. Thus, as Waddell grew ever more hysterical, Whittle grew ever more calm. He had, in effect, launched into his own modest version of the Reconstruction.

❧

Few of his comrades seemed to notice this at first, or care. The "Longitudes" and the "Latitudes" grew ever more hardened in their opinions as the ship churned on.

By Wednesday, September 27, *Shenandoah* was nearing another point of decision. Still barely below the southern tip of Africa at latitude 41.14 south, longitude 24.40 west, she was drawing parallel with Cape Town, now some 2,000 miles away. Her course over the next twenty-four hours would tell the officers and crew all they needed to know. Isolated, Waddell shared nothing.

On that night the "Longitudes" could stand the suspense no longer. Seventy-seven of them, a little more than half the souls on board, signed a 6,000-word petition urging the captain to sail for Cape Town. Six officers were among the signers, effectively announcing their independence from their commander. The highest-ranking was Francis Chew, the fourth-ranking lieutenant behind Lee, Grimball, and Whittle. The other signatories were the sailing master, Irvine Bulloch; the ship's surgeon, Charles Lining; the chief engineer, Matthew O'Brien; the paymaster, Breedlove Smith; and midshipman Oris A. Browne. Stressing the "anxiety and regret" with which the crewmen regarded their prospects, the letter went on:

> So long as we had a country and a Government to support and sustain it was done cheerfully . . . so long as there was an object to be gained that object was sought for by none more eagerly than ourselves. . . . Now we respectfully submit, all these motives for exertion are gone.

The document went on to argue essentially that the horrors of capture were too great for *Shenandoah* to risk the long—over 8,000 miles—northward "gantlet" to England. The gothic rumors, and in

certain cases the vivid memories, of the Union prison camps filled
these formerly intrepid combatants with dread.

> It is a well-known fact that during the war, with threats of retalia-
> tion sounding in their ears, the United States authorities frequently,
> almost generally, treated our prisoners with great rigor and severity.
> How much more will be the case now that the war has been concluded
> in the present manner?

What was to be gained by sailing on to England, the petition
asked, and what would not be gained "by proceeding there in some
neutral vessel from a neutral port?" It cited the prospects of terrible
weather—they would be sailing directly into the North Atlantic's fall
hurricane season—and the instability of a ship whose weight had
been depleted along with the stores of coal and fuel. It ended with
rhetorical flourishes of good intentions and respect.

Waddell received the letter the following morning. He glanced at
it, folded it up, and ignored its contents.

Shenandoah had now passed the optimal point of a course change.
Her destination—England—was clear, yet still unannounced.

Hours later, Waddell received a second petition. This one was
shorter, blunter, and more overtly demanding. The identity of its author signaled to Waddell that his adversaries extended virtually into
his cabin: it was written by his clerk Blacker, who personally thrust it
toward him. It bore ten signatures, all by noncommissioned officers.
Blacker remained boldly in Waddell's presence, obliging the captain to
read it while he watched.

It greeted the captain peremptorily as "Sir:" and declared, after the
obligatory opening pleasantries: "The ship has now arrived at a position where we feel the urgent necessity of impressing you with our
feelings as to the destination." The petition restated some of its prede-
cessor's arguments in favor of Cape Town, and laid out new ones with
clipped precision.

The document pointed to the heavy volume of mail and merchan-
dise steamers passing between the South African port and the British
Isles, which would afford the men plenty of transportation chances;

the proximity of Cape Town (about fourteen days' sailing, compared to over forty days to England). Then it got down to brass tacks, forcefully restating the central theme of the first petition: the pervasive horror of capture.

> [A]s this ship has gained for herself great notoriety, we may readily conclude that ships are already on the lookout for us on the usual route. . . . We can not reasonably expect any good treatment if we fall into the hands of the U.S. government. Their treatment of prisoners already has sufficiently shown how we will be dealt with, and as there are several paroled prisoners on board [from Yankee camps] it will go doubly hard with them.[42]

The captain finally grasped the glaring truth: the ship was close to insurrection, and he could no longer afford to wave away the signs. He sputtered a painfully impotent threat to Blacker: "I will be captain, sir, or die on this deck." But even Waddell could see that his authority was critically weakened. He had chosen to stand aloof while the crew split into factions, and now he was reaping the whirlwind.

Soon to come were the petitions arguing for England. The first of these virtually completed a sweep of the officers and midshipmen. It contained the names of Lieutenant Grimball, the highest-ranking lieutenant behind Whittle; Lee, next in rank to Grimball; Scales, the fifth lieutenant; Frederick McNulty, the assistant surgeon; and the midshipman Mason, whom Waddell had needlessly tried to intimidate in the watch-shuffling incident. The second represented seventy petty officers and seamen who, satisfied that the ship's course was to their liking, offered oily flattery and assurances of "complete reliance and trust in whatever it should please you to do."[43]

⚜

The crisis had exposed James Waddell—in case anyone remained in doubt—as a weak man, if not a coward. (His prewar naval credentials made a strong argument against physical cowardice.) In the traumatic wake of the two Cape Town petitions, he had summoned—once again!—a small circle of officers: Chew, Grimball, Scales, Lee, and

Whittle. To these men, Waddell finally made a clean breast of his choice for a port: Liverpool. But these petitions—they had cast things in a different light. Waddell's new decision was to let these officers decide.

In Waddell's travesty of leadership lay a heaven-sent opportunity for Conway Whittle, should he want it: the chance to seize control of the ship from its faltering commander, restore stability, and bring *Shenandoah* to port as a hero.

Nothing was farther from his mind.

Whittle was the only officer who had signed no petitions. Though he privately favored Cape Town as the logical destination, the better angels of his nature expressed themselves in his logbook entry for Friday, September 29. This was the day, as it happened, that *Shenandoah* crossed her outward-bound track of November 29, 1864—eleven months, 45,000 miles, and the girth of a planet behind them. Whittle wrote:

> The minds of a good many who were in favor of going to Cape Town seem very little quieted. There is a position approaching panic among them which I consider very disgraceful and imperious. Some look as though they had already been hung. In the name of honor, truth and propriety let us support the Captain. Even if we are caught and hung, why are we not men? Cannot we stand our fate like men, a fate which unjust tho' it would be, has been stood and met by men of all countries. No! let us throw aside this childishness, and trusting in God, stand like men to brave all consequences of our participation in the struggle now ended by Divine will, for all that is dear to man. God has afflicted us for some just & holy cause; by his will alone can even a sparrow fall. If we are captured, which is most improbable, it will be by his will; trust in him and him alone!!!

Noting the seventy-seven signatures in favor of sailing to England, and the confidence the writers expressed in Waddell, Whittle continued:

> Tho' I differed with him for reasons well known to all, and thoroughly canvassed in my own mind, he has my unbounded support. I am willing to run any risk that he may incur.

Papers, petitions, &c., &c., are not my forte as Executive Officer. I will have nothing to do with them for he has my support in everything, except one, & that would be any attempt to go to a Yankee port.

❧

October washed in on a dark wave. *Shenandoah* was making superb time under sail—well over 200 miles a day—yet she crackled with tension; hostility. Men found reasons to insult one another, take grievance, spread rumor. Waddell had made a feeble attempt at festivity when the ship recrossed her outbound route; he'd sent champagne and a note of congratulations[44] to the officers' wardroom. When it arrived, three of the officers walked out. John Minor started a rumor that Cornelius Hunt had hoarded several hundred dollars found on a Yankee whaler. Men called one another names, nursed grudges and suspicions, stole things from one another; somebody lifted sailmaker Alcott's opera glasses. The ship had now gone more than five months without being resupplied. Food and water were beginning to run low.

Whittle, fighting to maintain his officer's stoic dignity, was no less immune to the prevailing dark cloud than anyone. He processed the growing dread not through anger, but through grief. His journal fairly palpitated with laments for Pattie, whom he had by now given up as lost. "Oh! How awful it is that there seems to be no prospect of my ever being able to ask her to be mine. When I asked before I had a profession to support us, but how changed! . . . Oh! how sad & heartbreaking to give up all hope of her being mine." By October 5, he was imagining his father and brother and sisters lying in pools of their own gore. "My dear father, have they bathed his silvery locks with blood; my dear brother, have they slain my dear sisters and brothers . . . these thoughts harrow my brain."

Worse and more immediate burdens awaited him.

He marked October 8 sadly: "One year ago today, I sailed in this ship from London. It has been a year of constant anxiety and labor from then till now. And to have such a sad, inglorious, pitiable & miserable end is truly heartbreaking." No other Rebel had been aboard the ship longer than William Conway Whittle.

Three days later, *Shenandoah* crossed the equator for a fourth time.

Hardly anybody took notice. Of more interest were the three cases of scurvy that erupted.

On Tuesday, October 10, as *Shenandoah* cut through the tricky currents of the Brazilian Basin, the miniature civil war raging around the raider's decks at last swept Conway Whittle into its maw. The crisis began as a routine case of drunkenness. The hard-drinking and hot-tempered surgeon McNulty, the Irishman who had decked "Father Neptune" for hazing him, and who had triggered the hotel brawl in Melbourne, walked around now in a stupor, or sat slumped; he could no longer perform a doctor's duties. Worse, his drunkenness brought out his dark side.

> Dr. McNulty got on one of his periodic drunks, and was so abusive to some, that he was reported to me. I, by order of the Captain, ordered him to confine himself to his quarters. He is a poor unfortunate, whom I greatly pity on account of his weakness.

This entry made no mention of what had really happened: Whittle had interrupted the surgeon's liquor-fueled tirade and escorted—perhaps carried—the doctor to his cabin as other crewmen looked on. There he relayed Waddell's order to stay put. The half-stupefied McNulty drew a pistol on the lieutenant and threatened to shoot him if he didn't rescind the order. Whittle, risking his life, snatched the gun away and carried it to Waddell, along with a brief summary of what had happened. He assumed that the incident was over and would be forgotten—a routine case of a drunken seaman lashing out.

It wasn't over. The next morning McNulty, sober now, sought out Waddell and insisted that he had not been drunk; his abusiveness to his fellow crewmen had been in defense of the captain—whom they had disparaged—and as for the pistol, he'd produced it only with the intention of showing it to the lieutenant. Whittle's version of the story? Why, it was nothing but cruelty!

McNulty was lying, bald-faced, on all counts. Conway Whittle disliked lying; he abhorred the surgeon's implication that he himself was a liar, and he certainly had no intention of seeing his good name besmirched in the ship's record because McNulty wanted to absolve himself. Whittle acted at once, but carefully. He checked with two witnesses who affirmed that McNulty had been intoxicated. Then, with Dabney Scales in tow as a witness, Whittle knocked on Mc-Nulty's cabin door.

> *I asked him if he intended to deny my report. He said, "All I say, Sir, is that I was not drunk." I asked him if he was not intoxicated, he said he was.*

This was clear insolence: McNulty, confident that Waddell was now safely on his side, was toying with Whittle, mincing words to provoke his superior, daring the lieutenant to call him on the double-talk—or call him a liar. McNulty was an expert at goading people.

> *I asked him why he did not tell the Capt. so [that he was intoxicated], instead of leading him to believe that my report was false, he simply said, "Well, didn't I?" I replied no.*

Here things began to escalate. Whittle grilled McNulty on whether he'd actually just drawn the pistol "to show me," as McNulty had also told the Captain. McNulty said that was also true. Whittle, being the man the gun was pointed at when he took it away, took the taunting no longer, but he took the bait.

> *I said that he did not. He asked, "How do you know?" I replied that I was certain of it and that I believe furthermore that he knew that he did not. He said, "Well, Sir, when we get on shore there is a way to settle this thing." I said yes, and that at any time or place I should be ready to do so. He said, "Well, then, do you waive [the class privileges of your superior rank]?" "Yes, Sir," I replied, "I waive everything."*

The "way to settle this thing," of course, was via code duello: the duel. Dueling was one of the darker rituals of Whittle's beloved Southern culture. With its roots in medieval concepts of manhood, its rules codified and recodified over the centuries (the ten rules of "code duello" were established by an Italian in 1595), dueling fit perfectly with the Southern embrace of chivalry. Gentlemen whose honor had been insulted did not cower; they did not run—nor did they call on friends or relatives to back them up in taking vengeance. Instead they sought "satisfaction" according to the elegant, lethal rules of code duello: the formal challenge, usually delivered by a "second"; the meticulous selection of weapons, often ornate pistols handcrafted for just this purpose; the rendezvous at the appointed site—usually a remote field, and usually at dawn; the elaborate courtesies of speech and gesture that preceded the bloodletting.

Conway Whittle had just completed a historic around-the-world mission on behalf of the Southern nation that he venerated. He had left behind—perhaps forever—a young woman he'd loved. He had survived epic storms, Yankee intrigue at Melbourne, and the irrational wrath of his own commanding officer. He had conducted himself with chivalric restraint and perfect decorum in dealing with hundreds of hated Yankee prisoners, including wives and children, who had fallen prey to *Shenandoah*.

He was nearly at the voyage's end. And now, having acted bravely and out of recognition of his duty, Conway Whittle faced the prospect of death—at the hands of a fellow Southerner, under rules of honor that were sacred to his beloved nation.

A further, crowning irony lay in wait for Whittle: the bearer of the formal challenge from McNulty, the "second" chosen by the alcoholic surgeon, was to be none other than Sidney Smith Lee.

19

D r. McNulty's written challenge, worded in the absurd, self-regarding gentilities required by code duello, arrived at Whittle's cabin the following morning. The bearer, as rumored, was Lieutenant Sidney Smith Lee, "who is the only man in the mess with whom I am not on good terms," Whittle noted. "I demand an explanation," McNulty's letter began, and progressed through the prim suggestion that "should the demand appear extravagant, such other satisfaction as is looked for between gentlemen is expected at your earliest convenience."

Conway Whittle played his role in the macabre little pageant with dutiful resignation. He consulted Dabney Scales, whose Mississippi roots presumably qualified him as an expert on the subject, to find out "if it were possible to settle this thing on shipboard." Scales said no. Whittle then sought out McNulty's fellow surgeon, Charles Lining, "and asked him to be my friend [second]."

He handed Dr. Lining a written reply for Lining to deliver to Mc-Nulty, and he recorded its exact language in his log:

> *Sir,*
>
>   *I have to acknowledge receipt of your note. . . . My language to you last evening . . . explained itself. Under the circumstances I have but to accede to your demand for such satisfaction as you desire. As the ship is not a place where such a thing can be settled, as soon as we get on shore, full satisfaction will be given you.*

They would meet on some "field of honor"—if they met at all. Whittle's phrasing of his request to Lining—to be his "friend" rather than his "second," as code duello would prescribe—was both subtle and shrewd. He'd provided Dr. Lining a title crucially different from that of "second." Given that solving matters of misunderstanding by mortal combat was increasingly frowned upon, this "softer" term allowed the principals to keep the references to an actual duel to the death somewhat ambiguous.

There was poignancy, as well, in Whittle's naming Dr. Lining a "friend." Friends had been few and far between for the lieutenant on this voyage. Distance and impartiality were part of the price he paid for his rank as executive officer of the ship.

Nor did Whittle expect to return home to find any friends, relatives, his sweetheart Pattie, or any intact social structure, for that matter. Isolation, disjunction from the world, and the prospect of the gallows—these were Conway Whittle's portion in the year 1865. In this context, fighting a duel was only one in an endless series of dismal obligations. It was his duty. He was honor-bound. He would face his responsibility—but he would face it with a "friend," rather than an accomplice, at his side.

In his journal on the night of October 12, Whittle was typically soul-searching, and typically forbearing of his adversary:

> *Thus ends, for the present, this disagreeable affair. It must come off when we get on shore. I have always been opposed to dueling but I have given an insult. . . . I must give him satisfaction and will meet him. I may have been wrong in not keeping my opinion that he had lied to myself, but I could not do it. . . .*

Whittle, who had taken several pages to detail the events of the preceding two days, as the crisis unfolded, made only a cursory, two-line entry—recording their course and describing the weather—for the following day, Friday the thirteenth: "It is very hot."

On the afternoon of the fourteenth, their reliable winds vanished entirely and the *Shenandoah* fell becalmed under clear blue skies. Now only a few miles north of the equator, and almost precisely halfway between Africa and South America, they were at the crossroads of the Atlantic Ocean's two vast maritime highways. They were sitting ducks. Reluctantly they began to fire the boiler and make steam. However, it was not a Yankee cruiser they had to fear, but the strange pinwheeling storms in what is now known as the equatorial counter-current, where conditions of sea and sky will change in a matter of moments from dead calm to something decidedly different.

As the first wisps of *Shenandoah's* smoke climbed straight up from the stack, the motionless ship swayed smoothly, almost imperceptibly, on the calm ocean. All eyes swept the horizon, and the few sails upon it, for signs of other smoke. Nothing, all sails slack, no smoke showing. Then, surprisingly, a light breeze sprang up from the southwest, from Brazil. It swung rapidly around to the west-northwest, from the North Atlantic. They watched the western margin of the clear, mild sea as a line of clouds rose above the far edge of the ocean and pushed toward the ship. In moments it stretched across the entire northwestern horizon. The approaching cloud deck divided the prospect into three tiers: the blue dome of heaven; a world-wide ribbon of pastel gray hues; and the turquoise green of the tropical Atlantic.

Below the dark gray top half of the storm wall, the men could see a much lighter band of gray rain that reached from the bottom of the clouds to the surface of the sea. The storm front was growing higher by the moment, and moving toward the ship far faster than *Shenandoah's* top speed. The crew, watching in the bright sunlight, knew that soon it would be raining in torrents. And as the wall of water—for it was more like being submerged than being rained on—moved inexorably from the bow to the wheelhouse, *Shenandoah* was drenched by an immense downpour, and the sunlight vanished.

In one way the storm was a godsend: the ship was light on potable water. Whittle had already taken action. He'd called out the crew to rig clean canvas sailcloth as catch-sheets. Stretched into funnels to form chutes, the cloth was used to direct as much of the fresh rainwater as possible into the ship's water casks.

"Slow to start, slow to end," the old weather-watcher's rule of thumb, applied here in the reverse. This storm struck with the immediacy of a slap to the face. In less than fourteen hours the temperature of the air would rise more than forty degrees, up to one hundred twenty by the following afternoon, and the storm would vanish by morning, leaving the air once more as balmy as the tropics.

It was this enormous exchange of energy between the two colliding fronts that *Shenandoah* still had to traverse. When the two oceanic walls finally intersected that night in the dark, they almost sank the CSS *Shenandoah*.

At midnight Whittle was awakened by frantic screaming. It was Lieutenant Chew, who was on watch as officer of the deck. Whittle heard the junior lieutenant shouting orders to re-rig the ship's sails, orders Whittle knew immediately were wrong. He jumped on deck in the driving rain, headed for the wheelhouse.

Unexpectedly the storm had pivoted almost 120 degrees and was now assaulting the ship from the northeast. Instead of having the wind in their sails, they suddenly had a gale in their faces. Chew, astonished, and even after this many months at sea still inexperienced, was yelling orders that were dangerously wrongheaded, given the lashing winds and high seas: to "hand down the Topmast studding sail jacks . . . and let go the Royal & Topgallant halyards."

Chew had called for misadjustment in the sails. Whittle saw that as he ran, his nightclothes now soaked through. The wind had come around from port and was blowing in from starboard; worse, it was shifting direction capriciously. Chew's adjustments had never caught up with the wind. The gale was trapping *Shenandoah* with her sails rigged to the left when they should have been set for the right, and then vice versa. The crisis quickly escalated: the wrong sides of the out-of-control sails filled with wind; and the gale, blasting into *Shenandoah*'s prow, began shredding her rigging, forcing her backwards in the turbulent ocean—backwards against her rudder. Backwards toward disaster.

Conway Whittle seized command just as the gale was starting to take control.

"I took the deck," his matter-of-fact notes read, "shortened sail, keeping the ship off before the wind, and then brought by. The squall was very fresh & blew our miz. royal away, & carried away the m'n royal studding sail boom." Those terse words barely hinted at Whittle's rapid strokes of seamanship. Within moments he had relieved Chew (a fact his notes imply but do not mention); got the crew activated in purposeful sail-setting; taken the helm and changed the direction of the rudder, probably saving it from snapping apart; and, in sum, kept the vessel upright. "I was as wet as a drowned rat," he allowed, "and caught cold. I never saw it rain so in all my life."

His quick thinking and decisive action may have saved the lives of everyone on board. Including the life of Dr. Frederich J. McNulty.

Whittle spent the following day, Sunday, in his room, reading.

With the passage of the front, the doldrums then set in again: temperatures of more than 100 degrees, mild winds giving way to almost perfect calm. The ship was nearly immobilized by currents: the north equatorial current and the equatorial countercurrent, colliding. Everyone prayed for the trade winds, as they had on the voyage south along the American continent. On the sixteenth, someone calculated the total distance *Shenandoah* had run: 39,282 knots, or more than 44,000 miles.

Two days after that, Whittle made a deeply layered sentimental entry in his log:

> *This with all of us, and particularly myself, an important anniversary. It is the day on which the little steamer "Laurel" and this ship met at Madeira a year ago. The day on which we took on board our battery, stores & officers and, in fact the birthday of the "Shenandoah." Since this day 12 months ago, how many changes have we gone through.*

He summarized them: an initial wave of pride and rejoicing at "having an opportunity of saving our country," followed by "the most heartbreaking despair at having no country to serve." And then he turned to his other sustaining obsession:

> *To me the day is more dear in as much as it is the birthday of the dearest being on earth to me. This day twenty two years ago my darling Pattie was born.*

After invoking (yet again) God's blessing and protection on his sweetheart, with his characteristic rhythms of the Anglican prayer book, Whittle concluded:

> *At dinner today, I filled my glass with port wine, and silently drank her health. Oh! May she have many happy returns of the day. Many anxious thoughts has she had for me, for she loves me most dearly. And only to think that if the Yankees refuse us permission to enter the country, which I think more than likely, I may never see her again. The thought almost maddens me, but her motto "hope on, hope ever" shall be mine.*

"Hope on, hope ever." The motto could easily have been Conway Whittle's, as well.

Northward. A little wind, roasting sun. *Shenandoah* tacked west, out of her true course north by east, seeking trade winds, but also seeking solitude—she was now moving into seas of heavy traffic. The shoulder of Africa had for centuries attracted and dispatched uncounted merchantmen, and even in these early post-slavery years, trade was brisk. At noon on the nineteenth, less than 200 miles off Praia, the main port of the Cape Verdes, she recrossed another nautical marker: "We were almost exactly where we were one year ago . . . which was . . . the day after we took *Alina,* our first prize." Whittle squinted upward at the total eclipse of the sun that afternoon, "one of the most beautiful sights I ever saw. . . . In the middle of it, the moon's disk was right in the center of the sun, with a bright circle of the latter all around it." He wondered whether his dear ones might be looking at the same sight.

North of the Cape Verde islands under moderate trades, *Shenandoah* encountered one ship, and then another; but neither proved to be a dreaded Yankee. The ocean surface was like glass. On the twenty-second, Whittle estimated the ship to be fifteen days out of an English port. "What will become of us after we get there, God alone can tell. For myself, I have little or no faith in the existence of honor among nations, when the honorable course may clash with interest." He agonized again about "my little brothers, sister, and dear old father," and prayed again for the strength of Christian resignation.

The dying was about to begin.

"Two of our men are very ill," Whittle wrote. One of them, delirious from advanced venereal disease, his body covered with ulcers, was William Bill, sometimes known as Bill Sailor, a Kanakan from the Sandwich Islands. The other was the mysterious marine sergeant George P. Canning, who had joined the crew at Melbourne, and had been bedridden with his festering gunshot wound to the lung that he claimed to have suffered under General Polk at Shiloh. Whittle had been no more successful than anyone else at figuring out Canning's true background. The lieutenant described Canning as "a well educated young Englishman," and understood him to have been on the staff of General Albert Sidney Johnston. Of the two sufferers, Whittle remarked, "Oh how I pity the poor fellows, because neither is prepared to die." The comparison to himself was unstated, but clarion-clear.

William Bill was moribund the following day, Canning not much better. The trade winds themselves were dying. Whittle calculated the ship's distance from Charleston, South Carolina, at 2,300 miles— "We are now nearer our dear ones than we have been for a long time. . . . I wonder if we will get any nearer." He made some further calculations: 112 days since the crew last had seen land, 195 since they'd been ashore (at Ascension [Ponape]) in the South Pacific; 248 days since being ashore in a civilized place; and, out of the 365-day year, a total of 330 days at sea. "That's right 'hefty,' " he concluded.

On the twenty-fifth, as *Shenandoah* plodded along under light winds, the lookouts espied a menacing shape on the horizon. Standing to the westward two points off the port, lee, bow, this ship was clearly no merchantman: "She was made out to be a brig with great drift between her masts, no mainsail, staysails, or studding sails, with royals set."

It was obvious that the vessel had turned toward the Rebel ship. "Very soon she was on the same tack as ourselves, and standing higher than we, was crossing our bow." She was going to intercept them, there could be no other reason for such a mid-ocean course adjustment.

Officers and crew assumed the worst. They looked on with dread as the brig bore steadily down on them over a four-hour stretch.

To alter their course or to switch to steam, under these circumstances, would have the same effect as semaphoring, "WE ARE SHENANDOAH." The "great drift between her masts" that Whittle mentioned—he did not say what lay between, but, by implication, the "drift" was wide enough to accommodate a steamer's hoisting smokestack.

For *Shenandoah* to fire her boiler, risky at best, it would first require raising her own smokestack. This action would have changed *Shenandoah*'s profile immediately. She would no longer appear to her adversary as a harmless merchantman. Hoisting the stack would announce her warrior status. Steam was not an option.

Indeed, any visible change in *Shenandoah*'s course could prompt this stranger, now almost certainly a Yankee man-of-war, to launch a full-speed chase. And so the Confederate ship sailed on toward the Yankee's intercept point with feigned indifference, while all aboard strained to contain their anxieties.

Luckily for the southerners, first contact had occurred late in the afternoon. If the disarmed Rebel fugitive could just manage to maintain her ruse until nightfall, escape became a possibility. She managed.

> *As soon as it was dark, we wore short around* [turned off course]*, got up steam, steamed dead to the windward for 16 miles, and then went our course, putting out all lights. If she be a Yankee, she will be somewhat astonished tomorrow morning to find no vessel in sight . . . she will have a sweet time finding us, as we will remain under steam until we get a good breeze.*

At first light, all eyes scanned the horizon for the brig. Gone.

A close call. How many others lay ahead, on this high-risk, open-sea scramble toward Liverpool?

William Bill died at 5:00 p.m. the next day. "He was such a sufferer that we cannot regret that he is relieved. God have mercy on his benighted soul, I pray." A day after that, Bill was buried at sea. The sight of the Rebel naval colors—white field, with the Stars and Bars in the upper left corner—at ceremonial half-mast unleashed wrenching thoughts in Whittle:

> When I saw our poor flag weeping, I could but be plunged into the depths of thought connected with it, which made me still more melancholy. Our poor downtrodden country, our weeping flag, we are as it were, the rear guard of the armies of the South.

North of the Azores by October 28; indeed, north of Boston, *Shenandoah* could at last shape her course on a line for Cape Clear, the southern coast of Ireland. But the ocean had one more trial for *Shenandoah* and her men before they sighted land. Two weeks to the day after the midnight storm that shredded her rigging, a gale struck her at noon, accompanied "by a tremendous sea, the height of which I never saw equated except off these very islands when I was in the str. *Nashville* in February 1862." Perhaps Whittle was forgetting Cape Horn, or South Africa's Cape Rollers, or the violent Christmas gale in the Indian Ocean; perhaps not. Shenandoah survived again, and they sailed on.

As much as he longed for their arrival at Liverpool, he worried at the same time that the English government would give them up to the Federals. He lapsed into French as he expressed his concern and resignation: "Nous verrons, J'espere que non mais je le croit." ["We will see, I hope not, but I believe so."]

The mysterious, nettlesome Sergeant Canning died at 5:30 on the thirtieth. "His death is very sad," wrote Whittle. His next thought unconsciously spoke to the complex moral reckonings that could bedevil an officer whose defeated homeland was founded on slave labor, yet who recognized the humanity of all men. "The poor old Negro (Weeks) who waited on him, was by him terribly abused and he cursed him most terribly up to the very last. Oh! it is a terrible sight at anytime to see a soul take flight, but when you see a man die who up to his last breath is a sinner the sight is awful. Oh! God let us prepare to die."

It was Canning's unceasing, graceless abuse of the loyal Weeks, even as the moment of death approached, that so distressed the young lieutenant. Whittle saw the old veteran giving up his last chance for absolution, for forgiveness. That was what made him a "sinner" from his Episcopalian perspective. And it was death that awaited all of humankind. Perhaps it was a sense of being a fellow "sinner" with Canning, and a sense that his own imminent death was likely, that renewed Whittle's constant struggle to attain Christian grace.

Canning joined Bill in the oceanic grave the next day. The Catholic burial service was read by Dr. McNulty, as Whittle noted without comment.

❧❀❦

Nine hundred miles from Liverpool by noon November 1—about four days out from land, Whittle calculated. He was plunged in gloom, as he confessed in his log: "Some how or other, I look forward to our safe arrival in an English port with very little hope." The feeling had only deepened on the following day: "I feel that we are men with something awful hanging over us. I do not look forward to our arrival at an English port with as much hope and good cheer as the rest. Why is this? I can't say." But he did say, "I fear that upon our arrival, if the Yankees were to declare a refusal to give up our persons a just cause for war, and England's interests were opposed to a war, the English government would make a sacrifice of honor to interest." *Shenandoah*'s unawareness in the Bering Sea that the war had ended, in other words, could very well count for nothing when the officers and crew were brought before a Yankee or even British court or tribunal. No innocence. No innocents. Sinners all, in the law's eyes and perhaps God's as well. The gallows would do Dr. McNulty's work for him, for all of them, Dr. McNulty included. Honor and interest. Soon the mulling of it became almost too much to describe: "Of the future I will only think, without putting my thoughts on paper."

Two hundred eighty miles out from Cape Clear by noon November 3. Two hundred ten by 8:00 p.m. Sails all around them by now. Whittle continued to brace for the worst.

One was a six topsail yards ship, with very white canvas, and every indication of her being a Yankee.

Whittle was clearly counting the miles. "We are gradually approaching the end of our journey." As always, routine maintenance was the order of the day. He ordered the spar deck holystoned, "and it really looks very well."

On that day, Captain Waddell commenced the payment of *Shenandoah*'s officers and men for their services on the mission. The coffers were woefully sparse. "Upon calculation, it is found that it would take some $30,000 to pay, [of] which we have about $4,000. This, deducting the probable cost for pilotage, etc., will get every man in the ship $1.00 for each $7.10 he has due him." Whittle himself received $45.90, "having some $326.00 due me." It would be the last money he'd have for a long time, he figured, "and it only grieves me to know why. I do not love money, and have no desire to be rich. All I want is enough to live on and support my darlings at home."

The gale-force winds were long behind them now. The skies had ceased to breathe, as though the spell of Appomattox were slowly spreading its stillness around the globe. *Shenandoah* became a creature of the night in the final days of her voyage—hanging listless in the water by day, sails limp, her captain unwilling to draw attention via smoke from her engines. Only after sunset did the firemen belowdecks heave into the ship's dwindling supply of coal, and make the propeller turn. She crept in this petty pace for three days.

The last entry remaining in Conway Whittle's logbook sums up both his sense of desolation and his unquenchable determination to somehow surmount it.

"Where there is a will there is a way," and this shall be my motto. I am sure not to starve on it.

Scarlett O'Hara, screaming out from Southern literature sixty-one years in the future, hardly put it better: "As God is my witness, I'll never go hungry again!" Eighty-five years on, another southerner, William Faulkner, far more elegantly consecrated the hopes of the Conway Whittles of that era: "I believe that man will not merely endure: he will prevail. He is immortal, not because he alone among creatures has an inexhaustible voice, but because he has a soul, a spirit capable of compassion and sacrifice and endurance."

Doomed, enduring, defeated, willing their way, Conway Whittle and the men of *Shenandoah* edged toward Liverpool and whatever fate awaited them there.

20

E ndgame:
  She had breached the Irish Sea, home waters of the British
Isles, but both England, to the east, and Ireland, to the west, remained invisible under a nighttime fog. On November 5, *Shenandoah*
entered St. George's Channel.

Cornelius Hunt's log noted that Bulloch steered the ship brilliantly
via chronometer and patent log. No one slept. Officers and crewmen
alike scrambled about, organizing their possessions, making ready to
depart the ship for a last time. Some men battled their fears of what
awaited them by thinking of good things to eat on shore.

Friendships forged on board were annealed: Dabney Scales handed
John Martin a drawing he'd made of *Shenandoah* as a memento of the
voyage.

But some of the officers' anxieties ran toward darker things. What
was the true mood among this grab-bag crew? It was hard to tell, but
clearly the meager pay-out of their salaries had made no one happy.
"Hadn't there been a chest of gold sovereigns aboard at one time?"
They asked one another, and, "What of the money from the prize
boats?" What was the extent of grudges held against Waddell? Worse,
what of perceptions that in the final weeks he had risked everyone's
lives on this long dash north to England? Where did their loyalties lie,
if they had loyalties, these sailors-of-fortune, these transfers from captured ships, these hardened vagabonds from the world's nations, these
brawlers, these drunks? One might have imagined a formidable core
of ringleaders just by counting Conway Whittle's punishment victims.

There was the fireman George Silvester, triced and gagged,

demoted. And second midshipman Thomas Hall, accused of "scandalous conduct" and triced, gagged, and disrated; then triced again in an embrace with his fighting opponent Raymond; then triced again, for eight hours, after tormenting the Frenchman Rowe. Then Silvester again, for insolence. Then the gunner's mate Crawford, for insolence. Then seaman James Fegan for refusing to obey orders. Then two officers and several men, for getting drunk on *Abigail*'s liquor. Then second carpenter Lynch, clapped in irons and gagged for drunkenness and insolence. Even the convalescent Henry Canning had been triced, essentially, for getting on Whittle's nerves.

Canning, at least, was dead. As for the others, and the crewmen sympathetic to them—were they perhaps a more immediate threat than the gallows?

Was *Shenandoah*'s final drama to be a mutiny?

Landfall.

Tuskar Light. They marked the time. Bulloch had brought them home with perfection. Running lights at midnight diverted everyone's thoughts. A Liverpool pilot boat. Now came the moment that all aboard had yearned for and dreaded: contact, at last, with the world they had left behind. Waddell ordered rockets fired to draw the boat's attention. He then signaled his own ship's identity via lights—but it was a false identity. Waddell's nerve had failed him again. His ship was called *America,* he signaled; it was ninety days out of Calcutta.[45]

An interesting choice of names, that: *America.*

The pilot boat approached the raider in the dark. Its lone passenger—the Mersey River harbor pilot—scrambled up *Shenandoah*'s rope ladder. The ship's junior officers told him the raider's true identity. Hunt's reconstruction of the conversation between the pilot and Whittle, who greeted him, has been widely quoted:

"Good morning. What ship is this?"

"The late Confederate steamer *Shenandoah.*"

"The hell you say. Where have you fellows come from last?"

"From the Arctic Ocean."

"And you haven't stopped at any port since you left there?"

"No, nor been in sight of land, either. What news from the war in America?"

"Why, the war has been over so long people have got through talking about it. Jeff Davis is in Fortress Monroe, and the Yankees have a lot of cruisers out looking for you."[46]

Whittle escorted the pilot to Waddell, who asked him to corroborate the reports of the war's end. The pilot did so. All of *Shenandoah*'s options were now voided, except one. Waddell was gripped with a desire to exercise it while he still had some control of the ship. He instructed the pilot to bring *Shenandoah* on into port.

The pilot hesitated; the tide was low, he warned. The ship was likely to bottom on the sizable sandbar that rose between the sea and the entrance to the bay.

Waddell replied that he didn't care. He was not about to wait hours for high tide when any Yankee cruiser in the vicinity would most certainly show no hesitation in attacking. He ordered the pilot to make a run for it anyway. The pilot, perhaps with a shrug, went with Waddell and Whittle to the wheelhouse, where the pilot pointed out a course that would bring them to the lowest part of the still-submerged bar. How low was the bar, at this time of day, at this phase of the moon? The pilot could only guess. How deep was *Shenandoah* riding? At her bow, *Shenandoah*, fully loaded, needed a minimum of twenty feet of water under her keel. She needed more at her stern. When she was properly loaded, her bow rode some ten inches higher than her rudder, and when she was taken by the wind, the wide, flat bottom of her long, thin clipper hull would raise her bow farther, and she would plane upward a bit above the water. Even such a small effect helped make her faster, and in the 18,000 miles they had covered since they left the ice, that small amount of tail droop had mattered. By now, having consumed much of her coal and all of her perishables, they would need much less than twenty feet. They could proceed slowly. Or so they rationalized.

They moved. Whittle relayed the compass headings to the Officer of the Deck for the helmsman, as eager to get to land as anyone, who had already spun the huge wheel dead on course before the OD could even finish speaking.

Shenandoah's bow swung precisely toward the Mersey channel, the ribbon of river that would carry them to Liverpool. Captain Waddell went below to his cabin.

The night was dark, but the ship's company blazed with inner thoughts. James Waddell, to his credit, turned his thoughts to the preservation of lives. He began to compose a carefully worded letter of surrender to the new prime minister of Great Britain, Earl Russell, at Whitehall. Russell, unfortunately for the men on *Shenandoah,* had succeeded Lord Palmerston, their erstwhile supporter who had died a month earlier.

> *I have the honor to announce to your lordship my arrival in the wa-*
> *ters of the Mersey with this vessel, late a ship of war under my com-*
> *mand, belonging to the Confederate States of America. The singular*
> *position in which I find myself placed and the absence of all precedents*
> *on the subject will, I trust, induce your lordship to pardon my hasty*
> *reference to a few facts connected with the cruise lately made by this*
> *ship.*

Waddell summarized the commissioning of the raider and her for-ays against United States merchantmen around the globe over the preceding year. Taking care to specify *Shenandoah*'s location from May through July—"the Okhotsk Sea and Arctic Ocean"—the captain made the case that his ship was far removed from any possible source of news when the Civil War ended. "Your lordship can imagine my surprise," he wrote (presumably without irony), upon his learning of the war's end only on August 2, from the officers of *Barracouta.* "I de-sisted immediately from further acts of war," he assured the prime minister, and headed for a European port, "where I would learn if that intelligence were true." Finding that it was true, he surrendered "the ship with her battery, small arms, machinery, stores, tackle and apparel complete, to Her Majesty's Government."[47]

The letter's unstated message was simple: we are not pirates. We are honorable men of war, and have acted according to the rules of war as we understood them. Spare our lives.

Waddell was still working on his letter at 4:00 a.m. on November 6 when a tremendous jolt slammed through the ship and sent everyone stumbling. *Shenandoah* had run aground on the sandbar, exactly as the pilot had predicted.

Her immobilization reignited the fearful tensions among the officers. Conway Whittle imagined he'd picked up on a plot among the crew to plunder the ship for anything of value—a plot imagined by Lining as well. He hurried from cabin to cabin, telling his fellow officers to keep their sidearms handy.

No plundering occurred.

Shenandoah floated free of the bar with the morning tides and steamed past the mouth of the Mersey. The fog lifted briefly, and there lay the green pillows of England on either side, under constellations of seagulls: the first dry land since the Aleutians 124 days and 18,000 miles earlier.

She made her way carefully toward the inner harbor and, by 8:00 a.m., as the fog re-enveloped the landscape, *Shenandoah* anchored directly astern the British warship *Donegal.* Hunt later wrote that no one minded the fog, "for we did not care about the gaping crowd on shore witnessing the humiliation soon to befall our ship."[48]

The formal denouement to *Shenandoah*'s voyage into history came two hours later.

At around 10:00 a.m., *Donegal*'s captain, James A. Paynter, climbed smartly aboard the black raider. James Waddell, painfully stiff with humiliation and scurvy, stood impassive in his worn gray dress uniform and nodded to the perfectly tailored British officer. They exchanged salutes, and Captain Paynter officially informed Lieutenant Waddell of the Civil War's end. Waddell showed no emotion as he acknowledged the information. He handed Paynter the letter that he had written to Lord Russell, asking that it be delivered to the British foreign minister in London. Waddell also handed the British captain a bag filled with gold and silver coins of several nations, which he said totaled $820.38. This was the money taken from ships after the date of the South's surrender.

Then Lieutenant Commanding James I. Waddell performed what surely was the single most odious duty of his long naval career. He formally surrendered the CSS *Shenandoah* to Captain Paynter. Paynter acknowledged the surrender. The men saluted each other again. It was done.

For *Shenandoah* and her crew, the authority of the Confederate States Navy had ended. Their Civil War was now actually over.

Cornelius Hunt averted his eyes from this ceremony, and his glance fell on Lieutenant Conway Whittle. Whittle had turned his back to the proceedings. From his vantage point, Hunt could see the tears streaming down the young Virginian's face.

᠅᠅᠅

The unspeakable duty performed, James Waddell turned to address the ship's crew. They stood before him in orderly rows, perhaps the last time they would be so assembled. Waddell gazed at them, and they gazed back: a jumbled collection of jacks and tars and gobs and salts plucked from the merchant ships of the world; ordinary seamen who, by the simple caprice of fate, had found themselves caught up in one of the most fantastical naval escapades ever. Volatile, hard-drinking, quick-fisted men, cold-eyed strangers to one another for the most part, transients and opportunists who sailed with the Rebels not out of national loyalty but out of self-interest, convenience, release from leg irons, a little adventure. Yet these men had, in the end, melded into an entity that was more than the sum of its parts. Their self-discipline had often bent but never had been broken. Their cohesion as a sailing unit had been repeatedly stressed to the point of rupture, but, in the moment of crisis, never torn. Against all the probabilities of human nature, they had ceased to become many, and were one.

What would Waddell say to them—to redeem himself from things he had said in error, or things he had left unsaid—on this last opportunity to say anything to them? Would Waddell mask himself behind his familiar façade of icy, distant formality?

No one recorded his exact words. They were reported to have been brief and respectful. He simply thanked them for their loyalty and declared that they had nothing to be ashamed about.[49]

In his memoirs, Waddell was gracious toward his junior officers, some of whom had given him cause for bitterness. Speaking of "those noble men who were officers under my command," Waddell declared, "The circumstance of age and rank, not superior merit or greater devotion to our cause, made me their commander. For thirteen long months we were thrown into a connection so close that the narrative I write seems rather a souvenir of our intercourse than a statement of historical events."[50]

His brief remarks at an end, as Whittle and others wept, *Shenandoah*'s Confederate colors were lowered from the mizzen gaff: the last flag down.

Now, what was to be the fate of these dreaded, celebrated captives? Freedom? Incarceration? Execution? The long hours of waiting commenced.

They had surrendered. But they were not yet free

⁂

If any Confederates had been expecting a heroes' welcome at Liverpool, they were mistaken. No one was even going ashore. Any lingering affection from the British government toward the rebels had been swept away by the bombast of Charles Francis Adams, who for months had been pressing Her Majesty's government for massive reparations to the United States. Adams took the clearly valid position that Britain was responsible for permitting *Shenandoah* and other raiders (such as *Alabama*) to be built in British shipyards—never mind the clandestine nature of these projects—and thus liable to the United States for the huge economic toll taken by them. As for the presence and surrender of *Shenandoah* at Liverpool, Adams could hardly wait.

He wanted the British to incarcerate all hands immediately and turn them over to United States agents in Britain. The British ministers, perhaps understandably disinclined to honor every one of Adams's demands as soon as he made them, demurred on this, pending talks with legal experts at Whitehall.

Adams's reparation crusade, which he would pursue over several years, promptly infuriated British public opinion, and the British press, which turned its wrath on the raider and its crew. "The inability of the United States navy to catch this light-heeled enemy is an apt commentary on the pending claims for compensation on account of damages inflicted by Confederate vessels," the *Telegraph* fulminated, "[claims] almost as extravagant as if London policemen were expected to aid those of Paris and New York in repressing crime in those cities."[51] The *Star* growled that "if the commander of the *Shenandoah* imagines that in England he is to escape with impunity, the action of Her Majesty's government will promptly undeceive him . . . these men must not be permitted to walk abroad unchallenged as if they had been engaged in a meritorious enterprise. . . . It is disheartening to reflect how much the cause of maritime rights has been prejudiced by the fatal apathy we exhibited toward these Confederate cruisers."[52] The *News* wondered "how it is that this cruiser has been able to pursue her course without the least interruption from the navy of the United States. We have learned of her in various parts of the world dealing destruction and scattering dismay among merchantmen, whalers and other unarmed vessels, but no war-vessel of the United States appears to have molested her." The paper went on to propose a sinister answer: "It is possible that the expectation of recovering from this country compensation for the losses . . . has made the Government and the people of the United States less eager for her capture than they otherwise would have been."[53]

The London *Times* perhaps put the matter most coldly. Calling the raider's arrival an "unwelcome event," the newspaper remarked, "It would have been a great relief to ourselves . . . had the *Shenandoah* been simply excluded from the Mersey and left to roam the seas till she should fall into the hands of her pursuers." The *Times* closed with a modest proposal: it suggested that the men be tried as pirates.

The ministers at Whitehall read the papers.

The boiling hostility from the British press, coupled with Adams's public lusting to get his hands on the Southerners, could only worsen the anguish of the officers and men as they waited. They were trapped, and quite likely facing the ends of their lives. Escape was nearly out of the question. *Shenandoah* rode at anchor, and since there had been no formal response to Waddell's letter, no one was allowed to disembark that first night. Malnourished, many weakened by scurvy, the sailors made poor candidates for escape in any event. They would have been virtually naked in this suddenly alien country. And so these swashbuckling seamen, recently the terrors of the world's seas, were reduced to staring back blankly at the gawkers who appraised them from the safety of small boats. Lining thought that the spectators regarded them as wild beasts.[54] Lambs awaiting slaughter was closer to the truth.

⚓

On the morning of the second day, the men watched with an escalating sense of dread as the British navy brought up a bristling gunboat, HMS *Goshawk*, and lashed her to *Shenandoah* on the far side of *Donegal*. Sailors on the gunship rigged a gangway to *Shenandoah*, and one Lieutenant Cheek marched aboard. With Cheek and a few customs agents came a squad of some fifty British marines and armed sailors. As the might of the British navy stood in formation on *Shenandoah*'s deck, Lieutenant Cheek asked that her officers be assembled.

Cheek addressed the officers in the wardroom. He told them that he was now in command of *Shenandoah*, and that the marines with him were in charge of the ship. He added that he would remain in charge until the Prime Minister had replied to Waddell's communiqué. Then he made things crystal clear:

"You understand that you will be held as prisoners until Her Majesty's pleasure regarding you is known. Also, you will understand that you will not be permitted to take the vessel out of the port again without permission."[55]

Later, some of the southerners found dark hilarity in this—as if, having circled the globe and submitted themselves to the indignity of surrender, they might be planning another excursion.

The former Rebels were not entirely dehumanized; a few British naval officers took pity on their brothers of the sea, and brought some luxuries aboard for them: fresh eggs, fresh milk, whiskey, tea, sugar, tobacco.[56] The cook Marlow somehow managed to slip ashore the first day and heroically returned with hampers of gleaming vegetables from the market. A young officer later remembered how, "as the hampers of onions, big, red, strong kind, were passed up . . . they were grabbed by officers and men alike, and eaten as though they were the finest apples." The pretty English wife of the sailmaker Alcott was allowed to board the ship briefly, and the men gazed at her as though she were a mermaid.

But after Lieutenant Cheek took over, he virtually locked the ship down. He even refused a boatload of additional foodstuffs, sniffing, "We'll feed our own prisoners." And the malnourished, angry, fearful men watched as the supply boat moved off. And more hours passed. And Whitehall deliberated. And the men of *Shenandoah* continued to await their fate.

On the night of November seventh, however, a handful of Rebel officers carried out what seems to have been a gambit to escape. Perhaps working through the same channels as Alcott and Marlow, they arranged for a dinghy to pull up beneath *Shenandoah*'s bow under cover of darkness. Irvine Bulloch, Sidney Smith Lee, Charles Lining, and midshipman Orris Browne dropped on board, and were ferried to Liverpool.

Shortly before they departed, the officers invited Whittle to join them. Whittle refused.

Browne remembered making the offer, and he remembered Whittle's reasons for refusal, and he remembered the words with which he expressed that refusal, for the rest of his life. And Browne remembered the aura of nobility that underlay Whittle's words, that unbending Southern chivalric sense of duty that set Whittle apart from everyone else who sailed with *Shenandoah* around the world.

Browne repeated those words back to Whittle nearly thirty years on.

At dawn the next morning Browne and Bulloch returned to await their fate.

Smith Lee rejoined the ship at midmorning. Cornelius Hunt never returned. He alone made a clean escape, and years later published his vivid memoirs of the voyage.

The British marines doubled their guard, planted the offending dinghy on the raider's deck, and made it clear that any other craft that approached the captive ship would face their gunfire.

And the men of *Shenandoah* continued waiting for their futures to be decided—life or death.

The officers were the first to learn. The news arrived at 7:00 p.m. on November 8, as they stared moodily at their dinners belowdecks. It arrived in the person of Captain Paynter, who clambered aboard the ship and descended upon the group, clutching a telegram. The telegram was from Lord Clarendon, the foreign secretary at Whitehall, and it announced the Crown's verdict regarding the captives.

The officers doubtless stood nervously as Paynter began to read them the wire. History does not record their reactions, but stunned speechlessness would be a good guess.

What had impelled the foreign secretary and his peers toward this particular verdict? Was it their memory of England's long history of profitable trade with a slaveholding society? Was it Britain's long tradition of impersonal but ultimately evenhanded justice? Had the blood lust of the British press affected their judgment?

The telegram didn't say. What it did say was that *Shenandoah*'s mariners were to be set free.

Free, with the exception of one category: British subjects. Any son of England aboard the ship would face the wrath—and almost certainly the gallows—of his government. For an Englishman to fight in the navy of another country meant death.

As Waddell and his junior lieutenants struggled for control of their emotions, Captain Paynter spoke again: it was required that this sorting take place at once. On deck.

Chairs scraped and cutlery clattered as the officers brushed through the wardroom and hustled into the dark, chilly Liverpool air. Paynter had instructed one of their number to assemble the crew on deck and call the roll. Tellingly, it was not Captain Waddell, but Lieutenant Whittle, whom the British captain selected for the task.

In foggy winter mist pierced only by the orange glow of shipboard lanterns, the shadowy, shambling figures materialized from their bunks, from their mess, from whatever cramped nook or cranny of the ship they'd chosen as their waiting-place. They floated into their ranks like bearded, gray-garbed ghosts. In stark contrast to their gaunt shabbiness, a detachment of Royal Marines, imposing in bell-shaped shakos and red tunics, armed with muskets and fixed bayonets, stood at the ready on either side of the ship.

As the *Shenandoah* men fell into place, a thought struck Whittle: *For all they knew, they'd been gathered to receive their death sentences!*

He watched through the gloom as Captain Paynter, his brass buttons catching the oil lamps' glow, ordered them to attention and snapped to his full military bearing. The British officer turned his gaze on the crewmen, and then on Whittle, who stood with the ship's articles in his arms. Paynter indicated that Whittle was to begin.

Whittle opened the ledger. He would skip the uniformed officers, whose nationality was as obvious as it was damning. He prepared to start with the noncoms. He looked at the names in lamplight. He knew full well where the first man was from. The first would be John L. Guy, the gunner. Guy was English born and bred. Would Guy know what to say? Of course not. Whittle understood now why Paynter had ordered this polling to commence at once.

The men did not know the consequences of their answers! Paynter had wanted it that way: to announce that he was culling them for British subjects, or even to give the word time to circulate, would be an open invitation for any Englishman to lie.

Whittle's suspicion of Paynter was mirrored by the crew. The huddled captives could only assume the worst. This was a cold-blooded inquisition, a ransacking of the helpless ranks, for Southerners. What else could it be? The fire-breathing British newspapers . . . the well-known fulminations of Charles Adams . . . the incontrovertible truth that they had plundered American merchant ships in peacetime . . . they were going to hang.

Certainly, from their point of view, they would just as likely hang if they announced themselves Confederates as they would if they said Englishmen.

Whittle looked into the ranks of the men. He spoke the gunner's name clearly: "Guy." As soon as he heard his name, the gunner left ranks, walked uncertainly across the deck, and stood in front of Captain Paynter. The man Whittle had punished brutally, the man who had most probably fired the last shot of the Civil War, waited to learn his fate.

"What countryman are you?" Paynter asked.

And Guy may have hesitated, or he may not have, but in an accent without a hint of drawl the gunner said clearly, "I'm a southerner."

Paynter looked at the gunner. This was no Dixie-born Johnny Reb. Paynter glanced at the hundred or so men standing on deck in the November air.

"Next."

The gunner made his way to the far rail, and Whittle called the next name, "Harwood." The ship's boatswain came forward. He was as much an Englishman as Paynter himself.

"What countryman are you?" Captain Paynter asked Harwood.

"I'm a southerner," came the reply. Paynter's eyes narrowed.

"Next."

Here was the sailmaker, the man whose wife had met the ship with fresh food three days earlier.

"Alcott."

The Liverpool native crossed to Paynter and drew himself up.

"What countryman are you?"

"I'm a southerner. A Virginian, sir."

Conway Whittle listened with gathering amazement and a kind of euphoria—an awareness that some motive higher than mere personal survival had taken collective hold of these men—a glimmer of belief, perhaps, that the distant God he'd prayed to throughout the voyage had indeed been attentive, and was now inspiring these men to consecrate their lives—when the answers to Paynter's question began to come back, one by one . . .

"Southerner!" "Southerner!" "Southerner!" "Southerner!"

"Southerner!" from the *Godfrey* Bostonians. "Southerner!" from the *Delphine* men of Maine. "Southerner!" from the Australian stowaways and the whaling men of *Edward Carey* and *Hector* and *Abigail* and all the great flaming roundup in the Bering. Only a few men, whose Polynesian features betrayed them, muttered the truth of their nationalities. These sailors-of-fortune, who had sailed uneasily together, were prepared to die together.

A silence after the final name had been called. Whittle, who had wept at the lowering of the Confederate flag, must have shed some tears in the darkness for the gallantry of these men. All eyes were fixed on Captain Paynter, who was struggling to form a response to what he had just heard.

Something about these ragtag devils must have moved him, pierced through his martinet's steeliness. Southerners, British . . . it no longer bloody mattered, did it?

Bugger all. He let every man-jack of them go free.

☙☙☙

Their last voyage together was on a ferryboat that took them from *Shenandoah* to Liverpool. And then they drifted off quietly and separately into a fog denser than any in the Aleutians, the fog of history. Many of the officers, faced with certain arrest and trial in the United States and uncertain of their safety even if they remained in Britain, tried their fortunes in South America. Francis Chew, Dabney Scales, and John Grimball lived for a while in Carlota, a haven for ex-Confederates not far from Vera Cruz, Mexico. Sidney Smith Lee, Orris Browne, and John Mason were among a group that headed for Argentina, where they lived as farmers in another Confederate enclave, Rosario, tending cattle, chickens, and vegetables.

James Waddell, hemorrhaging from scurvy, and weakened critically by weeks of deprivation, found a small house in Liverpool. He sent for Ann in America, who had been living under Federal restrictions in Maryland for the duration of her husband's voyage. She joined him and they took up residence in a town near Liverpool. After a lengthy recuperation in England, Waddell worked there for a shipping company until his pardon by the U.S. government in 1875. Returning home, he was appointed captain of a newly built passenger liner named *San Francisco*, a mail runner on a route linking San Francisco, Japan, and Australia. His first port of call was Australia, where people still remembered him and welcomed him with cheers and parties.

On her return voyage, *San Francisco* struck an unmarked reef fourteen miles off the coast of Mexico. Waddell remained the last person aboard, and brought the ship within three miles of shore before she sank. An investigation exonerated and commended him. He continued on with the company before retiring to Annapolis with his wife. Some years later, sea duty of a sort called him again: the governor of

Maryland asked him to command a nautical police force battling oyster pirates in Chesapeake Bay. Waddell won this war: surprising a small fleet of raiders one night, he ordered howitzer fire. He sank one boat and captured three others. He wrote his memoirs for his family's records, and died in 1886.

William Conway Whittle and Frederich McNulty never fought their duel.

Whittle's sisters and brothers all survived, far from Tidewater, safe in the Blue Ridge Mountains, and were united, eventually, with their father, Commodore Whittle.

Whittle never reencountered Pattie. He never mentioned her in his subsequent writings, and he never spoke of her to any of his descendants. He provided no indication that she was ever found.

Aware that he and all the officers still faced prosecution, even the gallows, in the United States, and fearing rendition at the hands of Adams, Whittle left for Europe immediately. After getting his strength back in Paris, and learning that any hope of returning to the States was lost, Whittle accompanied Browne, Smith, and Mason to Argentina and farmed with them there for a few years, until he had farmed the grief and bitterness out of his heart. After a general decree of amnesty in 1868, he came home to Virginia, where he became captain of a steamboat plying the route between Norfolk and Baltimore. He married a Norfolk woman in 1872—Elizabeth Calvert Page, the daughter of the renowned Confederate naval commander Richard Lucien Page. Page, his son-in-law-to-be Conway Whittle, and also Whittle's father Commodore Whittle, shared a curious and unwelcome Civil War distinction. All three had been defeated by the same man: Admiral David G. Farragut, a fellow prewar naval officer and their neighbor on Duke Street, in Norfolk, until 1861.

William Conway Whittle and Elizabeth Calvert Page had four children, and remained in Norfolk all their lives. They lived in an elegant brick house of Federal design that still stands, thanks to Whittle's descendants and admirers who linked arms a century later and stood in front of the bulldozers when developers threatened to raze it. In later life, Whittle founded the Bank of Virginia. In 1910 he published the story of his cruises on CSS *Shenandoah* and CSS *Nashville*. He died in 1920 at the age of eighty.

Shenandoah never regained her glory. Two days after Paynter released her crew, Thomas Dudley finally got his hands on her. The U.S. consul inspected her and found her in a squalid state of repair and sanitation. Perhaps his judgment was flavored with partisanship and frustration. He ordered her sailed to New York, but she was turned back by a storm. Eventually the government auctioned her to a wealthy dilettante, the Sultan of Zanzibar, who used her as a yacht for a while. In 1879 she struck a coral reef during a gale in the Indian Ocean, and sank.

Alone among all the men who sailed under *Shenandoah*'s flag, Lieutenant Conway Whittle returns history's gaze without lowering his eyes.

He fought for a cause condemned by the infallibility of the time-present perspective: a cause that claimed many and noble ideals, but a cause fatally compromised by its defense of human slavery. Yet Conway Whittle owned no slaves, nor was he ever known to align himself with that institution. Before the Civil War his mother, sister, and older brother had all died while his father, a Captain in the U.S. Navy, was at sea on a mission to stop the slave trade.

He was a man trapped in history, as all men and women are trapped in history: a man whose selfless loyalty to native ground and tradition placed him on the wrong side of history's ledger.

Yet he was as good a man as history seems able to produce: a warrior of courage inconceivable to most people; a naval officer of surpassing calm and intelligence; a seeker after Christian redemption; a steadfast lover; a student of human nature; a gentle soul; a custodian of virtue.

Whittle demonstrated these qualities again and again, through gestures as large in their way as the seas around him. Perhaps his most convincing demonstration was contained in a few quiet words that have been all but lost in history's oceanic fog: the words Whittle spoke to Orris Browne aboard *Shenandoah* on the night of November 7, 1865, the words that Orris Browne never forgot.

Browne reminded Conway Whittle of these words in a letter written on stationery engraved with Browne's elaborate, swirling letterhead, and dated November 8, 1893—twenty-eight years and a day after Whittle spoke them. The letterhead bore the return address of Browne's prosperous truck farm: Hollywood Place, Cape Charles, North Hampton County, Virginia.

Browne had been a guest at the home of John T. Mason, the *Shenandoah* midshipman who'd slipped into Liverpool with Browne and the others that long-ago November night. During his three-day stay, he and his host had been poring over Mason's logbook. Mason had hoped to assemble a reunion of the raider's officers, but Browne was the only invitee able to be there. ("We had looked for you, but Mason had your letter saying you could not attend.")

"You were missed more than anyone, for several reasons," Browne wrote to his friend, who was then fifty-three. "You were the nearest officer to the place of meeting who was absent." And then Browne turned to what he really wanted to say.

"You are now the senior officer of the crew," he began, "and you were, during the cruise of the ship, the real commander of her in many tight places, and at times, you were the only man that I know of who could've directed Waddell, our Captain.

"I never really understood Waddell, though I tried to. At times he did well, he was comfortable to the position that he held, at others he was entirely impotent and limp. Again, on plain propositions clear to almost anyone, he would rush off the wrong way, perfectly satisfied that the most profound wisdom was guiding him. I believe that he was honest, conscientious, and not lacking in courage, but still he was weak."

Browne reminded Whittle of the English marine guard that took charge of the ship, and the anxious waiting, over three days, while the British government debated the demand of Charles Francis Adams that the crew be handed over to the United States for trial as pirates. He fondly recalled some hijinks the young officers indulged in during the wait: A "little 'convention,' as Smith Lee would call it, in the Ward room," a "jubilee in the Steerage." And then he brought up the night of the aborted escape:

We . . . made our arrangements, which were to have a boat under the bow sprit at night, and drop down into it. But if the boat did not come by 12 o'clock, then with certain of our crew, we would cut away one of the Shenandoah's *boats. In this we would have been opposed by the English Marines, but we decided that we could get away with them, that we were going ashore.*

Browne reminded Whittle of a moment of decision he'd imposed on the lieutenant: a decision in which Whittle had been invited to choose between expediency and honor.

I invited you to join us after telling you of the plans. You replied, "There is no objection to the plan, or to your going, but I cannot join you. I am the Executive Officer of this ship, and I must stay here, let the consequences be what they may. If to hang is the end, I shall see the last of it. My position is different from that of you and your associates. You are the junior officers of the ship, and I advise you to go. Take this"—offering me your pocketbook with all your money—"you will need it. I may never want it." And when I declined to accept it, you insisted upon it, saying that the little you have will not go far. That occurred on the poop deck, abaft the mizzenmast, and a little on the starboard side.

That is where Browne and the others left Conway Whittle. In a sense, that is where he has quietly stood ever since, meeting history's gaze: on the poop deck of a fallen ship, abaft the mizzenmast, and a little on the starboard side, the Executive Officer eternal, under a flag of valor that will never go down.

NOTES

1. Letter from secret service agent James D. Bulloch to Confederate Navy Secretary Stephen Mallory, September 16, 1864, Confederate Navy Research Center, Mobile, Alabama.
2. James I. Waddell, *C.S.S. Shenandoah: The Memoirs of Lieutenant Commanding James I. Waddell*, edited by James D. Horan (Annapolis: Naval Institute Press, Bluejacket Books, 1996), 53.
3. Ibid.
4. Ibid., 55.
5. Ibid., 57–58.
6. Murray Morgan, *Confederate Raider in the North Pacific: The Saga of the C.S.S. Shenandoah* (Pullman, WA: Washington State University Press, 1995), 44. (First published as *Dixie Raider: The Saga of the U.S.S. Shenandoah* [E. P. Dutton, New York, 1948].)
7. Waddell, *Memoirs*, 78.
8. Ibid., 79–80.
9. Morgan, *Confederate Raider*, 60.
10. Waddell, *Memoirs*, 123.
11. Ibid.
12. Ibid., 124.
13. See Tom Chaffin, *Sea of Gray: The Around-the-World Odyssey of the Confederate Raider* Shenandoah (New York: Farrar, Straus and Giroux, 2006), 142.
14. Ibid., 143–45.
15. Waddell, *Memoirs*, 125.
16. Unidentified crew member of *Shenandoah*, quoted in The Patriot Files: Dedicated to the Preservation of Military History, www.patriotfiles.com
17. See Chaffin, *Sea of Gray*, 149.
18. Waddell, *Memoirs*, 130.
19. See Chaffin, *Sea of Gray*, 151.
20. Journal of Midshipman George Mason, quoted in Chaffin, *Sea of Gray*, 153.
21. See Chaffin, *Sea of Gray*, 157–58.
22. Waddell, *Memoirs*, 133.

23. Ibid., 134.

24. Ibid., 175.

25. Ibid.

26. Letter from James D. Bulloch to Captain James I. Waddell, July 19, 1865, Official Records of the Union and Confederate Navies in the War of Rebellion, quoted in Chaffin, *Sea of Gray*, 299–300.

27. Lieutenant Chew's diary, quoted in Chaffin, *Sea of Gray*, 292.

28. Waddell, *Memoirs*, 176.

29. Ibid.

30. Ibid.

31. Waddell, *Memoirs*, 177.

32. See Chaffin, *Sea of Gray*, 306–8.

33. Quoted in Chaffin, *Sea of Gray*, 308.

34. Ibid.

35. Waddell, *Memoirs*, 178.

36. See Morgan, *Confederate Raider*, 269.

37. Unpublished diary of midshipman John Thompson Mason, archived in the Library of the Confederacy, Richmond, Virginia, and quoted in Morgan, *Confederate Raider*, 270.

38. Mason, quoted in Morgan, *Confederate Raider*, 270.

39. Unpublished journal of Charles Edward Lining, Library of the Confederacy, quoted in Morgan, *Confederate Raider*, 271.

40. Ibid., 272.

41. As described by Lining in Morgan, *Confederate Raider*, 272.

42. As quoted by Morgan, *Confederate Raider*, 278–80.

43. Ibid., 284.

44. Ibid.

45. As described in Chaffin, *Sea of Gray*, 349.

46. From Cornelius Hunt, *The Shenandoah, or the Last Confederate Cruiser*, quoted in Chaffin, *Sea of Gray*, 293–94, 350.

47. As quoted in Morgan, *Confederate Raider*, 295–96.

48. Cornelius Hunt's memoirs, quoted in Morgan, *Confederate Raider*, 297, and Chaffin, *Sea of Gray*, 351.

49. As described by Morgan in *Confederate Raider*, 297–98.

50. Waddell, *Memoirs*, 185.

51. As quoted in Morgan, *Confederate Raider*, 300–301.

52. Ibid., 300.

53. Ibid., 301.

54. Ibid.

55. Stanley F. Horne, *Gallant Rebel: The Fabulous Cruise of the C.S.S. Shenandoah* (New Brunswick, NJ: Rutgers University Press, 1947).

56. As reported in Chaffin, *Sea of Gray*, 355.

GLOSSARY

---

abaft. Behind, or in back of. "Abaft the mizzen," for example, would refer to any area sternward of the rearmost (mizzen) mast.

beam. *Shenandoah*'s teak decks were supported by iron I-beams running from one side of the hull to the other. Hence, the longest beam determines the width of a ship at its widest point (*Shenandoah*'s was 32 feet). The "starboard beam" refers to the right side of the hull when facing forward, and the "port beam" refers to the left.

belaying pin. A wooden-handled hardwood pin about two feet long that was used to fasten ropes to the railing of the ship. Belaying pins were removable from the railing and could be used for other tasks, such as breaking ice away from the pulleys.

berth. A sleeping space, hammock, or bunk. Also the place where a ship, either anchored or tied to a pier, is at rest.

berth deck. The area below the exposed decks that is used for the crew's sleeping accommodations. *Shenandoah*'s berth deck had to be cleared of its cargo of coal before it was usable.

bluff-bowed. A term for a ship with a broad, flat bow, useful in nudging into slushy ice. The narrow, bladelike bow on *Shenandoah* could be pinched between the floes, while the bluff-bowed hulls of the whalers gave the ice very little to squeeze, and their barrel-like shape let them rise up away from the ice, unlike *Shenandoah*'s tall, flat-sided hull.

boatswain (bosun). A senior noncommissioned officer in charge of the anchors, rigging, and sails. *Shenandoah*'s combat-seasoned boatswain, George Harwood, was an Englishman; he'd also served two years as boatswain on CSS *Alabama*, and had survived her sinking in the English Channel. The boatswain serves as the go-between linking the crew's duties and the officers' orders. He is senior in rank to all other noncommissioned crew members, but junior in rank to all the officers.

bond. During a more chivalrous period in naval warfare, when an enemy ship had been captured, instead of being destroyed, it could be ransomed, or *bonded*. The owner or captain could avoid the ship's destruction by promising (giving a bond, creating a legal obligation) that he'd bring the vessel to the nearest port, sell it, and remit the funds to the country that had captured—but hadn't destroyed—the bonded vessel. It was a form of extortion, but the bonded ship, of course, never actually paid; certainly the Confederate government never survived long enough to collect on such bonds. Bonding was basically a humanitarian option giving countries at war a chance to protect the enemy's merchant mariners, and thereby their own. Bonding some of their prizes also allowed *Shenandoah*'s 1,000-plus prisoners a way off the raider, which wasn't equipped to carry one-fifth that number.

boom. A long horizontal spar (timber) to which the bottom edge of the spanker sail is fastened. *Shenandoah*'s boom pivoted near the base of the mizzenmast and swung out over the stern, passing above the wheelhouse. *Shenandoah*'s boom was 56 feet long.

bowsprit. The hollow, tubular, cast-iron projection extending forward from the bow. It carries a long round timber (spar) known as the jib boom, which points forward like a gigantic lance above the ship's bow. This jib boom in turn anchors the forestays (ropes) that support the foremast. The jib boom also provided the fastening points for *Shenandoah*'s four triangular jib sails. *Shenandoah*'s huge metal bowsprit was hollow and big enough for a man to wiggle inside, as did more than one of the stowaways in Australia.

brace. One of the lines (ropes) attached to the outboard ends of each of the yards, or spars. The yards are the horizontal timbers on which the square sails are hung. By pulling on the braces, or "bracing," the yards can be pivoted about the vertical masts, allowing the sails to catch the wind more effectively.

brig (brigantine). A sailing ship with two masts of which the forwardmost (foremast) is rigged with square sails, and the rearmost (mainmast) is rigged with triangular sails set fore-and-aft (parallel to the hull). A brigantine was called a "hermaphrodite rig" because it combined the two styles of sail (square and triangular).

brought by the wind. A sailing vessel is *brought by the wind* when it is stopped rapidly by turning directly into the wind so that the wind pushes the vessel and its sails backward, thus canceling all forward momentum.

bulwark. The part of the ship's side extending above the deck. It was this wall-like coaming that had to be cut open to let *Shenandoah*'s cannons stick out.

bunker. The large belowdecks area used to store coal aboard a ship. The bunkers provided access for the coal heavers to move the fuel into the boilers, but *Shenandoah*'s backup fuel supply, a cargo of coal, subsequently required "shifting" from the cargo decks to the fuel bunkers so it could be made available to the engine room.

capstan. A heavy winch mounted near the bow and used to raise the anchor. It is turned by sailors pushing on *capstan bars* (see below) and walking around the capstan, which, as it is turned, winds the anchor chain.

capstan bars. The removable heavy iron bars that are fastened spokelike into the top of the capstan. They allow many men, pushing on the bars, to raise a great weight.

chronometer and patent log. Chronometers are extremely accurate clocks that allow the navigator, called the sailing master, to locate the ship's position. The patent log is a mechanical device that calculates the rough speed of a sailing vessel. The device is dropped overboard while attached to the moving vessel, and a rotating member on the patent log allows the ship's speed to be calculated. Current, drift, waves, and other factors make it a less-than-accurate device. Bulloch, *Shenandoah*'s sailing master, navigated "by chronometer and patent log" from the Aleutians to Liverpool with only those two instruments. There was never a point where he could check his navigation against a known landmark. It was a remarkable feat of seamanship.

clipper. A sailing ship with long, smooth lines, a narrow beam, and a sharp, graceful bow built specifically for speed.

close-reef [v.]. To shorten sails. In order to reduce the amount of sail exposed to the wind, the canvas sailcloth is gathered up and tied to the yard, with short lengths of rope that have been sewn to the sails. These ropes are called *reefs*. Thus, to *reef* a sail means to shorten it, to *double-reef* means to shorten it more, and to *close-reef* means to shorten sail as much as possible.

copper. Wooden ships are subject to worms, barnacles, and algae that create drag and slow them severely. Copper plates nailed over the wooden hulls helped prevent such formations and were invaluable to the shipbuilder. When Whittle refers to "our copper," he means the copperplated hull. When *Shenandoah*'s crew burned the whalers on Ponape, they left the wrecks on a reef, above the low-tide line, so the locals could pry off the copper and resell it.

double-reef. See *close-reef,* above.

dumb-trucks. The wheels of a gun carriage, these allow for movement of the cannon during loading, aiming, firing, and recoil.

ensign. Whenever the flag of a particular nation is flown on a ship, it is called an *ensign.* When *Shenandoah* entered Melbourne harbor, the other vessels showed their respect by dipping their ensigns. An ensign is also an officer trainee, a sub-lieutenant or midshipman.

fore-and-aft. Anything parallel to a line drawn from the bow to the center of the stern is called *fore-and-aft*. The small triangular staysails on *Shenandoah*, found at the bow and between the masts, were rigged fore-and-aft. Except for the square-rigged sails on a clipper ship, the rigging on almost all sailboats is arranged fore-and-aft.

forecastle (fo'c'sle). The raised part of the ship in front of the foremast. It is usually one deck above the main deck, and is found directly behind (abaft) the bow. The crew often has its quarters inside the forecastle, and on *Shenandoah* it also provided a bit of shelter for the pig house and manger, part of the livestock carried on the ship for food. The anchors are handled from the forecastle, and it is where the ship's bell is located.

fore rigging. The wires, ropes, and chains that support and are carried on the bowsprit and jib boom. When Whittle climbed on board *Sea King* in London, he was undercover, and, rather than using the gangway, which was being watched, he was able to climb on board unseen using the many lines that are found at the very foremost point of the ship. When berthed, large sailing ships frequently had their bowsprits and fore rigging extending high over the piers and streets that serviced the vessels.

forestay. Wires or ropes that are connected from the top of the foremast to the very front of the ship. Jib sails are hung from it on some ships, but they were not on *Shenandoah*.

frigate. A warship of medium size, built for speed, and carrying as many as 60 guns. U.S. Navy frigates and steam frigates posed a serious threat to *Shenandoah*.

gale. Technically, a wind blowing between 34 and 47 knots, it is characterized by high waves that break at their crests.

gangway. A hinged opening through the coaming, or bulwark, in the side of the ship, provided so that a gangplank may be extended to a pier or other vessel.

gig. A longboat, rowed as an auxiliary craft. Waddell used a gig to inspect the outside of the hull during a calm spell. *Shenandoah* had the pick of fast whaleboats from the captures, and kept several on deck to offload their prizes.

goosewing. When the wind is too strong to keep a square-rigged sail fully opened, the center part of the sail can be raised in the middle and the outer corners left exposed. The resulting configuration resembles the wings of a flying goose.

grapnel. A metal hook, much like a small anchor, but having several sharp, opposed points. The Rebel crewmen were once able to pull *Shenandoah* out of the ice by rigging a grapnel to a long rope, and rowing the grapnel away from the ship in a small boat. They brought the hook out through the ice floe and fastened it to an iceberg. The men back on board were thereby able to reel *Shenandoah* out of the pack ice and into open water.

gun deck. The deck where a ship's cannons were located. *Shenandoah*'s gun deck could also be called her spar deck, or her weather deck.

halyard. One of the ropes used to raise or lower a sail.

hawser. A large rope, having a circumference greater than five inches, by which a ship is moored or towed.

hoisting propeller. *Shenandoah* had a propeller that could be lifted off its drive shaft and brought inside the ship. Because she was faster under sail than under steam power, hoisting the propeller meant the sails could be used without the drag the propeller would create if left in place.

holystone. Sandstone blocks roughly the size and shape of an old-style family Bible, used as primitive scouring tools. By sliding holystones back and forth over the wooden decks, crewmen working on their knees could clean the boards.

ironclad. A generic term for any steam-powered naval ship covered with metal plating that protected the vessel's superstructure and allowed the ship to fire its cannons through closable armored openings.

jib boom. The long, lancelike spar that is carried fore-and-aft at the bow.

keel. The lowest element of the ship's hull. The bottom of the ship.

leeward. The direction toward which the wind is blowing. A floating object such as a ship, or a cork, will be blown to leeward.

lubber's hole. Where a two-section mast is joined, an open wooden platform is built out to carry the lines and stays supporting the upper member of the mast. The platform is called the *top*, and on a warship, marines could stand on the tops and fire muskets at the enemy. This platform has an opening near the mast that a clumsy person, a "landlubber," could squirm through when climbing. It was also possible, but much more daring, to swing out away from the mast using the stays, and climb up over the outside edge of the platform and avoid the indignity and awkwardness of using the lubber's hole.

manila. Ropes, or lines, may be made from many plants. Manila is rope made from the wild banana plant of the Philippines, called *abaca*, and is extremely rot-resistant. Hemp makes excellent rope, but it rots and stretches more rapidly than manila.

midshipman. A trainee officer, a sub-lieutenant, an ensign. The most junior of a ship's officers.

mizzenmast. The rearmost mast on a three-masted ship. On *Shenandoah* it was just in front of the wheelhouse.

mizzen royals. The topmost sails on the mizzenmast.

monitor. A type of *ironclad* (see above). Monitors were characterized by an

extremely low hull, almost level with the waterline, and a cylindrical gun
turret mounted amidships.

pintle. One of the heavy metal hooks on the hinge of the rudder by which
it is attached to the stern of the ship, and upon which the rudder pivots
to change direction. *Shenandoah*'s pintles were badly damaged long before the ship reached Australia.

pipe over [v.]. A mini-ceremony involving a whistle called a *bosun's pipe*,
used to alert the crew that something important is happening. When a
dignitary boards a vessel, it is customary to pipe him over the gangplank,
or "pipe him on board." When Waddell went over the side to inspect the
hull, he was "piped over" the side.

plain sail. Sail or sails used under normal weather conditions.

poop deck. A raised deck at the stern of the ship. On *Shenandoah* the poop
deck formed the roof of the officers' cabins and the wardroom, and upon
it stood the wheelhouse. The mizzenmast rose out of the poop deck.

port. The left-hand side of a vessel when one is facing the bow.

ratline. Ladderlike rope steps tied between the shrouds (see below). The
ratlines are used to climb the shrouds in order to adjust the sails.

reef. One of the short lengths of rope tied in rows across the front of a sail
and used to tie the canvas to the spar when shortening sail.

reef down [v.]. To use the reef lines to tie down part of a sail and thereby
reduce the amount of canvas exposed to the wind.

rove. When Whittle had to replace much of the original rope that had
come with *Sea King*, it meant taking the ropes—called "lines" at sea—
out of all the pulleys and threading new lines back in. The word *reeve*
means to pass a line through something, specifically a ring or pulley.
Reeving new lines was difficult, dangerous, high-altitude work. There
were hundreds of complicated pulleys, called *blocks*, all over *Shenandoah*.
These formed the critical control elements of the ship, and without
reliable lines, the sails would have been useless. In a storm, when certain of these ropes break, it can mean the loss of an entire sail, or even
a mast.

royal. On a square-rigger like *Shenandoah*, the sails on each mast are
named in ascending order as follows: *sail, topsail, royal, topgallant.* Many
extreme clippers had even more courses of sails, the next highest were appropriately known as *skysails*, and even above that another set could
sometimes be used if the wind was just right; this highest sail of all had
two names, based on its shape. It was known as a *skyscraper* if it was triangular, and if it was rectangular it was called a *moonsail*. All sails have two-
part names, for example *main royal*. The first name indicates the mast to
which the sail is attached, and the second name gives the sail's position

above the deck; hence, the *foresail* is the lowest sail on the foremost mast. The *mainsail* is the lowest sail on the mainmast. The *mizzen royal* is the highest sail on the mizzenmast, and the *main royal* was *Shenandoah's* topmost sail on her mainmast. It would need to be knotted in place by a seaman working the equivalent of 14 stories above the ocean.

schooner. A ship with two or more masts, generally carrying triangular sails rigged fore-and-aft—that is, a ship without a clipper's square sails.

sheet. A line—rope—used to control the bottom edges of a sail.

shorten [v.]. To take in, or reduce the area of, the sails exposed to the wind, is to shorten them, thereby slowing the ship.

shrouds. The heavy ropes, or even wires, that attach the top of a mast to the point where the hull meets the deck, bulwark, or coaming. Shrouds have thinner ropes tied between them known as *ratlines* (see above).

six-top sailer. Whittle has spotted a ship carrying so much canvas that he counts as many as six topsails, which means it is probably a Yankee clipper. The more "top-yards" Whittle spots on a potential target, the bigger the ship.

sloop. A small sailing vessel with a single mast.

spanker. A large, fore-and-aft rigged sail mounted to the mizzenmast. Rather than a square sail carried on yards, the *spanker* is a four-sided sail that pivots over the wheelhouse at the stern, and is carried on two long spars, the topmost being the *spanker gaff*, and the bottommost being the *spanker boom*. When *Shenandoah's* damaged propeller had to be pulled up through the roof of the wheelhouse to be repaired, the crew rigged the spanker boom as a hoist to lift it.

spar. Any pole or timber, such as a *yard, mast, gaff*, or *boom*, that is used to hold a sail. The spars carrying *Shenandoah's* square sales are called *yards*.

spar deck. The upper deck of the ship, open to the weather, where the spars, yards, and sails could be handled.

square-rigger. Ships carrying square—actually rectangular—sails that are arrayed in columns and carried perpendicular to the hull are called *square-riggers*. The term differentiates such ships from those with triangular sails arranged fore-and-aft.

stern copper. The copper plating protecting the stern of *Shenandoah* from teredo worms and marine growth. It was not heavy enough to protect the ship from ice.

starboard. The right-hand side of a vessel when one is facing the bow.

stay. A line, rope, or cable that holds a mast upright is called a *stay*, also known as a *shroud*. The stays are further described by the names of the masts they support: *mainstay, forestay, mizzenstay*.

staysail. Any fore-and-aft sail carried on the mast's stays, the cables holding the masts upright. Staysails are frequently used when the square-rigged sails would present too much canvas to the wind, particularly in a gale.

steerage. The compartments or spaces inside the ship's hull near the rudder and steering mechanism. Accommodations for crew and passengers are frequently found in steerage, and they are the least desirable quarters.

stove [v.]. From a nautical term, *stave,* meaning to puncture or break. Whittle is concerned that the ice might have "stove in" or punctured the hull's planking.

studding sails. In light wind, *Shenandoah* could extend a series of auxiliary sails outboard of the yards that held the square sails. These were called *studding sails,* and as with all sails, they are named by the masts and sails they are flown from, thus the *main royal studding sail* would be carried on an outrigger from the royal sail on the mainmast.

tackle. A system of two or more pulleys, called *blocks,* and the ropes that attach them. Block and tackle are used to lift heavy objects.

yard. One of the spars that carry the sails on a square-rigged ship. *Shenandoah*'s main yard was over seventy feet long.

yardarm. The outer third of a yard. *Yardarm* is the term often used to describe any of the long spars that a square-rigger uses to support the top edges of the sails.

BIBLIOGRAPHY

———◆———

Bowcock, Andrew, *CSS* Alabama: *Anatomy of a Confederate Raider,* Annapolis: Naval Institute Press, 2002.

Chaffin, Tom, *Sea of Gray: The Around-the-World Odyssey of the Confederate Raider* Shenandoah, New York: Farrar, Straus and Giroux, 2006.

Davis, Burke, *The Civil War: Strange and Fascinating Facts,* New York: Random House Value, 1988.

Horan, James D., editor, *C.S.S.* Shenandoah: *The Memoirs of Lieutenant Commanding James I. Waddell,* Annapolis: Naval Institute Press, 1960.

Konstam, Angus, *Confederate Raider 1861–65,* Oxford, UK: Osprey Publishing, 2003.

———, *Confederate Blockade Runner 1861-65,* Oxford, UK: Osprey Publishing, 2004.

Morgan, Murray, *Confederate Raider in the North Pacific: The Saga of the C.S.S.* Shenandoah, *1864–65,* Pullman, WA: Washington State University Press, Reprint Series, 1995 (originally published by E. P. Dutton, 1948).

Norman, Andrew E., general editor, *The Autobiography of Charles Francis Adams, Great American Autobiographies,* New York: Chelsea House, 1983.

Schooler, Lynn, *The Last Shot: The Incredible Story of the CSS* Shenandoah *and the True Conclusion of the American Civil War,* New York: HarperCollins Publishers, 2005.

Whittle, William C., *The Voyage of the CSS* Shenandoah: *A Memorable Cruise,* Tuscaloosa: The University of Alabama Press, 2005.

———, *Cruises of the Confederate States Steamers "Shenandoah" and "Nashville,"* published privately, 1910.

ACKNOWLEDGMENTS

ACKNOWLEDGMENTS are intended to tell people who have been instrumental in helping to create a book know how much their participation means. In this sense, it would be impossible to acknowledge how much Ron Powers contributed, for his work meant everything to this story. He can never know how much his effort impressed, focused, inspired, and informed this project, and me. Thank you, Ron, from my heart.

I'd like to thank Rick Horgan and Julian Pavia at Crown for their patience and professionalism. John Talbot, my agent, and Jim Hornfisher, Ron's agent, both deserve recognition and gratitude for bringing this project together. My dear friend Tim Murphy showed me such enthusiasm, optimism, and support throughout the entire process that I fail to see how he is not as much a critical part of the story as Whittle himself.

My family has helped me work on this story for years, and Cousin Beverly Dabney, by providing me her records and motivation, really was as much an inspiration as Whittle's own writing. I truly could not have done this without her. Robert and Kennon Baldwin, my brothers, have provided material and psychic support, and also did a fine job of reading the early versions; thanks also go to Catlin and Alison Baldwin for the use of KWB. My cousins Jim and Melody Baldwin, and Ann Blade Stauffer, who made my visits in Norfolk possible, and Frank Blackford, who made such an important research contribution when the going was toughest, all get my heartfelt thanks.

My good friends Ed and Nan Lazaron, Connie Fisher, Peter Campanaro, Ashe Gupta, Patricia, Chris and Madeline Valando-Meech, and Margo McFarland also deserve acknowledgment, all for vastly different reasons.

In addition, Robert Hitchings and Troy at the Norfolk Public Library, and the folks at The Museum of the Confederacy in Richmond, were very helpful. Also, I am so grateful to Ann Morgan at the Taylor-Whittle Home in Norfolk, who escorted us through the wonderful old house. It revived memories of my boyhood when we would visit my cousin Beverly Dabney, Conway Whittle's granddaughter, while she still lived there.

I would also like to thank the pros who helped translate my garbled diction: Transcribers are Cindy Kimball of Kimball Office Services, Inc., Bristol, Vermont, and Meredith Fletcher of Castleton College, Castleton, Vermont.

These next friends have made various contributions, and I am grateful to them all: Dr. Linus Abrams, Lawrence Altman, Jamie Arcuri, Keith and Stuart Baldwin, Dave Barnes and Alanna, Danny Barror, Ron Bernstein, John and Ann Blackford, Frank and Polly Blackford, Cary Baldwin Blade, Joe Blumenthal, Dr. Joseph Boldt, John Boswell, Rick Boucher, Stefan and Chisuko Broinowski, Stuart Bronfeld, H. Lee Browne, Mary Calderhead, Chris Canavan, Debbie Choate, Mike Collins, Paul Dadonna, Ward and Diane Davol, Dick Dickerson, Art Doumtjes, Loren and Mickey Dubno, Nicole Eisenman, Ken Eshelman, David Eyre, Susan Fisher, Sheila Fortune, Alfred Franci, Patricia Fullerton, Josh Greenstein, Vena Gupta, Drew Haluska, Dr. William Hampton, Judy Hart, Ron and Jim Hollar, Craig Hurley, Moira Incorvaia, Angela Ingrao, David and Ken Jacobsen, my uncle Whittle Johnston, my aunt Martha Johnston, my uncle Jim Johnston, Rebecca Johnston, Sarah Kernochan, Georgie Koulianos, David Lewis, Jane Lewis, Marci Mansfield, Molly March, John Markham, Skip McNomee, JR Meadows, Andy and Pat Micek, Maureen "Nanni" Micek, Dave Miles, Joe Mulvey, Dr. Mark Newberg, Dr. David Nocek, Joe Ossorio, Aldo and Henry Pascarella, Rob and Gale Penn, Dee Pridgon, Dr. Sunil Rana, Samantha Richardson, Eric and Rosemary Spahr, Dr. John Sparks, Ron Strahn, Ed Tedeschi, Susie Fisher Thorness, Dr. Larry Toder, Rob Toohey and Krissy Clarke, Gary Trageser, Derek Uhlman, Petion Vitillus, Ron Warzoha, Anne A. White, Bailey White, Susanne Coloneri Whittle, Knox Wibberley, Dr. Felice Zwas.

I also want to acknowledge the support, suggestions, and intelligent criticism I received from my son, John Macky Baldwin IV.

—John Baldwin

INDEX

Abigail (barque), 224–225, 232, 243, 316, 327

Adams, Charles Francis, 5–7, 67, 121, 164, 204, 321, 322, 326, 329, 331

Adventures of Philip (Thackeray), 212–213

Agincourt, Battle of, 7

Alaska, 223, 245, 250

Albert, Prince Consort, 32, 33

Alcott, Henry, 138, 169, 327

Alcott, Mrs. Henry, 323–324

Aleutian Islands, 85, 261, 268, 284, 319

Alina (barque), 51–54, 70, 144, 308

"Amazing Grace" (Cowper), 192

American Colonization Society, 262

Amphitrite Strait, 223, 234

Anadyr Bay, 236

Andersonville National Cemetery, Georgia, 287

Anna Jane (brig), 72–73

Antietam, Battle of, 223

Anton Lizardo reef, 26, 29

Appomattox, 240

Arctic Circle, 175, 256, 257

Arctic Ocean, 223, 226, 230, 245, 256, 318

Armstrong, Captain, 47

Army of Northern Virginia, 142–143, 158

Ascension Island, 197–200, 202–205, 209, 214, 249, 309

Atlanta, Georgia, 1, 86, 201

Atlantic & North Carolina Railroad, 36

Australia, 85, 126, 148, 151, 153–174, 253, 281, 282

Azores, 311

B-17 bomber, 148

Babushkin Bay, 230

Baker, Captain, 200

Barracouta (barque), 276, 281, 286, 289, 292, 318

Barron, Samuel, 3, 85, 161, 162

Barton, Clara, 287

Bass Strait, 156

Beaufort, North Carolina, 34, 38, 47

Benjamin, Captain, 245

Bering Sea, 206, 223, 226, 230, 231–235, 238, 239, 241–243, 245–253, 255–256, 267, 273, 279, 312

Bering Strait, 223, 245, 250, 256, 260

Bermuda, 34

Beverage, J., 34

Bipolar disorder, 185

Black soldiers, in Civil War, 264–265

Blacker, I. C., 246, 293, 296

Blanchard, William, 163–164, 168, 172–173

Blockade, 3, 5, 8, 17–21, 30, 34–36, 40–41, 47, 84

Bogue Island, 35, 40

Brazilian Basin, 300

British-Confederacy relations, 4–5, 7, 19, 30–33, 66, 159

British Royal Observatory, Greenwich, 149

Brooke, John Mercer, 83–84

Brown, George (alias) (*see* Whittle, William Conway)

Brown, Mr., 73

Browne, Oris A., 293, 295, 324, 328, 329, 330–332

Brunswick (barque), 251

Bryson, Andrew, 27

Bull Run, Battle of, 12–13, 47, 57

Bulloch, Harriet, 14

Bulloch, Irvine S., 29–30, 113–115, 125, 149–150, 183, 189, 221, 229, 230, 234, 270, 281, 290, 292, 295, 315, 316, 324

Bulloch, James Dunwoody, 13–14, 20–21, 29, 49, 50, 52, 53, 84, 85, 113, 121, 126, 268, 269

Burnside, Ambrose, 36, 37, 39

Butler, Benjamin "Beast," 56

Cannibals, 189, 191, 193

Canning, George P., 175–176, 309, 311–312, 316

Canning, Henry, 275

Cape Clear, 311, 312

Cape Dezhnev, 256

Cape Horn, 85, 268, 288, 289, 291, 311

Cape Howe, 175

Cape Lookout, 41

Cape of Good Hope, 104

Cape Otway, 154

Cape Rollers, 136, 165, 311

Cape Roman, 42

Cape Thaddeous, 236

Cape Verde Islands, 308

Capetown, South Africa, 125, 135, 136, 282, 292, 295–298

Carlota, Mexico, 328

Caroline Islands, 197

Casualties, of Civil War, 285, 287

Catherine (barque), 246, 248

Cats, 140, 270–272

Chancellorsville, Battle of, 199

Charbrol Harbor, 197–198

"Charity" (Cowper), 191–192

Charleston, South Carolina, 29, 36, 41, 44, 45, 203, 240, 244, 309

Charleston Harbor, 42

Charter Oak (schooner), 61–64, 70

Chase, Captain, 200

Cheek, Lieutenant, 323, 324

Chew, Francis Thornton, 74, 130–134, 139, 143, 190, 199, 227, 229, 270, 281, 287, 293, 295, 297, 306–307, 328

Chile, 288

Clarendon, Lord, 325

Codd, Mr., 86

Coleridge, Samuel Taylor, 192

Colombia, 283

Congress (barque), 251

Corbett, Peter S., 4, 67

Cornwallis, General Charles, 5

Cotton trade, 5, 7, 19, 30–32

Covington (barque), 251, 255, 256

Cowper, William, 191–192

Craven, T. A. M., 33, 34

Crawford, William, 96, 184, 196, 316

Crew, of *Shenandoah*, 8, 9, 14–16, 18, 50, 52, 54, 55, 69, 72, 74, 75, 82, 86, 88, 91–97, 99, 107, 118, 148, 175–176, 180, 186–187, 193, 211, 215, 218–219, 233, 234, 244, 294, 315–316, 320, 325–328

CSS *Alabama*, 18, 30, 49, 149, 321

CSS *Atlanta*, 99

CSS *Florida*, 18

CSS *Laurel*, 9, 66, 67, 282, 307

CSS *Louisiana*, 46, 56, 57, 178

CSS *Nashville*, 29–48, 149, 178, 230, 253, 271, 311, 329

CSS *Rattlesnake*, 46

CSS *Shenandoah*, 30
   Abigail episode, 224–225, 232
   Alina episode, 51–54, 308
   appearance of, 10
   at Ascension Island (Ponape), 197–200, 202–205, 209
   barometer readings, 146–147, 226
   Bering Sea captures by, 238, 239, 241–243, 245–253, 255, 256, 269, 273, 279, 312
   boiler on, 114–115
   British press reaction to return of, 321–322, 325
   captain of, 11–12
   cargo of, 90, 203, 210, 286, 296
   cat on, 140, 270–272
   caulking on, 164–166
   Charter Oak episode, 61–64
   Christmas on, 140–143, 146
   code of conduct on, 50
   commissioned, 9
   conflict of command on, 73, 126–135, 177–185, 190–191, 216, 217, 231–232
   course set after war's end by, 280–292, 295–300, 304–314

CSS *Shenandoah* (*cont.*)

crew on, 8, 9, 14–16, 18, 50, 52, 54, 55, 69, 72, 74, 75, 82, 86, 88, 91–97, 99, 107, 118, 148, 175–176, 180, 186–187, 193, 211, 215, 218–219, 233, 234, 244, 294, 315–316, 320, 325–328

D. *Godfrey* episode, 68–69

deaths on, 309–312

Delphine episode, 144–145

disarming of, 276, 278, 282–283

discipline on, 59, 60–61, 95–97, 100–101, 106–108, 123, 124, 146, 151, 173, 177, 184, 193, 196, 225, 246, 275, 288, 315–316

at Drummond Island (Taputeouea), 194–196

drunkenness on, 55, 141, 173, 177, 184, 194, 214, 224–225, 300–301, 316

in east-west shipping routes, 210–214

equator crossed by, 85–86, 196, 283, 286, 299

females on, 62, 71–72, 77, 144–145, 151–153

final days of, 330

fog encountered by, 220–224, 230, 232–235, 239, 243, 244, 256–260

guns on, 69, 124, 125, 136, 138, 184, 274, 282–283

ice encountered by, 226–231, 235, 247, 256–260, 291

Kate Prince episode, 76–78

in Liverpool, 315–319, 323–328, 331–332

in Melbourne, 154–174, 253

miles sailed by, 284, 292, 307

Mogul episode, 49–50, 51, 53

navigator of, 149–150

near-collision of, 97–99

"no name" episode, 78–81

"Norwegian" episode, 94, 95

payment of officers and crew of, 313, 315

prisoners of, 71–72, 77–78, 116–118, 159, 160, 163–164, 205, 209, 241–243, 246–248, 252, 256, 267

propeller of, 120–122, 125, 135, 151, 260, 261

rudder on, 127–129, 135, 148, 227, 258–259, 307

sails and rigging on, 58–59, 90–91, 101–102, 109, 110, 211, 215, 219, 284

scurvy on, 300, 319, 322

search for, 292

sister ships of, 18

southward course of, 83, 85, 86, 88–93, 96, 97, 101, 102, 104, 108

speed of, 8, 10, 108

storms encountered by, 58, 93, 128–131, 136–141, 143–144, 185, 197, 211, 215–221, 225, 253, 270, 289–290, 305–307, 311

surrender of, 318–321

tacking prowess of, 75, 76

transformation from *Sea King*, 7–9, 67

whaling ships and, 84, 85, 102, 105, 112–115, 238, 239, 241–243, 245–253, 255, 256, 269, 273, 279, 312

CSS *Thomas L. Wragg*, 46

Cuba, 25

Cunningham's Patented Self-Reefing Topsails, 101–102

D. *Godfrey* (barque), 68–70, 123, 173, 327

Darling, Sir Charles Henry, 159, 160, 164, 166, 168, 170, 172–174

David Brown (barque), 162–163

Davis, Jefferson, 13, 20, 69, 131, 177, 208–209, 244, 276, 317

Declaration of Independence, 5

Delphine (barque), 144–145, 162, 163, 238*n*, 327

Deserta, 9, 14, 21, 157, 284, 292

Dickens, Charles, 140

Diomede Islands, 250, 256

Diplomacy, 5–6

Discipline, on *Shenandoah*, 59, 60–61, 95–97, 100–101, 106–108, 123, 124, 146, 151, 173, 177, 184, 193, 196, 225, 246, 275, 288, 315–316

Disease, 18, 24, 46, 247–248, 285, 300, 319, 322

Drake Passage, 288, 289

Drummond Island, 194–196

Drunkenness on *Shenandoah*, 55, 141, 173, 177, 184, 194, 214, 224–225, 300–301, 316

Dudley, Thomas H., 5–6, 66–67, 204, 330
Dueling, 301–304

Early, Jubal, 1
East Cape, 256
East India Dock, London, 4
East India Squadron, 12
Easter Island, 288
Ecuador, 284
Edward (barque), 112–115
Edward Carey (whale ship), 199, 200, 204, 327
Egg Islands, 46
Eldridge, Captain, 200
Emancipation Proclamation, 265
Emerson, Ralph Waldo, 274
English Channel, 6, 7, 30, 49
Eniwetok, 189
Equator crossings, 85–86, 196, 283, 286, 299
Eskimos, 246
Espionage, 4, 6, 33, 66, 67, 253
Euphrates (whale ship), 239, 243
Evans, Thomas, 288
Extreme clippers, 10–11
Eye of the Needle, 154

Farragut, David G., 46, 56, 57, 99, 329
Faulkner, William, 313–314
Favorite (barque), 251
Fegan, James, 193, 316
Fiji Islands, 188, 189, 191
Finlayer, Captain, 150, 156
First Kansas Colored Volunteers, 265
First Louisiana Native Guards, 264
Fletcher, Christian, 287
Flood, George, 123
Fog, 220–224, 230, 232–235, 239, 243, 244, 256–260
Ford's Theater, Washington, 209
Foreign Enlistment Act, 20, 66, 68, 173
Fort Fisher, North Carolina, 201–203
Fort Macon, North Carolina, 35, 36, 38–40
Fort Sumter, South Carolina, 29
Fort Wagner, Battle of, 265
Fort Warren, Massachusetts, 46, 57, 99, 130
Fox, Charles James, 47
Franklin, Tennessee, 142, 201

Fraser, Trenholm & Company, 36–38, 45–46
Funchal, Madeira Islands, 9, 14

Gage, Frank, 62, 63, 69, 76, 77
Gage, Mrs., 62, 63, 69, 77
General Miramon (steamer), 28
Gen'l Pike (barque), 247, 248
Gen'l Williams (whale ship), 245, 248
Georgetown, South Carolina, 42–46, 48, 253
Gettysburg, Battle of, 223, 261
Gilbert Archipelago, 195
Gilbert Islands, 189, 197
Gilman, Mrs. Samuel, 61–63, 69, 71, 76, 77
Gilman, Samuel, 61–63, 71
Gipsey (barque), 247, 248
Glover, Mr., 195
Goldsborough, I. L. N., 47
Goldsmith, Oliver, 179
Gone with the Wind (Mitchell), 313
Gooding, Captain, 38–40, 46
Grant, Ulysses S., 62, 143, 206, 240, 261
Grattan, Henry, 68
Gray (whale ship), 251–252
Great Australian Bight, 153
Green, Peter, 118–119
Grimball, Jack, 73, 74, 78, 123–125, 141, 152–153, 159, 161, 173, 188, 190, 192, 199, 200, 210, 211, 229, 258, 270, 272, 294, 295, 297, 328
Guadalcanal, 189
Gulf of Mexico, 12
Guy, John L., 138–141, 144, 326–327

Hall, Thomas, 94–96, 99–100, 106, 107, 138, 316
Hallock, Captain, 71
Hampton Roads, Battle of, 84
Harris, Clara, 209
Harvest (barque), 199, 200, 204, 205, 212
Harvey Birch (merchant ship), 30
Harwood, Mr., 115, 327
Hatcher's Run, 158
Hawes, Captain, 243
Hector (whale ship), 199, 200, 204, 327
Hett, Lane & Company, 77
Hillman (whale ship), 251

HMS *Bounty*, 287
HMS *Donegal*, 319, 323
HMS *Goshawk*, 323
Hobson's Bay, 157, 160, 172
Hokkaido, 222, 223
Honey Springs, Battle of, 265
Hood, John Bell, 143, 201, 203
Horreicks, Thomas, 198
Hunt, Cornelius E., 52, 107, 246, 293, 299, 315, 319, 320, 324

Ice, 226–231, 235, 247, 256–260, 291
Impressment, 16, 31, 50
In Search of the Castaways (Verne), 105
Independence Day, 261–262
Indian Ocean, 49, 85, 108, 311, 330
Insurance rates, 21, 94
International Date Line, 236
Iony Island, 225
Ireland, 311
Irish Sea, 315
Ironclads, 5, 17, 46, 56, 67, 268
Isaac Howland (whale ship), 251
Isabella (barque), 247, 248
Island Mound, Battle of, 265
Islands of Refreshment, 105

Jackson, Stonewall, 199
Japan, 198, 222, 223
Jarvis, Joe, 26
Jas. Maury (whale ship), 251
Jim California, 234
Jireh Swift (whale ship), 242, 243
Joe Long, 234
John Boy, 234, 272
John Frazer (supply ship), 126
Johnson, Andrew, 287
Johnston, Albert Sidney, 309
Jones, William, 151
Juarez, Benito, 25–26, 28

Kamchatka Peninsula, 222–226, 230–231
Kate Prince, 76–78
Kennard, Joel, 26
King Lear (Shakespeare), 240
Kohola (brig), 257
Kraepelin, Emil, 185
Krill, 102–103
Kuril archipelago, 222, 234

Laird Brothers Shipyards, 17, 67
Langland Brothers & Company, 171, 173
Lee, Robert E., 1, 8, 36*n*, 130, 142, 143, 158, 206, 208, 240, 244, 257, 261, 293
Lee, Sydney Smith, Jr., 8, 58, 76, 86, 130, 151, 173, 183, 199, 226, 229, 257–258, 293–295, 297, 302, 303, 324, 328, 331
Libby, Captain, 77, 78
Liberia, 262, 265
Lincoln, Abraham, 5, 8, 13, 20, 25, 65, 67, 86, 158, 185, 202, 204, 209, 239, 243–244, 257, 265, 275, 287
Lincoln, Mary, 209
Lining, Charles E., 109, 163, 176, 192–194, 281, 282, 287, 292–294, 303–304, 323, 324
Liverpool, England, 6, 17, 18, 21, 36, 66, 67, 281, 282, 292, 298, 312, 318–323
Lizzy M. Stacey (schooner), 81
Lynch, Mr., 60, 140, 141, 225, 316
Lynn, James T., 78–80

Madden, Walter, 92
Madeira Islands, 9, 22, 68, 157, 307
Madison, James, 16
Magellan, Ferdinand, 236
Mallory, Stephen R., 13, 19–20, 45, 48, 65, 84, 85, 161, 268
Manigault, Colonel, 44, 45
Manning, Thomas S., 233
March to the Sea, 86, 143, 201
Marin, Admiral, 28
Marlowe, James, 177, 323, 324
Marquis de Habana (steamer), 28
Marshall Islands, 189
Martha II (barque), 251
Martin, John, 315
Mason, James M., 31
Mason, John Thompson, 52, 63, 140, 141, 170, 281, 282, 297, 328, 329, 331
Maury, Mathew Fontaine, 84
McDougal, Charles, 268–269
McGuffney, Mr., 184
McNulty, Frederick J., 86, 150, 151, 170, 194, 297, 300–304, 307, 312, 329
Meade, George Gordon, 261

Melbourne, Australia, 85, 126, 151, 153, 154–174, 253, 281, 282

Mersey River, 316–319

Mexican War, 12, 24

Milo (whale ship), 241–243, 267, 273

Miner, R. D., 28

Minor, John F., 96, 108, 113, 115, 124, 130, 131, 299

Miramon, Miguel, 25

Mississippi River, 56, 57

Mobile Bay, 18

Mogul, 49–50, 51, 53

Moran, Mr., 91–92

Morehead City, North Carolina, 36, 44, 45, 48

Morse, Samuel, 93*n*

Mozambique Channel, 135

Mustang (merchant ship), 172

Nananierikie, King, 202–204, 214

Nashville, Battle of, 201, 202

Nassau (whale ship), 251

Naval Academy, Annapolis, 12, 25

Neuse River, 37

New Bern, North Carolina, 37, 38

New Guinea, 197

New Hebrides, 191

New Orleans, Battle of, 29, 46, 48, 56–57, 99, 110, 130, 178

New Testament, 277

Newton, John, 192

Nichols, Mrs., 144–145, 151–152, 159, 163–164

Nichols, Phineas, 144, 159

Nichols, William, 144, 159, 162–163

Nichols (harbor pilot), 158, 160, 161, 166

Nile (barque), 251, 252

Nimrod (barque), 150, 156, 162, 246, 248

"No name" (barque), 78–81

Nome, Alaska, 245

Norfolk, Virginia, 2, 161

Nye, Ebenezer, 224, 233

O'Brien, Mathew, 108, 120–123, 150, 151, 184, 295

Ogeechee River, 46

Old Testament, 263–264

Oregon, 267

O'Shea, Mr., 8, 9, 60–61, 135, 138, 140

Ossabaw Sound, 46

Ounkatan, 222

Page, Richard Lucien, 329

Page family, 2

Palmerston, Henry Temple, Lord, 5, 32–33, 67, 318

Panama, 284

Pattie (Whittle's sweetheart), 81, 89, 101, 109, 125, 142, 145, 147, 150, 155, 161, 180, 188, 193, 235, 241, 252, 272, 284, 299, 304, 307–308, 329

Paynter, James A., 319–320, 325–328, 330

Pearl (barque), 199, 200, 204

Pearl (schooner), 34

Pegram, Robert Baker, 29–31, 33–37

Pendergrast, Mr., 78–80

Pennsylvania (man-of-war), 12

Peters, First Mate, 53

Petersburg, siege at, 157

Pickett, George Armstrong, 257

Pitcairn Island, 287

Poe, Edgar Allan, 236, 257

Polk, Leonidas, 309

Ponape, 197–200, 202–205, 209, 214, 249, 309

Port Hudson, Battle of, 265

Port Phillip Bay, 154–156, 175

Porter, David D., 56, 57, 201, 202

Porter, John L., 83–84

Portland, Oregon, 267

Praia, Cape Verde Islands, 308

Prisoners, of *Shenandoah*, 71–72, 77–78, 116–118, 159, 160, 163–164, 205, 209, 241–243, 246–248, 252, 256, 267

Propeller, of *Shenandoah*, 120–122, 125, 135, 151, 260, 261

Puget Sound, 273

Rathbone, Henry, 209

Rawlinson, Mr., 184

Raymond, Peter, 215, 234, 288

Reconstruction, 265, 287, 295

Richmond, Virginia, 1, 29, 36, 45, 142, 143, 158, 206, 240, 244

Rio de Janeiro, Brazil, 71, 292

Rio Grande del Sol, Brazil, 74

Rip, the, 156–158, 175

Roaring Forties, 105, 109

Robert Fowades (whale ship), 239

Robert Gilfillan (schooner), 34

Robt. Cummings (barque), 247–248, 251

Roosevelt, Martha, 14

Roosevelt, Theodore, 14

Roosevelt, Theodore, Sr., 14

Rosario, Argentina, 328

Rowe, Louis, 106, 124, 215, 234, 316

Rudder, of *Shenandoah*, 127–129, 135, 148,
    227, 258–259, 307

Russell, Lord, 318, 319

Russia, 223, 230

St. Elmo's fire, 271

St. George's Channel, 315

St. Jonas Island, 228

St. Lawrence Island, 237, 245–246

St. Paul, 146

St. Thomas, 31

Samoa, 189

San Francisco, California, 267–269, 273,
    276, 281

San Francisco (mail runner), 328

San Juan Ulua, 25

Savannah, Georgia, 143, 201–202, 232,
    240, 244

Scales, Dabney Marion, 98–99, 130, 170,
    183, 190, 191, 193, 194, 199, 216,
    224, 225, 229, 292–295, 301, 303,
    315, 328

Scotia Sea, 292

Scurvy, 300, 319, 322

Sea King (merchant steamer)
    appearance of, 4
    cargo of coal, 1, 3, 7
    innovations of, 11
    passage to Atlantic, 4, 6–7, 14
    sold to Confederacy, 2
    speed of, 10, 11
    transformed to *Shenandoah*, 7–9, 67

Sea of Okhotsk, 222, 223, 225, 226, 230,
    231, 234, 318

Searsport, Maine, 53, 144

Semmes, Raphael, 18

Seward, William, 16, 67, 239

Shag Rock, 290

Shakespeare, William, 240

Shenandoah (*see* CSS *Shenandoah*)

Shenandoah Valley, 1

Sheridan, Richard Brinsley, 1, 201

Sherman, William Tecumseh, 1, 86, 143,
    201–203

Shiloh, Battle of, 223, 309

Siberia, 223–227, 230, 231, 245, 250

Silvester, George, 59, 60, 70, 75, 107, 108,
    315–316

Sinclair, Arthur, 232

Sinclair family, 2

Slavery, 23, 31, 32, 192, 263–266, 330

Slidell, John, 31

Smallpox, 247–248, 285

Smith, Captain, 238, 239, 243

Smith, Edmund Kirby, 209

Smith, William Breedlove, 78–79, 91–92,
    161, 287, 295, 329

Solomon Islands, 189

Sophie Thornton (whale ship), 241–243, 255

South Orkney Islands, 290

South Shetland Islands, 290

Southampton, England, 30, 31, 33

Southern Indian Ocean, 139

Spain, 25

Spring Hill, Tennessee, 201

Staples, Captain, 53–55, 57, 63, 71, 144

Stars, importance of, 273–274, 286

State of Georgia (steamer), 34–35, 44, 47

Storm riding, 10–11

Storms, 58, 93, 128–131, 136–141,
    143–144, 185, 197, 211, 215–221,
    225, 253, 270, 289–290, 305–307,
    311

Strong's Island, 197–198

Stumptown, Oregon, 267

Sullivan, Barry, 167

Sultan of Zanzibar, 330

Superstitions, 270–271

Susan (brig), 73–74

Susan Abigail (brigantine), 243, 244, 248

Tahiti, 283

Taputeouea, 194–196

Tarawa, 189

Tasman Sea, 180

Tausk Bay, 226, 230

Tea market, 10

Tenerife, 67, 68

Tennessee River, 201

Textile mills, 19, 30
Thackeray, William Makepeace, 212–213
Thomas, George H., 142
Thompson, Edwin P., 200
Tierra del Fuego, 290
Tobacco, 32, 88, 148
Tonga, 189
Trent (packet), 31, 32
Tristan da Cunha, 105, 112, 114, 116–118, 120
Tropic of Capricorn, 288
Twain, Mark, 88
Twelve Tribes of Israel, 264

Union blockade, 3, 5, 8, 17–21, 30, 34–36, 40–41, 47, 84
USS *Adams*, 13
USS *Camanche*, 268–269
USS *Germantown*, 12
USS *Indianola*, 26–28
USS *Kearsarge*, 18, 49
USS *Merrimack*, 84
USS *Monitor*, 46
USS *Niagara*, 6–7
USS *Preble*, 25
USS *Sacramento*, 6–7
USS *Saginaw*, 268
USS *Saratoga*, 26–27
USS *Savannah*, 26
USS *Tuscarora*, 33–34
USS *Virginia*, 84
USS *Wachusett*, 18, 292
USS *Wave*, 26–28

Valparaiso, Chile, 68
Vanavery, Mr., 288
Vera Cruz, Mexico, 12, 24
Verne, Jules, 105
Vicksburg, siege of, 261
Victoria, Queen of England, 3, 32–33, 62, 159

Waddell, Ann Seligman Inglehart, 12, 128, 134, 179, 328, 329
Waddell, James Iredell, 18, 50, 58, 60–62, 71–73, 77, 78, 81, 85, 89, 90, 109–112, 114, 115, 118, 119, 123, 145, 150, 175, 176, 210, 229, 239, 242, 246, 247, 313, 331
    appearance of, 11
    background of, 12
    on Confederate navy, 16–17
    course set after war's end by, 280–283, 292, 295–299
    in Melbourne, 157–164, 166, 168, 169, 172–174
    memoirs and journal of, 15, 24, 63, 157, 159, 168, 173, 268, 277, 280–281, 290, 291, 320–321, 329
    news of fall of Confederacy and, 277–278
    personality of, 13, 15, 63, 127, 128, 133, 177, 179, 181, 292–294
    plan to attack San Francisco of, 267–269
    in private life, 328–329
    resignation from U.S. Navy by, 13, 23
    Whittle, relationship with, 14–15, 82, 126–135, 141, 156, 190–191, 216, 217, 231–232, 253, 269–270, 274
War of 1812, 5, 16
Washington, George, 176, 177
Waverly (whale ship), 251, 252
Weeks, Edward, 176, 311
Welles, Gideon, 13, 20, 23
West, William, 144
Whaling fleet, 6, 84, 85, 102, 105, 113–115
White, Moses J., 39
Whittle, Arthur Sinclair, 24
Whittle, Beverley, 276–277
Whittle, Commodore William Conway, 3, 24, 25, 28, 29, 56, 155, 161, 276, 285, 329, 330
Whittle, Elizabeth Beverly Sinclair, 24
Whittle, Elizabeth Calvert Page, 329
Whittle, Jennie, 177
Whittle, William Conway
    action off Mexico, 25–29, 253
    capture and imprisonment of, 46, 48, 57
    childhood of, 25
    children of, 329
    code of conduct of, 50–51, 54, 65, 70–71, 94, 96
    death of, 329
    as Executive Officer of *Shenandoah* (*see* CSS *Shenandoah*)
    fall of Confederacy and, 206, 208–209, 276–278, 329

Whittle, William Conway (*cont.*)
  fantasy of own ship of, 81–82, 183,
     185–186, 269
  female passengers and, 151–153, 182
  hatred of Yankees by, 53, 54, 56, 57, 69,
     72, 122, 182, 249–250, 252, 261–263
  health of, 65, 87–88, 185, 193
  journal/log of, 8, 21, 26–28, 34, 35,
     38–43, 46–48, 69–76, 79–81,
     86–89, 91–120, 122–125, 127–134,
     139–148, 150–155, 157–158,
     161–164, 166–169, 174, 176–206,
     208–217, 219–221, 223–225,
     227–241, 243–246, 248–255,
     257–264, 269–278, 280, 281,
     283–289, 291, 294, 298–300, 303,
     304, 306–313
  marriage of, 329
  McNulty incident and, 300–304
  Mersey River harbor pilot conversation
     with, 316–317
  as midshipman, 25–29
  on *Nashville*, 29–30, 32–35, 37–48, 178,
     230, 253, 271, 311
  at New Orleans, 46, 48, 56–57, 178
  physical appearance of, 2–3
  poem by, 206–208, 209
  racism of, 262–263
  religious faith of, 65–66, 89, 101, 125,
     228, 235, 260, 263–264, 272–273,
     277
  resignation from U.S. Navy by, 29
  ship's cat and, 271–272
  sweetheart of, 81, 89, 101, 109, 125,
     142, 145, 147, 150, 155, 161, 180,
     188, 193, 235, 241, 252, 272, 284,
     299, 304, 307–308, 329
  twenty-fifth birthday of, 150
  voyage on *Sea King* by, 1–4
  Waddell, relationship with, 14–15, 82,
     126–135, 141, 156, 177–185,
     190–191, 216, 217, 231–232, 253,
     269–270, 274
Whittle family, 2
Wilkes, Charles, 31
William Bill (Bill Sailor), 309, 310,
    312
Williams, John, 123, 146, 151, 172–173,
    264
Wilmington, North Carolina, 158, 201,
    202, 232, 240, 244
Wirz, Henry, 287
Wm. C. Nye (barque), 246, 248
Wm. Thompson (whale ship), 238, 239,
    243
Wood's Hotel, London, 3
Worth, Charles, 112–113
Wright, Richard, 4

Yeats, William Butler, 147
Yellow fever, 18, 24, 46
Yorktown, Virginia, 5